C000009416

"Change . . . fear not! The inspirational experi⟨ book help us to unleash the tremendous power own way, we can generate the leadership to prepare ourselves for this age of great changes."

Beng Neoh, *Managing Director, Challenger Funds Management (Asia), Singapore*

"*Mastering the Power of You* brings together an extraordinarily diverse range of leaders to deliver the perfect go-to contemporary leadership guide for the 21st century; insightful and enlightening, expect this book to arm leaders at all levels with the winning concepts, skills, and behaviours to deliver significant and lasting change."

Lieutenant General Richard Wardlaw, OBE, *Chief of Defence Logistics & Support, Strategic Command, Defence Support, Ministry of Defence, UK*

"In a world where books on leadership fill libraries with biographies and memoirs, and 'how to' volumes are in abundance, this distillation of *Mastering the Power of You* is powerfully succinct. In a time when clear advice on how to be mindful of one's own leadership journey is generally in short supply, this collaboration fills that void in an easy-to-read, compelling way. I recommend this book to every leader as a way to remember why your leadership is so important, and why bringing your thoughtful, authentic self to the problems we all face is powerful."

Clair J. Moeller, *President and Chief Operating Officer, Midcontinent Independent System Operator (MISO), USA*

"We all have power to influence others. *Mastering the Power of You* is a book that explores the motivations and practices of leadership. Why do we assume these leadership roles? What's in it for us? If you need guidance about how your leadership can be used to influence others, for the collective good, then this book is for you."

Louisa Wall, *Member of Parliament, New Zealand*

"If you are looking for a read that will help you adapt and succeed in today's fast-changing and challenging world, whatever your stage of career might be, then this is the book for you. I was particularly struck by the rich content of the book which included valuable insights on different parts of strategic decision making and leadership, all based on personal experiences and analyses of the contributing authors."

Marios Demetriades, *Financial Services Expert and Entrepreneur, Former Minister of Transport, Communications and Works, Republic of Cyprus*

"*Mastering the Power of You* is a diverse and helpful toolkit that is usable across cultures and contexts. It contains experience, advice, and practical exercises – something to help any of us to become better versions of ourselves and to have a better impact in the world."

Air Vice Marshal Andrew Clark, *Chief of Air Force, Royal New Zealand Air Force, New Zealand*

"This wonderful book serves as a source of inspiration to senior leaders as well as a tool set for emerging leaders. With the modular approach chosen, the interested reader will find practical and actionable advice for the current leadership issues. Its content is both easily accessible and state-of-the-art thinking."

Christian Schäfer, *Director and Global Head of Payments, Corporate Bank, Deutsche Bank, Germany*

"*Mastering the Power of You* is a must-read for all who are interested in cultivating their leadership skills to succeed in the 21st century. Leaders from around the globe in diverse fields share their real-world experiences, lessons learned, and guidance on the skills and behaviors that are essential to delivering results and sustainable change with long-lasting positive impact. It is an inspiring and thought-provoking guide."

Sherry Maple, *For-purpose Brand and Business Development Leader in Emerging and Developed Markets; former Director CPG and Food Service - Latin America, Starbucks, USA*

"Leadership opportunities are increasingly complex and fast-changing. *Mastering the Power of You* provides rich perspectives for all current and aspiring leaders to think deeply about the environment in which we operate and provides insights and ideas to help you lead with purpose and with authenticity."

Neil Tomlinson, *Vice Chair, Deloitte, UK*

"*Mastering the Power of You* is a must-read for those entrusted to lead during a period of massive disruption and uncertainty. Leading any organization in the best of times can be a real challenge. However, leading in a world fueled by war, social upheaval, and a pandemic will require skills and qualities that were unthinkable just a few years ago. The leadership journey into the future has begun. How we succeed in making this critical transition will have implications that may last for generations. This book is a must-read to help us understand the past, but also how we embrace a very different future."

Gary A. Officer, *President and CEO,*
The Center for Workforce Inclusion, USA

"*Mastering the Power of You* breaks the topic of leadership into thirty-two bite-sized themes, each of which covers invaluable principles and tips that will definitely serve as a perfect leadership guide for leaders in all spheres of life."

Oyinkan Adewale, *Independent*
Non-Executive Director, Lafarge Africa

"*Mastering the Power of You* is a fine collection of personal experiences and stories of well-established leaders from around the world; highlighting critical leadership concepts, behaviors, and skills. The book is an excellent guide for anyone aspiring to be an effective leader and a better person."

Alan L. Barretto, *Managing Director, Nilpeter India*

"There's a vital role for progressive, values-based leadership to help tackle pressing global challenges from economic and racial inequalities to the climate crisis. Any leader who wants to make a positive impact should draw inspiration from this book about how they can play their part in shaping a fairer and more sustainable world."

Dhananjayan Sriskandarajah, *Chief Executive, Oxfam GB*

"Exploring and embarking on a leadership journey is one of the biggest adventures in everyone's life. The expedition prepares for every eventuality that we meet in this uncertain world. Don't forget to pack this magnificent book with you. *Mastering the Power of You* guides you to reach far and higher destinations."

Chiaki Sakurai, *Senior Vice President, Otsuka Pharmaceutical, Japan*

"*Mastering the Power of You* is a thought provoking and compelling read for any leader in the 21st century. Bringing together a diverse group of leaders, who share their practical and inspirational insights on how we can all be better leaders for the benefit of others and ourselves; irrespective of your role, sector, or stage in your career and life more broadly."

Sean Cruise, *Managing Director, Global Head of Data & Digital, Apex Group, UK*

"*Mastering the Power of You* is an inspiring collection of insights from leaders generously sharing their wisdom and experience. I highly recommend that you read this book if you want to tap into those very special qualities we all possess and can develop beyond those we learn in formal education. It will be a game changer for you as for me!"

Amanda Ellis, *Senior Director, Global Partnerships, Julie Ann Wrigley Global Futures Laboratory, Arizona State University; and Professor of Practice, Thunderbird School of Global Management, USA*

"I really enjoyed dipping into *Mastering the Power of You* and learning from the insights of leaders from around the world. I learned a great deal from the experiences that have been shared, the practical insights that are described, and the valuable self-help exercises that are offered in each chapter."

Mike Thomas, *Chair, University Hospitals of Morecambe Bay and Visiting Professor of Organisational Leadership, University of Chester, UK*

This delightful book *Mastering the Power of You* is a must-read for everyone, from graduates to senior executives. In our uncertain world, this book will inspire you to become a better leader, support your team, and navigate pandemics, conflicts, and other unpredictable, adverse economic and social situations. The strength of the book lies in the diversity of the authors from around the world, the depth of experiences shared, the leadership topics covered, and plenty of examples and exercises to practice your skills. As they say, the only constant in the world is change, and this book provides tools to equip all leaders and future leaders to deal with our ever-changing environment.

Reinette van der Merwe, *CEO, First Capital Bank, Botswana*

"*Mastering the Power of You* gives you insightful thoughts behind the leadership expected for today's business environment. Great reading for all business leaders who need to deal with diversities and inclusiveness."

Masaya Fujimori, *CEO, Cornerstone Japan*

"*Mastering the Power of You* is an insightful book on leadership with many chapters contributed by leaders from diverse background and industries around the world. This book is a useful resource written in an engaging and enlightening manner with practical examples. A highly recommended reading for recent graduates as well as seasoned professionals."

Eng Hui Ti, *Chief Executive Officer, Baiduri Bank, Brunei*

MASTERING THE POWER OF YOU

The world of the 2020s is complex and demanding. We are faced with a myriad of difficult decisions about our present and future, driven by the impact of the COVID-19 pandemic, the economic downturn, rising unemployment and inequalities, digital disruption, uncertain political environments, and climate change. In this book, leaders from around the world share their experiences in adapting to the changing world and the lessons they have learnt. They offer advice on mastering a diverse range of leadership concepts, skills, and behaviours to prepare for the challenges of the 21st century.

The easy-to-follow format is grouped around the core concepts of Leadership, entrepreneurship, and volunteering; Purpose and values; Authenticity, trust, and presence; Strategising, thinking, and decision-making; Mentoring and development; Mental resilience; Diversity and inclusion; Negotiating and collaborating; and Social and environmental impact. Each of the 32 chapters takes you on a voyage of discovery to a wide range of "powers" and inspires you to use them to open new opportunities in your life and workplace.

If you are a recent graduate aspiring to gain meaningful employment in a rapidly transforming workplace, or a mid-career professional whose job may soon change or disappear with increasing automation, this book is for you. If you are a consultant, coach, mentor, or trainer, looking for new approaches, this book will provide valuable guidelines. If you are a seasoned professional navigating the new norms, this book will give you many inspiring insights.

Lalit Johri is a strategic advisor to national and international organisations and former Senior Fellow in International Business, Saïd Business School, University of Oxford.

Katherine Corich is Founder and Chair of Sysdoc Group, a non-executive Director of the UK Civil Aviation Authority, and Chair of global anti-trafficking charity, It's a Penalty.

Gay Haskins is former Dean of Executive Education at Saïd & London Business Schools and a co-author, with Mike Thomas and Lalit Johri, of *Kindness in Leadership,* Routledge, 2018.

MASTERING THE POWER OF YOU

Empowered by Leader Insights

Edited by Lalit Johri, Katherine Corich, and Gay Haskins

Routledge
Taylor & Francis Group

LONDON AND NEW YORK

Cover design by Jasmin Milne, Sysdoc Group

First published 2023
by Routledge
4 Park Square, Milton Park, Abingdon, Oxon OX14 4RN

and by Routledge
605 Third Avenue, New York, NY 10158

Routledge is an imprint of the Taylor & Francis Group, an informa business

© 2023 selection and editorial matter, Lalit Johri, Katherine Corich and Gay Haskins; individual chapters, the contributors

The right of Lalit Johri, Katherine Corich and Gay Haskins to be identified as the authors of the editorial material, and of the authors for their individual chapters, has been asserted in accordance with sections 77 and 78 of the Copyright, Designs and Patents Act 1988.

All rights reserved. No part of this book may be reprinted or reproduced or utilised in any form or by any electronic, mechanical, or other means, now known or hereafter invented, including photocopying and recording, or in any information storage or retrieval system, without permission in writing from the publishers.

Trademark notice: Product or corporate names may be trademarks or registered trademarks, and are used only for identification and explanation without intent to infringe.

British Library Cataloguing-in-Publication Data
A catalogue record for this book is available from the British Library

Library of Congress Cataloging-in-Publication Data
Names: Johri, Lalit M., editor. | Corich, Katherine, editor. |
  Haskins, Gabrielle, editor.
Title: Mastering the power of you : empowered by leader insights / edited
  by Lalit Johri, Katherine Corich and Gay Haskins.
Description: New York, NY : Routledge, 2023. | Includes bibliographical
  references and index.
Identifiers: LCCN 2022021148 (print) | LCCN 2022021149 (ebook) |
  ISBN 9781032112992 (hardback) | ISBN 9781032113005 (paperback) |
  ISBN 9781003219293 (ebook)
Subjects: LCSH: Decision-making—Social aspects. | Organizational change. |
  Covid-19 (Pandemic)—Social aspects. | Covid-19 (Pandemic)—Economic
  aspects.
Classification: LCC HD30.23 .M3722 2023 (print) | LCC HD30.23 (ebook) |
  DDC 658.4/06—dc23/eng/20220805
LC record available at https://lccn.loc.gov/2022021148
LC ebook record available at https://lccn.loc.gov/2022021149

ISBN: 978-1-032-11299-2 (hbk)
ISBN: 978-1-032-11300-5 (pbk)
ISBN: 978-1-003-21929-3 (ebk)

DOI: 10.4324/9781003219293

Typeset in Bembo
by Apex CoVantage, LLC

To the many leaders around the world who have crafted the enlightening chapters of this book and whose thoughts, insights, and experiences have inspired its content.

All royalties received from sales of this book will be donated to charities.

CONTENTS

List of contributors   *xvi*

Foreword   *xxix*
Lalit Johri, Katherine Corich, and Gay Haskins

Part I: Leadership, entrepreneurship, and volunteering   1

1   Mastering the power of leadership   3
    Lalit Johri

2   Mastering the power of digital entrepreneurship   22
    Thomas Abraham

3   Mastering the power of entrepreneurship   35
    Kelly Keates

4   Mastering the power of volunteering   46
    Mads Roke Clausen

Part II: Purpose and values   59

5   Mastering the power of purpose   61
    Katherine Corich

6   Mastering the power of kindness   74
    Gay Haskins

7   Mastering the power of moral value   88
    J.R. Klein

Part III: Authenticity, trust, and presence 105

8 Mastering the power of authenticity 107
   Wanda Hamilton

9 Mastering the power of trust: evolving your leadership 118
   Paul Matthews

10 Mastering the power of presence 132
   Karen Glossop

11 Mastering the power of storytelling 142
   Gabrielle Dolan

Part IV: Strategising, thinking, and decision-making 153

12 Mastering the power of strategising 155
   Josef Bruckschlögl

13 Mastering the power of analytical thinking 166
   Prasad Ramakrishnan

14 Mastering the power of creative thinking 179
   Anshul Sonak

15 Mastering the power of sensemaking 191
   Sunil Deshmukh

Part V: Mentoring and development 203

16 Mastering the power of mentoring 205
   Victoria Wall

17 Mastering the power of people development 220
   Shawn D. Mathis

Part VI: Mental resilience 237

18 Mastering the power of mental fitness 239
   Mark O'Brien

19 Mastering the power of self-confidence 251
   Chloe Phillips Harris

20 Mastering the power of courage to turn your dreams to reality 260
   Avril McDonald

21 Mastering the power of challenging the status quo   269
    Mai Chen

Part VII: Diversity and inclusion   **281**

22 Mastering the power of inclusive thinking   283
    Rebecca Oldfield

23 Mastering the power of diversity and inclusion   294
    James Burstall

24 Mastering the power of gender equality   305
    Alina Nassar

Part VIII: Negotiating and collaborating   **317**

25 Mastering the power of negotiations   319
    Josef Bruckschlögl and J.R. Klein

26 Mastering the power of human collaboration   335
    Desiree Botica

27 Mastering the power of community   344
    Jensine Larsen

28 Mastering the power of partnerships   354
    Marita Lintener

Part IX: Social and environmental impact   **367**

29 Mastering the power of freedom of information for
    social justice   369
    Amrita Johri and Anjali Bhardwaj

30 Mastering the power of impact investing   380
    Giles Gunesekera

31 Mastering the power of social equity   396
    Marsha Marshall

32 Mastering the power of sustainability   410
    Kishan Nanayakkara

Index   *421*

CONTRIBUTORS

Part I: Leadership, entrepreneurship, and volunteering

Lalit Johri, Professor, has been an innovative academic for over 45 years. His areas of expertise include strategy and leadership in international businesses, alliances including public–private partnerships, public policy, and institutional reform. He holds an MSc degree in physics and MBA and PhD degrees in Business Policy and Strategic Management.

Until October 2019, Lalit served as Senior Fellow in International Business and Director of the Oxford Advanced Management and Leadership Programme (OAMLP) at Saïd Business School, University of Oxford. Currently, he is based in Thailand, leading research and people and team development initiatives and advising policymakers and business leaders in public and private enterprises in several countries. Earlier, Lalit served as Professor of International Business at the Asian Institute of Technology (AIT), where he was a Founding Director of the School's Executive MBA. He was also a tenured professor at the University of Delhi in India. He has led research, consulting, and executive education programmes for senior leaders in private and public sector organisations and government agencies in the USA, UK, Europe, Middle East, and Asia. He has attended the Aspen Seminar and was awarded the Aspen Scholar of the Year by the Aspen Institute, Washington, USA, for his outstanding professional accomplishments and public contributions.

Thomas Abraham is the founder of technology advisory companies, T-Ventures and HR2Tech. As a digital entrepreneur and "catalyst", he advises technology start-ups on their business strategy, go to market, partnerships, and global expansion.

He has held senior leadership roles in India with multinational companies, including as Managing Director at Wolters Kluwer Tax & Accounting and Sage Software. Thomas spends his weekends making videos for his YouTube channels "Musings with Thomas Abraham" on business and strategy and "The living room music" that brings out his passion for music. Thomas is a graduate in Science from St. Stephen's College in India and has an MBA from Faculty of Management Studies, University of Delhi, India.

Kelly Keates is Managing Director of Zonge Engineering & Research Organization (Aust) Pty. Ltd. She has a demonstrated history of working in the mining and metals industry and started working underground at Roxby Downs before being employed at Zonge in 1991 as a junior office assistant. In 2006, she purchased the company. Zonge provides electrical ground geophysical survey solutions in Australia and around the globe conducting surveys for mining exploration and environmental and geotechnical applications. This has developed into a new business venture developed to protect the environment, Liquid Integrity Systems Pty Ltd. She is also a director at MinEx CRC.

Kelly recently completed senior leadership programmes at Harvard and Oxford Business Schools and received an Outstanding Alumna Award from Saïd Business School. She has also been awarded Premiers Leadership Excellence Awards, Industry Leadership Grants, a scholarship with the Australian Institute of Company Directors, and has been a Telstra Business Awards Finalist and a Mentor for the Curious Minds Program. She is passionate about taking on the challenge of constant improvement.

Mads Roke Clausen is an experienced civil society leader and CEO for the Association of Danish Private Social Services. He is also a board member of The Hive Foundation, a cutting-edge foundation seeking to transform how we organise social efforts, and the Liljeborg Foundation, which has a strategic focus on scaling up voluntary organisations. He has also served as the chair of the National Council for Volunteering and doing research in the new financial landscape for voluntary organisations.

From 2006 to 2018, Mads served as the CEO for Mothers' Aid (MA), the leading Danish charity for vulnerable pregnant women and families. In 2015, he received the Danish National Centre for Social Research's Anniversary Prize on behalf of MA for developing research-based consultancy and the use of impact data, and in 2019, he received the Oxford Advanced Management and Leadership Programme Outstanding Alumni award from Saïd Business School, University of Oxford. In 2021, H.M. Queen Margrethe II of Denmark awarded Mads Roke Clausen The Order of Dannebrog for his leadership within the social and voluntary sector. He also has a PhD in Social Finance from Roskilde University.

Part II: Purpose and values

Katherine Corich is the Founder and Chair of the Sysdoc Group, a global consulting and IT business. Her expertise is in the fields of business transformation, whole-system thinking, digital disruption, leading change, simulation-based learning, and cross-border working, and she has led transformation programmes for major global corporates and the public sector in UK, NZ, and Australia.

A recipient of several awards, a few of Katherine's greatest achievements include being twice awarded the Ernst & Young Entrepreneur of the Year Award (Finance, Services & Arts [2003] and Master Entrepreneur [2010]). She was named as the UK New Zealander of the Year in 2015 and was Inducted into the Hi-Tech Hall of Fame. Katherine won Aveeno Business Women of the Year and was UK National Business Awards finalist. Katherine's leadership of performance-based philanthropy programmes is seen as ground-breaking. This includes It's a Penalty anti-trafficking and child protection campaigns run during major international sporting events, and the programmes: Common Protect, Student Ambassadors, and Safe in Sport.

Gabrielle (Gay) Haskins has worked for over 40 years in the field of management and leadership development. She has been Dean of Executive Education at major business schools including London Business School, Saïd Business School, University of Oxford, and the Indian School of Business in Hyderabad. She has also served as Director General of the European Foundation for Management Development (EFMD) in Brussels, a global association driving excellence in management development worldwide.

Earlier, Gay was Director of *The Economist* Newspaper's conferences and before that, worked for the Government of Ontario, Canada, and as a consultant for what is now Deloitte's, she obtained an MBA degree from the Schulich School of Business in Toronto. She is a member of the International Advisory Board of the University of Dublin's Innovation Academy and an associate of the Societal Innovation and Enterprise Foundation, St Aidan's College, Durham University. She is the co-editor, with Mike Thomas and Lalit Johri, of *Kindness in Leadership* (Routledge, 2018).

J.R. Klein is Principal of J.R. Global, a consultancy committed to facilitating global transformation through local initiatives that strengthen communities by emphasising leadership and systemic change. He has been active in social impact finance for more than 40 years. J.R. is an Oxford University Press-published author with expertise in organisational structure, cultural sensitivity, pragmatic leadership, planning, and social impact. His expertise is recognised worldwide.

J.R. Klein has an MBA degree and has continued his post-master's education at the Harvard Business School and Saïd Business School, University of Oxford. He has been awarded three master-level qualifications – postgraduate awards in Performance Measurement (HBS), Strategic Perspectives (HBS), and Advanced Management and Leadership (Oxford Saïd). He has received various awards including the 2011 Smart Leader Award from Smart Business magazine, the United States Small Business Administration 2011 Financial Services Champion of the Year, 2017 Outstanding Alumni Award from the Oxford Advanced Management and Leadership Programme, and the 2020 Distinguished Alumni Award from Northern State University.

Part III: Authenticity, trust, and presence

Wanda Hamilton is CEO of the Canada–UK Foundation in London and is passionate about creating social change through philanthropy and education.

She has held senior leadership positions with both Canadian and British charities, including the Royal National Institute of Blind People, United Way, and CNIB. She is a graduate of Carleton University in Ottawa, and in 2019, she was recognised by Saïd Business School, Oxford University, as an Outstanding Alumna following her completion of their Advanced Management and Leadership Programme in 2015. Wanda is a SheEO activator, part of a global community of radically generous women investing in societal change. She is also a senior mentor for *Women of the Future* and was listed in 2019 in the *Financial Times* as one of their *50 Leading Lights in Kindness* – building organisations through kindness, authenticity, and collaboration.

Paul Matthews believes that trust is the essence of leadership. He helps leaders and teams build impact and trust using powerful conversations.

Paul has worked for more than 25 years as a leader or leadership advisor at every level in large and complex businesses across Europe and Australia. He now runs his own practice as a speaker, mentor, and coach. He helps leaders lift performance using communication and leadership that ignites the workforce and empowers teams to go further faster on change, innovation, and success. Learn more at paulmatthews.com.au or start a conversation at paul@commscoach.org.

Karen Glossop has been developing people's skills in communication and leadership since 1997. She trains groups and coaches individuals across the corporate, public, and non-profit sectors. She operates independently as Resonance Training and also in association with UK universities and business schools. Karen blogs regularly about public speaking, communication, and influencing. Also working as a training consultant, Karen is a co-artistic director of award-winning theatre company, Wishbone.

Recently, Karen has been exploring how speakers can engage and make an impact on others in an online setting.

Gabrielle Dolan is a highly sought-after international keynote speaker and educator on real communication and business storytelling. Her clients include Accenture, EY, VISA, Vodafone, Uber, Amazon, and the Obama Foundation. She is the best-selling author of five successful business books, including *Stories for Work: The Essential Guide to Business Storytelling* and *Real Communication: How to Be You and Lead True*, which was a finalist for Australia's Business Book of the year 2019. Her latest book *Magnetic Stories: Connect With Customers and Engage Employees With Brand Storytelling* debut in Australia at number 2 in best-selling business books in March 2021.

Bringing humanity to the way people communicate isn't just a career, it's a calling. The ultimate expression of Gabrielle's passion for the cause is her Jargon Free Fridays Movement (jargonfreefridays.com). Her dedication to the industry was recognised when Gabrielle was awarded the 2020 Communicator of the Year by the International Association of Business Communicators Asia Pacific region.

Part IV: Strategising, thinking, and decision-making

Josef Bruckschlögl, FH-Hon.Prof. Dipl.Ing., is CEO of KWAK Telecom Ltd., a telecommunications company based in Cyprus in the field of payment services. The firm serves clients in more than 100 countries and is at the forefront in bringing micropayment services into emerging markets. Earlier, Josef has served in leadership roles at Telekom Austria and Deutsche Post and has consulted global companies such as Deutsche Telekom, Magna, and BMW. He is also a founding partner of the international consulting firm Transformation Paradigms, where he is in charge of European markets.

Josef is Chairman of the Endowment Association at St. Pölten University of Applied Sciences and Professor of Innovation and Business Development. He has a master's degree from St. Pölten in telecommunications and media economics and is an alumnus of Oxford University Saïd Business School's Oxford Advanced Management and Leadership Programme where he was awarded "Outstanding Alumnus" in 2016. CV magazine has named him the "most influential CEO in Telecoms 2019".

Prasad Ramakrishnan is Chief Operating Officer of Motiv Power Systems, a Silicon Valley-based electric powertrain company in the commercial truck industry. After a distinguished career at Ford, Triumph International, Alstom, and General Electric, he has taught at the Swiss Federal Technological University (ETH) in Zurich. He is currently an Adjunct Lecturer at Babson College in Boston and also mentors start-ups in Asia, Europe, and North America.

Prasad's education has been in physics, electrical engineering, and administration. He is an alumnus of Oxford's Saïd Business School's Advanced Management and Leadership Programme. He has lived with his family and worked in several countries in the Americas, Europe, and Asia and enjoys reading, tennis, travel, and learning about different cultures.

Anshul Sonak is Principal Engineer and Global Director of Digital Readiness Programs (Global Government Affairs Group) for Intel Corporation. Based in Singapore, he advises social enterprises, start-ups, government bodies, and multilateral organisations on making technology inclusive and expanding digital readiness for all.

Anshul has implemented several social education programmes in the area of digital literacy, inclusion, STEM disciplines, youth techno-entrepreneurship, and technology for good. He is a regular speaker on social impact at programmes organised by UNDP and the Asian Development Bank. He has a master's degree in rural management from the Institute of Rural Management, India. He has completed the Oxford Advanced Management and Leadership Programme. He is UNDP Asia's first regional Youth Co-Lab Champion from the private sector.

Sunil Deshmukh is a member of the Global Board of the Institute of Management Accountants (IMA) USA. He teaches at the IMA Leadership Academy and is Associate Dean of IMA's Mentoring Programme. As a certified coach (International Coaching Federation and Marshall Goldsmith, USA), Sunil runs mentoring and coaching programmes for start-ups and business leaders based in India.

Sunil has held senior leadership positions in different industry segments in Africa, the Middle East, ASEAN, and India. Throughout his career, he has won several awards. The most recent is the "IMA Champion Award" 2020. He is a qualified Management Accountant with certifications from the USA and India and Fellow Member of the Institute of Company Secretaries of India (FCS). He has completed executive leadership programmes from Saïd Business School, University of Oxford, and the Aspen Institute, USA.

Part V: Mentoring and development

Victoria Wall has a keen interest in potential performance and career development, which led to the establishment of Victoria Wall Associates Ltd – Victoria's first business enterprise, 32 years ago. Advising on organisational change, recruitment, and development programmes, her experiences brought about the creation of VWA Consulting in 1994, a London-based leadership development consultancy that works with a broad range of clients including FTSE 250 corporations, pharmaceuticals, private equity investors, hedge fund managers, and exhibition companies.

Her career portfolio includes executive coaching, career coaching, mentoring, leadership assessment, and development, and also talent mapping, team building, and facilitation of strategic "off sites". She has designed many mentoring training workshops and also mentors occupational psychologists in executive coaching, having developed a scientific and structured approach to understanding leadership behaviour. She is a coach and trustee to two South African-based charities, The Kusasa Project (http://www.thekusasa project.org) and mothers2mothers (http://www.m2m.org), and is passionate about helping to educate the next generation.

Shawn D. Mathis is the founder, Chief Digital Officer, and the board director at OnSomble™ Inc., based in Nashville, TN, which provides an enterprise-level, cloud-based professional behaviour assessment and adaptive-learning healthcare solution. Shawn is Adjunct Professor in the healthcare MBA at Freed-Hardeman University and serves on the Business Advisory Council for the College of Business. He formerly served as Adjunct Professor of Advanced Research Methods and Director of Doctoral Capstone Projects in the Doctor of Behavioral Health programme.

Shawn earned the Doctor of Philosophy in humanities at Faulkner University. He has a Diploma in organisational leadership and certificates for the Oxford Executive Leadership and Oxford Advanced Management and Leadership programmes at Saïd Business School, University of Oxford. He attended the Aspen Institute's Executive Seminar on Leadership, Values, and the Good Society in Aspen, Colorado. He has also completed the Board Directors' Programme at Henley Business School, University of Reading, and studied corporate governance at The Wharton School, University of Pennsylvania.

Part VI: Mental resilience

Mark O'Brien is Programme Director of the Oxford Healthcare Leadership Programme and Associate Fellow at the Saïd Business School, University of

Oxford. He is also Adjunct Professor at the Faculty of Business, Economics and Law at the University of Queensland and Non-Executive Director of St John of God Healthcare Australia. In his 37 years since graduating as a medical practitioner, he has transitioned from a busy doctor and medico-political advocate in rural Australia to an internationally recognised expert in building cultures of empathy, safety, and professionalism within the healthcare industry.

His passion has seen him provide advice and training in Australia, the United Kingdom, Ireland, South East Asia, New Zealand, Canada, and South Africa. An estimated 300,000 healthcare professionals in 13 countries have undertaken courses developed by him in topics as diverse as leadership, culture change, communication skills, and professionalism. Previous roles include the Medical Director of Cognitive Institute (a company he co-founded) and International Programme Director for Education of the Medical Protection Society. *www.linkedin.com/in/mark-obrien-ci*

Chloe Phillips-Harris is an author, a wild horse trainer, and an expedition leader from the Bay of Islands, New Zealand. She works with New Zealand's wild horses, the Kaimanawas of the Central Plateau and the Aupouri horses of the Far North to tame, train, and help them transition to a domestic life. As an equestrian, she has ridden in events nationally and competed across many disciplines. Her greatest achievement is competing in the world's toughest horse race, The Mongol Derby, a 1000-km endurance race that pushed her to her limit. In 2018, Chloe published a best-selling book on it called, *Fearless* (Harper Collins).

Chloe has led many expeditions in remote areas, including a crossing of the Gobi Desert in winter on camels, where temperatures dropped as low as −45 C. She worked with the Dukha people, the last reindeer riders in the mountains of northern Mongolia and filmed for the first time their winter and spring migrations. She also helped set up farms in Kazakhstan and run large animal welfare programmes in the South Pacific working with rural communities and helping to improve livestock and equine health. She is always up for a challenge and loves seeing just what we are capable of. If there is a way to explore extreme environments with animals at her side, Chloe will be there.

Avril McDonald is the best-selling award-winning author of the "Feel Brave" series of books (Little stories about big feelings) and the founder of www.feelbrave.com. Feel Brave has the vision to give *all* children access to tools that help them manage tough emotions and reach their potential. The Feel Brave books have been translated into seven languages and her video resources are used and loved in schools around the world and are broadcast on television and safe global children's streaming apps.

Avril is a trained teacher, an experienced businesswoman, and a mum. She is an ambassador of the Life Education Trust New Zealand (who uses her books and strategies in all their mobile classrooms), an ambassador of the New Zealand Fire Fighters Welfare Society, and a patron of the Westminster Children's University in London.

Mai Chen is Senior Managing Partner of Chen Palmer, Australasia's first public law specialist firm, which she co-founded in 1994. Her specialist areas of expertise include advising statutory bodies, the New Zealand Bill of Rights Act 1990, human rights, Treaty of Waitanga issues, judicial review, education law, employment law, and white collar fraud.

She is also Adjunct Professor at the University of Auckland School of Law, and Founder and Chair of the Superdiversity Institute of Law, Policy and Business, New Zealand Asian Leaders (NZAL), SUPERdiverse Women, and New Zealand Asian Lawyers.

Part VII: Diversity and inclusion

Rebecca Oldfield is CFO and Executive Vice President of Business Transformation at Infineum International Ltd. She joined Infineum in 2000 after completing a PhD degree in material science at Pembroke College, Cambridge, and has since explored many aspects of business management through roles in Sales, Logistics, Portfolio Management, and HR, located in the UK and USA.

Rebecca is a mother of three children, and is determined that her daughters and son experience a more inclusive and creative work environment than she did! As the Executive Committee sponsor of Inclusion and Diversity within Infineum, she aims to disrupt traditional models of talent and capability to improve innovation, empowerment, and well-being for individuals and teams. Rebecca is passionate about realising these untapped opportunities, at work, in her community and within her family. She hopes that this book, and all its fantastic contents, will spark ideas and opportunities for those ways beyond her current network, and enrich the lives of its readers and those closest to them.

James Burstall is CEO and the founder of multi-award-winning, hyper-converged super-indie Argonon, one of the UK's largest truly independent groups, with offices in London, New York, Los Angeles, Liverpool, and Glasgow. He founded Argonon in 2011, bringing together world-class independent production companies, spanning all genres, producing for broadcasters and platforms around the world.

Argonon's eight production companies include Bandicoot (*The Masked Singer*), Leopard Pictures (*Worzel Gummidge*), Windfall Films (NASA's Mars Landing), Like a Shot (*Abandoned Engineering*), BriteSpark Films (*Dispatches*), Leopard USA (*House Hunters International*), Studio Leo, and branded content expert Nemorin. Previously, James founded Leopard Films, specialising in returnable factual series including the international formats *Cash in the Attic* and *Missing* and Leopardrama, producers of the global award-winning *An Englishman in New York*, starring John Hurt and Cynthia Nixon.

Alina Nassar is a partner at Nassar Abogados, Costa Rica. She chairs the Aviation practice and co-chairs the Competition practice, both at regional level. Besides her work as an attorney, Alina actively participates as speaker and panellist in international conferences on air transport and on diversity and inclusion, and volunteers for several non-profit organisations.

Alina has held different positions in the Board of Directors of the International Aviation Women's Association (IAWA) and was its first Latin American President (2018–2019). She is passionate about creating and supporting educational and labour opportunities, advocating for diversity and inclusion, and contributing to programmes for the development of emerging economies. She holds a Master of Laws (LL.M.) degree from the University of Texas at Austin; a Juris Doctor (J.D.) degree with honours from the *Universidad de Costa Rica*; and has completed the Oxford Advanced Management and Leadership Programme, Saïd Business School, University of Oxford. She is currently pursuing a Master of Science degree in space studies at KU Leuven, Belgium.

Part VIII: Negotiating and collaborating

Desiree Botica is a foundational member of the Sysdoc Group and has been involved in the ongoing development and growth of the company for over 29 years. In her role as Sysdoc CEO, she is responsible for effective delivery of Sysdoc's core management consulting services. Effective collaboration is a key to the success of service delivery to Sysdoc clients, as they are most frequently engaged in delivery of programme management, change management, business process optimisation, and end-user training and support.

As Sysdoc CEO of New Zealand and Australia, she leads all aspects of Sysdoc business in the region. Her inspiring and focused leadership enables teams to deliver quality solutions to clients, ensuring operational excellence company-wide. She is passionate about people and people working together to create solutions to solve complex business problems and to create excellent work environments. Desiree is a mother of two wonderful strong young women who are attending University in New Zealand. She is also the founder of the Pump Up the Volume charity to support children with Type 1 diabetes and is a mentor for the Auckland University Women's Mentoring Programme.

Jensine Larsen is an award-winning digital social impact entrepreneur, a journalist, and a global speaker on the power of technology to speed up global women's power. She is the founder of World Pulse, a safe social network connecting women worldwide for a greater global voice. Today, World Pulse is powered by more than 870,000 women from 190 countries who are speaking for themselves and collectively improving the lives of 172.46 million people. In the best-selling book, "Half the Sky", New York Times columnist Nicholas Kristof recommends joining World Pulse as one of the top four things you can do in ten minutes to support women globally. For her work, Jensine received the 2018 Media Social Impact Award from the United Nations.

Jensine's ambition is to ensure that digital technology unleashes the untapped creative potential of women everywhere. She is a leader in digital communication, women's leadership, online communities, reciprocal philanthropy, and strategic partnerships. She founded World Pulse magazine in 2003, growing that platform into the pioneering WorldPulse.com, a global social network and leader in grassroots women's digital empowerment training.

For more than 15 years, Jensine has made it her job to listen to women in forgotten communities around the world. She is a frequent speaker on how social networking and technological innovation is a powerful accelerator for women's global power, appearing in media and on stages from NPR and BBC to TED.

Marita Lintener is Head of International Affairs at Skyguide, the Swissair Air Navigation Service Provider. She is also the founder and Managing Director of Lintener European Aviation Consultancy. She serves as Member of the Board and Vice-President Europe and Africa of the International Aviation Women's Association (IAWA).

Marita holds a master's degree in economics from the University of Bonn and is an alumna of the Oxford Advanced Management and Leadership Programme of Saïd Business School, University of Oxford. In September 2019, she was honoured by the EU Commissioner for Transport as "EU diversity ambassador".

Part IX: Social and environmental impact

Amrita Johri Amrita Johri leads information and research initiatives at Satark Nagrik Sangathan (SNS), a citizen's group in India working to promote transparency and accountability in government. She is a member of the working committee of the National Campaign for Peoples' Right to Information (NCPRI), which plays a pivotal role in campaigning for effective implementation of the Right to Information (RTI Act) in India. She has co-authored several national reports on the implementation of the RTI Act in India, including those on the performance of information commissions, judicial interpretations of provisions of the law, and assessments of the use of the law. She is associated with various rights-based struggles in India and is part of the convening group of the National Right to Food Campaign and Delhi Rozi Roti Adhikar Abhiyan (Delhi Right to Food Campaign).

Amrita is a recipient of the Meeto Memorial award for young South Asians in recognition of her commitment to promote communal harmony, peace, justice, and human rights. She has a master's degree in social policy from the London School of Economics & Political Science and a bachelor's degree in journalism from Lady Shri Ram College, Delhi University.

Anjali Bhardwaj Anjali Bhardwaj is the founder of Satark Nagrik Sangathan (SNS), a citizens' group working in the slum settlements of Delhi, with a mandate to promote transparency and accountability in government functioning and to encourage active participation of citizens in governance. She has been closely associated with the Right to Information (RTI) movement in India for over two decades and has been anchoring efforts to monitor the implementation of the RTI and has co-authored several national reports. She is also Co-Convenor of the National Campaign for Peoples' Right to Information (NCPRI). As part of the NCPRI, she was involved in campaigning for an effective RTI Act in India, and since the passage of the law in 2005, she has been working to ensure its effective implementation.

Anjali is associated with various rights-based struggles in India and is a member of the Steering Committee of the National Right to Food Campaign. She was one of the 12 global recipients of the "International Anticorruption Champions Award, 2021" from the US State Department in recognition of "leadership, activism, and advocacy for the Right to Information Movement in India". Anjali has master's degrees from Oxford University and Delhi School of Economics, Delhi University.

Giles Gunesekera Giles is Founder and CEO of Global Impact Initiative. The business creates Impact Investments, seeking both a positive financial return and intentional social impact for its stakeholders. Giles has over 25 years of experience in building teams and businesses for global enterprises.

Giles has a unique blend of leadership and business skills gained in the corporate environment married with financial and governance skills gained in the Not-for-Profit sector. He holds numerous Volunteer Not-for-Profit Directorships ranging from the Environment, International Aid and Human Rights to Disabilities, Education, Arts, and Sports. Giles is on Advisory Boards for the United Nations for Climate & Health and Sustainable Finance. He has received an Outstanding Alumnus award from Oxford's Advanced Management and Leadership Programme for creating an innovative, sustainable business that generates a positive social impact. Giles has formal academic qualifications from Melbourne University, Monash University, the Financial Services Institute of Australia, and the University of Oxford.

Marsha Marshall Marsha Marshall is CEO of Manawanui Support Ltd, a disability support organisation in New Zealand that facilitates and supports self-direction for over 6,000 disabled people and their families.

Originally from Canada, Marsha immigrated to New Zealand in 1997, where she has led the implementation of self-direction in a variety of roles. With a background as a paediatric nurse, Marsha has over 30 years of experience in health and disability and is passionate about self-direction, social impact, and social equity.

Kishan Nanayakkara Kishan Nanayakkara is Managing Director and a major shareholder of Resus Energy PLC, a renewable energy company listed on the Colombo Stock Exchange, which he founded in 2003. Kishan has over 30 years of experience in sectors ranging from manufacturing to financial services at senior management and board levels. He served on the Board of the Sri Lanka Sustainable Energy Authority, as an advisor to the National Council for Economic Development and as a consultant to the Public Enterprise Reforms Commission of Sri Lanka.

Kishan is Chartered Accountant in England and Wales and Chartered Management Accountant with an MSc degree in finance from the University of Birmingham. He is an alumnus of the Oxford Advance Management & Leadership Programme, Saïd Business School, University of Oxford, and, in 2019, he was accorded the Programme's outstanding alumnus award. As a life-long learner, he is currently following the master's degree in sustainability leadership at Cambridge University.

For further information on the contributors and contents of this book, please contact LMJOHRI@GMAIL.COM

FOREWORD

How delighted we are that *Mastering the Power of You at Work* is now published! Its preparation has been a mammoth task, involving contributions from leaders around the World, in 15 countries.

Many of the contributors of the chapters are alumni or faculty of the Oxford Advanced Management and Leadership Programme (OAMLP). This senior-level leadership programme is run through the Saïd Business School, University of Oxford, and was directed by Dr. Lalit Johri between 2007 and 2019.

The genesis of this book lies in Lalit's dream of taking education to people when a senior executive on the OAMLP asked him *"how can people around the world benefit from the important knowledge created and shared at Oxford University?"*

The ideas and concepts for the book were generated through vigorous discussions between Lalit and the alumni of OAMLP and young graduates Lalit met during his travels. Katherine and Gay, faculty of the OAMLP, joined Lalit eagerly to bring this project to fruition. Later, other well-known leaders within our networks were invited to contribute chapters in the book. This we feel has provided a rich mix of worldwide perspectives.

The purpose of each contributor is to share their knowledge and expertise with people who are aspiring to make a difference in their organisations, communities, and society. Each chapter is based on their personal experiences, analyses, and learnings. We would like to heartily thank all those who have contributed chapters and those who have assisted "behind the scenes", including Amrita Johri, Anjali Bhardwaj, Bernadette Stevenson, Philippa Bonay, Rose Barnett, Jasmin Milne, Sukanya Lee, Jodie Platts, and Vichak Phongpetra.

Mastering the Power of You is a unique look at the positive powers of leadership within us all. It is written for everyone who aspires to succeed in helping to make the world a better place but may feel the need for new insights to deal with the challenges occurring in their workplace, region, or country. It is written to inspire you to kindle your passion as a leader.

Your personal challenges may range from securing a meaningful employment, enhancing your skills to cope with changes in your workplace, maintaining your sense of well-being, and to thriving as a respected and trusted person in your community. As a responsible citizen, you may be inspired to address some of the social, economic, technological, environmental, and political challenges in our society.

The simple and easy-to-follow format of each chapter is grouped around the core concepts of Leadership, entrepreneurship, and volunteering; Purpose and values; Authenticity, trust, and presence; Strategising, thinking, and decision-making; Mentoring and development; Mental resilience; Diversity and inclusion; Negotiating and collaborating; and Social and environmental impact. This will inspire you to master these concepts, skills, and behaviours and use them to open new opportunities in your life and workplace.

Reading *Mastering the Power of You* will give you an extraordinary lens into the insights of leaders around the world. You will be taken on an expedition of discovery, guided by insights, with 32 chapters on a wide range of "powers" such as "the power of mental fitness", "the power of digital entrepreneurship", the power of leadership" "the power of purpose", "the power of creative thinking", "the power of kindness", "the power of negotiations", and "the power of sustainability".

The crucial nature of each power is revealed, as each chapter unfolds, assisted by personal experiences, plentiful examples, further readings, and valuable exercises to assist your personal mastery, vitally important to thrive in today's workplace and world. Through greater insight into the experiences of others, you will find that you are not alone.

Our objective is that reading *Mastering the Power of You* will play a valuable role in helping all readers to draw on some unique personal powers to deal with a broad spectrum of challenges. We have aimed to equip you with a broad set of leadership skills that you can apply in your life and work. And above all, we hope that it will inspire you all to have the courage to stand out and thrive in our challenging but wonderful world.

Read on, explore, and master the power of you!

Lalit Johri, Katherine Corich, Gay Haskins,
and all our worldwide contributors

PART I

Leadership, entrepreneurship, and volunteering

1

MASTERING THE POWER OF LEADERSHIP

Lalit Johri

Abstract

The power of enlightened leadership is everywhere, in every society, community, organisation, and family. Leadership skills drive our responses to solve the problems faced by humanity. They provide direction and inspiration for the evolution and fulfilment of peoples' objectives.

Anybody, irrespective of their position in a hierarchy, can be a leader. It is through their purpose, character, and deeds that they attract followers. The followers make leaders – "a leader without followers is a voice in the wilderness".

The field of leadership knowledge is vast and changing. We can learn about leadership by studying literature, by reading the biographies of great leaders, and by watching the leaders in our organisation. We can also develop leadership skills by putting ourselves in a leader's position in a project. This chapter explores the leadership discipline and how we can master the power of leadership.

Keywords: Leadership, mission, orchestration, self-awareness, positive difference

Outstanding leaders

It was the news from Wuhan, China, in the first days of 2020, that made Sarah Gilbert sit up and think. As Professor of Vaccinology at the

DOI: 10.4324/9781003219293-2

University of Oxford in the UK, and a leading scientist at the university's Jenner Institute, her research team wasted no time in getting involved.[1]

By mid-January when the genome sequence of the unknown virus was released by the Chinese scientists, Professor Gilbert and her team deployed their ongoing scientific research to design a vaccine to fight against the unknown virus. Later, the World Health Organization named the virus as COVID-19.

In the next few months, the Oxford vaccine team stitched up partnerships and garnered financial resources to develop a vaccine to prevent COVID-19 virus infections. In a record time of less than 12 months, Professor Gilbert and her team gave to the world a precious gift to protect life – a vaccine named Covishield.

In the first 11 months after the emergency authorisation of the vaccine in UK, more than two billion doses of Covishield were supplied to 170 countries preventing an estimated 50 million infections and saving a million lives.[2]

I regard Professor Sarah Gilbert amongst the outstanding leaders of the year 2020 in the field of science. She and her team foresaw the threat posed by the virus and successfully orchestrated the development of the vaccine. Her leadership is truly a remarkable story of modern times.

Ten years ago, in 2012, social activist Malala Yousafzai, 11 years old at that time, survived a fatal attack on her life when she was campaigning for girls' right to education in Pakistan. This fearless young woman did not give up and has "*continued her struggle and become a leading advocate of girls' rights*". This is another great example of exemplary leadership driven by strong belief, courage, and determination.[3]

According to the World Bank and the World Health Organization, half of the world's population lacks access to essential health services. Fortunately, there are some exceptional leaders who are involved in solving global-scale problems. One such leader is Dr. Devi Prasad Shetty, a cardiac surgeon and the founder of Naryana Health in India.

Dr. Shetty pioneered the mission – *Health for all. All for health*. Inspired by this mission, he and his team are on a journey to build a nationwide network of hospitals and health centres to provide modern healthcare services to people, irrespective of their economic status. His goal is to become a "*high-quality healthcare service provider at the lowest-cost in the world*". Using state-of-the-art technologies and medical practices, and management techniques, Naryana Health is showing the way forward for providing high-quality and affordable healthcare services to billions of people in the world.[4]

In the field of civil rights and social justice, there are two great leaders whose leadership contributions have changed the course of world history. Mahatma Gandhi championed the philosophy of nonviolence and "fought against" racism, discrimination, and colonial rule. His unique leadership philosophy of nonviolence and his resolve to get rid of colonial powers became a beacon of hope for people of colonies to strive for their country's independence from colonial occupiers. Millions of people were inspired by Mahatma's leadership and joined him in the freedom struggle in India. India gained independence in 1947, paving the way for many countries in Asia and Africa to seek independence from colonial rulers.

Reverend Martin Luther King Jr. was a religious leader and civil-rights activist in the United States. He followed Mahatma Gandhi's philosophy of nonviolence. He led several protest marches against racism. In 1963, he delivered the famous speech "I have a dream". A year later, the United States passed a law prohibiting all forms of racial discrimination.[5]

The lessons I have learnt

The leadership stories of these great men and women are inspiring. For more than four decades, I have been studying the leadership journeys of leaders in different fields. My objective is to understand the spirit and meaning of leadership and learn lessons from the great leaders. Here are six of the important lessons I have learnt.

The essence of leadership is to make a positive difference in the lives of people giving them a sense of safety, identity, dignity, purpose, and hope. It may sound philosophical but, in my opinion, effective leaders in political or business or social organisations focus on people. The people are the main actors in the success of an organisation and its positive impact on the society. The men and women leaders I have described earlier have led causes to benefit people.

Leadership is getting immersed in reality. Being sensitive to situations and events sets the stage for leaders to reflect and act. They are curious to know how these emerging situations are impacting people and the planet. They ask questions like "Is there something that is not right? What if we don't challenge or do something?" Mahatma Gandhi hated the tyranny of colonial rule on powerless people. Martin Luther King Jr. fought for equal rights to people, irrespective of the race and colour. Professor Gilbert foresaw and was working to protect people and the world from "disease X".

Leadership is seizing the opportunity. This is a very important lesson. When real leaders see something that is wrong or inappropriate or missing, they see it as an opportunity to correct it. We call it a "defining moment". Such moments inspire leaders to do something! Their resolve sows the seeds of a mission or purpose. Dr. Devi Prasad Shetty saw abysmal health care services in India as an opportunity. His "*Health for all. All for health*" mission laid the foundations for providing affordable high-quality health care. These six words summarise his purpose and strategy for providing health care to all by seeking collaboration of different actors in the healthcare ecosystem. Professor Gilbert and her team at Oxford lost no time and seized the opportunity to develop a vaccine to fight against COVID-19 virus.

Leadership is striving to achieve the dream. This is the orchestration stage when leaders put all efforts behind a cause to fulfill their purpose. They show their dream and seek support from people and institutions. They experiment with new ideas. They make mistakes and learn and refine. They are relentless in the pursuit of their goal. To test, mass produce and distribute the Covishield vaccine at a global scale, Oxford University entered in a not-for-profit partnership with the British Swedish pharmaceutical and biotechnology company AstraZeneca. Through their intense effort the vaccine was designed, tested and approved in a record time of ten months. Mahatma Gandhi organized mass demonstrations to protest against the discriminatory policies and practices of the colonial rulers in South Africa and India. He was sent to prison several times, but it did not break his resolve. He was steadfast in demanding independence for India.

Leadership is a collective act. Great leaders build strong leadership teams by attracting people from different backgrounds with diverse expertise. They develop future leaders. The leadership teams rally around a compelling purpose and virtuous principles. We are facing many wicked problems affecting our lives in unprecedented ways. We need collective leadership at different levels in our society to address these complexities. Mahatma Gandhi attracted many national and international activists to support him in leading the freedom movement in India. He enjoyed the support of millions of ordinary people who participated in the protest marches he organised. Instead of the usual 10 years it takes to develop a vaccine, the Oxford vaccine Covishield was developed in 10 months, largely due to great teamwork on the part of virologists and scientists at Oxford University.

> **Explore:**
>
> The Oxford Vaccine
>   https://www.research.ox.ac.uk/area/coronavirus-research/vaccine

Leadership must be dynamic to the situation and context. Leadership does not follow a rigid path. As the context changes, leaders must adapt. This requires constant unlearning and relearning at all levels in the organisation. While exhibiting resilience in the face of threatening environment strong leadership teams embrace change. Rejuvenating their dream, building, and acquiring new expertise, innovations and seeking new frontiers is the essence of dynamic leadership. To fulfill the mission of high-quality healthcare at the lowest cost, Narayana Health is using advance data analytics based on machine learning and artificial intelligence.

> **Explore:**
>
> Narayana Health uses data analytics and AI to provide affordable high-quality health care
>   https://news.microsoft.com/en-in/features/narayana-health-uses-data-analytics-and-ai-to-provide-affordable-high-quality-healthcare/

In December 2021, the Oxford vaccine team published a blueprint for developing a new vaccine within hundred days of the identification of a new virus. The accelerated design, testing and manufacturing based on process innovations will not only reduce the cost of the vaccine but also potentially minimize the damage we have seen during the COVID-19 pandemic.

For dynamic teams, leadership is a journey of a constant pursuit of higher aspirations based on learning and innovation.

> **Explore:**
>
> Oxford team publishes blueprint for making millions of doses of a new vaccine within 100 days
>   https://www.ox.ac.uk/news/2021-12-22-oxford-team-publish-blueprint-making-millions-doses-new-vaccine-within-100-days-0

I have been in higher education for more than four decades. During this period, I have learnt hundreds of lessons in leadership, and I will discuss some of these lessons.

Leadership and risk

In 1976, as a young lecturer at the business school in the University of Delhi in India, I established a trekking club in the school. This was our "leadership simulator". I was inspired by my curiosity when I read about the flight simulators used for training pilots. My logic was that we can give real and augmented experiences in leadership to our young students by organising high-altitude trekking expeditions in the Himalayas for them. This was also meant to address the students' demand for an experience-rich curriculum in building team leadership skills. I personally led the first two expeditions in 1976 and 1977 and learnt many lessons in leadership that the conventional pedagogical techniques could not teach.

Unlike today, in the 1970s, the Himalayan high mountain ranges lacked infrastructure and life support services. Mounting a high-altitude trekking expedition is no less daunting than leading a business enterprise in a high-risk environment. The element of surprise and speed associated with risk situations is such that it can instil fear or at worst inflict fatalities. Fortunately, I and several members of the expeditions had prior experience in trekking, and none lacked confidence, which is very important for undertaking risky ventures.

For launching the inaugural expedition, our first challenge was the lack of material resources. We approached our school's alumni network with an inspiring story – how the "leadership simulator" will help young students and why the alumni should support us. Our story worked and we received enough food rations, medicines, and sponsorships. For equipment, I approached my cousin at the Youth Hostel Association of India, and he was extremely generous in lending equipment. It was a low-budget venture, and our strategy was simple – "go frugal and do-it-yourself" without the help of porters, guides, and cooks.

We were ready to go and "take" risk! Thirty years later, my colleague at Oxford, Pete Goss, a pioneering British yachtsman, explained the meaning of risk taking. He said, "Successful adventure leaders 'embrace' risk. They prepare and train for every possible scenario by playing and replaying risk situations in their mind". As leaders, we can't be irresponsible and push our team members into unknown situations unprepared. Pete's words made lot of sense and I learned how to "master" risk.

The trekking expeditions have taught me many lessons in leadership. Every moment, the members of the expedition experience physical, mental, and emotional stress. The leader must keep the spirits of every one high and lead the way to the destination. During extreme crises situations, fear sets in. The leader must get everybody together, rebuild the confidence, and consult and chart the course of action to get everyone out of harm's way.

The leader is responsible for the safety, well-being, and confidence of each member of the team. The leader must listen all the time. When the members are extremely tired, they go quiet . . . the leader must observe, ask, and respond. The leader must make sense of how each member is doing. Empathising, helping, and encouraging go a long way in restoring energy and enthusiasm. In the 1977 expedition, I faced a situation when a member of the team was very sick. He could not move, and I decided to take him back to base. It was a difficult decision, but it was my responsibility as a leader to ensure that he got medical help at the base station. He recovered and reached home safely.

The "leadership simulator" in the University of Delhi business school has produced many great leaders who are leading business enterprises in many countries. My former student Sunder Hemrajani, the deputy leader of 1977 expedition and the leader of the 1978 expedition, has published a book giving a detailed account of these expeditions. He has organised case discussions on crises situations faced during expeditions.[6]

Leadership and change

In 2001, I was chairing the AIT Reforms Steering Committee at the Asian Institute of Technology (AIT) in Thailand, where I was serving in the business school as a professor in international business. The reform programmes were focused on improving the financial and administrative management of the Institute and enhancing the impact of its academic programmes.

In educational institutions, the researchers and teachers enjoy considerable autonomy on academic matters. Keeping this in mind, we laid down principles underpinning the reforms, projects, and processes.

- Generate broad consensus on why reforms are necessary and what we should aim for.
- Invite academics to propose and champion change projects.
- Design change projects with clear roadmap, milestones, and measurable outcomes.

- Use intense consultation processes with stakeholders to generate new ideas for each change project.
- Organise regular meetings to review the progress and address the concerns of the teachers, students, and administrative staff.
- The Chair of the Reforms Steering Committee and project champions are accountable to the President's Council and the Board.

Leading change in an international educational institution was an invaluable experience. I learned many crucial lessons in leadership for change:

- Most people resist change. They require and take time to understand and accept the need for change. As a leader, don't force change. Create a widely shared understanding of the rationale for change.
- The change projects must be people-centric. They should be for the benefit of the people, the organisation, and society.
- People don't like ambiguity associated with change. As a leader, be transparent and communicate the right information about what will change and how it will change.
- People associate risk with change. As a leader, don't sweep risk under the carpet. Be upfront and explain to different stakeholders what the risks are and the steps that will be taken to mitigate the risk.
- People see change from their personal perspective. As a leader, explain what will change for people, how they will be trained to play the new roles, what kind of support will be made available to them to perform in new jobs successfully.
- Change should minimise stress on people. Too many change programmes, complex change processes, lack of clarity, and lack of trust in the leadership team are some of the sources of stress. As a leader, weigh the pros and cons of scope, scale, and speed of change; keep change processes simple and engaging; communicate clearly and frequently; ensure that project champions enjoy high levels of respect and trust.
- Gather feedback on how effective the change actions are. Be flexible and adapt to changing circumstances.
- When a change project achieves the desired objectives, acknowledge the efforts of the people and celebrate the success.

Leadership for educating leaders

In 2007, I was invited by Gay Haskins, Dean of Executive Education, to apply to be Fellow at Oxford University's Saïd Business School. To my delight, the panel appointed me! One of my tasks was to transform the flag-ship programme of the school for senior leaders – the Oxford Advanced Management and Leadership Programme (OAMLP).

It was an honour for me to steer the programme and orchestrate the edu-cation of senior leaders from all over the world. Over the next 12 years, we experimented with new ideas, and in the end, the OAMLP team was success-ful! We were ranked amongst the top open programmes in the world. On the last day of my last OAMLP in October 2019, Andrew White, Associate Dean of Executive Education, summarised my leadership in a letter to the alumni:

> *Given that the World has so many challenges, Lalit is someone who can have a quiet sense of happiness and satisfaction about his achievements. He has dedicated more than ten years to evolving our OAMLP into often a life changing experi-ence for senior professionals, often working late into the night to build session content or case studies for topical debate. His inclusive style of leadership has created a high-impact experience applauded by senior leaders since 2007. . . . Lalit's professional mentoring has contributed to the development of many staff across Executive Education, many of whom have been promoted to more senior positions within our own and other institutions.*

The reward I cherish most from my role at Oxford University is meeting hundreds of outstanding senior executives from countries around the world. We became great friends and we have continued our conversations and research on contemporary challenges faced by the leaders. They have made seminal contributions in the preparation of this book. I am delighted to share some examples of our recent work and the leadership lessons we have learnt.

Leadership in teams

In 2020, Philippa Bonay, Director of People and Business Services, Office for National Statistics, UK Government, and an alumna of OAMLP, and I wrote a working paper on pillars of team collaboration and the roles of a team leader within organisations. In the paper, we have discussed nine roles of a team leader to create a culture of collaboration and high performance.

Orchestrator

The symphony of the organisation is orchestrated by team leaders and played by the team members. The orchestration role of leaders is chal-lenging. In our research, we discovered that many team leaders were so focused on daily work routines and output that they can forget to take a broader view of the operating context of their teams. Team leaders must elevate their thinking to distil the complex external trends, the organizational purpose and communicate with high clarity to team members. They are the interface and manage "boundaries" between their own team and other teams in the organisation. The team leaders provide a very important bridge between the strategic leaders at the top and functional teams at the ground level. They manage competing demands, creating boundaries and protection for the work to be done and build trust through ensuring participation – they act as the bridge for two-way communication.

Inspirer

It is tremendously important that team members do not lose sight of the purpose, vision and goals of the organisation. The team leader, who has a wider mandate in the organization, has the responsibility to keep the deeper meaning of the work top of mind for members: the vision of the organization and how far they have achieved their goals. The organisational goals are achieved when the team leader inspires team members to achieve results and milestones incrementally and cumulatively. The team leader facilitates the connection between the day-to-day work, the wider context, the societal role and contributions of the organisation and how and with whom the team needs to collaborate beyond themselves. The team leader inspires team members as important links in fulfilling the purpose of the organisation: a coalition for the greater good.

Enabler

As enabler, the team leader has to ingrain the organisational ethos, work ethics and values in the minds and hearts of the team members. In addition to providing resources and working tools, the leader has to provide social and psychological space for team members to perform their tasks. Friction within teams can be caused by a range of factors. It is not necessarily a bad thing – creative tension, constructive and courteous disagreement are key factors to a high-performing, highly collaborative team. Collective problem solving enhances sustainable decision making. For this to work successfully, the team leader must enable psychological safety – being able to be oneself, share one's ideas and views without fear of humiliation or retribution – this leads to greater sharing and collaboration, supporting the team to coalesce around issues and draw on the richness of its collective knowledge beyond individual expertise. Productivity, continuous learning and innovation are enhanced as a result.

Mediator

The human system in every organisation has constantly changing dynamics. Often differences surface and act as psychological barriers to collaboration; the team leader has a role in creating the environment to surface and share differences. Often, at least initially, this will require the team leader to observe and sense conflicts. Sometimes tensions can be kept from the team leader or indeed harboured by individuals, which can fester and create strained work environments. Drawing on empathy and the greater knowledge of its members, the team leader must surface issues and work to diffuse them. Aligned to the educator role, they will look to increase the team's ability to self-mediate and auto regulate. The team leader may also find themselves mediating between the team members and the senior leadership. This can be the most challenging element of the mediator role, requiring a level of independence from both sides in order to present a compelling way forward to both. Basing the proposals around the benefits of collaboration and inclusivity of ideas will increase trust and lead to a high-performing organisational system.

Curator

The team leader has a central role in facilitating collaboration through creating a culture of mutual respect, mutual trust, mutual understanding and kindness. At the core of teamwork is the concept of collaboration. We define collaboration as an ethos or spirit where team members accept and respect, trust and complement each other and radiate kindness to accomplish team tasks. The spirit of collaboration rests on complex person-to-person interaction.

The team leader has the responsibility to curate the team, ensuring maximum diversity across the whole range of possibilities which ensures appropriate levels of challenge and new learning. Diverse teams are more innovative and show greater levels of customer service, long-term growth and employee engagement. In short, diverse organizations outperform less diverse counterparts and provide benefit across the whole system. The team leader must consider the wider benefit an individual can bring to a team beyond their expertise – complementarity rather than similarity. This will also guard against the mutual understanding element leading to groupthink.

Carer

The Covid-19 pandemic has brought the health and wellbeing of employees on the centre stage. Wellbeing is now an essential leadership capability, attending to it can positively impact the experience and productivity of individuals and therefore teams. The leader has to constantly enquire, listen, sense and pay attention to the health and wellbeing of the team members, embedding it in the culture of the team so it is not a response to extreme response to distress or crisis but the essence of team ethos and interaction between the members and the leadership of the team. The team leader must know when it is important to slow down, to check in with members and prioritise work accordingly. They must also create community connections for support across the team and beyond.

Every member represents a crucial link in the human chain for processing work and accomplishing team tasks. Taking a human-centred approach means a deeper understanding of motivations, aspirations, personal circumstances, emotions and also blockers, all of which influence individual thinking and action. The team leader must pay attention to individual as well as collective needs and do so authentically. The need to listen, but also know what to listen for.

Educator

In the age of social-media we are constantly bombarded with billions of bytes of information which may be difficult to navigate; determine right from wrong, necessary from distraction, and fad from enduring. A trusted leader in a team setting is in an ideal position for educating and influencing the behaviour of the team members. As an educator, not only can the team leader change the social behaviour of the members, but also shape their values and role in the context of society. The team cannot support the organisation's mission and success in isolation. The team leader must understand and translate the systemic space within which the team operates elevating its members' corporate knowledge to that of their individual expertise in order that they may better collaborate and work in, and across, the system.

The team leader drives the culture of the organisation through their own behaviour and that of the team. A myriad of micro cultures exists within organisations: it is the role of the team leader to elevate the strength of the team level culture to the level of organisational success. They must also weave the corporate expectations and corporate culture into the ethos and behaviour of the team to attain the levels of collaboration across the system that lead to a high-performing culture. They must call out and address behaviour that is not aligned and further challenge themselves on their own behaviour.

Mentor

The nature of a mentor is to foster an environment of collaborative learning and shared endeavour. This takes the role of the team leader beyond task, situation and immediate outcome to that of builder of a learning organisation. In this role, the team leader's experience and wider knowledge are transferred daily to the team through the very act of work. This should be done deliberately, and the members should purposefully use this learning to enhance their own approach.

When employees return to work after extended periods of lockdown, team leaders need to mentor the employees in adapting to new work methods and health and safety protocols. Many companies are introducing new technologies, new workplace environments and new ways of working requiring employees to upskill their competencies. Some of these changes and innovations are disruptive causing psychological stress amongst the employees. The team leader has a critical role in restoring the self-confidence of the team members and giving them a sense of mastery of the work processes and team tasks.

In a collaborative environment, everyone learns from the knowledge and skills of others. Therefore, mentoring can become distributed across the team rather than being held solely by the team leader. This also increases diversity of thought yielding stronger outcomes and greater inclusion. Trust is built. By encouraging collaborative mentoring, the team leader will enhance the social environment, transformational learning and openness to the wider system.

Evangelist

Evangelists have the best interests of everyone at heart. This role is the cumulative role of the other eight; it also extends explicitly across the whole system. The pivotal role of the team leader in the middle of the organisation makes them ideal for evangelising. The evangelist team leader develops a clear and coherent message about the organisation, its work and the benefits of collaboration for high performance. They democratise the work, the organisation, its values and its products and federate others around them with the added objective of increasing collaboration to improve the system and its outputs. The team leader may also play a crucial role in sensitising team members to the external environment, extending the work of the organisation beyond its corporate boundaries, for example helping them in planning and organising voluntary work in the communities that depend upon it or would see benefit from the organization. Evangelism can be contagious, it's fun, it empowers and creates a true sense of belonging. The evangelist inspires, federates diverse voices and ensures inclusion of all the stakeholders in the system.

Inspiring messages for women leaders

During January 2022, Phillipa Bonay was in conversation with Hanaa Al Kharusi, General Manager, Corporate Banking at Ahlibank in Oman and an alumna of the OAMLP. Besides her role as a senior woman leader, Ms. Al Kharusi mentors young professionals and women leaders in Oman. One of her leadership missions is to encourage them to aspire for higher responsibilities in organisations. In the conversation, Ms. Hanaa Al Kharusi described ten inspiring messages she has for the women leaders.[7]

- Believe in yourself. Focus on your positive psychology.
- Anchor yourself in your cultural roots and values. It helps in building your self-identity.
- Develop a sense of purpose and pursue it actively. Your purpose will guide your thinking and leadership actions.
- Be authentic as a person. This will help in building mutual trust.
- Nurture global outlook with deep respect for people from diverse cultures.
- Pursue and value new knowledge. Invest in acquiring new skills.
- Strive to break the glass ceiling. The sky is the limit!
- Stand tall amongst people. Do not underestimate yourself. Seize opportunities to demonstrate your expertise and commitment.
- Drive the business agenda by balancing economic, financial, and social gains and impacts.
- Lead calmly with humility and compassion.

Deep thinking skills for leaders

In September 2020, Philippa Bonay and I wrote another working paper on the importance of deep thinking for leaders. Since the onset of the COVID-19 pandemic, we are at the inflection point when leaders have to focus on nurturing deep cognitive skills to thrive. Continuously fade-in–fade-out nature of the business landscape threatens our mental models (internal algorithms). As leaders, we build our mental models based on our life experiences, successes and failures and get stuck in the groove. Very few leaders have natural agility or deliberate commitment to change their mental models. The "burning platform" does not always work. The impact of the pandemic can be exhausting as it impacts both our strategic thinking and our emotional resilience, the latter being essential for success in the former.

Human beings love the status quo. This is precisely why leaders are currently more challenged than they have ever been. As leaders, we need to sharpen our mental agility, to constantly refresh and adopt new mental models and develop flexibility to work simultaneously with diverse sets of mental models in our strategy teams.

So, what deep cognitive skills do we need to nurture to frame challenges and make context specific choices? These choices should not only address the current and emerging realities but also be consistent with deeper purpose of the organisation.

In our work, we have identified several thinking skills that can help leaders to respond:

- Ability to reflect and conceptualise
  - What leadership lessons have you learnt since the onset of the COVID-19 pandemic? Why are these lessons important?
- Learning from failures
  - What leadership lessons have you learnt in the situations during the COVID-19 pandemic where your organisation failed to achieve its objectives?
- Agility of mind
  - During the COVID-19 pandemic, what leadership lessons that you had learnt prior to pandemic have you had to unlearn? Why?
- Judgement to characterise and differentiate
  - Who are your preferred leaders in public space who have led their country successfully during the COVID-19 pandemic? How are they different from those who leaders who have failed?

- Framing and reframing
  - How would you frame the challenges posed by the COVID-19 pandemic on your organisation? How would you frame this narrative purposefully for your teams?
- Purpose as a leader
  - As a leader of an organisation, what gave you the sense of fulfilment prior to the COVID-19 pandemic? Has there been a shift in your purpose during the COVID-19 pandemic?
- Critical thinking and innovation
  - What are the weaknesses of executive training and development programmes in their present form? What changes would you recommend in the design of the programmes in the wake of the COVID-19 pandemic?
- Depth in curiosity
  - To lead your organisation in the coming years, what are your curiosity questions?
- Depth in logic
  - How deep is your understanding about how the COVID-19 pandemic has impacted our world? What changes do you anticipate in your industry?

Leadership in the age of distraction and destruction

In February 2022, during a webinar discussion, J.R. Klein, principal of J.R. Global Associates, and an alumnus of the OAMLP, argued that spiritual energy can help leaders in maintaining a sense of balance, motivation, and purpose.

The pressure of leadership in an age of distraction and destruction can end up being a primary reason for anxiety, frustration, burnout, and failure. The negative narrative of myopic ideologies causes the loss of a sense of community, the increase in ideological echo chambers and crowd mentality, the attention deficit syndrome, and egocentric individuality.

This age requires personal discipline to rise above the norm. Traditional belief systems provide relevant models for leaders to strengthen performance and cope with situational pressure and anxieties. The spiritual energy builds habits that build character. Character is the catalyst to managing willpower, serving others, and intentional introspection. It is the foundation of higher performance and relational relevance.

The understanding that we are all part of something bigger than ourselves is the driver of spiritual behaviour and energy. Finding our role in the bigger picture will change our behaviour, approach to leadership, and make us better leaders.

Mastering the power of leadership

There is a leader in everyone! To stand out as a leader, you must kindle your spirit of leadership. In our daily life, we experience situations that are against the spirit of a modern progressive society. Living in the crucible of life, how we respond to opportunities and threats defines us as leaders. These external influences and our internal thinking shape and refine our character, values, and dreams as leaders.

How to master the power of leadership? There is no set prescription. A good starting point is to read books on and by famous leaders. There are thousands of books written on great leaders. You can select your favourite leaders and dive deep in the life and learn from their speeches and actions.

You can start shadowing leaders and observe them at work. Follow their speeches and ask questions – what is their purpose and mission? What are their values? What are their actions? Leaders attract followers in an ethical way and with kindness rather than manipulation, coercion, or through imposing hierarchy – these are not the attributes of good leaders.

The leader in you evolves over time. It is *learning by doing and reflecting*. As a leader, you are constantly making decisions then you review the impact of your decisions and change. This is a process by which you refine your leadership choices and style. Take time to reflect about situations, reactions, and your leadership style, because great leadership is about great self-awareness. Continually look to improve, adapt, and envision – leadership is as much about preparing the future as the here and now or the past – great leaders challenge themselves and their assumptions, constantly.

To help leaders improve their skills, many organisations conduct psychometric assessments and 360° feedback surveys. The survey data help in identifying the areas for improvement. In the next stage, these organisations provide coaching and mentoring support to the executives.

Participating in senior leadership executive programmes is a very effective way to master the power of leadership. At Oxford, my mission in the OAMLP was to facilitate the journey of leaders from being successful to becoming significant. We created a safe environment for comprehensive dialogues amongst senior leaders. We encouraged the participants to slow down and reflect deeply on their purpose and role in the society.

I started this chapter with a discussion on great leaders. During the COVID-19 pandemic, we have witnessed many "leaders" holding positions at the highest levels in politics have failed their people. The crisis triggered by the COVID-19 pandemic has proved that leadership holds the key to human success.

To master the power of leadership and to enhance your effectiveness as a leader, you will need to focus on building your character and skills. In this book, we have a wide collection of chapters on mastering leadership skills written by leaders from different fields. I invite you to read and reflect!

Meanwhile, my own leadership journey continues. Since late 2019, I am leading a team of researchers and policymakers in developing a blueprint for reviving and rejuvenating their economy and enterprises. We have developed a multisector "Living with the Pandemic" series of reports for a South East Asian country. The focus of my people development initiatives is on leadership and creating culture of safety and performance in organisations.

Summary

Leadership is essential for the success of human endeavours and evolution of humanity. There is a leader in everyone of us. When we nurture and use our leadership potential, we can achieve wonderful results at every level in the society. You can build and lead a sports team. You can become an activist to spearhead social causes. You can become a mentor, educator, or evangelist to build people and great teams. You can use the emerging technologies and become a start-up entrepreneur. Leadership skills can be learnt through formal methods of education and through experience. Start with a purpose and mission, build a team, and make a positive difference. Let us build strong leaders who create a vibrant society.

Reflection exercise: Develop your leadership manifesto

The objective of this reflection exercise is to write your leadership manifesto on a poster and discuss with your colleagues.

Start by writing your leadership **edge (E)**, that is, what are your unique strengths as a leader?

Next, write your leadership **values (V)**, that is, what are your guiding principles as a leader?

And then, write your leadership **agenda (A)**, that is, what are your purpose and your goals as a leader?

Discuss your leadership EVA with your colleagues and refine it.

Notes

1 Lane, Richard (2020), Sarah Gilbert: Carving a Path toward a COVID-19 Vaccine. *The Lancet*, 395(10232), 1247, April 18, 2020.
2 Two Billion Doses of AstraZeneca's COVID-19 Vaccine Supplied to Countries across the World Less Than 12 Months after First Approval. Available at: https://www.astra zeneca.com/media-centre/press-releases/2021/two-billion-doses-of-astrazenecas-covid-19-vaccine-supplied-to-countries-across-the-world-less-than-12-months-after-first-approval.html
3 Malala Yousafzai (2022), Nobel Prize Outreach AB 2022. Facts. *NobelPrize.org*, Tuesday, February 15, 2022. Available at: https://www.nobelprize.org/prizes/peace/2014/yousafzai/facts/
4 Narayana Health. Available at: https://www.narayanahealth.org/leadership/board-of-directors/dr-devi-shetty
5 Martin Luther King Jr. (2022), Nobel Prize Outreach AB 2022. Facts. *NobelPrize.org*, Tuesday, February 15, 2022. Available at: https://www.nobelprize.org/prizes/peace/1964/king/facts/
6 Hemrajani, Sunder (2021), *Beyond the Mountains – Overcoming the Challenges within*. Allied Publishers Private Limited, India.
7 Oxford Leadership Knowledge Club Podcast 6 – Hanaa Al Kharusi. Available at: https://anchor.fm/philippa07/episodes/Oxford-Leadership-Knowledge-Club-podcast-6-Hanaa-Al-Kharusi-e1cuidc

Further reading

1 Respect (Stanford Encyclopedia of Philosophy). Available at: https://plato.stanford.edu/entries/respect/
2 Trust (Stanford Encyclopedia of Philosophy). Available at: https://plato.stanford.edu/entries/trust/
3 Tett, Gillian (2021), *Anthro-Vision: How Anthropology Can Explain Business and Life*. UK: Penguin Random House.
4 Bennis, Warren (1989), *On Becoming a Leader*. Basic Books, published 1989 and reprinted many times.
5 Gilbert, Sarah and Green Catherine (2021), *Vaxxers: The Inside Story of the Oxford Astra Zeneca Vaccine and the Race against the Virus*. UK: Hachette.

2

MASTERING THE POWER OF DIGITAL ENTREPRENEURSHIP

Thomas Abraham

Abstract

In this chapter, I have discussed my own transformation from a corporate leader to a digital entrepreneur. The transition has been a fascinating experience in having to cope with a constant stream of challenges, the phenomenal pace of change and innovation, and a multitude of opportunities. In the digital space, life changes very fast, and therefore, as a digital entrepreneur, one has to be a constant learner. In the absence of ready-to-use textbook solutions, you have to use your imagination and experiment with new ideas. You are always learning by doing. Another important lesson I have learnt is the value of networking and seeking business partners. The digital technology landscape is very diverse with applications in every sector of a modern economy. I share lessons from my experiences working with other digital entrepreneurs who faced roadblocks and overcame them to build great products and services.

Keywords: Digital entrepreneurship, technology entrepreneur, innovation, consumer experience

The beginning

It all started in 1987 when I embarked on my career with American Express in Mumbai in India. I was given the task of selling corporate credit cards to business travellers. With high humidity and incessant rains in Mumbai,

DOI: 10.4324/9781003219293-3

selling door to door was physically taxing. The market opportunity was limited to exporters and the sales cycle was long as we were trying to sell a concept. This challenging assignment inspired me to think of trying something different. I set up a tele sales unit in the branch to improve my productivity. In those days, selling on the telephone was not very common in India. I used to dial potential customers manually. It was a successful experiment and it paved the way in my career to look for roles where I could try new ways of marketing and selling. There was a growing realisation that I was not comfortable with status quo. I started to nurture the idea of leaving the world of big companies and find new pastures where I could be more like an entrepreneur. I believe that I was inspired to do this by the words of the great American Baptist minister and activist, Martin Luther King Jr (1929–1968). He famously said, in his final speech before his assassination, delivered on April 3, 1968, "Only when it is dark enough, can you see the stars".[1]

The leap into the digital world

My leap into the world of digital technologies started at Wolters Kluwer in India after we took over the content of a well-known publishing house specialising in taxation. Prior to this takeover, our business was largely selling books on taxation for accountants. The book business was not sustainable due to the high cost of material, high distribution cost, return of unsold stocks, payment delays, and unpaid credit. Furthermore, the life of the printed content in the books was between 6 and 12 months, as the tax laws were changing constantly. Our research showed that users wanted up-to-date information on tax laws anytime and anywhere and therefore marketing content on a digital platform was the ideal medium.

The content that we acquired from the publishing house was in the form of tax journals and digital video discs (DVD). Our objective was to convert the content to an online product that would meet the expectations of the buyers and users in terms of up-to-date information accessible anytime, anywhere.

In transition from physical selling to digital selling, we faced many challenges:

- How to enhance the benefits of the content sold through the digital platform to accountants and tax consultants?
- How can we make them successful as tax consultants?

- How to re-train our sales staff and agents who were very comfortable selling books and journals face-to-face and now had to sell the new concept of content on digital platform?
- How can we charge a premium price for content which was continuously updated on the digital platform?
- And a big challenge was: how can we train our teams to convert and migrate from physical format to digital platform in order to deliver a rich experience to tax consultants?

As the leader of this business, I had to address these challenges. I set up an internal team comprising experts in content, technology, marketing and sales, and customer service to design strategies for migrating from a physical format to a digital format. It became an exercise in business transformation and meant building an entirely new organisation with fresh ideas and energy to provide the necessary momentum.

The transformation process posed many challenges! Many senior members of the team had strong views and I found myself getting pulled into discussions to reconcile differences. The project manager in charge of transformation often expressed his frustration at not being able to make any progress. We took the transformation team for an outdoor team building exercise. The objective of the exercise was to improve inter-personal relationships, to promote mutual trust, and to converge around common goal to make the transformation from physical to digital successful. We also established rewards for achieving intermediate milestones in the transformation journey. The prospect of mastering new technology, the opportunity to grow, and increasing trust in the team fired up everybody and we started to make good progress as a team.

As part of the retraining of the sales staff and agents, we had a series of brainstorming meetings to determine creative ways of selling the digital content. We launched a multi-year subscription that included content on DVD and our online digital products. This helped us earn revenues for multiple years upfront, thereby ensuring customer loyalty over the period, keeping out our competitors, and substantially improving cash flows.

Everybody was very happy that we were able to successfully move from physical to digital content, a unique strategy that made us a major player in the business.

In retrospect, the migration from physical to digital was a big step for me and our employees. We were on an unchartered territory. We faced many challenges and we were behaving like a bunch of entrepreneurs to resolve these. I learnt many lessons:

- Digital technologies offer new avenues for growth and higher profits to traditional brick and mortar businesses. However, if the migration from physical to digital products and channels is not successful, it presents high risks.
- To avoid the risk of failure, the traditional businesses have to upskill their employees and business partners to handle the digital infrastructure, business strategies and processes.
- For successful transition from physical to digital, the customers, the employees, the business partners, and the organisation should be convinced about the benefits of transition.
- Digital technologies have opened up enormous opportunities for entrepreneurs to start new businesses.

This was a turning point. I truly fell in love with the digital technologies and saw a new future for myself as an independent entrepreneur.

My journey as an independent digital entrepreneur

The decision in my mind was clear. My background in business software and digital content also fuelled my passion to start on an entrepreneurial journey. This led to several conversations with my wife Radhika who was more than supportive. It meant that I would end up taking a steep cut in my earnings in the near term. But that would also give me far more flexibility in time and the ability to focus on the work that I enjoyed.

During the last six months of my career in business enterprises, I had been mentoring aspiring young entrepreneurs who were creating unique digital products. This gave me a deep understanding of the digital space and the challenges that early-stage entrepreneurs face. I started my own company and worked with digital entrepreneurs who were developing business solutions offering "software as a service" (SaaS). The trend globally had shifted from buying software to subscribing for "software as a service". What followed over the next five years has been an exceptional ride working with SaaS start-ups helping them with their business strategy, business development, and international expansion.

There is no short cut here. I had to live in the trenches while working with these early-stage entrepreneurs, getting my hands dirty and do a lot of heavy lifting particularly when it came to getting them early customers. I developed relationships with resellers, consulting firms, and advisors in many countries to expand these start-ups into these markets. Business networking is an important skill for digital entrepreneurs looking to grow and expand in domestic or overseas markets.

Based on my experiences as a digital entrepreneur, I would recommend aspiring entrepreneur to answer these seven questions:

1. **Are you disrupting the market?** Are you developing a product or service that will change the way people buy and consume these? Make products and services easily accessible and offer new benefits and higher satisfaction. For instance, Uber changed the way we hire and use taxis.

2. **Are you using technology to differentiate?** How will technology give your product and service superiority over existing choices for customers? For example, when you buy books from Amazon, you can easily search the book you want, you can browse chapters, and you can read reviews and take an informed decision. Furthermore, it will recommend books that you may like and want to read.

3. **Can you claim high market share in a product or service category?** Are you able to focus on a specific segment and become a specialist and therefore become the best provider of products and services to customers? Amazon started their online business by focusing on books and claimed a high share in the book sales. An early success in dominating in the market gives confidence to diversify products and services.

4. **How fast can you build a team capable of delivering unique products and services?** To take advantage of digital technologies, you need talented people with diverse skill sets. You have to ensure that they work as a team and complement each other.

5. **How quickly can you grow and scale up your business?** Will technology help you reach more customers rapidly? Can you build a wide network of business partners who will enable you to grow quickly?

6. **What features will you incorporate in your start-up to ensure that all partners, products, and processes enjoy high levels of trust?** On a taxi service platform, technology-enabled features such as service ratings, reviews, information about the training of taxi drivers, the shortest travel route, and real-time human–technology interactions are as much part of the service experience and go a long way in building trust with the platform and its members.

7.   **How will you ensure the data of your customer is protected?**
     With stringent data privacy laws, it is important for digital products to
     take permission from users for using their data. In many instances, the
     data will have to be kept in the country of the user. You will also have
     to ensure that these data are used only for your product and not for any
     other purpose.

An underlying principle in answering these questions is to start with a
"Minimal Viable Product" (MVP), or a product with a basic demonstrable
benefit to the customer. If your product or service is now growing rapidly
then you have to be flexible and improve it until you can deliver higher value
to the customer. Consumer feedback plays a very important role in continuous improvement.

Despite changes and improvements, if the product or service does not
attract customers rapidly, then you have to change direction completely or
maybe even move out. Not carrying on with the original idea should not be
a matter of the "ego". Changing direction or shelving a project is an integral
part of the evolution of digital entrepreneurs.

Learning from experience

Let me demonstrate these points with one of our own experiences. Our
business partner Deepak Singh, Co-Founder of Spotmentor, helped organisations determine the gaps in employees' skills. They had developed a library
of "ideal skills" for jobs in specific industries by using standard job descrip-
tions. Their technology identified the actual skills that employees had by
using assessment tests, feedback from peers, and employees' self-assessment.
Based on the skill gaps, Spotmentor was able to identify a personalised list of
courses and content sourced from the internet that would help the employee
develop those skills identified as gaps. This was exciting. We had some initial
customers who used the MVP offering and gave feedback that helped make
changes to improve the value of our services. Over time, the product had
greater functionality and maturity.

We, however, hit a roadblock. Large organisations were also looking for
someone to guide them on identifying present and future employee roles
relevant for their organisation, and then to define the appropriate skills for
developing employees for those roles. This was important as businesses were
undergoing rapid changes and needed to be quick in determining the right
employee roles and skills keeping the future in mind. While technology

played an important part of the solution, these organisations wanted consultants who understood the skilling, learning, and human resources subjects to work with them on an ongoing basis.

We discovered that some large training and consulting firms were already providing this service, but they did not use any technology. That gave us an idea. Can we collaborate with them? I knew several consulting firms and suggested to Deepak that we should start meeting with them and explore and service potential opportunities jointly. Several conversations later, our partnership with a global consulting firm was forged. This partnership paved the way for offering Spotmentor's services for training and developing employees – a unique proposition!

The ability of Deepak Singh and his team at Spotmentor to understand early in their lifecycle that this was the way to go helped in creating a product of value and for driving success.

"*Successful people find value in unexpected places, and they do this by thinking about business from first principles instead of formulas*" (Peter Thiel, Co-Founder, PayPal, and Venture Capitalist).[2]

The changing landscape of digital entrepreneurship

There have been three stages in the evolution of digital entrepreneurs.

- During the internet boom in the 1990s, the entrepreneurs merely explored the possibility of using Internet to sell products and services, for example, airline tickets, hotel reservations, and other services on their internet portal. This was in addition to what they sold from their brick and mortar offices. Majority of customers were not familiar with online services, and the adoption of the products and services was relatively slow.
- In the subsequent decade, entrepreneurs were focused on "digital replication of a physical experience". For instance, we had websites, also known as platforms, specialised in areas like recruitment for jobs, buying and selling of shares in the stock market, and selling of tickets and hotel rooms. Consumers had better purchase experience and started transitioning from the physical to a digital experience. The growth in the use of mobile phones and the Internet was immensely helpful.
- These days, we are getting used to virtual markets where buyers and sellers come together, for example, taxi aggregators like Uber, short-stay aggregators like Airbnb, and movie aggregators like Netflix who have

transformed travel, stay, and entertainment for consumers. This is a new and more efficient way of delivering value to consumers.

With the growing number of "digital first" consumers who use their mobile phones for purchases, movies, news, and entertainment, the digital entrepreneurs are also becoming "digital first" producers. For example, entrepreneurs have started building solutions like cloud kitchens that offer food as a "delivery only" service.

Explore:

Grubhub Delivery dance, but I made it worse – Bing video (https://binged.it/3espwv3)

A wide range of business models

As a digital entrepreneur, you can adopt many alternate business models to build and grow a venture. In a *B2C (business to consumer)* model, you have a large audience to reach out to. You may have an idea that changes the way products and services are consumed. Or it could be a new or significant variant of an existing product or service. An example of this would be furniture store that sells online. The key challenge is to develop your value proposition, brand, and implement efficient processes. The possibility of competitors entering your space could be high. Businesses may not have exceptional success in the long term, as these ideas are easy to replicate. They also require significant investment on a recurring basis.

In a *B2B2C (business-to-business to consumer)* model, your value proposition is part a larger proposition for customers. The possibility for a competitor to be part of this larger proposition would be lower, as it would be difficult to dislodge you in case you are already established. Returns could be potentially high in case the overall proposition can show greater value to their customers because of what you bring to the equation.

Explore:

Meet the New Degreed – Bing video
   https://binged.it/3xSiqYs

In a *B2B (business to business)* model, there is an opportunity to be disruptive and become a market leader. This model may require lower investments to get to profitability. But would require substantial investments for growth. However, very often entrepreneurs fall into the trap of "building a better mousetrap" and fail to sustain innovation and differentiation from their competitors.

Explore:

Salesforce Platform Overview | Salesforce – Bing video
   https://binged.it/3xLWluz

Opportunities for freelance work

Over 60% of millennials do freelance work, better known as "gig work", on the side, and over 80% of them would become full-time gig workers if it paid more than what they make now. This explosive growth in the gig economy has been facilitated by demand for digital skills in the new economy, presence of gig platforms like Upwork, and the rapidly changing hiring culture of organisations, who are now more than ever, embracing the gig workforce. This fundamental change in the approach to employment is driving the entrepreneurial engine even more.

(Deloitte's 2019 Global Millennial Survey)[3]

Explore:

Brand ID: Up We Go | Upwork – Bing video
   https://binged.it/2ThsdYV

The challenge of rapid innovation

While it is easy to set up a digital business, growing it is extremely hard for several reasons:

1.   Technology is rapidly evolving and requires constant investment to stay ahead of the curve.

2. The entry barrier for competition is getting halved every 18 months with easy access to technology.
3. Product development timelines are getting shorter, and we may need to shift focus within our products to ensure customers get the best of innovation.
4. All digital businesses are relevant and profitable only if we can get significant volumes. Something entrepreneurs often forget.

I spoke with Mangesh Panditrao, Co-Founder of Shoptimize, who is leading the Digital technology revolution in Retail. There has been an unprecedented rush to automate the store in front end, as shoppers have been forced to go digital due to COVID-19. He however told me about the conundrum of being a digital entrepreneur in Retail.

• Retailers may have a lack of understanding of the true problems they are trying to solve.
• Retailers often have a simplistic solution about making their catalogues available online in the attempt to go digital. That may not be the solution.
• The question for Shoptimize has been: how can they build a marketing ecosystem around the retail store and get incentivised on gross merchandise value (GMV) or total sales. And therefore, be a co-creator with the brand?

Explore:

Shoptimize – The complete end-to-end D2C eCommerce Platform – Bing video
    https://binged.it/3erTfEk

The age of data

> *"Information is the oil of the 21st century, and analytics is the combustion engine".*
>
> Peter Sondergaard, Former Executive Vice President,
> Gartner Research & Advisory[4]

In an increasing era of data and digital pervasiveness in the way consumers and businesses are solving problems and consuming products and services, there is an enormous opportunity for digital entrepreneurs to play a role in the entire cycle. Devices and the related data generated are growing at an exponential pace, making data the new variable in designing products, services, and solutions.

How do we improve the productivity of farmers?

Explore:

How Aerofarms' vertical farms grow produce – Bing video
https://binged.it/3BcGYNS

The age of artificial intelligence

Artificial Intelligence (AI) is a powerful tool used to improve business decision-making, business performance, and customer service. One of the main uses we are seeing today is the ability to offer customers a more intuitive and personalised customer experience. AI refers to the ability of a computer or machine to mimic the capabilities of the human mind, learning from examples and experience, making decisions, solving problems, and combining these and other capabilities to perform functions a human might perform.

I spoke with Antoine Paillusseau, CEO, FinChatBot, a South African start up, on how he has been using Digital and AI to deliver this experience. "We do that by positively transforming people's lives through creating intelligent digital solutions to guide customer experiences".

Explore:

An Introduction to FinChatBot's Conversational AI Solutions – Bing video
https://binged.it/3xO79rQ

Accelerators and incubators

Accelerators "accelerate" growth of an existing company and are focused on scaling a business. Incubators "incubate" disruptive ideas with the hope of building out a business model and company. Their programmes have a methodical approach and timeframe in which companies spend a few months working with a group of mentors to build out their idea, business, address challenges, and build scale.

Explore:

Y Combinator | Incubated – Bing video
https://binged.it/36KVsXb
Why Does Idealab Work So Well? – Bing video
https://binged.it/3eopeoM

As a digital entrepreneur who is playing the role as "accelerator", I would conclude by saying that digital space is a fertile ground. Any person, irrespective of age and educational background, can look for new opportunities for creating business ventures. Digital entrepreneurs and enterprises are playing significant roles in advancing the future of humanity.

Try this thought experiment

Identify an existing product–service offering where you think you can develop a digital solution to enhance the consumer experience. Take some paper and a pencil and scribble your thinking around these questions:

1 Are you enhancing the consumer experience? How?
2 Are you disrupting the market? How?
3 Are you using technology to differentiate? How?
4 Can you claim high market share in this product–service space? How?
5 How fast and how will you build a team capable of delivering your unique product–service solution?
6 How quickly and how will you grow and scale up your business?
7 What features will you incorporate in your start up to ensure that all partners, products, and processes enjoy high levels of trust?
8 How will you protect the data of your customers?

> 9 Can you describe the "Minimal Viable Product" (MVP) profile of your product–service solution?
>
> 10 Do you need assistance of an incubator?
>
> If you have clarity on these questions then you are ready to take the plunge! Good luck!

Summary

The digital world presents enormous opportunities and challenges for starting your own ventures. The digital space is a fast-changing space. As an entrepreneur, you have to be a keen observer of latest trends, a constant learner, an engaging networker, and a strong commitment to take risks. You should be ready to swim in unchartered waters and make the most of it.

Acknowledgements

I am thankful to several leading digital entrepreneurs and professional colleagues who have shared their valuable insights in preparing this chapter. Amongst these are Atul Kunwar, an advisor to tech start-ups; Christopher Orchard, WGP Global, London; Arindam Bhattacharya, BCG Henderson Institute; Ajay Shukla, Higher Education UAE; Antoine Paillusseau, FinChatBot, Johannesburg; Mangesh Panditrao, Shoptimize; Prajakt Raut, Applyifi; Deepak Singh, Spotmentor.

Notes

1 "I've been to the Mountaintop", the last speech delivered by Martin Luther King Jr. on April 3, 1968, Mason Temple, Memphis, Tennessee, prior to his assassination on the following day. See www.americanrhetoric.com top 100 speeches and https://www.afscme.org>about>mlk
2 https://www.forbes.com/sites/ralphbenko/2014/10/13/peter-thiel-we-dont-live-in-a-normal-world-we-live-under-a-power-law/?sh=47d1b7667a7d
3 https://www2.deloitte.com/cn/en/pages/about-deloitte/articles/2019-millennial-survey.html
4 https://www.springboard.com/blog/data-analytics/41-shareable-data-quotes/

Further reading

Clark, Duncan (2018), *Alibaba*. UK: HarperCollins Publishers.
Hoffman, Reid and Chris Yeah (2018), *Blitzscaling – The Lightning-Fast Path to Building Massively Valuable Companies*. HarperCollins Publishers.
Horowitz, Ben (2014), *The Hard Thing About Hard Things*. UK: HarperCollins Publishers.
Thiel, Peter with Blake Masters (2014), *Zero to One*. UK: Penguin Books.

3

MASTERING THE POWER OF ENTREPRENEURSHIP

Kelly Keates

Abstract

Fifteen years ago, I bought my business. In the years since, I have experienced constant personal and business growth. My journey was not straightforward or what I had initially expected. I had to find confidence in myself, harness the freedom of being an entrepreneur, find inspiration from the people around me, and constantly seek opportunities to get where I am now. In this chapter, I will explore key concepts that have helped my business grow. I hope that, by sharing my experience, I can inspire budding and existing entrepreneurs.

Keywords: Women in business, entrepreneurship, personal business development, risk taking, change, knowledge, challenge, grow, relationship value

Introduction

In my quest for success and achievement, I have been inspired by the words of two successful women, both of whom are entrepreneurs. The first is Michele Ruiz, an American businesswoman, an entrepreneur, and a co-founder and CEO of BiasSync, a science-based solution designed to help organisations effectively assess and manage unconscious bias in the work environment. Michele said, "*If people are doubting how far you can go, go so far that you can't hear them anymore*".[1] The second is Sara Blakely, an American

DOI: 10.4324/9781003219293-4

businesswoman and the founder of Spanx, the well-known underwear maker. Sara is quoted in Forbes as saying, "*Don't be intimidated by what you don't know. That can be your greatest strength and ensure that you do things differently from everyone else*".[2]

I never imagined myself as an entrepreneur, "*A person who attempts to make a profit by starting a company or by operating alone in the business world, especially when it involves taking risks*" (Cambridge Dictionary[3]). Throughout high school, I was discouraged from choosing science subjects. Even though I enjoyed the content, my teachers doubted my ability to get good grades in science classes. When I reached university, my options were limited, leading me to choose a bachelor of arts degree. I didn't have excellent grades, but I had fantastic subjects like history of art, women in politics, and structural geomorphology (study of earth's crust).

After graduation

The summer after graduation, I was given the opportunity to work underground at a large mine, in the middle of rural Australia. I loved the remoteness of the work and the challenging environment I was in. I was completely out of my comfort zone, a young girl working for a huge corporation. First day, I walked into the mess hall to be introduced to my new colleague. "Kelly!" he said as he spotted me. "How did you know it was me?" I replied. "Well, look around, you're the only woman here".

I had not noticed the lack of women. I was shocked and disappointed when later told by some of the older miners over an after-work beer that they believed it was bad luck to have women underground. Since then, I have never let myself be concerned about being the only woman in the room, and in fact often don't notice anymore.

At the end of the short-term contract, I looked for something in the mining industry and was employed as a part-time office assistant in a small mining services company, which had branches across the world. It wasn't long before I put in systems and processes to ensure that cash flow was stable and had the support of the business owner to look for ways to extend the services we provided into new markets. I was appointed a director of the Australian branch and opened a new branch in Indonesia within a few years of starting.

Fifteen years later, Dr. Ken Zonge, the owner, approached me to purchase the business Zonge Engineering and Research Organization (Aust) Pty Ltd. I had three small children and was not actively seeking to be a business owner but hated the thought of having someone else be my boss. I travelled to USA and had a very long meeting with the owner. I detailed all the reasons I didn't want to buy the business. After listening to me for three hours, the owner quietly asked me if I wanted to buy the business or not. "Okay" I said.

I was given the opportunity, and I said yes. In a survey conducted by the Centre for Women's Business Research, most women start their business based on market opportunity rather than necessity[4] (Kituyi, 2021). After much negotiation, the sale was complete, and the funds were transferred but my confidence took a hit. The transition from manager to entrepreneur was tougher than just the change in title name, and finances at risk. I had to completely change my mindset and outlook on the company. I was met with hostility from significant people around me, clients, staff, and family. Many didn't hold back sharing their opinions. The bank even pulled the pre-approved loan, and my mother had to lend me money from her secret account to get me started.

My big challenge

This was truly one of the toughest moments of my life, but I was determined not to fail. Telling me I can't is the best way to make sure I can.

I didn't and still don't have the technical skills required for the core business we conduct. All I had was my Bachelor of Arts degree. I had imposter syndrome, fuelled by the men constantly asking how I could have possibly landed this role. It took me years to understand that, actually, I don't need to know how to fix a generator or interpret geophysical data to be able to successfully run this business.

Once I believed that I was an entrepreneur, I felt energised and ready to make modifications to the business model by expanding the technologies and markets with support from the management team. We said yes to every opportunity and challenge that came our way. I knew that "people are central to the success of any organization"[5] (Haskins, Thomas and Johri, 2018) and worked hard to create a team that is great to work with but also are committed to our continued success.

We implemented a business strategy and worked to actively differentiate ourselves from our competitors and took the time to understand our clients and their needs. The expansion to different markets overseas and the introduction of environmental services locked, in the businesses, long-term sustainability. This has been supported by consistent research and development to design new equipment and methods. We focus on providing the best outcome for our clients via a range of techniques with the largest range of latest equipment whereas our competitors mostly specialise in one technique. We are constantly reviewing technologies and equipment to ensure we provide the latest technology to our clients.

On reflection, I already had the knowledge to be a successful entrepreneur, I just needed to believe that and be confident in my ability and role. I don't normally concern myself with specific growth statistics for my business, as I focus more on overall business gauges like lead indicators, cash flow, and retention. Some interesting facts though are that we doubled our revenue in my first year of ownership. Revenue continues to grow year after year despite the downturns in the industry, reaching the highest level ever last year.

Some of my favourite entrepreneurs

Australia has a high percentage of entrepreneurs. We are ranked sixth out of 24 developed countries in terms of entrepreneurial activity. An estimated 12 per cent of the Australian adult population is engaged in starting and running a business[6] (Steffens, 2021). Mining billionaire's Andrew Forrest and Gina Rinehart are two of the major players that have taken very different paths to success with outstanding results.

At the start of his career, Forrest faced huge failure and subsequent criticism from the industry. He was able to take strength in the face of adversity. To me, it seems like this initial failure installed a sense of fearlessness, which enabled him to ignore the rules and take on the big miners. He built a train track right next to his competitor's when they refused to share. Forrest's fearlessness is an entrepreneurial trait I greatly admire and am constantly inspired by. His successes show that there are no limits when expanding and diversifying, and even without prior experience, no industry is out of reach.

Rinehart inherited her father's financially troubled company and transformed it to a diversified innovative portfolio including investments in iron ore, copper, potash, coal, gold cattle, dairy, and property[7] (Rinehart, 2021). Last year, Rinehart doubled her net worth to a whopping 36 billion AUD (Australian dollars). Although Gina and I don't share a bank account unfortunately, we do share a similar entrepreneurial beginning, starting with a small exploration company that has been successful from diversifying.

Governments can get a lot wrong, but the one thing they get right here is support for entrepreneurs and small businesses, and encouragement for collaboration with the Universities. I feel incredibly grateful for the supportive entrepreneurial spirit and many opportunities to share experiences in Australia. I am able to regularly meet with groups of managers and CEOs from all walks of life to share experiences and knowledge. Entrepreneurs in Australia are greatly valued, evidenced by the opportunities given to me to expand my knowledge and capacity. I have received government and industry grants to study at the world's top universities, export overseas, develop technology, and hire more staff.

Some of the local entrepreneurs in Adelaide who inspire me most include:

Kris Lloyd from Woodside Cheese Wrights taught herself not only how to make cheese, but also how to develop and grow her business into an internationally renowned company with her world champion cheeses.

Jim Grose from Axiom Precision Manufacturing transformed his business from car component manufacturing to the production of equipment for the defence and medical industries.

Zoe Detmold from Detmold Ventures was able to quickly diversify her company's products to meet the unprecedented demand for face masks to help prevent the spread of Covid-19.

Concepts of entrepreneurship

"Almost all entrepreneurs have that one thing: A core concept, idea or tenet that drives them and their business forward, and lies at the foundation of every major decision they make".[8]

(Forbes/Young Entrepreneur Council, 2017)

My entrepreneurial repertoire has expanded over the years, thanks to the shared knowledge of my network, opportunities for further study, and real-time experiences in my business. The key concepts that I have used to grow my business include shared vision, empowerment, risk, hunger, cognitive adaptability, and lead change.

Shared vision

Studies have proven that firms with a higher degree of shared vision ensure that all participants share goals, values, and drive innovation[9] (Stresse, 2021).

The first lesson I had to learn as a young entrepreneur was to trust myself. Although I wasn't an expert in geophysics, I could be an expert in strategic and business decisions. Once I had that down, the next step was a workshop for all my staff to contribute to the shared vision for the company. As a group we worked on what we felt was a key to the business. The whole team all had the opportunity to add or challenge the new vision document. This ultimately gave us a reference point for our purpose and behaviour as a collective.

Empowerment

Working in a male-dominated industry, typically run by autocratic ruling, I was deeply concerned that my leadership style and core personality traits would have to change in order to manage the trickier personalities. I tried being authoritarian, but it felt disingenuous and just didn't work for me or my staff.

I was relived to find that when I ditched the typically male style of management and opted for my own methods, everyone around me responded better. Thirty-eight per cent of entrepreneurs participating in a recent study believe transformational leadership has a great impact to the success of their enterprise[10] (Paladan, 2015). Transformational leaders use a full range of leadership styles to achieve superior results.

I believe that the path to being a successful entrepreneur is to show empathy, be genuine, and actively listen to others while holding my values at the core of every decision I make. For me, this approach has contributed to the continued success and growth of my business.

Hunger

While taking on the day's challenges, it's easy to forget the bigger picture. One of the most valuable decisions I made for the business was to conduct an internal review, to establish successes, failures, and future direction. Like any business owner, I expected glowing results. I cannot describe the complete shock that rippled through the whole organisation when the results came back, with low scores in almost every category. These results created a resolve for change and a unanimous motivation or hunger for improvement. The initial disappointment was hard, but I could not let this defeat me or my team; we needed to harness this collective disappointment into urgent action. John P Kotter defines the number 1 reason for why transformation efforts fail is not establishing a great enough sense of urgency[11] (Kotter, 2021). My business can always do better. Even when we are surrounded by success, I still keep seeking improvements. This hunger for excellence removes complacency, and pushes us forward.

Invest in yourself

You are your businesses' greatest asset. You are always capable of doing more than you know given the right tools. Take time to learn, grow, and create value in yourself. It can be hard to step aside from the day-to-day operations to invest in your personal development, but both you and your business will thank you for it. After 20 years in business, I had the opportunities to attend Harvard and Oxford Business Schools. I came back with increased confidence and brand-new tools that I could implement immediately.

Cognitive adaptability

My business requires continual critical decision-making. On a daily basis, new equipment or people may be required in a remote location immediately, our client may change the survey format, unforeseen weather or terrain may require changes to our plans. We are always learning to manage a different situation, and this has helped us develop our cognitive adaptability. Entrepreneurs with increased cognitive adaptability have an improved ability to adapt to new situations[12] (Nash, 2021).

COVID-19 presented unexpected and unknown risks to all businesses across the globe. I quickly realised that, without quick adaptation, we would be doomed. Things were changing so quickly, and no one knew what to expect. Other businesses just shut their doors, and the risks to continue were too great. I fought on. I convinced clients to not cancel contracts, and reassured staff that there would always be work, and together we can come out of this hard time even stronger.

Everyone around me was feeling the effects of the Virus, but each had very different experiences. I had to be there for my staff, listen with empathy, and adapt to their needs and the constantly changing situation. We were in this together, and although I didn't have all the answers, they could trust that I would make the best decisions for them and for the business.

I believe my ability to recognise and act quickly, adapting to the ever-evolving situation that has allowed my business to continue to grow during COVID-19 adversities.

Risk

I wouldn't be an entrepreneur if I hadn't taken the initial risk to buy the business. I remember expressing my concerns to my accountant during the buying process. I was concerned about the impacts it would have on my young family, but he reassured me that being the owner would not change the hours required or have any impact on my family life. Luckily, I was naive enough to believe him and take the risk, perhaps if I knew the truth, I wouldn't have. Although it has been a rewarding journey, I have spent more time at and on the business than anticipated.

Lead change

Continual change and improvements are necessary as an entrepreneur; for growth and sustainability, there is no time to put our feet up and declare all the work done and finished, and there is also no such thing as a perfect company.

I saw a gap in the market that I knew I could use my current businesses' technical expertise to fill. For the first time in our history, we developed a brand new, innovative piece of technology that would detect leaks in large liquid holding facilities. Just like that, my business was diversified, we entered into a brand-new market, and we were dubbed "technopreneurs".

Once again, I was surprised by unanticipated issues arising from the industries' reluctance to embrace new technology from "newcomers". Our unique in-house system provides leak detection different from the way things have always been done and challenged the establishment. Although we had a strong business plan, the demand hasn't been there for our initially designed system, so each one has meant new learnings and developments. We struggled to understand who our client really is because the system protects the environment, but the environment doesn't have a purchase order book. Persistence and results are helping to build the business but our projected business plan is taking more than our initial optimistic spreadsheet showed.

Explore:

How to master the power of entrepreneurship:

1   **Find the confidence and feel comfortable in yourself as an entrepreneur**
    When you have confidence in your own authentic self, you can bring your best game. There is no need to confine or compare yourself to others style, be confident in your abilities and work to your strengths.

2   **Harness the freedom of this title and take risks**

Once you are comfortable being an entrepreneur, embrace every opportunity that arises. Trust in yourself to make the right decisions, and take on risks that challenge you and your business.

3   **Expand your knowledge and experiment with new ideas**

Invest in yourself and in your continued education. But remember that expanding your knowledge is not just limited to formal education. You'll find that the experts are right in front of you, your staff and your clients and the people around you. Don't be afraid to ask for their insights and ensure you take the time to consider and research their suggestions.

4   **Create new opportunities to grow**

You have the best understanding of your company's assets and skills. Think outside of your already existing business box, and consider how you can transfer that knowledge into a completely new space.

5   **Expand your network of friends and don't hesitate to take help from them**

Asking for help doesn't make you any less of an entrepreneur. People love sharing advice, it's up to you to find the right people to really listen, encourage, and support. You'll often find advice in places you least expect it.

6   **Value your team and business partners**

A business is nothing without its people. Value them, their time, and their contributions. Each person has a fresh perspective, unique experiences, and individual motivators.

7   **Listen and understand your clients**

We created a survey to see where we could make improvements to our services, and have since moved to a less formal system talking to clients to understand what is important to them and the project.

8   **Never be complacent, always challenge, and improve**

Even when your business is successful, remember what you learnt as a young entrepreneur, invest in your knowledge, take on challenges, and expand your limits.

Summary

Mastering the power of entrepreneurship has been an unexpected and challenging but overall rewarding journey. I'm grateful for the experiences it has given me and the opportunities to be in charge of my future. Fear of failure, losing respect, and possibly losing everything financially made the first years tough. Eventually, I learnt that you need confidence to fully harness the freedom that comes as an entrepreneur. I'm grateful that I can take control of the business' future and help the team develop, the financial results grow and diversify into new technologies. I'm no longer as driven by the fear of failure, but find so much fulfilment in the constant pursuit of improvement. Have confidence in your abilities, constantly seek opportunities to learn, and take risks.

Follow-up actions

How to master the power entrepreneurship: follow-up actions for your organisation and run a business diagnostic:

1   Find an external business advisor who can conduct an internal review.
2   Bring in the entire team, every opinion is important.
3   Use a tool to rate yourselves on marketing, finance, compliance, operations and leadership.
4   Once each person gives these categories a score they can be totalled for an overall result.
5   Review the results, beware they may be much lower than expected
6   As a group, agree on priorities for urgent action
7   Workshop the solution to improvement using what, who, where, how strategies, implement an action plan
8   Accept failures and make a plan for improvement

Notes

1   https://twitter.com/michelruiz01/status/665267707344883712?lang=en
2   *Forbes.* Available at: https://www.forbes.com/sites/lizelting/2020/02/28/it-pays-to-be-bold/?sh=40f749f51ab3
3   Cambridge Dictionary. Available at: https://dictionary.cambridge.org>entrepreneur

4 Kituyi, M. (2021), Unctad.org. Available at: https://unctad.org/system/files/official-document/diaeed2013d1.pdf. Accessed on: April 18, 2021.

5 Haskins, G., M. Thomas and L. Johri (2018), *Kindness in Leadership*. Routledge.

6 Steffens, P. (2021). Available at: https://eprints.qut.edu.au/127058/1/GEM%20AUS%20Report%20CLIENT%20corrected.pdf. Accessed on: April 18, 2021.

7 Rinehart, G. (2021), *Biography*. Ginarinehart.com.au. Available at: https://www.ginarinehart.com.au/biography/. Accessed on: April 18, 2021.

8 Forbes (2021), *Forbes*. Available at: https://www.forbes.com/sites/theyec/2017/12/18/seven-essential-concepts-that-define-modern-day-entrepreneurs/?sh=58b7165f4dd4. Accessed on: April 18, 2021.

9 Stresse, S. (2021). Available at: https://www.researchgate.net/profile/Steffen-Strese/publication/307549002_CEOs%27_Passion_for_Inventing_and_Radical_Innovations_in_SMEs_The_Moderating_Effect_of_Shared_Vision/links/5dc9c01892851c818046cefa/CEOs-Passion-for-Inventing-and-Radical-Innovations-in-SMEs-The-Moderating-Effect-of-Shared-Vision.pdf. Accessed on: April 18, 2021.

10 Paladan, N. (2015). Transformational Leadership: The Emerging Leadership Style of Successful Entrepreneurs. *Journal of Literature and Art Studies*, 5(1).

11 Kotter, J. (2021). Leading Change: Why Transformation Efforts Fail. *Harvard Business Review*. Available at: https://hbr.org/1995/05/leading-change-why-transformation-efforts-fail-2. Accessed on: April 18, 2021.

12 Nash, S. (2021). Entrepreneurship 10e (2017) Hisrich, Peters and Shepherd 9780078112843.pdf. *Academia.edu*. Available at: https://www.academia.edu/38249418/Entrepreneurship_10e_2017_Hisrich_Peters_and_Shepherd_9780078112843_pdf. Accessed on: April 18, 2021.

Further reading

- Drucker, P. (1999), *Innovation and Entrepreneurship*. Oxford: Butterworth Heinemann.
- Dubner, S. and S. Levitt (2015), *Think Like a Freak*. USA: HarperCollins.
- Fagerberg, J., D.C. Mowery and R.R. Nelson (2005), *The Oxford Handbook of Innovation*. New York: Oxford University Press.
- Hisrich, R.D., M.P. Peters and D. Shepherd (2016), *Entrepreneurship*. 10th edition. Boston: McGraw-Hill Irwin.
- Christensen, C. (2013), *How Will You Measure Your Life?* Kennett Square, PA: Soundview Executive Book Summaries.

4

MASTERING THE POWER OF VOLUNTEERING

Mads Roke Clausen

Abstract

New social risks are on the rise, such as increasing loneliness and frag-mented family structures. The ability of volunteers to create "togetherness" often renders them the best and most effective first-line response to such challenges.

In this chapter, I share my experiences with leading volunteer efforts, including some of my mistakes and what I have learned from them. You also receive three profound examples of successful volunteer efforts.

I present many benefits that volunteers provide to society and what you yourself can get out of being a volunteer. And I give my best advice on how to maximise social impact by involving volunteers and how to avoid so-called "voluntary failures".

Keywords: Social impact, voluntary failures, new social risks, togetherness

Preface

You will find, when reading this chapter on the Power of Volunteering, that togetherness is a key to success. In this, I am reminded of the words of the great South African theologian, Desmond Tutu:

> I am, because we are. We are made for togetherness. We are made for complementarity. I have gifts that you don't have, and you have gifts that

DOI: 10.4324/9781003219293-5

I don't have. We are different in order to know our need for each other.
To be human is to be dependent.

Desmond Tutu (1931–2021), former Archbishop of Cape Town[1]

What I have learned from volunteers?

Until a few years ago, I was the CEO of Mothers' Aid, the largest charity for
vulnerable families in Denmark. One late afternoon in 2012, I was standing
in my office looking at the bulletin board and the diplomas documenting
our organisational success. Among the items on the bulletin board was a
newspaper clipping – an article featuring the Danish Prime Minister, who
declared: "*If I weren't in politics, I would work for Mothers' Aid*". Some of our
results were also posted on the bulletin board – how we had tripled the number of families receiving our help and other metrics documenting the very
high impact of our work. In short: All evidence of how Mothers' Aid had
become recognised as one of Denmark's most successful charities.

But that afternoon, I was worried. The results of recent years had been
achieved by the "professional section" of the organisation, while the volunteer section of Mothers' Aid had been overlooked in the new strategy, which
had its primary focus on the professional social workers. The volunteers
made up almost half of the organisation's resources in terms of the number
of hours of work that Mothers' Aid had at its disposal. And the whole local
structure was built on volunteers. But now, the volunteers had challenged
the new strategy. They felt neglected and that the Mothers' Aid leadership
failed to recognise the work being carried out in the local associations.

In 2012, Mothers' Aid consisted of two almost equal organisational units.
The one unit was counselling, staffed with paid social workers. The employees were proud of their professionalism and considered themselves among
the most skilled advisers in the social sector. This could also partly be attributed to the practice in Mothers' Aid, whereby the effects achieved by the
professional counselling were continuously measured to provide the best
help to the most vulnerable families.

In the voluntary local associations, care and presence were paramount.
The decor in the local associations and second-hand shops was "*homely and
cosy with good coffee and a bowl of sweets*", as one volunteer once told me. And
I remember a volunteer leader once describing the ideal volunteer: "*You
can have a volunteer who is really good at her work, but if she doesn't manage to be
present, caring and creates relationships, it just doesn't work*".

But the culture of compassion among the volunteers was not shared by everyone. I still remember a senior employee who criticised this culture among the volunteers:

> It can be difficult to address poor performance due to the very friendly and caring environment in the voluntary local associations. . . . The volunteers just want to be together with the people they know. We could do more activities if the volunteers were less social and more willing to try new things.

Fortunately, the board of directors and I chose to listen and engage in dialogue with the volunteers and with the families who received our help. I can clearly remember a single mother telling me:

> The help I get from the Mothers' Aid volunteers is so important to me because this has been the first time in my life that I get help from someone who isn't paid to help me. They see me as a human being – and that makes me grow.

The dialogue with the users and volunteers made me realise that our definition of how we provided the best help for our target audience was too narrow. In doing so, we had overlooked the volunteer's unique human resources, for example, their ability to provide compassionate care and build meaningful relations. We learned from the dialogue that professional methods and scientific methods to measure impact are essential, but care and relationships are just as crucial for effective social work.

In response to the leader who criticised the culture among the volunteers, I could say that while the commercial companies may be more efficient than the voluntary organisations, I think that there is a positive correlation between having a social culture and doing effective social work. Organisations that provide human care are not credible if their culture is not in harmony with this care. It is therefore also important that the volunteers are involved in developing the organisation's strategy. This insight changed our strategy to have a dual focus on both professional social workers and volunteers. And Mothers' Aid could subsequently register a significant increase in the number of volunteers. Because of that, we were able to provide more effective help for vulnerable families in Denmark.

A few years later, I left Mothers' Aid and became the chairman of The Voluntary Council, which advises the Danish government on how the voluntary sector can help alleviate social challenges in Denmark. More recently, I have joined several foundation boards working with social impact investments. In all of these functions, I have taken the message from the Mothers' Aid volunteers and the families with me: that care, presence, and relationships are as important as professional social workers and scientific methods to create effective social help. Therefore, the best strategy for both voluntary social organisations and modern welfare states is to let professionals and volunteers complement each other.

Volunteering to address social risks

Many industrialised countries have developed welfare states, which in various ways help their citizens to obtain education, to receive necessary health care, and a pension when they are no longer able to work. The classical welfare states can help their citizens overcome the so-called "old social risks" that result from living in an industrialised society. However, in recent decades, there has been a focus on *"the new social risks"*.[2] Loneliness is one of the new social problems, and while many fail to understand how severe a problem of loneliness can be, studies have found that around one-third of all people in industrialised countries are affected by loneliness, with one in 12 being severely affected.[3] And severe loneliness has been documented to be as harmful to one's health as obesity and smoking. Other examples of new social risks include the fragmentation of family structures and having a sense of being disconnected, and life having no meaning.[4]

It is my clear belief that these new social risks are best addressed by volunteers who can create social communities, facilitate activities, provide mutual help, and not least a sense of meaning. In short, volunteers have the key to tackling many of the new social problems that arise in modern society. On a more philosophical level, they have the key to a richer form of welfare than that provided by professional social workers. They create the sense of "togetherness" to which Desmond Tutu refers to in the introductory quote, the existence of which is the essence of being human.

One can volunteer in many different ways: as a scout, as an environmental activist, as a swimming coach, helping kids with their homework, washing dishes in a soup kitchen, or something completely different. In my eyes, no one single kind of volunteering is better than others. The world is full of various ways of volunteering and voluntary organisations. I will describe various examples to show how volunteering can address diverse social challenges.

Meals on Wheels

Meals on Wheels delivers meals to those who are unable to prepare their own. The target group is primarily comprised of homebound elders. The *Meals on Wheels* mission is to support well-nourished, independent, and connected communities through the delivery of nutritious meals, social connections together with a well-being check by a trained and dedicated volunteer workforce. The programme operates in many countries around the world.

Meals on Wheels is one of my favourite organisations. It is a simple and effective programme with a documented impact on nutrition and social capital. A scientific study in 2013 found that home-delivered meal programmes for seniors improved diet quality and nutrient intakes, strengthened socialisation opportunities, and enhanced quality of life.[5]

Explore:

Meals on Wheels in the USA
    https://www.mealsonwheelsamerica.org

Southall Black Sisters

Based in West London, Southall Black Sisters (SBS) is a leading non-profit organisation for black and minority women and girls in the UK. SBS is committed to the principles of equality and justice for all, but especially for abused black and minority women, who represent one of the most marginalised groups in the UK. SBS offers outreach services about family law, housing, immigration, and domestic violence.

SBS is a small organisation with some ten employees and a similar number of volunteers. The modest revenue is a deliberate choice made by the organisation's leaders, as they want an independent voice and, therefore, avoid entering into contracts that could be at odds with the organisation's values. But as an organisation, SBS is punching above its weight and is known throughout the UK for their fight for women's rights. And that is one of the things I respect and admire about SBS – they provide vital help to women in vulnerable positions while at the same time showing that a huge budget is not required to have a considerable impact. In this way, SBS is an example of how an effective and realistic strategy can create a profound impact without requiring a large organisational bureaucracy.

> **Explore:**
>
> Southall Black Sisters
>   https://www.southallblacksisters.org.uk

Civic action

The first two examples are about voluntary efforts that are rooted in an organisation. But voluntary efforts can also take place outside of a formal organisational framework. This form of voluntary engagement is termed "civic action". It includes activities such as political agitation, gathering knowledge on important topics and then launching campaigns to change the behaviour of public and private institutions, and getting citizens to become more active in their communities as well as in times of crisis to provide everything from health care to technical assistance.

American sociologists Nina Eliasoph and Paul Lichterman argue that "civic action" is a more appropriate way of understanding civic engagement than seeing volunteering solely as something that only happens in "formal" voluntary organisations.[6] Eliasoph and Lichterman define civic action as activities in which *"the participants are coordinating action to improve some aspect of common life in society, as they imagine society"*.[7] A concrete example could be a community of interest, where volunteers work together to improve housing conditions in a local community.

"Civic action" is relevant here in terms of the incredible variety that exists in the volunteering opportunities.

Famous volunteers

Many famous people do volunteer work. This is important, because it provides awareness and recognition of volunteer efforts.

My own favourite remains Princess Diana, who, as a Red Cross volunteer, helped shine a light on the fact that 2,000 people were being killed or maimed by landmines around the world every single month. In 1997 – six months before her death – she visited Angola, where she walked through a minefield, met with amputees, and brought necessary worldwide attention to a treaty signed later that year banning landmines.

Insights from the examples

- Volunteers represent the best and most effective way to address some of the new social risks, not least loneliness.
- Small organisations, such as Southall Black Sisters, can make a significant impact. Therefore, keep your organisation simple and avoid building up a large bureaucracy.
- Combining the volunteer's capabilities to create social relations and service delivery (e.g. Meals on Wheels) creates a richer kind of welfare.
- Giving voice and attention to important causes can be a vital volunteering contribution, as we have seen with Princess Diana's support of a global landmines ban.
- You don't always need an organisation to create positive change. My mother is a teacher, and she was often helping neighbourhood children with math throughout my childhood! That was volunteering in a simple but valuable way.

Voluntary failures

I am sure that many would agree with me that Lester Salamon (1943–2021) from Johns Hopkins University was the *Grand Old Man* of research in the voluntary sector, and he was excellent at articulating how we conceive volunteering. Lester believes that voluntary organisations are the most effective "*first line of response*" to many social challenges. But in a ground-breaking scientific article from 1987, he also describes four voluntary failures, which represent a "*central failing of the voluntary system as a provider of collective goods*", which possibly necessitates state intervention in certain situations.[8]

Whether you are volunteering yourself or leading volunteer efforts, you must be aware of the potential voluntary failures. Here is a brief introduction:

Philanthropic insufficiency: Funding that is both inadequate and unreliable and therefore does not provide the opportunity to meet society's existing social needs. For example, it is less than optimal to initiate a project for lonely young people but only have funding to run it for a year.

Particularism: Organisations favouring particular groups. An example could be an organisation that helps lonely mothers but fails to pay attention and offer assistance to lonely fathers.

Paternalism: It occurs if special considerations or certain moral requirements characterize the relief work. For example, you are not perceived as really poor if you smoke cigarettes since you would have more money if you didn't spend it on tobacco.

Amateurism: Providing relief efforts that are not based on the necessary professional insights into the social problem that one is trying to solve, such as letting unqualified volunteers help traumatised victims of violence instead of necessarily providing help from trained psychologists.

The voluntary failures you risk running into as a voluntary organisation depend on your target group and how you are trying to help. On that background, there is no standard solution to address these errors. My best advice is to ensure that your organisation has a skilled board and possibly an advisory board familiar with the target audience and their social needs.

What is a volunteer and what are the benefits of volunteering?

The most common definition of volunteer work comes from the International Labour Organization's Manual on the Measurement of Volunteer Work. Here, "volunteer work" is defined as *"unpaid, non-compulsory work; that is, time individuals give without pay to activities performed either through an organization or directly for others outside their own household or family"*.[9] This definition thus implies that unpaid work that you perform for your family (e.g. next of kin – brothers, sisters, parents, grandparents, and their respective children) does not count as voluntary work in the formal sense.

A few years ago, Salamon and Sokolowski carried out a tremendous research project, where they estimated the global scale and economic value of volunteer work throughout the world. They found that nearly one billion people worldwide are volunteering in public, non-profit, or for-profit organisations, or directly for friends or neighbours, in a typical year. The volunteering force is undoubtedly very large.

One of the key benefits of volunteering is social capital. One of the foremost thinkers on this subject is Robert Putnam, who wrote *Bowling Alone*, one of the seminal works on volunteering and social capital (you can find the reference to the book in the section on "Further reading"). According to Putnam, social capital refers to *"connections among individuals – social networks and the norms of reciprocity and trustworthiness that arise from them"*. According to this view, social capital is a key component to building and maintaining democracy.

But being a volunteer is not only good for the economy and the citizens who receive help from volunteers, but the volunteers themselves also enjoy a wide range of benefits. New skills are acquired, networks are expanded, and some volunteers acquire managerial experience. This is all good in itself, but it can also help to find new employment easily. And last but not least, I know many people who have met their husband or wife through volunteer work – which isn't the worst thing in the world!

Mastering the power of volunteering

Here are five tips for anyone interested in creating a high-impact organisation with the use of volunteers.

1   *Create a caring, holistic organisation*
    Organisations that provide care must themselves have a caring organisational culture. In my interpretation, this entails a leadership style that is patient, curious, and helpful, but at the same time also purposeful.[10] A caring culture also contributes to good collaboration between volunteers and professional staff.

2   *Create a financing strategy that supports the organisation's values*
    An increasing share of funding for voluntary organisations comes from social impact programmes (e.g. social impact bonds). The disadvantage of this type of funding is that it is often very bureaucratically demanding and rarely motivating volunteers.[11] Avoid funding that is at odds with the organisation's values. Remember the Southall Black Sisters, an organisation with a significant impact despite limited revenue.

3   *Evaluate your organisation for voluntary failures*
    Each year, the board should conduct a critical review of the organisation's impact and whether you are committing any of the voluntary failures mentioned earlier. Involve your target group and volunteers in this evaluation.

4   *Remember diversity when recruiting volunteers and create different types of jobs for volunteers*
    Remember that diversity is a strength – and this also applies to the composition of your volunteer corps. By promoting diversity and inclusion, you will have a broader recruitment base for

volunteers, which will enrich your organisation with various perspectives and experiences. At the same time, you must design volunteer positions suitable for both those who want a long-term relationship with the organisation and ad hoc jobs for those who just want to help for a shorter period (e.g. at a summer camp).

5   *Find good partners*
No single organisation can solve all social challenges. So be sure to develop good collaborative relationships with other organisations, which will make you more resilient; for example, by lending volunteers to each other when needs are acute.

How can you master the power of volunteering?

Here are five recommendations for how you, as an individual, can master the power of volunteering.

1   **You can contribute in many different ways**
The examples presented in this chapter reveal how volunteers contribute in many different ways to creating a better, more compassionate society. In my eyes, all kinds of voluntary contributions are important. The first step towards mastering the power of volunteering is to volunteer!

2   **Small contributions are also important**
I have always been a volunteer myself. But I also know that there are periods where I'm very busy – sometimes due to my work, at others because of my family – where it can be challenging to find the time. My solution in this situation is to find a volunteer gig that only requires a few hours per month. So my message is: Keep volunteering! Even when you're busy.

3   **Use your professional skills or learn new skills.**
Whether you are a nurse or teacher, you possess administrative skills or something completely different; I'm sure your professional skills can also be useful somewhere in a volunteering job. But, conversely, many volunteers find satisfaction in doing something different from what they do in their paid work, because it allows them to learn new skills or simply provides a little variation in their lives.

4   **Help to recruit more volunteers**
    The most important factor to becoming a volunteer is being
    asked to be a volunteer. That's more important than the educa-
    tional background, age, and gender. If you are a volunteer, you
    can therefore make an important difference by inviting others to
    become volunteers.

5   **Volunteering is good for your community and your health**
    Volunteering helps your community. But research has also
    found that it is good for your health. For example, a scien-
    tific study found that older adults who volunteer lowered
    their risk of early death, became more physically active, and
    improved their sense of well-being compared to those who do
    not volunteer.[12]

Summary

I thought that I was a rather successful CEO at Mothers' Aid, because the
professional part of the organisation enjoyed high economic growth rates
and created good results.

But the volunteers and vulnerable families taught me that volunteers'
abilities to create relationships and "togetherness" can contribute as much
impact as professional social workers. The most significant effect is obtained
by combining these resources and, at the same time, creating a caring culture
in your organisation.

I am grateful for this insight, which I have taken with me in my later functions as an adviser to governments, foundations, and non-profit start-ups.

Follow-up actions

The next time you meet the volunteers in your organisation, try to
raise some of the following questions:

- Why should anyone volunteer in our organisation?
- What impact do you make – you as a volunteer and we as an
  organisation?
- Would anyone miss our organisation if it closed tomorrow?

Notes

1 Tutu, D. (2011), *God Is Not a Christian: And Other Provocations.* New York: HarperOne, Chapter 2, pp. 21–22.
2 Taylor-Gooby, P. (2004), *New Risks, New Welfare: The Transformation of the European Welfare State.* Published to Oxford Scholarship Online: January 2005. doi:10.1093/0199267 26X.001.0001.
3 Cacioppo, J.T. and S. Cacioppo (2018), The Growing Problem of Loneliness. *www.the lancet.com*, 391, February 3, p. 426.
4 Sandbu, M. (2019), *Economics of Belonging.* Princeton University Press.
5 Zhu, H. and R. An (2013), Impact of Home-Delivered Meal Programs on Diet and Nutrition Among Older Adults: A Review. *Nutrition and Health*, 22(2), 89–103. doi:10.1177/0260106014537146.
6 Eliasoph, N. and P. Lichterman (2014), Civic Action. *The American Journal of Sociology*, 120(3), 798–863.
7 Ibid., p. 809.
8 Salamon, L. (1987), Of Market Failure, Voluntary Failure, and Third-Party Government: Toward a Theory of Government-Nonprofit Relations in the Modern Welfare State. *Nonprofit and Voluntary Sector Quarterly*, 16(1–2), 29–49.
9 International Labour Organization (2011), *Manual on the Measurement of Volunteer Work.* Geneva: ILO, p. 13.
10 Haskins, G., M. Thomas and L. Johri (2018), *Kindness in Leadership.* Routledge, p. 92.
11 Clausen, M.R. (2021), How Funding of Non-Profit Social Organizations Affects the Number of Volunteers. *VOLUNTAS: International Journal of Voluntary and Nonprofit Organizations (Manchester, England).* doi:10.1057/9781137346926_1.
12 Borgonovi, F. (2008), Doing Well by Doing Good. The Relationship Between Formal Volunteering and Self-Reported Health and Happiness. *Social Science & Medicine*, 2321–2334.

Further reading

Here is a beautiful vision about a PACT for civil society in England, created by civil society and written under the leadership of the insightful Julia Unwin. Available at: https://civil-societyfutures.org/pact/
If you are interested in a global perspective and an introduction to the variation in the civil society: Mary Kaldor: *Global Civil Society: An Answer to War.* Cambridge, UK: Polity Press.
This is *the* classic book on social capital – a must-read: Robert Putnam: *Bowling Alone.* New York: Simon & Schuster.

PART II
Purpose and values

5

MASTERING THE POWER OF PURPOSE

Katherine Corich

Abstract

In this chapter, I share how we can find purpose; whether this is in everyday life or in the broader context of the contributions that we strive to make in our work, in communities and organisations. The journey to living with purpose comprises many learnings, taking the time to observe small daily practices of gratitude and understanding the difference between one's inner purpose and the concept of outer purpose.

One of my key observations is that purpose is uniquely our own. It can shift like the sands of time on an ocean current, over the course of your life. That said, when you discover your purpose, it can carry you like an ocean wave, and anything is possible.

I hope that the stories I share, which illustrate where I have witnessed purpose, will help to inspire you to formulate your own beautifully fulfilling purpose.

Keywords: Purpose, meaning, entrepreneur, innovation

Introduction – the power of purpose

Few things are as important to our lives as living with a sense of purpose. In the words of Myles Munroe, "*The greatest tragedy in life is not death, but a life without purpose*"[1] (*Myles Munroe [1954–2014], pastor, teacher, and best-selling author specialising in the topics of leadership and purpose*).

DOI: 10.4324/9781003219293-7

Purpose is a driving force inside every one of us. It's that strong feeling that a sea current might one day propel you forward and another day make you feel like it could drag you under. Purpose is at once a sense of urgency, the voice challenging you to change something for the better, as it is a brake that is holding you back.

A need to strive for purpose is an essential part of being human. This tension that is at the core of purpose is the very thing that can make purpose both endearing and overwhelming. When we meet a person whose life is overtly driven by purpose, it can sometimes make us feel as if we are a lesser being. We might compare ourselves to this person who seems to be relentlessly driven by something greater than themselves. They seem to do so much, achieve so much, and they inspire awe. But who is this person and how have they mastered the power of purpose? Or have they? Are they exhibiting only one dimension of purpose? Are they, not you, at a different stage of their journey?

And what of the person who is quiet, calm, reflective, and self-aware? Do they not exhibit a life that is fuelled by purpose?

The German-born spiritual teacher, Eckhart Tolle (2008) in *"A New Earth, Awakening to Your Life's Purpose"*, describes an inner and an outer purpose. "Inner purpose concerns Being and is primary, outer purpose concerns Doing and is secondary". Yet he goes on to say, "inner and outer purpose are so intertwined, it is impossible to speak of one without referring to the other to the other".[2]

So what then are the dimensions of purpose? I see purpose as having four dimensions, inner and outer as described by Tolle; plus personal and global.

We'll refer to these concepts throughout the chapter and refer back to the diagram from time to time.

According to Tolle (2008), *"your inner purpose is to awaken. It is as simple as that. . . . Awakening is a shift in consciousness in which thinking and awareness separate".*[3]

The intersection of indigenous and western cultures is perhaps where we see the contrast of inner and outer purpose most poignantly. Growing up in Aotearoa, New Zealand, I was blessed to be raised amongst people who are deeply and spiritually connected to their land and lineage. We call this "whakapapa".

According to the Founder and Director of Haka works (a company which utilises tools from the Māori culture to motivate, inspire and build teams), Karl Burrows (2021) Whakapapa helps us understand our life's purpose.[4] It's an idea at the heart of our Māori culture. "Know thyself" – meaning know

FIGURE 5.1: The Dimensions of Purpose: Inner/Outer/Personal/Global. Black and White Image.
Source: Artwork by Nik Hannay. © Concept of inner and outer Purpose Eckhart Tolle.
© Concept of personal and global purpose and diagram Katherine Corich

your ancestors, what is their story? How does it connect with your story? What legacy have they left? How has it impacted you and informed your drivers and motivations? How will you realise your purpose today in your work/life? What foundations will you leave for future generations to stand upon?

Each of us intuitively knows that we have the seeds of great purpose inside of us, and we long to find a meaningful way to allow it to be nurtured and grow. We may not yet know where on the continuum of purpose our ambition sits, but let's frame that as a positive so we can continually seek joy in exploring our inner, outer, personal, and global purpose.

In this chapter, I am going to describe how I constantly seek purpose in everything I do, while trying also to live in the present and enjoy the beauty and simplicity of everyday living.

Being driven by purpose can be an unsettling way to live, as we are constantly seeking to change things, to make the world a better place, to know that our life has a meaning. However, when we master the power of purpose, we can feel stretched, balanced, and empowered.

The Oxford Learner's Dictionary defines "Purpose" as "The intention, aim or function of something; the thing that something is supposed to achieve". This, according to the aforementioned definitions, is therefore more closely aligned to "outer purpose".[5]

But what does it mean to achieve? Does it need to be world-changing or can it be as simple as making a difference in another person's life? My early years taught me that it can be the latter and that this is, in fact, the very essence of the concept of purpose. Once you have mastered this, you will find that scaling your purpose-led life is so much easier.

Purpose brings meaning to your life and, in the words of Viktor Frankl, *"Striving to find meaning in one's life is the primary motivational force in man"*[6] *(Viktor Frankl [1905–1997], Austrian neurologist, psychiatrist, philosopher, author, and Holocaust survivor).*

My personal experience

Born number 6 in a blended family of seven children, my feet were always the sixth pair of feet to climb into pre-loved boots, my arms slipped on woolly cardigans that had been worn a 1,000 times and childhood adventures: tree-climbing escapades, harvesting blackberry from hedgerows, creating sandcastles on the beach, and digging for pipi (shellfish) kept us all busy.

I learned from a young age that every one of us has a strong sense of something that I would later learn is called "purpose".

We all yearn for meaning in our lives, and at different ages and stages of our lives, we will discover new aspects of ourselves, of others, and of the world around us that help us to define our path, and by implication our unique purpose. Purpose is like a tectonic plate; it can move and change. Your evolving priorities and multitude of experiences help you to shape your purpose as you ask yourself existential questions such as "Who am I?", "How and where do I belong?", and "When do I feel alive?"

Motherhood – a powerful purpose

My mum is always full of wisdom and one of her most enduring and often repeated statements is "Love is service". I often thought about this as a young girl growing up, surrounded by people who said that equality is everyone's right, and feminism is the good fight for equality for women. So, to be raised in a family where we were told to reach for the moon, academically, sporting-wise, and in extra-curricular activities, mother's statement seemed somewhat at odds with the ambition.

Never short of sage words, other favourite expressions included "Love is not a pie with 6 finite slices; it's an ocean wave, that rolls continuously", and "Love is a verb, so just love". The world needs more people like my mum and there are millions and millions of people doing the work of loving and nurturing their families. This is purpose of the highest order.

Samoa – an equal opportunity

We moved to live in Western Samoa when I was 11. As the only white European child in my year 7 class, I didn't think of myself as different and I certainly didn't feel excluded in any way, until the day of the school photograph. As our class of giggling girls lined up for our photo to be taken, the photographer asked me to step forward and out of the group. Initially, I presumed that he needed help with something, then quickly realised that he was clicking his camera without me in the frame. At that moment, I felt an overwhelming feeling of injustice, sadness, confusion, and longing to belong. Why had this man deliberately wanted me outside of the photo? Was it the colour of my skin, or was it that I wasn't yet wearing the complete school uniform? To this day, I cannot be sure what his motivation was, but I do know that that moment will be forever etched in me as the moment I said "I hope that I will never make another human being feel excluded in their differences". This experience definitely helped to shape my purpose.

Accidental entrepreneur or pilot – decisions to make

I created a company called Sysdoc when I was 25. Sysdoc is a business transformation company, striving to make positive change to create successful organisations. I was a qualified pilot and I believed that taking the principles of aviation into everyday business could help organisations operate safely and efficiently. The Sysdoc journey has been purpose-driven from day one. We've been operating for 35 years and every day we see examples of our fundamental DNA being drawn upon to improve safety.

Let's explore purpose more in the context of being an accidental entrepreneur. How did it help give me the courage to establish a business and to continue in the times when things inevitably get tough?

Initially, the purpose seemed to come very naturally, an almost organic transfer of what I had learned during my training to become a commercial pilot. I utilised things that were very natural and obvious in aviation: using simulators for training, understanding of how human factors affect behaviour, whole-system thinking, and a deep understanding of the importance of the end-to-end process, especially when multiple people are involved in keeping you safe.

Over time, the organisations that we started working with would ask for more and recommend us to others. Staff numbers grew and Sysdoc had its' own energy and momentum. At this point, I realised that purpose can grow and become something even greater than you imagined. Sysdoc now had its own purpose, and that was to provide employment for people and to challenge the status quo in the ways of working.

We designed and introduced employment models that were unique at the time in the consulting industry, and as time passed, we recognised that our new purpose was to be a challenger and a disruptor. Fast forward to the present and we realise with a renewed sense of urgency that while the principles underpinning the Sysdoc business haven't changed, the impact we can have on the world, has an even greater sense of, now collective, purpose. Every person, every action, united and moving in the same direction.

Drawing again on the words of Karl Burrows (2021) and the Māori concept of "whakapapa":

> The same questions apply to teams/organisations, looking to how the ancestors (founders and leaders) of the past have left a legacy to inspire us in the now. What can we leave for those to come through our collective work? And it is the role of leaders to align individual purpose with the team's purpose and in doing so inspire cohesion, collaboration and massive achievement.[7]

My journey to mastering the power of purpose

In my experience, mastery of the power of purpose is an incremental journey. With each new experience, we add to our collection of knowledge and wisdom. When we experience injustice, we grow from the experience. When we have suffered unkindness, we can start to recognise that another person's desire to humiliate or diminish you is their issue and not yours. Perhaps we can help them uncover the source of their angst? When we grieve, we walk a well-trodden path to eventually build resilience. When we have been made to feel inferior, we can resolve not to let anyone we know feel a similar feeling. Adversity helps us to become the person we are today; it strengthens our resolve and purpose.

I am not sure that I have yet fully mastered the power of purpose, but I do have a deep sense of understanding about what it means to live a life with purpose. My sense of purpose helps guide my decisions about how and where I spend my time; it influences my behaviour and helps me to bring out the best in others. In summary, it enables me to create meaning in my life.

Mastery of purpose may be different from one person to another. For one person, purpose might be connected to their vocation, being in meaningful, satisfying work. For another, purpose may lie in their responsibilities to and love for family or friends. Others seek meaning through spirituality, meditation, or religious beliefs. You may find your purpose clearly expressed in all these aspects of your life.

The key point to remember is that your purpose can move, grow, and change throughout your life. It is uniquely your purpose.

Examples of people with purpose

Nelson Mandela – a life's working fighting for equality

My first example is of a very well-known person and one for whom little introduction is required. His life was filled with purpose, as he fought against apartheid and endured years of imprisonment. In his own words, "*The purpose of freedom is to create it for others*"[8] (*Nelson Mandela [1918–2013], anti-apartheid revolutionary statesman and philanthropist*).

For the remaining examples, I have deliberately chosen role models for the power of purpose who are less well known.

Sarah de Carvalho – it's a penalty and Happy Child International

Sarah is the founder and CEO of two linked charities, Happy Child International (HCI) www.happychildinternational.org and It's a Penalty www.itsapenalty.org.

Sarah established 14 children's homes in Brazil, which take in young homeless girls who have been sexually exploited. For 28 years, Sarah and her teams have rescued over 10,000 young girls. Many of these girls are pregnant and have no means to care for themselves and their babies. HCI gives them a safe home where they stay until they are ready to be reintegrated into their wider family and community.

Sarah is driven by a sense of great purpose. Most people who have done as much to help others as she has would start to slow down. However, her sense of purpose led her to establish "It's a Penalty" to raise awareness about child sex exploitation globally and to harness sport as a force for good, by running campaigns during major international sporting events. Every working every day and waking moment, Sarah strives to improve the lives of others.

Maarten van der Bas – raising children

Maarten, a father of four children, gave up his career to be the home parent at a time when it was definitely not a popular choice for men. He did so with quiet dignity and often suffered the silent mirth of other's disapproval.

At 31 years of age, he had the world at his feet. Selected as one of ten young people for a high-performing graduate programme in a global bank, his leaders had seen something special in his character. Yet he chose parenthood.

I regard Maarten as one of the greatest purpose makers. He put service over self and ego to do what he knew to be the right thing for our family. It was not until 25 years later when the children were grown up and he was attending a dinner of highly accomplished global leaders, that Maarten was able to share his very deliberately articulated purpose

> I was working and enjoying my role, but I wasn't being driven by a higher sense of purpose, so when I could transition into a home based primary carer role, I knew that I was liberating Katherine to make a big difference in her work as an entrepreneur.

This is a snapshot of the many examples of living life with purpose that we see on a regular basis.

Some insights on finding your purpose

Purpose and passion sit side by side. In the words of Bishop Jakes, "*If you can't figure out your purpose, figure out your passion. For your passion will lead you right into your purpose*"[9] (*Bishop TD Jakes [1954-present], American bishop, author, and filmmaker*).

Your life purpose is your contribution. It's the thing you wake up thinking about in the morning and it feeds your energy levels throughout the day. In the diagram, we showed that purpose can exist at different levels, let's explore here the personal or global dimensions. However, let's not favour one over another. All manifestations of purpose are important to those who find purpose and those who receive a benefit from another's purpose.

Examples of personal purpose:

- Living consciously
- Growing food and feeding your family
- Looking after your loved ones
- Caring for your community
- Sharing your means with people in need
- Being a role model for younger people

The idea of purpose as contribution is emphasised in the following quote from Richard Leider, the founder of Inventure – The Purpose Company. "*Genuine purpose points to the end of the self-absorbed, self-serving relationship to life*"[10] *(Richard Leider [1944-present], author, pioneer in the field of career coaching, and spokesperson for the power of purpose).*

In summary, every one of us should feel that our contributions are purposeful and important. Small, daily acts of kindness are of equal importance. Humanity would not exist without them.

If you are born in a slum and every day is a challenge to get enough to eat, how can you still have a sense of real purpose? Your purpose may be about survival, or your small acts of kindness to improve the lives of people in your world.

If you are in a refugee camp, how do you have a sense of purpose? How can purpose help to improve the daily grind of sitting and waiting? Is there a role to lead others in daily practices of meditation or physical fitness? Do meditation and inner purpose become more important? Whatever is the answer, try to be kind to yourself. From small personal gestures, tall trees can grow.

Now let's look at collective or global purpose. Here are some examples:

- Campaigning for peace
- Fighting for equality of all people's
- Fighting against human trafficking
- Fighting against abuse of women and children
- Fighting the decline of species biodiversity
- Fighting against warming of the planet
- Fighting against political corruption
- Fighting against fraud
- Feeding the planet
- Reducing waste and recycling

All of these seem like grand, noble causes, but none of these can be achieved without the small purposeful acts of humanity, which are delivered every day, everywhere. We must never diminish the central role of these.

Concepts

Defining high-impact purpose

Great purpose is the ability of a person to see beyond their own self and ego and into the heart of humanity, in a way that enables them to know the type of contribution which they can make. The purpose becomes high-impact purpose when the contribution of a person makes a material difference in the lives of others.

Principles of high-impact purpose

- Your purpose is unique to you
- Purpose can evolve over time and life experiences

Purpose can have many different dimensions: responsibility to family and friends, your vocation – meaningful work, or your spirituality.

Benefits of purpose

- It has the ability to change your life and that of others for the better
- It enables you to challenge the status quo when the norm lacks integrity of purpose
- It enables us to collectively work towards greater good for the planet

Purpose gives you energy and confidence.

List points to highlight great purpose

- Finding serenity inside yourself
- Finding true meaning in what you do.
- Contribution
- Making a difference
- Overcoming fear to drive positive change

Methods to prescribe to be a purpose maker

You can become a purpose maker by consciously thinking about the difference you want to make in yourself and in the world. It doesn't need to be a high-profile action; it can be something very simple.

Here are some positive steps that I use when I am at a crossroads:

1. Think consciously about what really motivates you. Is there something that you would love to be, do, or change?
2. A useful way to think about this is to write down: What gives you a sense of calm and then what puts the fire in your belly?
3. Write a list of the top five things you would like to do to make a difference.
4. Think carefully about which one of these you are ready to tackle.
5. Put the plan into action (volunteer, study something you love, and start something new).
6. Finally, remember to take time to be kind to yourself.

Measuring the impact you are having

An example which stood out for me was in a town of 40,000 people where there were high levels of reported family violence. Over time, the charity sector's response was to create many charities. At one time, this reached a total of 45 charities whose stated "purpose" was to "reduce family violence". Yet incident numbers were on the increase and show-ing no sign of abatement. Was individual purpose over-shadowing greater good and impact?

While every individual and charity were stating that they were working with "purpose", it was clear that they were not working in a joined-up way, resulting in no changes in the negative statistics – just an over-supply of workers who were failing to make a difference?

So does it also require "collective intent and collaboration"? I believe it does.

Summary

I hope that some of my insights on the power of purpose have inspired you to think about how your own life experiences – your life story – all the things which you have lived and breathed shape who you are and the con-tribution that you want to make. I hope too, that they inspire you to reach your full and purposeful potential.

Let your purpose be your guiding north star. Be kind to yourself as you do so. At times, the fire in your belly to improve something will manifest as great flames. At other times, just let the embers warm you as you sit quietly and reflect. Trust yourself and you will find your purpose.

Follow-up actions

1. Practical exercise – Keep a diary for a month

On a daily basis, keep a diary and write down:
At the beginning of the day . . .

What are you grateful for?
What are your intentions for the day?
What would make today a great day?

As the sun goes down:

What you did today? Can you add something tomorrow that might move you gently towards feeling more purposeful?

At the end of the month, summarise the things you did, give yourself a pat on the back, and set a stretch target for the upcoming month.
Draw a circle on a page and divide the circle in two:

- In the left-hand half circle, place a summary of "what you did" each day. This can be one sentence or a short list.
- In the right-hand half circle, write one sentence that summarises what you dream of doing.

2. Plan how you can start doing more of what you dream of doing

For example, if you are already in a job, speak to your boss and ask them whether you can start to lead on the implementation of sustainability ideas.

If you are not working, research the types of companies that you would like to work for and plan how you might help them to achieve positive wins.

Draw a timeline of your life, and on it, show the different types of "purpose" that have motivated you at different times.

Reflect:

Do you share the "best version of you" with the world?

Are you living authentically, according to your values and beliefs?

When you wake up in the morning, do you jump out of bed ready to start the day?

Notes

1 Munroe, Myles (1992), *In Pursuit of Purpose: The Key to Personal Fulfilment*. 2nd edition. Destiny Image.
2 Tolle, Eckhardt (2008), *A New Earth, Awakening to Your Life's Purpose*. Reprint edition. Penguin Books.
3 Ibid.
4 Karl Burrows (2021), *Haka Works: Whakapapa*. Haka Works Education. Available at: https://www.facebook.com/hakaworks/posts/2982640288686237
5 Oxford Learner's Dictionary (2021), *Definition of Purpose Noun From the Oxford Advanced Learner's Dictionary*. Oxford Learner's Dictionaries. Online. Available at: https://www.oxfordlearnersdictionaries.com/definition/english/purpose
6 Frankl, Viktor E. (1992), *Man's Search for Meaning*. 4th edition. Boston, MA: Beacon Press.
7 Karl Burrows (2021), *Haka Works: Whakapapa*. Haka Works Education. Available at: https://www.facebook.com/hakaworks/posts/2982640288686237
8 Mandela, Nelson (1979), Original Quote: *The Purpose of Freedom Is to Create It for Others*. Nelson Mandela Foundation. Available at: https://www.nelsonmandela.org/?fbclid=IwAR24lrQ7okuKxY5qzAvfNKtqF9OxFa-zNhf00eTdiFpWMY5qgZN4tf3Pgi0
9 T.D. Jakes Ministries (2021), *Bishop T.D. Jakes.org*. Available at: https://www.tdjakes.org
10 Leider, R. (2010), *A Year of Living Purposefully. Living on Purpose*. Available at: http://richardleiderblog.info/

Further reading

• Beck, Martha (2008), *Finding Your own North Star: Claiming the Life You Were Meant to Live*. Reprint edition. New York: Harmony Books, Crown Publishing Group.
• Garcia, Hector and Miralles, Francesc (2017), *Ikigai: The Japanese Secret to a Long and Happy Life*. Penguin Life.
• Joly, Hubert (2020), A Time to Lead With Purpose and Humanity. *Harvard Business Review*, March 24.
• Oprah's Super Soul Conversations (Podcasts). Available on the Appstore or via: https://podcasts.apple.com/us/podcast/super-soul/id1264843400
• Parks, S.D. (2011), *Big Questions, Worthy Dreams: Mentoring Emerging Adults in Their Search for Meaning, Purpose and Faith*. New York: Jossey-Bass.
• Saïd Business School at the University of Oxford (2020), *Oxford Saïd Team Creates New Framework to Govern Purpose*. Available at: https://www.sbs.ox.ac.uk/news/oxford-said-team-creates-new-framework-govern-purpose
• Steiner, Brandon (2018), *Living on Purpose: Stories about Faith, Fortune and Fitness That Will Lead You to an Extraordinary Life*. USA: Lioncrest Publishing.
• The Enacting Purpose Initiative (2021), *Enacting Purpose Within the Modern Corporation: A Framework for Boards of Director*. Available at: https://www.enactingpurpose.org

6

MASTERING THE POWER OF KINDNESS

Gay Haskins

Abstract

Acts of kindness can give us all a real boost. They are never wasted.

Nonetheless, until recently, kindness has seldom been mentioned as a leadership trait, not discussed in leadership development programmes. This chapter discusses what kindness is and the positive role that it can play in organisations. It looks at the leadership traits of kind leaders and the positive impact that an emphasis on kindness can have on organisational commitment and performance.

It provides examples of kind acts that individuals and organisations have carried out before and during the pandemic, calling for all of us to make kindness integral to our values and philosophy going forward.

Keywords: Kindness, listening, honesty, fairness, compassion

Introduction

> *"No act of kindness, no matter how small, is ever wasted"*.
>
> Aesop, slave and storyteller living in Ancient Greece 620–564 BCE, *The Lion and the Mouse, Aesop for Children* (translator not identified), 1919[1]

Aesop was right. In 2020, in the early months of the pandemic, I came home from a wintry walk in the English countryside to find that one of my neighbours, Pat, had dropped off the Sunday newspaper for me. Another

DOI: 10.4324/9781003219293-8

neighbour, Doran, knocked at the door with some delicious cherry cake. I'm not a baker, so this was a special treat! And then, a lovely bouquet of flowers arrived from my nephew, Andrew.

Simple random acts of kindness such as these seem to have heightened during the Pandemic. They give both the giver and the receiver a real boost. As well, they have a boomerang effect: kindness begets kindness. As Aesop wrote, kind acts are never wasted.

The enduring influence of kind people

The idea of kindness having a positive effect on humanity is conveyed throughout religious thinking. All world religions (including, among others, Buddhism, Christianity, Judaism, Hinduism, Islam, Sikhism, and Taoism) have similar concepts of the application of kindness, which can be broadly summarised in the Golden Rule of "Do unto others as they would do unto you".[2]

My own early life was strongly influenced by the Quaker faith. Quakers belong to a historically Protestant Christian set of denominations known formally as the Religious Society of Friends. Members believe that there is something transcendent and precious in every person: God is in everyone.[3] Their weekly gatherings are called Meetings and can be held anywhere. They begin with all the group sitting in silence, with no leader and everyone able to contribute during the hour together. Anyone can join in: you don't have to be a Quaker to attend Meeting.

Quakers have strong values: peace and love at the centre of our exist-ence; speaking the truth at all times; being guided by integrity; ensuring sustainability; and living life simply. Their adherence to a simple life leads to a belief that everyone, whatever their age, cleverness, talent or eloquence has "*magnificent opportunities to be kind and patient and understanding*".[4] "This", they believe, "is a vocation just as truly as some more obviously seen as such – the call of everyone to continual unspectacular acts of loving kindness in the ordinary setting of every day".[5]

My parents were Quakers and, at two months old, I was taken to the Friends Meeting House in Dorking, Surrey, in June 1945. There were about 35 families who were members of the meeting at that time, and, as I grew up, I became increasingly aware of their goodness, their simplicity of life, and their kindness. I remember vividly: dear Jessie Cheston who used to invite me over to lunch and let me wander endlessly around her cottage garden; the Kohler family who opened up their old-fashioned caravan to the children each Sunday after Meeting had taken place; and James and Phyllis Topping whose deep belief in peace, love and kindness were an inspiration to my father and mother.

These Quakers were my role models. I always admired and respected them and they are etched deep in my memory. I grew up, therefore, highly influenced by a group of very kind people.

The role of kindness in my own leadership

As a result of the Quaker influences on my own behaviour, I have tried to be kind in my life, both at work and at home. Quaker values have stuck with me always, affecting the way I managed and led in organisations. Thanks to them, two words that colleagues have used to describe my leadership style (whether at the European Foundation for Management Development [EFMD], The Economist, London Business School or Oxford University's Saïd Business School) are "*caring*" and "*kind*".

About caring: I have always derived great pleasure from seeing members of my team progress. In early 1990, I hired a bright young German graduate, Adolf Ihde, from the London School of Economics to join my team at EFMD. He progressed well and went on to join Airbus, ending his career there as Senior Vice President of Human Resources. When I joined Oxford University in 2006, I invited Dr. Lalit Johri, who was working at the Asian Institute of Technology, to apply for a position at Saïd Business School. Lalit was hired and went on to become the leader of the Oxford Advanced Management and Leadership Programme for 12 great years. I have found as much joy in seeing these colleagues progress in their careers as I have in my own development.

About behaving kindly: I have always tried to encourage a warm and friendly environment in the teams I have led, as much as possible without hierarchies. I have encouraged celebrations: of birthdays; of success stories; of simple human kindness. I have also always tried to listen to others and give them time and I have derived great motivation through being a mentor to others. I believe strongly in the strength of international cultures and have therefore tried to build diverse and inclusive teams.

About fairness: I have come to understand that kindness to others must include fairness to others. This isn't always easy. For instance, anyone in a leadership position will know how precious their time is. My own biggest challenge (and one that I sometimes failed to overcome) was divvying out my time: giving all members of my team an equal opportunity to come to me and discuss things, not showing favouritism.

Food for thought

- *Think of some of the kindnesses that have enhanced your life. Who did they come from? What impact have they had on you?*

A journey into kindness

I became particularly involved in a journey into kindness in 2014.

The journey was ignited through a conversation with Professor Mike Thomas of the University of Chester. Mike told me that he had recently examined the use of the word *"kindness"* in academic research on organisational leadership. He had found that it was hardly ever mentioned! My own experience corroborated this.

Over many years of involvement in leadership programmes in business schools around the world, I had never heard the importance of kindness mentioned in the classroom. *"Surely"*, we thought, *"the importance of kindness is not limited to the home? It must be important in the workplace too"*.

We put together an outline for a book on *"Kindness in Leadership"*.[6] We presented the outline to the publisher, Routledge, and, to our delight, they accepted it. We spoke with friends and they eagerly agreed to contribute. Writing and editing *"Kindness in Leadership"* was exciting. We felt that we were breaking new ground. All the team of writers became convinced that being kind is an important leadership attribute and that kind organisational cultures lead to commitment, engagement, and trust. Let me share some of the findings of our conversations and interviews. But first of all, let us briefly reflect on the meaning of kindness.

Kindness defined

The words "kind" and "kindness" are words that we hear frequently in our daily lives. *"How very kind!"* we say. Or, *"That was a real act of kindness"*. Indeed, "kind" is among the top 500 most frequently used words in the English language.

The *Cambridge English Dictionary* and the *Merriam-Webster Dictionary* provide a number of definitions for the adjective "kind", showing that it has several meanings and underpinnings:

- "Generous, helpful and thinking about other people's feelings".
- "Arising from, or characterised by, sympathy or forbearance".
- "Gentle, considerate, forbearing, humane".

For "kindness", in the same dictionaries, we find two definitions:

- "The practice or quality of being kind". ("She treated people with kindness".)
- "A kind considerate or helpful act or deed". ("They did me a great kindness".)[7]

Kindness, therefore, can be a quality particularly linked to being helpful, compassionate, empathetic, and humane. Importantly too, it frequently has an action orientation to it. As well, it is a relational behaviour: it is only possible to demonstrate kindness in the context of an interaction with one or more individuals.

In our research for *Kindness in Leadership,* we found that there is actually a host of words that relate to kindness and being kind. Kindness can manifest itself in many ways: altruism, care, compassion, decency, empathy, fairness, forgiveness generosity, goodness, honesty, humility, loyalty, and respect, for instance.

As a private sector leader said to my colleagues Clare Murray and Alison Gill, in the course of an interview for our book, "*Kindness is a bland word, but the meaning is fabulous. The word is small but what it represents is fabulous*".[8]

Food for thought

- *What does kindness mean to you?*

Kindness in organisations

If kindness is important, is it incorporated into the values of your present organisation or where you have worked in the past? If you are thinking about setting up an organisation, will kindness be a core value which you will espouse as a founder?

Values can be described as "*a small set of timeless, guiding principles*".[9] They strongly complement the purpose of an organisation, endure over time, and can be described in behavioural terms. Organisations which most frequently cite kindness or compassion as a core value are hospitals, schools, and a few universities. The values of London's famous University College London Hospitals (UCLH) are: *safety, kindness, teamwork, and improving.*[10]

Some organisations are set up with a kind purpose at their core: charities, social enterprises, and not for profits, for instance. But when we wrote *"Kindness in Leadership"* between 2015 and 2018, we found that kindness was not cited as a core value in many private sector organisations. However, some famous large companies have been *"built for good"*: the Nationwide Building Society in the UK was specifically formed in 1844, to provide members of the cooperative movement with the opportunity to purchase homes. The famous retail store, the John Lewis Partnership, is owned by its employees and was established as a *"genuine partnership for all"*.[11]

But I scoured the internet for for-profit businesses with kindness as a core value without much success. Finally, I came across Agency H5 in Chicago, a small PR company "founded on kindness". Excitedly, I got in touch with its CEO and Founder, Kathleen Scarpy (formerly Kathleen Kenehan Henson), and talked with her at length. Kathleen had worked for several years in large PR companies in the US before she decided to set up her own business in 2001. As a mother of five children, she did not aim to build the biggest or most profitable PR agency in the world. But she deliberately aimed to set up an organisation that valued and exemplified kindness. The box here shows some of Kathleen's inspiring thoughts and actions.[12]

Everyone deserves to be treated with respect and love. I believe in practicing the Golden Rule in business by treating others as you would want to be treated. . . . I'm a big believer that bestowing kindness breeds stronger, more long-term relationships.

You will never go to bed with a concern or worry if you choose to do the kind thing during your workday. Sure, sometimes you might get taken advantage of, but that's rare, and the benefits far outweigh the risks. . . . I've always focused on the principle of kindness and the business grew and the profits followed. . . . I simply wanted to create an agency where people could be their authentic selves and choose to be joyful outside of work and bring that joy into the office every day.

As a leader, I've found that when people are genuinely happy, they practice kindness to each other and that ultimately makes our clients happy and it's an ongoing cycle of kindness. . . . I've never focused on the profits first. . . . I've always focussed on the principle of kindness and the business grew and the profits followed.

Kathleen Scarpy, Founder and CEO, Agency H5

Agency H5 is not a large organisation: at the time of writing that statement in 2017, it employed fewer than 50 people. It is possible that the ability for companies to exemplify kindness both internally and externally may be affected by their size. Having a comparatively small number of employees may offer the opportunity for a wider and more intimate understanding of the personal circumstances of employees and therefore greater possibilities to act with kindness. "*In large institutions, the layers mean that people at the top are so distant from the others' daily lives that they cannot really know how their decisions will affect people in real life*", said Bill Marley, Chief Executive of The Employability Trust in a roundtable on kindness at St Aidan's College, Durham University in 2016.[13]

Food for thought

- **Can you think of an organisation that you would describe as kind?**

Kindness-based behaviours

In 2018, Saïd Business School joined with Hall and Partners and the Women of the Future Programme to produce a booklet called *The Power of Kindness*. For this booklet, Professor Lalit Johri and I interviewed a number of UK leaders who had been named in an annual list of 50 Leading Lights of Kindness and Leadership, established by the Women of the Future Programme in 2018.[14]

We identified ten behaviours that exemplify kindness in organisations:

1. Listening to others and valuing their views;
2. Communicating with a personal touch;
3. Celebrating and recognising, being encouraging and responsive;
4. Being honest;
5. Accommodating personal issues;
6. Treating others with respect;
7. Championing and encouraging others;
8. Being inclusive;
9. Being humane and compassionate;
10. Making kindness a philosophy.[15]

About listening: it is interesting that "Listening" came at the top of the list. In today's soundbite world, really making time to listen to others can be hard. But, as Ruth Shaw, General Manager, of The Premier League

(Football) Charitable Fund has said, "*The best leaders always make you feel like they have time for you, no matter how busy they are or how much is going on*".[16]

About honesty: the importance of being honest was also frequently mentioned. Kindness is not about being "soft" or about avoiding frank and firm discussions. An honest and kind leader is strict and kind; analytical and kind; tough yet kind. In addition, as frequently mentioned in our discussions on kindness, it is vital for the kind leader to be honest, forthright, and clear: these are all key underpinnings of kind behaviour.

About strength and courage: For some kind leaders, this honest, frank, and open aspect of kindness comes as a challenge. In 2018 and 2019, I had the pleasure of supervising the MBA dissertation of Emma Carter. Emma was working as Workshop Coordinator at a small Lancashire-based business called Atkinson Vos, specialists in the sale and servicing of all-terrain vehicles called Unimogs. Her dissertation was on the Role of Kindness in Small Manufacturing and Engineering Companies in the North East of England.

At the outset of the project, Emma's definition of kindness was: "*Kindness is a smile, an acknowledgement: it's being there*".[17] However, when she had completed her research and interviews, her definition had changed. She wrote: "*Kindness is a balancing act. It takes great strength but with the help of others, kindness will prevail*".[18]

What Emma had found in the course of her investigation was that being kind is not simple. It is not just about a smiling "Hi, how are you?" to your colleagues in the morning, asking about their families and listening to their concerns. It's much more than that. It's about being firm and fair, presenting feedback with honesty, making decisions that may not please people but for the greater good. It requires courage and as Emma wrote in her dissertation: "*the strength part is the hardest part of kindness*".[19]

Making kindness a philosophy: the leaders that Lalit and I interviewed for *The Power of Kindness* all shared a belief in the value of kindness as an underlying philosophy for our lives and our work. Kindness as a philosophy guides leaders to be respectful of others, to show empathy and be compassionate. It leads to beliefs that people are central to the success of any organisation; equity and fairness are important ideals in enhancing employee confidence and loyalty; and that respect and care stimulate ownership and commitment.

Food for thought

- *Which of the ten kindness behaviours particularly resonate with you?*

The impact of kindness in organisations

What about the impact of kind and compassionate behaviours – do they increase commitment and trust in organisations? Interviews carried out with leaders around the world by Professor Lalit Johri suggest that they do. Lalit found a causal relationship between acts of kindness and positive outcomes. Through interviews with 47 leaders based in both emerging and developing countries, a wide range of positive impacts of kind leadership were suggested. These included:

- *Impact on employees*: greater happiness, higher motivation, energy, willingness to go the extra mile, higher commitment, engagement and participation, and increased loyalty and productivity;
- *Impact on teams*: greater stability, application of collective wisdom, higher order creativity and motivation, transformation;
- *Impact on management*: acceptance and trust, cordial relationships with workers;
- *Impact on culture*: less stressful work environment, collaboration and compliance, and transformation;
- *Impact on the reputation of the organisation*: attract and retain customers, "great place to work", attract best talent, attract strong business partners;
- *Impact on the performance of the company:* reduced transaction costs, better social and economic performance;
- *Impact on customers*: increase in the number of satisfied customers, higher satisfaction levels, and loyal customers;
- *Impact on business partners:* enduring long-term relationships and transformational relationships.[20]

Research carried out in the United States supports the conclusion that compassionate leadership has positive outcomes on productivity and financial performance. In their 2017 book, *Awakening Compassion at Work,* Monica Worline and Jane Dutton provide examples:[21]

> *In a study of eighteen organisations that had recently engaged in downsizing, the extent to which employees characterised their organisations as more virtuous was correlated with higher profitability, greater productivity and enhanced customer retention.*

*Another study examined performance over two years across forty busi-
ness units in the financial services industry. It found that, when compassion was part of the values of the business units as rated by the members,
the compassionate units exhibited better financial performance, executives
perceived the compassionate unit as more effective and those units realised
higher employee and customer retention.*

Monica Worline and Jane Dutton, Awakening Compassion at Work

Role models for kindness

Let me now share a little information on two people, who for me are or have
been role models of kindness.

**Jean François Poncet, former Director General, European Foun-
dation for Management Development (EFMD) – a humble leader:**
when I think back on my own working life, Jean François Poncet stands out.

In 1980, I was working in Brussels for the European Foundation for Management Development (EFMD), an international association of business
schools and companies focusing on best practice in management education.
EFMD is quite a large organisation nowadays, but in those days, there were
fewer than ten staff members, and, being mainly reliant on annual member-
ship fees for our income, we were not well off.

The Director General at that time was Jean-François Poncet, a charming
and charismatic Frenchman. Jean-François was one of the humblest men
that I have ever met. He had no desire for power, or for putting himself first:
was a true servant leader with a missionary zeal for bringing others to the
fore. He led from behind; and was passionate about putting people together
and growing international networks. As a network manager, he knew that
kind leadership involved getting others to excel.

Every evening, when we were not travelling to meet with the members,
Jean François would gather the small team into his office and ask for our
thoughts from the day, or for ideas on a key issue, we were grappling with.
He treated us all as equals, he listened to our ideas, and he encouraged
us. And when times were tough and the organisation faced financial difficulties, Jean François did not ask any members of the team to cut their
pay: he cut his own. I have never worked with a kinder, or better, leader.
As a result of Jean Francois' kind leadership, I became totally committed
to EFMD.

Jacinda Ardern, Prime Minister of New Zealand – a compassionate leader: Over the past four years, Jacinda Ardern has won worldwide admiration for her compassion, empathy, and kindness. In her initial tenure as Prime Minister, she has impressed the world with her compassion, especially during the Christchurch terrorist atrocity, the Whakaari volcano eruption, and the COVID-19 pandemic. In her interview in the eBook by Geoff Blackwell (*I know this to be true) on kindness, empathy, and strength,*[22] Jacinda Ardern consistently emphasises the importance of kindness, empathy and inclusivity in our fast-paced and digitised world. She also underlines the commitment and strength that kind leadership requires. **Angela Merkel,** Germany's Chancellor for many years also stood out for her decency and kindness during her tenure. Her decision to encourage large numbers of refugees to come to Germany required great strength and courage.

In an interview with The Guardian newspaper in 2020, Jacinda Ardern was asked about the key qualities that underpinned her path as a leader. Her response is shown in the following box:[23]

> *Kindness, and not being afraid to be kind, or to focus on, or be really driven by empathy. I think one of the sad things that's I've seen in political leadership is – because we've placed over time so much emphasis on notions of assertiveness and strength – that we probably have assumed that it means you can't have the other qualities of kindness and empathy. And yet, when you think about the challenges that we face in the world, that's probably the quality that we need the most.*
>
> *Jacinda Ardern, Prime Minister of New Zealand, 2020*

Food for thought

• *Who has been an exemplar of kindness in your own life?*

Summary

In this chapter, I have shared some of my experiences and research findings about kindness. "*Kind*" is a simple word understood by all English speakers throughout the World and is one of the 100 most frequently used words in our vocabulary. The impact of kind actions at the individual, family, team, organisational, and community levels can be enormous. Kindness has a boomerang effect: kindness begets kindness.

Kind leaders make kindness part of their core values and philosophy of living. They exemplify it within the organisations through compassion, empathy, listening, fairness, and honesty. Their impact is positive, leading to greater organisational commitment and motivation. Exemplars of kind leadership make a huge contribution to our lives whether at the friends and family level or within organisations and communities.

A global need for kindness

Ever since the Pandemic broke out around the world, acts of kindness have featured with increasing prominence in the news: the care and commitment of health care staff and other front line workers has been amazing; businesses have given back to their employees and to society at unusual levels;[24] governments have introduced extraordinary measures to keep economies going; food banks have increased their activities and/or sprung up around the world in an effort to feed the impoverished; simple acts of kindness by neighbours and friends seem to have increased enormously; and individual and group efforts to raise money for charity feature on the news on daily basis.

But we have a very long way to go if we are to create a truly kind and compassionate world. Poverty, crime, corruption, etc., are still all around us. They too feature on the news on a daily basis.

I believe that each of us has it within us to play a part, however small, in making the world a better place. In 1970, American country's music singer/guitarist released an album called "*Try a Little Kindness*". The lyrics were written by Curt Sapaugh and Bobby Austin and the song became a hit around the world. I can hear Glen Campbell singing as I write and I've included a link to the song in my references so that you can sing along too![25]

You've got to try a little kindness,
Yes, show a little kindness,
Just shine your light for everyone to see
And if you try a little kindness
Then you'll overlook the blindness
Of narrow-minded people on the narrow-minded streets.
        Song by Curt Sapaugh and Bobby Austin recorded
        by Glen Campbell, 1970

We need to keep worldwide acts of kindness at centre stage. We need to think about the long-term value of kindness and to put kindness to the fore in our lives – at home, in our organisations, in our communities, in our own countries and in our cooperation around the world.

Kindness can change a life for the better. Being kind is a powerful mantra to guide us forward. Try a little kindness. Make kindness core to your leadership philosophy.

Follow-up exercise: creating a kind organisation from scratch

In the post-pandemic times, many existing and potential entrepreneurs will be thinking of starting up their own business, or, hopefully, trying to create a culture of kindness in their existing organisation. Here are a few questions to think about along the way:

- *Is kindness a principle of your life and do you want this to carry over into the organisation you create and develop?*
- *Do you want your organisation to have kindness as a core value?*
- *What kind behaviours will you seek to exemplify as a leader?*
- *How can you work with others to create a culture of kindness in your organisation?*
- *How can you ensure inclusiveness in your organisation*
- *How can you build kindness into your customer relations, into your community relationships and towards the planet as a whole?*

Notes

1 Aesop (620–564 BCE), *The Lion and the Mouse,* Aesop for Children (translator not identified), 1919. Illustrations by Milo Winter (1886–1956). Available at: https://www.guten berg.org.ebooks/19994

2 The Golden Rule stems from the thinking of the great Chinese philosopher, Confucius (c551–479BC).

3 For further information on the Quaker faith, see: https://www.quaker.org.uk and https://en.wikipedia.org/wiki/Quakers

4 Haigh, Clifford (1962), *Quaker Faith and Practice.* 5th edition, Chapter 21 >21.43 available from Religious Society of Friends, Friends House, 173 Euston Road, London NW1 2BJ. Available at: https://gfp.quaker.org.uk>21-43

5 Ibid.

6 Haskins, G., M. Thomas and J. Johri (2018), *Kindness in Leadership.* Routledge.

7 *Cambridge English Dictionary* (2017). Available at: www.dictionary.cambridge.org/dictionary/english/kind and *Merriam-Webster Dictionary* (2017). Available at: www.merriam-webster.com/dictionary/kind

8 Haskins G., M. Thomas and L. Johri (2018), *Kindness in Leadership*. Routledge, p. 48.

9 Collins, J. and J. Porras (1996), Building Your Company's Vision. *Harvard Business Review*, September–October.

10 Haskins, G., M. Thomas and J. Johri (2018), *Kindness in Leadership*. Routledge, pp. 30–32.

11 BBC (2014), Video clip, John Spendan Lewis on "a Better Way of Managing Business", May 2. Available at: www.bbc.co.uk/news/av/uk-wales-27245930/john-spendan-lewis-on-a-better-way-of-managing-business

12 Scarpy (formerly Kenehan Henson), Kathleen, Founder and CEO, Agency H5, in *Kindness in Leadership* (2018). Routledge, pp. 199–200.

13 Ibid., p. 119.

14 Saïd Business School, Hall and Partners and The Women of the Future Programme/Kindness and Leadership Leading Lights (2019), *The Power of Kindness: Kind Leaders Shaping the Future* For copies and information on the annual UK Kind Leaders awards, contact The Women of the Future Programme. Available at: https://www.womenofthefuture.co.uk

15 Ibid., p. 15.

16 Ibid., p. 19.

17 Carter, E. (2019), *The Role of Kindness in Small Manufacturing and Engineering Companies in the North West*. MBA Dissertation, May.

18 Ibid.

19 Ibid.

20 Haskins, G., M. Thomas and J. Johri (2018), *Kindness in Leadership*. Routledge, p. 80.

21 Worline, M. and J. Dutton (2017), *Awakening Compassion at Work*. Oakland, CA: Berrett Koehler, pp. 14, 15.

22 Blackwell, G. (2021), *(I Know This to Be True) Jacinda Ardern on Kindness, Empathy and Strength*. Chronicle Books.

23 Blackwell, G. (2020), Political Leaders Can Be Both Empathetic and Strong. *The Guardian*, interview with Jacinda Ardern, May 30.

24 Forbes (2020), *50 Ways Companies Are Giving Back During the Coronavirus Pandemic*. Available at: https://www.forbes.com>2020/03/17

25 Austin, B. and C. Sapaugh (1970), Try a Little Kindness, recorded by Glen Campbell, 1970. Available at: https://youtube.com>watch. Glen Campbell Try a Little Kindness Live 2002 – You Tube – With the South Dakota Symphony.

Further reading

Hamilton, David (2010), *Why Kindness Is Good for You*. UK: Hay House, David Hamilton is a doctor and expert in the science of kindness.

Haskins, Gay, Mike Thomas and Lalit Johri (2018), *Kindness in Leadership*. UK: Routledge, one of the first books to explore the concept and practice of kind leadership in organisations.

Worline, Monica C. and Jane E. Dutton (2017), *Awakening Compassion at Work: The Quiet Power That Elevates People and Organisations*. USA: Berrett-Koehler Publishers Inc., a valuable guide to research and practice on unleashing compassion at work.

7

MASTERING THE POWER OF MORAL VALUE

J.R. Klein

Abstract

The word "moral" comes from a Latin root, which refers to commonly accepted norms and customs. Historic examples of cultures and ideologies, however, present acceptable behaviors that are considered repulsive, such as killing in Nazi Germany or slavery in the United States old south. The contemporary view of moral value is wider than the Latin root and describes standards of "goodness" and rightness (right and wrong) in terms of character and behavior. Acceptable moral value, therefore, becomes conduct that is advantageous to society. If it does not meet the social test, it is considered immoral. This view puts a heavy burden on moral character, especially in leadership, and points directly at traits that drive moral value. Presented in this chapter is a contemplative conversation about defining, identifying, and building moral character. It presents essential conceptual and practical tools that can build character that help master your power of moral value.

Keywords: Truth, character, wisdom, self-control

Introduction to moral value

I am getting ready to travel back in time. It is something I do periodically, and each time, a new feeling of sensibilities appears, from the clouds, directly in front of my eyes. This trip is back to my hometown on the edge of the Chateau Hills overlooking vast American prairie lands. I will visit places that are in my memory yet almost not recognizable and somehow foggy.

DOI: 10.4324/9781003219293-9

It was on a small farm in these great plains that some of life's basic lessons began to take shape in my consciousness. Those lessons primarily caught and not taught were carried by the ritual of everyday life in a place that was sometimes harsh and unforgiving. Those practices carried by parents, family, elders, teachers, friends, and neighbors were the cultural community shaping my sense of moral value.

Moral values are critical in guiding and leading our lives.

> Morals are the rules which people use to guide their behavior and thinking when an individual is dealing with, or capable of distinguishing between right or wrong. Moral values are relative values that protect life and are respectful of the dual life values of self and others.[1]
>
> (The Sentinel, 2020)

What are moral values?

The process of defining moral value puts us soundly into the middle of a discussion that has been on the minds of humans, since we first stuck our heads out of the cave. What began with the relatively simple question "What is the right thing to do?" has become one of the most complex dilemmas faced by every culture on earth. From the Greek philosopher Aristotle to the German Nietzsche, from English philosopher J.S. Mill to the Swiss Rousseau, the simple question has turned into an overabundance of theories, ideologies, principles, rules, legislation, religions, and contradictory worldviews.

In its "everyday sense", morality refers to a code of conduct, by which human beings regulate their lives. Abstract interest in morality arises from the kinds of questions that might be asked about a code of conduct. In contemporary thought, this code has a social focus and stands on the test of benefit to society.

The first question is what kinds of useful rules people use to govern their lives. This question attempts to understand the real practices of societies, people groups, and individuals. The answer constitutes the meaning of "morality" perceived and believed. Different groups hold to different codes of conduct and therefore perceptually represent more than one standard of morality. Here is an example.

We had been working on the project for several years in a very rural unstable economic community of Appalachian America. The goal was to create a food store that had been closed for a decade. Residents with limited resources were forced to use any means they could to travel a considerable distance to buy groceries. The solution was simple, and it brings a grocer to the community. The stated values of all the partners attempting this feat were compatible. The community needs access to food.

The lack of food was causing health, education, relational, economic, and social problems. The moral value of the solution was indisputable.

However, the messages sent by venture partners presented the variation of real practice. The residents condemned "outsiders'" view of their plight as immoral. They had been without food service for a decade. Local businesses joined the narrative from an economic perspective and criticized the lack of willingness of banks to finance community business. Banks cited the reality of their business and the lack of asset collateral necessary to invest capital. They denounced the lack of government investment or assistance that could help local communities. The government wanted to help but was hampered by the lack of resources that fit the project and the bureaucratic inflexibility. Politicians just wanted to get re-elected and did their best to conjure up a solution. They complained about the social impact finance community for not doing their job. All of the players were convinced of their moral "rightness". They all understood the question but defined their code a bit differently.

Question number 2 examines the soundness of the codes of conduct that people stick to. These moral ideas try to discover the rules that people should use to guide their conduct. Interestingly, the rules as prescribed need not coincide with actual practices and accepted moral principles.

I have a friend, Mike, who belongs to an organization that has a strict code of rules of conduct based on long-held beliefs in the value of family, community, and people. They meet together, pledge together, and convince each other that their set of codes is the high moral ground. What they are not good at is behaving in compliance with the accepted community code of conduct. The message that they send is diametrically opposed to the aspirations.

The next question asks whether the rules constitute a kind of morality, or objective, or are simply statements of approval and disapproval. This inquiry seeks to discover if the rules are universally valid, or unique to the groups that adhere to them.

The last question attempts to understand the nature of codes of correct behavior. It seeks to discern the why of adherence. Its devotion is based on religion, sense of justice, ethnicity, nationalism, geography, or any other diverse items of difference. The interaction of the answers to these questions constitutes the definition of normal "morality"[2] (New World Encyclopedia, 2018).

But what values can be identified as universal?

I learned a lot from my father. Though his formal education was brief and consisted mostly of experience gained in Africa and Italy during the Second World War, his dedication to family and community were great teachers. He once told me that the most important things happen at home. His values had two faces, one was his set of rights and wrongs, and the other was the community defined. We have a poor history of grasping the basic importance of knowing ourselves and our collective connection to the community.

My father's sense of a code of conduct was specific to his experience and social group. Some theorize this obvious fact of cultural disagreement indicates that moral rules are nothing other than social conventions of particular cultural groups. In this thinking, something like believing that lying is wrong is simply an expression of the beliefs of a group of people. It is their belief that makes it true. This view is called moral relativism. According to moral relativism, there is no objective and universally valid moral principles. Morality itself is nothing but a matter of convention[2] (New World Encyclopedia, 2018).

In this view, there is simply no room for any kind of moral universality, and morality becomes little more than toleration of others' differences. My experience has presented me with another observation. In 2014, it was my honor to be part of the Oxford Advanced Management and Leadership Programme's June cohort. The cohort consisted of something like 17 nationalities from 22 different countries. Based on moral relativism the best we could have hoped for is tolerance of differences and little more. Yet, quickly upon the opening of the session, by listening and interacting, we discovered that in between our differences there were places where we thought the same. Amid difference, there was common ground.

A great example of a real universal leader who understands the complexity of moral value is Dr. Dambisa Moyo. Dr. Moyo is a Zambian economist with a master's degree from Harvard and a PhD degree from Oxford. She has served on the Board of Chevron, 3M, and Barclays. In a recent interview with the New York Times, she says,

> I am at the crossroads of many different perspectives. I'm on the board of a large global energy company. I serve on the board of the Oxford University endowment. I also was born and raised in Africa, and there's still 1.5 billion people on the planet who have no access to cost-effective energy, including my parents, who still live in Zambia.[3]
>
> (Dr. Dambisa Moyo [2021], Economist)

Discovering moral values

How do I know my morals are valued?

It is curious that physical courage should be so common in the world and moral courage so rare[4] (Mark Twain [1835–1910], American humorist). In a world that is no longer simply defined as local and presents an interactive global reality with cultural, societal, ideological, and theological differences, the challenge becomes what values are true? Everyone has their own story based on their frame of reference. We believe that our story is true but so does everyone else.

Narrative has supplanted reality, whether founded in truth or not. We even find ourselves mired in conversations about what truth is. To quote the Hebrew prophet Isaiah, *"truth has stumbled in the streets"*.[5]

I have a good friend named Jerry. I have known him for several decades with our relationship beginning with his influential leadership in my appointment to a social impact financial institution. As with all relationships, ours has evolved. In that evolution, we have come to a place where he has become my "canary in the coal mine". Miners would take caged canaries into the mine. If dangerous gases were present, the canary would die but the miners would be saved. Jerry has become my thought partner. He is always bringing my thinking back to what is valid and what I trust to be real. The shared experience has helped us define truth. His commitment to the relationship has been a validation of trust, honesty, and the value of cognizant dissonance in civil conversation.

The meaning of the word truth extends from honesty, good faith, and sincerity in general, to agreement with fact or reality in particular.[6] Truth is trusting that something is valid. This common recognition of truth can be identified inside most individual, cultural, and societal narratives. In each of the stories that are carried around by every human, there is a place, acknowledged or ignored, that we all share. Impudent as it may sound in a world that embraces differences, it is our similarities that will bring us together and in doing so define truth itself. Observation tells us that in the contemporary environment things like kindness, respect, and non-violence are not universally accepted concepts. That opinion is having harmful effects on the stability and civil evolution of society. What should be universal is the agreement on what we trust as being fact and reality. It becomes what we hold as moral value.

Recognizing moral values

What is the value of being moral?

My maternal grandfather was English and a proper bloke. He came to the States at 17 years old and never returned to Britain. He did, however, keep a lot of England with him over the next six decades. To my knowledge, he never came to the dinner table without his dinner jacket. I remember asking him after a long, dirty, tiring day farming why he would still change into his jacket before dinner. His answer was simple; "It is the proper thing to do". Recognition of commonly held values promoting stability, social evolution, and contentment is the proper thing. It is the moral foundation that allows for relationships based on shared values.

> Self-control is strength. Calmness is majesty. You have to get to a point where your mood doesn't shift based on the insignificant actions of someone else. Don't allow others to control the direction of your life. Don't allow your emotions to overpower your intelligence.[7]
>
> (Morgan Freeman [1937–], contemporary American actor)

The world's interactive global nature spawns change. It is not just one transformation every so often but continual change. Leaders are the primal element in navigating the complexities of the constantly changing technological and global world. They must possess or develop some unique tools and characteristics that facilitate the change journey.

Good leaders understand the importance of sharing a common set of values, and they recognize the value of differences. This foundation becomes the foothold of relationships that drive equity and civil dialogue. They are the right things to do.

To be a good leader, husband, wife, father, mother, or friend, your character must be seeded with the proper things. That means being in touch with the commonly accepted values of truth, justice, equity, and the whole list of moral values. It means more than knowing them but allowing them to become real when you behave like them.

The 37-year-old New Zealand Prime Minister, Jacinda Ardern, had been in office only 16 months when the unbelievable happened. Christchurch experienced the first of its kind in New Zealand, a mass shooting at two mosques that killed 50 and injured 40. Ardern showed her moral foundation swiftly labelling the attack "terrorism" and bluntly called out an Australian lawmaker who linked the violence to Muslim immigration.

She went to Christchurch the day after the attacks of visiting members of the refugee and Muslim community. Dressed in black and wearing a hijab, she tearfully told them that the whole country was "united in grief". It was not just her dress but her putting herself into the solution. Her pledge was to cover the funeral costs of all 50 victims and offer financial assistance to the families, as well as her swift action on gun control (Her government introduced gun measures in Parliament the next week.)[8] (Jacinda Ardern, 2021, Prime Minister, New Zealand).

This was not just politics, as Ardern has time and again voiced her value of "the importance of inclusivity and equality in society". She is an example of a leader whose drive is the moral values of mutually held truths.

Explore:

Five ways to step up and become a moral leader
https://www.weforum.org/agenda/2019/08/5-ways-moral-leader

Building moral value

What does it mean to have a moral character?

We have thought together about what moral values are, discovered what values are moral, and what the value is of being moral. Now, we begin to think about how we can develop our sense of morality by using simple tools. *The moment you wake up each morning, all your wishes and hopes for the day rush at you like wild animals. And the first job each morning consists in shoving it all back; in listening to that other voice, taking that other point of view, letting that other, larger, stronger, quieter life come flowing in*[9] (C.S. Lewis 1952). The ability to build our moral character is a matter of behavior. It begins with building new habits. It begins with the thousands of little things we have to make decisions around every day. By applying some simple concepts to these decision, habits form and become character traits. They become who we are. When we face large challenges, we approach them from what we know, our character. We must master our power of moral value.

On January 15, 2009, a potential disaster turned into a heroic display of skill and composure when Captain Chesley Burnett Sullenberger III (Scully) safely landed the plane he was piloting on New York City's Hudson River after a bird strike caused its engines to fail. About a minute after taking off from New York's La Guardia Airport on January 15, 2009, US Airways Flight 1549 collided with one of the aviation industry's most threatening foes: a flock of geese. Crippled by the bird strike, both engines lost power and went quiet, forcing Captain Sullenberger to make an emergency landing. When air traffic controllers instructed the seasoned pilot to head for nearby Teterboro Airport, he calmly informed them that he was "unable" to reach a runway. "We're gonna be in the Hudson", he said simply, and then told the 155 terrified passengers and five crew members on board to brace for impact. That is exactly what they did, and all 155 passengers and crew survived.

Captain Sullenberger, when confronted with a crisis, did not have to go back to the manual to find the solution. He did not have the time to text his friends or call the helpline. What he did have was hours of practice that build his character as a pilot. When the crisis struck, he instinctively knew what to do because it was who he was not what he was.

This is a great example of how moral value gets inculcated into character. It is about building habits that become character. Here are some guides to help in the formation of little habits.

The action arrow

If character is important, how is it achieved? Character simply means building good habits. Habits begin with the way we think about what we are doing. There is an axiom that lays out the foundation for any behavior. It is called the *Action Arrow*.

The point of the arrow, its head, is behavior. This is the way we act, the way we relate to people, and the way we communicate. The arrowhead is driven by the shaft of the arrow. The shaft is long, strong, straight, and narrow. If it is not straight or balanced correctly, the arrowhead will miss the mark. Even though the target may be perfectly aligned if the shaft has not

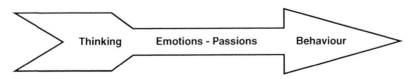

FIGURE 7.1: The Action Arrow
Source: Copyright J.R. Klein

been calibrated correctly, there is no way of telling where the arrow will fly. The arrowhead of behavior is driven by the shaft of emotion. If emotions are not adjusted correctly, behaviors will go wherever feelings drive them.

At the other end of the arrow is the fletch or feather. This possibly is the most important part of the projectile as it provides aerodynamic stabilization. The fletching of an arrow is an art unto itself. Its vanes or feathers must be made of an appropriate material for the type of arrow. It must be of the right shape and length and placed in a precise position on the shaft just above the nock or the piece that will hold the bowstring. Before the arrow flies a good deal of thought goes into the whole process, what and where is the target, where on the target to aim, distance, conditions, etc. Thinking serves the same purpose on our action arrow. Emotion, driven by thinking, always results in intentional behavior. Decisions on what action is appropriate, necessary, and beneficial should be made before initiating action. Thinking changes the direction of the arrow by transforming emotion into passion which will drive different behavior.

I have a new favorite saying. "Most people have no idea what they are talking about and those that do know what they are talking about usually get it wrong". Recently, I served on a committee that was charged with researching, analyzing, and creating a recommendation to leadership regarding a new sign for the front of a business. The team was manageable with five people including me as the lead. The process went smoothly until it came to the discussion of what content should be on the sign. One team member had a particular name format that was sure to be what leadership would want to adopt. The member was adamant that anything else would not be acceptable. The outcome was clear because of the member's close relationship with one of the leaders. As the process continued, it became evident that the sign content would be similar but different from what was offered by the member. The contention in the process was driven by emotion without thoughts consultation. At the end of the day, leadership accepted the recommendation of the committee without the detractor's content.

Thinking is the primary attribute that sets humans apart. The human mind is always trying to make sense of the torrent of information that pours into eyes, ears, nose, throat, and other senses constantly. We learn from infancy how to cope with our environment and in doing so build our perception of reality. Most of us gain a sense of justice, honor, goodness, and "rightness" that propels our thought process. Once thinking reveals its value it allows thinking to move to the front. Recognition of what is the right thing to do becomes a choice and that choice applied a 1,000 times a day on the small seemingly inconsequential situations become a habit. When the big choices present themselves, they are less traumatic because the right thing to do has become your character.

Thinking is the basis of good character, but it is not enough to just agree to the proposition until we spend some time fleshing out which moral values are the right things. As we have discussed earlier, it is the commonly held values that constitute our common truths and our shared values. Some commonly held values that seat themselves in character are present in three axioms, the Relationship Triangle.

The relationship triangle

Life in a world full of people is based on relationships. This structure operates on a basic assumption that people will get along. What we discover quite quickly is that the assumption has a flaw. People have always had problems with people. The key to relationships is thinking about these types of things: love, joy, peace, patience, kindness, goodness, hope, gentleness, and self-control.

The first side of the *Relationship Triangle* is to put others first. It is not a radical concept, and it is the bedrock of most "moral" societies. It is easier to see its implementation in social impact initiatives, charity work, or faith-based missions. It is a little harder to implement at the individual level, simply because we too often give way to emotion without thought. The sense of the matter is that if we all put others first our priority would be to take care of each other.

An example of this principle is not some set of rules and regulations. It can be as simple as opening the door for someone, helping without being asked, or being sensitive to someone else's needs before your own.

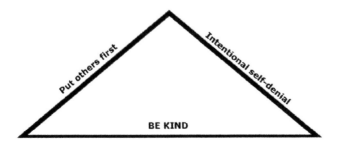

FIGURE 7.2: The Relationship Triangle
Source: Copyright J.R. Klein

The second side of the triangle is intentional self-denial. My mother would sum up the concept in a phrase offered to me each time I left home. "Remember who you are". Whether it is called meditation, introspection, self-improvement, or spirituality, it means you cannot have good relationships with people if you do not know yourself. Truly knowing your mind, character, and values is the starting point of understanding other people.

Again, this is not some mystical concept, but it is simply building the habit of learning who you are. This intentional introspection can be motivated by any number of things external or internal. The important part of the process is the "intentional" part. It is something that all relationships are built on. The first person you need to know is yourself.

The third side of our triangle completes the other two. It can be called by many names, consideration, compassion, gentleness, sensitivity, graciousness, or kindness. It represents the implementation of the other two sides of our structure. Being kind may not always be simple nor is it always accepted as an admirable trait. None the less it can become natural with practice and is the base upon which everything else rests.

A kind word, a hospitable gesture, or a friendly smile is a signal that sends a message of inclusivity. Kindness changes people's perception of the giver and the receiver.

The personal pentagon

There is no shortage of resources and information available that can continuously increase our knowledge. Knowledge has always been prized by cultures and civilizations. Most of what we know about our history and pre-history is a result of knowledge that has been obtained and recorded. Knowledge is the first side of the pentagon, the one with the door in it that provides an entrance to everything else. However, just knowing the right things only brings us to the front door. Even the phrase "*knowledge is power*" often attributed to the English philosopher and statesman Sir Francis Bacon, from his Meditationes Sacrae (1597),[10] has its limitations.

I am not a good reader, but I do like to read. It probably has something to do with the curiosity inherited from my mother. This curiosity has been dramatically enhanced by the technology I keep in my back pocket. Wow! The things that I know.

We have mountains upon mountains of knowledge, but until we understand what to do with it, how to apply it, or what it means, it is pretty much useless. This notion is the second tenant of the *Personal Pentagon*. Knowledge is nothing without understanding. Understanding what we know and how

FIGURE 7.3: The Personal Pentagon
Source: Copyright J.R. Klein

to put it into practice is the mystical key. This reality has changed the world ever since humans discovered they did not have to wait for lightning to start their fire.

There is a revelation emerging from that volume of information available to everyone. Data do not lie, and most of the time, data do not say anything at all. Being able to use data entails listening to the data. We are beginning to recognize that. A quick examination of the world of entrepreneurial start-ups will provide the revelation that many of them are focused on analytics. They are creating tools to make sense of meaning in the mountains.

Once we understand how to apply knowledge in alignment with the "arrow" and the "triangle", our character instinctively changes. It makes little difference what narrative from what age or culture is examined the right understanding and applying of knowledge is called wisdom. It is the third pentagon side. Wisdom is the right application of knowledge. The common recognition of being "wise", when practiced, becomes a habit and as we have realized, at the beginning of this chapter, builds our character.

Wisdom is simply listening, learning, being sensitive, and intuitive about what you know and how to apply it. One of the best examples of wisdom in leadership is to master the power of letting other people do their own thinking and then gently keep the conversation focused on solutions. This quiet leadership principle focuses on the wisdom of stretching people more than they stretch themselves while providing extensive positive feedback[11] (David Rock, 2018).

This simple equation introduces the fourth side of our pentagon. Wisdom internalized and exhibited changes how we think, and our thinking drives our emotion/passion, and we behave differently. Gradually we begin to see life through different lenses. Life's path begins to take on a more palatable complexion. Hebrew texts call this Halakha, living in the right way. Things that were of prominent importance begin to take on a different perspective and things that did not seem to matter much now take on another role. The values of kindness, sensitivity, and the value of other narratives fit into a view of the world that is more egalitarian. Wisdom changes life's path.

Explore:

Halakha, living in the right way.
   https://www.myjewishlearning.com/article/halakhah-the-laws-of-jewish-life/

Research suggests that wisdom is a beneficial psychological attribute that may be linked to a sense of well-being, happiness, and better overall health[12] (Mushira Khan, 2021). Wisdom is about learning to live life in a way that enables success and a good life. Most of us want to live an enjoyable and successful life. The only true way to accomplish and maintain it for a long term is through practicing and applying wisdom.

Wisdom paves the path of life with fertile ground that produces success. Walking this wisdom pathway creates the common-sense realization that so often escapes most of humanities teaming masses. Wisdom bears fruit. As we do the right things, the right things begin to happen. It is the final tenant, the fifth side of the pentagon. The blinding flash of the obvious is that by changing ourselves, we change those around us, and as they change, the chain reaction continues. This genius idea changes the world. It is this mastery of moral values that will allow us to live forever in the hearts and minds of those who come after us.

Mastering the power of moral value

How do you turn what you know into what you do? Why is it important?

At the risk of becoming overbearing, I offer one last metaphor, the Behavior Tree. The concept of the behavior tree attempts to sum up our mastery of moral value. The roots of our tree gain sustenance from the energy of commonly held

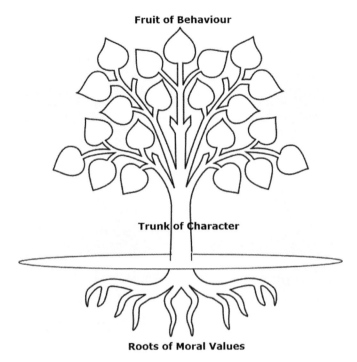

Fruit of Behaviour

Trunk of Character

Roots of Moral Values

FIGURE 7.4: The Behavior Tree
Source: Copyright J.R. Klein

truth. This energy enables the moral value roots to grow wide and deep and provide stability for the tree. Our character is the trunk. It can sprout straight and tall providing branches, big and small, and broad foliage providing shade and shelter. Importantly, the roots of moral value and the trunk of character will not sustain unless they can be replicated. The tree must bear the fruit of civil behavior, which when produced seeds new roots and new trees.

It is not enough to have the musical score, to know the words to the song, and to hum along with the melody. To be able to sing the song and carry the message through the music requires practice. Beginning with singing little pieces of the song and putting them together the whole work begins to take voice. We do not have to be perfect to practice but when we practice, we become perfect. It begins by learning the right thing to do and it becomes knowing to do the right thing. *Keep your thoughts positive because your thoughts become your words. Keep your words positive because your words become your behavior. Keep your behavior positive because your behavior becomes your habits. Keep your habits positive because your habits become your values. Keep your values positive because your values become your destiny*[13] (Mahatma Gandhi, 1869–1948).

Moral value is the foundation on which all other acumen is based. All leadership, if not life itself, is based on "*the ability to make good judgments and quick decisions*".[14] This acumen definition simply frames the essence of our entire discussion. This is the key to the future of the future.

Jacqueline Novogratz, the CEO of Acumen, a social impact investor, in her book, *Manifesto for a Moral Revolution*, calls it moral imagination. "*Moral imagination is the basis of an ethical framework for a world that recognizes our common humanity and insists on opportunity, choice, and dignity for all of us*".[15] This idea of being able to change the world simply by thinking differently about who you are and allowing it to change the way you interact with the world is significant.

But surely, we are not saying that in a world that is prone to deteriorate toward the lowest common denominator can be changed by one person accepting the idea of moral imagination? For perfect clarity, that is exactly what we are saying. "*Moral imagination offers a powerful lens through which to see the world's potential, recognize its disparities, and work to address them*".

The mastery of moral value will enable you to be more than just a leader. Leadership in an organization, group, community, or family is more than just a position or authority. It is more than telling others where to sit or stand. It is an opportunity to become more than you think you are. The prospect of being able to help people think for themselves and make better decisions is to change the world one step at a time. Mastery of the power of moral value will be one of the most important accomplishments you will ever make. You may never see the fruits of your labor and it will not be an easy road. I offer the advice given by my mother, "Try it you might like it".

Summary

Mastering the power of moral value begins with intension. Intension leads to focused action and building habits that change character. Character changes resolute thinking and results in passion that drives behavior. This chapter has framed the notion of what concepts, tools, and influencers build commonly accepted behavior that benefits society. That benefit is moral value.

Moral value leads to common ground that produces cultural sensitivity. Knowing and understanding what is perceived to be different and defining common space are the keys to civil dialogue. Civil dialogue produces tolerance, friendship, collaboration, and shared value and action. Working together makes a better world.

Follow-up actions

1   Think about your what is important to you and how it fits into the generally held definition of moral value.
2   Start building small habits that help you identify cues that trigger distraction.
3   Start building small habits that help you focus you attention.
4   Actively practice helping other people to think by asking questions and providing encouraging feedback.
5   Take time for introspection and do frequent internal inventories.
6   Remember who you are.

Notes

1   The Sentinel (2020), *Moral Values and Importance of Moral Education*. Available at: https://www.sentinelassam.com/editorial/moral-values-and-importance-of-moral-education/
2   New World Encyclopedia (2018), *Morality*. October 20. Available at: New World Encyclopedia: https://www.newworldencyclopedia.org/entry/Morality
3   Gelles, David (2021), At the Crossroads of Global Business, Corner Office *The New York Times*, October 10.
4   Twain, M. (1922), *Mark Twain in Eruption: Hitherto Unpublished Pages about Men and Events*. Harper & Brothers Publishers. Edited by Bernard DeVoto.
5   Klein, J.R. (2020), *Truth Stumbles in the Street*. August 4. Available at: J.R. Global Associates: https://www.jrglobal.co/post/truth-stumbles-in-the-streets, as cited Isaiah 59:13, The Tanach (TLV).
6   Oxford University Press (1884 Ed. 2019), *Oxford English Dictionary*. Oxford: Oxford University Press.
7   Steele, Ken (2020), *Train Up a Child*. Dorrance Publishing Co.
8   Fifield, A. (2019), New Zealand's Prime Minister Receives Worldwide Praise for Her Response to the Mosque Shootings. *The Washington Post*, March 18.
9   Lewis, C.S. (1952), *Mere Christianity*. Geoffrey Bles, (UK).
10 Bacon, Francis (1597) as cited in Susan Ratcliffe (Ed.) (2018), *Oxford Essential Quotations*. 6th edition. Oxford University Press.
11 Rock, David (2007), *Quiet Leadership: Six Steps to Transforming Performance at Work*. Harper Collins Publishers.
12 Khan, Mushira Mohsin (2021), *Investigate of Wisdom & Well-being: Personal Wisdom & Quality of Life In Chinese Older Adults*. Mather Institute. August 23. Available at: https://www.matherinstitute.com/2021/08/23/the-impact-of-wisdom-on-older-adults-quality-of-life/
13 Gandhi, Mahatma (2002), *Open Your Mind, Open Your Life: A Book of Easter Wisdom*. Andrews McMeel Publishing.
14 Novogratz, J. (2020), *Manifesto for a Moral Revolution*. New York: Henry Holt and Company.
15 Ibid.

Further reading

1   Novogratz, Jacqueline (2020), *Manifesto for a Moral Revolution*. New York: Henry Holt and Company.
2   Rock, David (2007), *Quite Leadership*. New York: Harper Collins.
3   Wild, Jennifer (2020), *Be Extraordinary*. UK: Robinson

PART III

Authenticity, trust, and presence

8

MASTERING THE POWER OF AUTHENTICITY

Wanda Hamilton

Abstract

Behaving authentically is a key ingredient in living a successful, productive business and personal life. The chapter discusses why behaving authentically is essential in today's business environment and how behaving authentically creates success. Examples of authentic behaviour in current and past leaders are given. The author argues that authenticity is a way of behaving that inspires people, and organizations to greater achievements. Examples of authentic leadership are shared, along with critical questions for self-assessment and reflection about developing skills as an authentic leader.

Keywords: Authenticity, self-awareness, transparency, empathy, vulnerability

Introduction

With sweaty palms and a racing heart, I slid the papers across the huge boardroom table. I forced a smile I hoped conveyed sincerity and openness, not fear. My Vice-Chair watched, not really believing I had given our business plans and our entire operating budget to the lead union negotiator, our "adversary" in the bargaining process that brought us to the table.

We were a troubled charity, in collective bargaining with a strong union. I was scared witless she was right to tell me I had just blown up the organization. Equally though, I was at my core convinced that unprecedented transparency was our best option, maybe in fact our only option.

DOI: 10.4324/9781003219293-11

Our organization was a mid-sized Canadian charity, struggling financially, and damaged by politics of race, gender, and ethnicity. As a housing shelter for women leaving domestic violence, we had an excellent reputation for service, but were struggling with a toxic culture and declining budgets. The union was asking for improved terms and conditions, including wages, that we just couldn't see a way to afford. We had to find a way to work together as a team, rather than adversaries. The huge gamble I had just taken was that we could build trust and collaboration through a sincere, radically candid approach to collective bargaining

My words matched my belief. I said that we could not find a way to meet their wage and benefit demands, but neither could we succeed without their expertise and contributions. We said plainly that we had looked at the budget every way we could, and we could not see how to offer the package they were looking for. We thought every possible financial option had been explored. We valued their review and input. We said honestly that we should look at it together if they could find a different way of approaching income and costs.

We held our breath for nearly three days while union officials and staff stewards reviewed the budget and developed their position. It was very unusual that not a word leaked back to us about their deliberations, and we were worried. We were finally called back to the negotiating table on the third day. The union agreed that they couldn't find any other way to proceed than what we had proposed. From that point forward, the culture shifted.

What is authenticity and why is it important?

As new models of successful leadership emerge, with authentic leadership at the forefront, it is understandable that research and teaching offerings also grow. Oxford Saïd Business School embeds concepts of authentic leadership across their executive development programmes, including their flagship Oxford Advanced Management and Leadership Programme. Harvard Business School now offers executive education programmes on authentic leadership as a stand-alone, alongside their traditional offerings in strategy, finance, and so forth.

There is general agreement that Authenticity is a critically important leadership trait. "Authenticity is so important it will be a career prerequisite in future", said Neil Heslop,[1] OBE, CEO at CAF Group, in conversation with me recently. "Authenticity, both in leadership and as a cultural value in the organisation, enables people to connect their own motivation and efforts to the work the organisation needs them to do".

Although we've been hearing much more about it in the last decade, authentic leadership is not an entirely new concept. We may have first heard about authenticity from ancient Greek and later philosophers including, Sartre, Kierkegaard, Heidegger, and Nietzsche who described the importance of knowing oneself.

In the current day, the foundations of authentic leadership were perhaps established by Harvard-based professor and author Bill George, who is thought of as a founding father of authentic leadership. In his early work (2004),[2] George drew on interviews with 125 executive leaders to argue that authentic leaders had four basic traits:

- self-awareness
- transparency
- balance in viewpoints, and
- an internalized moral compass.

In his later writing[3], he expanded this somewhat and spoke of five basic qualities, which demonstrated authentic leadership:

- understanding your purpose
- practicing solid values
- leading with heart
- establishing connected relationships, and
- demonstrating self-discipline

There is one huge reason why authentic leadership skills are critical. The new work force is demanding it. Richard Taylor, a leading executive coach in London, and Nigel Miller, global HR strategist at PR giant Edelman, agree. "Talk to anybody under 30 about what they've seen in their lifetime, and it's only disappointment from global leadership", said Nigel Miller in conversation with me. "Political crises, financial crises, environmental crises. Hierarchies of power have failed them. Miserably. We talk instead about narration and curation", he continued.

Richard Taylor agrees. He said to me in a recent interview, "The work force today has a world view where power is found in relationships and social spaces, in collaboration and having *a reason to believe*. And that can only come in trusting and trusted relationships". Trust is made up of three ingredients – authenticity, logic, and empathy.[4]

Authenticity and empathy are traits needed for success not just at work but in life as well. I spoke with award-winning social entrepreneur Dr. Mary Gordon,[5] who believes these are core executive competencies. "You can get in the corporate door with hard skills, but you'll be out the door fast without soft skills. The wheels will come off!", she said.

Are empathy, vulnerability, and authenticity all facets of the same qualities? Mary believes they are all connected or interrelated. Mary believes empathy allows us to connect with the vulnerability and humanity of other. "You can't be authentic unless you are basically connected to yourself and have the ability to read the other". "So", she says, "it's not a guarantee that if you are empathetic that you are also authentic, but there's a heck of a good chance!"[6]

> *Authenticity in leadership is not only about having your own core values and beliefs. It is equally about how you live these values. Authentic leaders behave in a way that inspires people and organizations to greater achievements. They see people in their full context and value their individuality. This involves building connections characterized by trust and mutual respect (Wanda Hamilton).*

Authentic leadership is a life-long journey

I never really thought of myself as an authentic leader. Job performance evaluations said words like warm, honest, open, friendly, tough but fair, a great relationship builder . . . but never the word "authentic".

It was some years after my union bargaining experience that I came to understand this as an important milestone in my own journey to authentic leadership. I realized that this sort of completely unexpected, "radical candor" was an example of authentic leadership. It was the beginning of my understanding that these behaviours were my core values. More than that, they were my leadership edge and the key to any success that followed.

I come from a Canadian military family. What this means is that we were uprooted from school, home, and community every two or three years during my childhood. We were planted in new schools and communities regularly. While many would see this as a significant disadvantage, in fact what it gave me (and many like me) is a great need to understand new situations and people quickly. I was able to relocate within Canada and easily travel anywhere as my career progressed. The skills I developed because of childhood need, in fact, became a great career strength.

The three qualities that I developed were the ability to make connections by quickly reading new situations, to draw on inner courage, and to adapt quickly to change. These skills, or values, were the essential building blocks of authentic leadership. Let me explain.

Connection is best when it comes from an honest place – a willingness to share yourself and your stories. No matter how rich you are, how famous you are, how intelligent you are, there's **always** someone who is more. The best thing you can be is your own unique self, because frankly the point is that nobody in the world who is honest with themselves and self-aware truly feels they are perfect. Everyone has got their Achilles heel. It is beyond the scope of this chapter, but further readings about the power of self-doubt in executive leadership are recommended.[7]

It takes courage to be authentic: courage to speak up, courage to learn, courage to stay and cope with change, and courage to go if the change is not right for you. Courage, and the willingness to be vulnerable, can be the birthplace of innovation and creativity.

Change is one of the top reasons for employee negativity. From Darwin, we know that it's not the strongest that survives, nor the smartest; actually, it's the one that is most adaptable to change. When the environment changes, we must change with it. The very thing that we've always been excellent at may, in fact, no longer be the thing that is needed for us to survive and thrive.

Effective leaders must harness change, and maximize its positive impacts, while at the same time coping with the negative side of change, uncertainty, and fear of the unknown. Authentic connections with each other, and courage, are essential ingredients in successfully coping with change.

What I have described are the first two steps, or phases, in becoming an authentic leader: developing your character and self-awareness . . . or as the ancient Greeks put it, "Know yourself" and then understanding this as authenticity and using it as a leadership edge.

There are a great number of management tools and tests to measure authenticity in leadership. Some are qualitative, some are quantitative, and, I would argue, all are possibly most useful in large well-resourced settings. Some further readings on the topic of testing are available.[8],[9] You may, however, be more interested in developing yourself with the follow-up activities and informal questions of reflection shared, also at the end of this chapter

Taking inspiration from others

Janice Charette is currently Canada's top public service, Clerk of the Privy Council and formerly High Commissioner of Canada to the United

Kingdom. She is regularly featured on such lists as 50 Most Important Canadians and Top 100 most powerful Women in Canada and is widely regarded as a highly authentic leader. In a recent interview with me, she said

> Mine is not a studied or theoretical approach, but rather I work on feelings and perceptions. I did not deliberately set out to be purpose driven – I worked in a way that was true to my values. Saying what you're going to do, and then doing it.

Janice says the biggest risk leaders face is a gap between what they say and what they do. She offered three powerful leadership insights:

- do the right thing, the right way. It might take you longer, but in the end, you will have a more sustainable, durable result.
- you must be able to look at yourself in the mirror, be accountable to yourself for what you do.
- Stretch yourself beyond your normal comfort zone, do what author Brene Brown[10] might have called embracing vulnerability. Janice emphasized this, saying, "Don't be afraid to hire people smarter and above all different than you. A diverse team is brilliant, they will do miracles".

I also recently caught up with Pinky Lilani[11], OBE, CEO of Women of the Future, a widely respected organization working in several countries. She says being authentic means being herself and upholding her values in everything she does. Her core values are integrity, empathy, respect, listening, and making others shine. "We as women cannot underestimate the power of people who know us and support us to be the best we can be, in both challenging periods and the good times".

Supporting people to be the unique best they can be is a theme I heard again from rising stars. Authenticity and empathy are important tools to make teams feel valued and elicit best performance. Melany Rose is a warm, charming outspoken environmentalist working in middle management at the British Museum. She speaks about the leaders who most inspired her, and she echoed what I had heard earlier from Pinky and Janice.

High-performance leaders recognize the importance of developing people based on their own aspirations, who they want to be in their career, rather than exclusively based on training courses that closely match their present roles. Melany Rose said this was what motivated her most. Melany spoke highly of leaders who understood her career aspirations, her personal circumstances, and above all, listened actively to achieve this understanding. She felt that this type of authentic leadership elicited the best performance from her, and all the teams.

Authentic leaders must understand and adapt to context

Authentic leaders create environments where people **want** to follow them. That understanding of followership, or as Bill George calls it, "the I to we" move, is what sets authentic leaders up for success.

Early in your career, you will be rewarded for your individual achievements. But as your career progresses, and you assume leadership positions, you need to take everybody along with you. Bill George explains this, saying

> to become authentic leaders we must discard the myth that leadership means having legions of supporters following us as we ascend to the pinnacles of power. Only then can we realize that authentic leadership is serving people by aligning them around a common mission and values and empowering them on their leadership journeys.[12]

This notion of followership and alignment rather than agreement is incredibly important in authentic leadership. Alignment has the potential to bring people together, while agreement is much more about who is right and who is wrong.

Nelson Mandela is a world leader greatly admired for his leadership and authenticity. Mandela understood the importance of alignment for all, rather than very binary right and wrong. He saw himself as a servant leader, a servant of the people. He had a great understanding of both context and the urgent need for alignment amongst all peoples of South Africa. If he were to act on the anger, he felt at his wrongful imprisonment, and he would be acting in retribution not in reconciliation. To act against his captors, and white people in the country, he would create greater conflict between peoples. Mandela understood that to achieve peace in the country – reconciliation – he could not mirror the treatment he had received in prison, but rather he needed to rise above the hatred, punishment, and inequality. Mandela understood his context, lived his own core values of peace and equality, and achieved his aims with authenticity.

Authenticity depends greatly on context and has limits. "Being authentic doesn't mean that you can be held up to the light and people can see right through you", says business writer Herminia Ibarra.[13] The first step in the journey to authentic leadership is knowing your own core values. The journey continues, as you put these values into action in your leadership and become more skilled at using the tools you have developed, in the right measure at the right time.

Mastering the power of authenticity

To the extent that it can be taught, reflection and inclusion are the best techniques for developing yourself as an authentic leader. The dictionary definition of reflection can mean both *serious consideration and thought* or *mirroring*.

Here are five ways of developing yourself and your authentic leadership through reflection and inclusion. You may also want to look at the reflection exercises and more specific questions at the end of this chapter.

1. **Start by reflecting on who you are and what you believe**. Do this at all stages of your life and career.

   Critical questions – do I really know and value myself? What are my strengths and weaknesses? What do I value and stand for? What is my purpose in life?

2. **Be an active, reflective listener**. Check your understanding by asking questions and mirroring back what you believe you heard.

   Critical questions – Am I listening well? Am I hearing not only what is being said but also observing what's happening in the culture and context? Am I genuinely achieving understanding and empathy for the unique circumstances of my team members?

3. **Retreat and reflect**. Don't underestimate the importance and benefit of being more deliberate and possibly slower in your decision-making. In the volatile, uncertain, and chaotic world of today, leaders must often make decisions for which there is no precedent. Quick intuitive decisions may be less suited for complex unprecedented situations – reflection and varied inputs may lead to greater wisdom and better decisions.

   In his groundbreaking book, *Getting to Yes*,[14] master negotiator William Ury talks about retreating as an essential component of successful negotiations as well. He calls it "going to the balcony", looking down at the situation and taking a moment to be certain you understand your position.

   A retreat and reflect way of working could be both immediate, as in taking a moment to think before speaking, or it could be longer term, as in taking your team away to give yourself both time and space to think together about more complex or longer-term decisions, and to develop as a team.

Critical questions – Am I taking a moment to pause and reflect before I speak, enabling me to react in a considered rather than intuitive way? Am I reflecting on my own decisions, behaviour, and actions and remaining open to feedback from others? Are we working together to create solutions that meet both business and personal needs?

4. **Include diverse opinions.** Including people from all levels of your organization and from all backgrounds is not only the right thing to do in the interests of equality and diversity; in fact, research shows that it may lead to better decisions.

    Research[15] looking at 600 business decisions made by 200 companies over several years backs this up:

    teams outperform individual decision makers 66% of the time, and decision making improves as team diversity increases. Compared to individual decision makers, gender diverse teams (make better decisions) 73% of the time. Teams that also include a wide range of ages and different geographic locations make better business decisions 87% of the time.

    Bottom line, inclusive teams are not only authentic in composition, but they also help leaders overcome their own biases and make better decisions.

    Critical questions – Am I creating value for my organization by building in the time and opportunity for varying viewpoints to be clearly heard and considered, especially where complex decisions need to be made?

5. **Make it a life-long journey, growing and changing. Remember that your greatest strength is also your greatest liability.** If taken in the wrong measure, or at the wrong time, every asset can be a liability. Take optimism and perseverance for an example. Taken in the right measure at the right time, the optimist has an essential "can-do" attitude. However, that optimism can also become your liability. If you are weighing up decisions through your optimistic lens, you may make a risk analysis biased by optimism. In other words, the asset of optimism becomes your "confirmation bias" and damages your decision-making. The qualities of perseverance and determination are another example. Might you be persevering too long and not correctly assessing when to let something go?

This is also the case with authenticity. Authenticity can be a double-edged sword. We have said that vulnerability is a component of authentic leadership. You need to decide for yourself how much vulnerability to show and when. Saying you don't have all the answers might be considered by some as showing vulnerability, while to others it shows the wisdom of knowing yourself, knowing your limits, and most importantly, respecting and valuing the expertise and inputs of others.

Critical questions – Am I learning from my mistakes? Am I open to challenging myself and making personal changes where needed? Before you can learn from your mistakes, you must let go of the need to always be right.

Summary

Authenticity is **NOT** an action, something you do or say, but rather it's a way of being. Very simply put, leaders are authentic when they are truthful – and that means truthful both to themselves and to others.

Being true to yourself is not a new concept at all. From the time of the ancient Greeks who said, "Know Yourself", to more contemporary great thinkers (Sartre, Kierkegaard, Heidegger, and Nietzsche) humankind has been reflecting on what it means to "be" – to live a meaningful life and contribute both to one's own world and to the greater community and society.

The important learning is that the greatest power we each can have is the power of independent thought and action, true to our own beliefs and value. What is a new way of thinking, however, is looking at it through the lens provided by modern management writers such as Bill George, who argued that leaders are at their most powerful when they are trusted, authentic, and true to themselves.

The key ingredient to leading authentically is knowing who you are and what you believe. Leading authentically means that there is powerful and observable consistency between your values, your words, and your behaviours.

This personal power, the power of you, becomes the reason for teams to believe in what you are saying and follow you. Authentic leadership, like any leadership, is not just about unlocking your own potential and career success, it should equally be about empowering other people because of your presence.

Follow-up actions

Reflect on the following questions:

1   *Who you are and what you believe in?*
2   *What is your purpose in life? How will you achieve your purpose in life?*
3   *How can you be true to yourself and others?*
4   *How do you feel when you are your authentic self?*

Notes

1   Biography of Neil Heslop. Available at: https://www.cafonline.org/about-us/governance/our-executive/neil-heslop
2   George, B. and Peter Sims (2007), *True North: Discover Your Authentic Leadership*. Jossey-Bass.
3   George, B. (2015), *True North: Discover Your True North*. Expanded and updated version. John Wiley & Sons.
4   Frei, F.X. and A. Morriss. *Harvard Business Review Magazine*, May–June 2020. Available at: https://hbr.org/2020/05/begin-with-trust
5   Biography of Dr. Mary Gordon. Available at: https://rootsofempathy.org/mary-gordon/
6   (ibid.)
7   The CEO Report: Embracing the Paradoxes of Leadership and the Power of Doubt, published by *Saïd Business School*, Oxford University. Available at: https://www.sbs.ox.ac.uk/sites/default/files/2018-09/The-CEO-Report-Final.pdf
8   Kernis, M.H. and B.M. Goldman (2005), From Thought and Experience to Behavior and Interpersonal Relationships: A Multicomponent Conceptualization of Authenticity. In A. Tesser, J.V. Wood, and D.A. Stapel (Eds.), *On Building, Defending, and Regulating the Self: A Psychological Perspective*. Psychology Press, pp. 31–52.
9   Neider, L.L. and C.A. Schriesheim (2011), The Authentic Leadership Inventory (ALI): Development and Empirical Tests. *Leadership Quarterly*, 22(6), 1146.
10 Brown, B. (2012), Daring Greatly, *How the Courage to Be Vulnerable Transforms the Way We Live, Love, Parent, and Lead*. Penguin Random House Books UK.
11 Biography of Pinky Lilani. Available at: https://www.bbc.co.uk/programmes/profiles/g1f5Hn25f6wrdRQyLNR4tP/pinky-lilani-obe
12 George, B. (2015), *True North: Discover Your True North*. Expanded and updated version. John Wiley & Sons.
13 Ibarra, H. (2015), *Harvard Business Review Magazine*, January–February. Available at: https://hbr.org/2015/01/the-authenticity-paradox
14 Fisher, R., W. Ury and B. Patton (1991 [1981]), *Getting to Yes: Negotiating Agreement Without Giving In*. 2nd edition. Penguin Books.
15 New Research: Diversity + Inclusion = Better Decision Making at Work, September 21, 2017. Quoted by Forbes Magazine, Erik Larsen. Available at: https://www.forbes.com/sites/eriklarson/2017/09/21/new-research-diversity-inclusion-better-decision-making-at-work/?sh=36b207754cbf

9

MASTERING THE POWER OF TRUST

Evolving your leadership

Paul Matthews

Abstract

Trusting others unleashes potential in a way that old school leadership approaches such as control and hierarchy cannot.

Leaders who are trusting of others embody behaviours that build trust in and around them, successfully lifting individual and organisational success. These "lifting leaders" trust others to bring their skills and expertise forward. The resulting trust acts as a catalyst for progress.

Leaders that evolve to the needs of their workforce elevate their results as they are more tuned-in to the needs of their teams. Evolved leaders can successfully lift their entire workforce in this way.

Recent changes at work have created barriers to trust building and to trusting others. The Trusting Leaders' roadmap outlines how current leaders can evolve, mastering the powers of trust, by trusting others to unlock a bounty of treasure for leaders.

Keywords: Trusting, evolving, lifting, limiting, leading

Introduction – my journey with trust

> "*If you're privileged enough to be in a position of leadership, it is paramount that you maintain the trust of the people for whom you have a responsibility*".[1]
>
> *Daniel Goleman (2015)*

DOI: 10.4324/9781003219293-12

My journey with trust started in Southern India. My wife Rhian and I had travelled there to welcome in the year 2000. But on the 23 December 1999, we found ourselves lost and injured in the middle of Karnataka.

Our bus to Goa crashed in the dead of night and rolled into the darkness of the jungle. We were terrified, dazed, and confused. But we were alive. We had no option but to put our trust and welfare firmly in the hands of the locals. Trusting others was our only strategy. Taking control, giving advice, or leading us out of there was not an option. Trusting others was all that we had.

It was their wisdom, insights, and action that got us out of danger and to safety. Their knowledge, motivation, and sense of care saved us. They got me to a doctor for emergency treatment and helped us find alternative transport to Goa and a safe place to stay. Trusting them made all the difference and brought us sanctuary in a disastrous situation. Trusting them lifted us up from danger.

Trusting to trust

Much has been written for leaders about trust: building or losing it. But few have focused on the need to be trusting of others and the benefits this brings. Being trusting of others, igniting their capability and enthusiasm to contribute, has become my default style of leading. It has unearthed many treasures for me in my career.

I have learnt that empowering others to create success by trusting them is the driving force that empowers teams to succeed in the most beneficial way.

But beware: trusting doesn't sit comfortably with everyone. It can be dangerous and risky[2] (Mcleod, C, 2020). Trusting others to do a "good job" can feel alien to some leaders. It doesn't always come naturally, especially if you are used to a less open style of leading. There are some that fear they might trust too much. Others that fear they won't be able to get the levels of trust right.

From conversations with hundreds of leaders, peers, and other coaches, I have come to realise that building trust and trusting others is a balancing act. The more trusting you are the more trust you can build, so long as you drive progress at the same time. When we gain the trust of others and know how to trust, we can achieve greatness, together. In the words of the renowned author, psychologist and science journalist, Daniel Goleman, "If you're privileged enough to be in a position of leadership, it is paramount that you maintain the trust of the people for whom you have a responsibility".[3]

Now more than ever

Lately, the need to trust others and be trusted has been magnified exponentially. Hybrid and remote working have pushed trust up the list of attributes for successful leadership. But few resources or help is available to enable leaders to build trust and harness its treasure.

Lately, many businesses have abandoned office working. Physical proximity to teams or leaders is no longer a daily feature. Human interactions are reduced. Our ability to build trust is limited by this. Technology has replaced many of the moments that matter for trust building. Training, workshops, watercooler moments, chats in the hallway, etc. all diminished.

New low-touch/high-tech working means invisible bonds like trust are more important than ever when employees or leaders are working remotely. With little motivation to return to the pre-2020 workplace, mastering the power of trust has become an essential focus for leaders.

Some timely questions from a few of my coaching clients include:

"How do I know if my team are actually working at home, not sunbathing in the garden?"

"Why do I need to build trust when they are paid to do a good job?"

"Trusting others feels high risk, why can't I just tell them what to do?"

> Trust is the currency that enables leaders and businesses to create the conditions for employees to deliver results.

Frei and Morris (2020) say trust is "the first step to becoming a genuinely empowering leader":[4]

> *Trust is also one of the most essential forms of capital a leader has. Building trust, however, often requires thinking about leadership from a new perspective. The traditional leadership narrative is all about you: your vision and strategy; your ability to make the tough calls and rally the troops; your talents, your charisma, your heroic moments of courage and instinct. But leadership really isn't about you. It's about empowering other people as a result of your presence, and about making sure that the impact of your leadership continues into your absence.*

Creating moments that matter in our remote world is a priority for leaders. If they fail to create interaction, occasions, and platforms to connect with employees, then they will never be trusted. It is vital that leaders proactively seek opportunities to involve, interact, and unite so that they can also be trusting.

Three leaders I learnt from

Over the years, I have worked for and with many leaders. Their ways have influenced and impacted me. These three provide a spectrum for my chapter.

Example 1: The limiting leader

I worked for a director in the transport industry who did not value my expertise. He had low trust in his team and in others generally. He was limiting his and his teams' results, because he had not evolved to meet their needs.

He made decisions without me and ignored my advice. He employed me because of my expertise but then failed to harness my value, because he was not a trusting leader. He was old school, preferring control and power over advice and alternative perspectives. His impact was limited by his lack of trust. His ego prevented him from empowering others. He was not trusted by his team because he did not trust them. He was very prescriptive and was restricting. My ability to add value in the business was limited.

He also gave others no option but to comply with his ways. This impacted morale and motivation. I felt excluded, isolated, and ignored. And I learnt quickly that the culture of that part of the business was the same. There were many others feeling what I felt. The limiting leader failed because he did not evolve to the needs of the team: too prescriptive on direction and control, not enough involvement from others. These leaders cannot build trust because they are not trusting of others and do not evolve their style to their teams. Their ways are limiting for themselves, their teams, and their businesses.

Example 2: The lacking leader

At the other end of this spectrum, I recently coached a Public Sector leader who was far too trusting but lacked direction. This made her ineffective. She listened, valued the expertise of others. She had clear vision and sound values. But she failed to lead in a way that held others accountable. She didn't move others along and in effect she got left behind.

She failed to assert her direction and decisions in a way that harnessed the energy and engagement of others. She was liked by many but was not respected because she failed to "land the plane" on critical decisions and strategies. She became irrelevant as a leader. She was lacking direction, accountability with too much consultation.

Example 3: The lifting leader

Lifting leaders trust others and build trust that lifts results. I worked for a National Director of Health. Her approach was to give me space, so I could add value and contribute. She was a trusting leader. But what was different to the other two types of leaders described was that she was clear on direction, expectations and goals, without being restrictive.

She held us to account and gave us responsibility. She recognised the importance of empowering others with trust so that they were able to contribute. This enabled the team to move forward trusting her. She balanced the need for direction with involvement. She had evolved to the needs of her team and trusted them. She evolved her style, which in turn built trust in her and lifted results.

Consequently, I thrived. She listened to my advice and involved me in decisions. She respected my insights, which made me feel valued. I felt part of the solution, elevated. I was lifted by her trust and so were our results. This had an influential impact and on my future leadership style. I saw the benefits that trusting others brought her and sought to emulate her lifting behaviours in my career.

This chapter reflects on the benefits achieved by lifting leaders and explores the recent changes at work that act as barriers to building trust or trusting others. I explore how to become a more trusting leader and most importantly how to step forward and master the power of trust using my trusting leaders' roadmap.

Forces preventing trust

To master the power of trust, we need to lead in a way that is fit for our times. Right now, leaders face huge shifts in the way we work. Many are bamboozled with endless change, new priorities, complex systems, and plans. This feast of data, information, and change brings with it a famine of attention in our teams. Trust and engagement are at risk.

Some leaders are struggling to keep up. There is no pause button. Others react by seeking to control everything. There feels like there is an expectation that leaders will somehow magically evolve, that they will learn or know how to stay relevant and thrive in complexity with little or no experience.

Lifting leaders recognise that they need to consistently evolve with their environment. Right now, many are busy reflecting on three important questions.

EVOLVE: ask yourself:

- How are these changes impacting trust in me?
- How can I change so that I continue to build trust?
- How can I become more trusting of others to unleash their success?

Evolving our ways

Understanding the changes taking place now is only one part of the solution. Proactively translating these into effective new ways to lead are the critical actions that will help leaders thrive. Knowing how to navigate the sea of change is what will set leaders apart this decade.

Evolving leaders are harnessing and mastering the power of trust. Their focus is on establishing deeper relationships from powerful conversations with employees. They are letting go of old school ways of hierarchy and delegation. Instead, they are using conversations to humanise and connect. They are creating bonds of trust with employees that unleash breathtaking results.

To evolve to trusting leadership, first we need to break through some barriers that might be limiting trusting behaviours.

Barriers to Trust:

1   Understanding the workforce.
2   Connecting in ways that build more trust in you.
3   Trusting others: letting go.

Challenge 1: Understanding the workforce

If we understand who we are leading, their needs, and motivators, then how to lead them and build their trust becomes easier.

The workforce is increasingly complex. Employees in the developed world are more educated and sophisticated than ever (McCrindle.com).[5] Their demography, education, learning preferences, and motivations provide the key to building trust and unlocking potential. Understanding them first, then connecting with them is what will enable leaders to thrive.

Changes in the DNA of our workforce are forcing more and more business leaders to rethink their leadership and communication styles. They recognise that a new way of influence, connection, and involvement is needed. Evolved leaders understand that there are multiple generations and learning preferences in our workforce and that their leadership impact is diminished if they do not respond to these.

> Ensuring that our leadership hits the mark with our fellow workers must be our primary focus, if we are to successfully evolve our leadership.

Evolving leaders lift their results by recognising that employees are motivated by the future, a purpose, their career, and a life outside of work (Ghandi, V. 2018).[6]

In the past, leaders needed much less trust, because they were seen as the superior authority and made most of the decisions at work. Trusting and being trusted was less of an issue.

The role of the leader has shifted. Learning to tap into employee knowledge, insights, ideas, and energy has never been so important. Trusting each other, not controlling, is the way forward. Trusting employees is the essence of leading for this decade. The leaders and businesses that succeed are those that will achieve higher levels of performance by building trust. Their focus is more on real and deeper employee connection, less on pushing old school ways or engagement gimmicks from the 1990s.

Challenge 2: Connect in ways that build more trust in you

Neuroscience has valuable insights for leaders who want to evolve their ways. Two very different reactions in the brain show how lifting leaders increase relevance, results and trust.

Primitive communicators

Old school ways of communication create reactions in the brain similar to fight or flight responses. This gets observed in employees' brains when a leader tells them what to do.

Leaders who have not evolved and continue to use one-way communication (such as telling and orders) will perpetuate this response in the brain of their teams. Their behaviour is negatively impacting results, effort, and ideas. These are the experiences I had whilst working for the Limiting Leader in example 1.

Leaders who behave in this way aren't trusting and don't build trust; they erode it. They cause employees to leave the organisation, because they feel undervalued or excluded from decision-making.

Evolved communicators

This reaction observed in the brain is experienced by employees working with leaders that have evolved their communication. Leaders using conversations and two-way communication (including questioning, listening, and inquiry) create a different reaction.

Leaders who have conversations with the 2020s workforce build deeper connections and get better results. This style of communication increases the emotional bond between leader and team – just like the example 3 (The Lifting Leader). Our conversations induced a desire in me to connect with the leader, innovate, go the extra mile, and take pride in the outcomes.

Conversations align with the needs of the current workforce. But the most important outcome for evolved leaders that are using conversations is way more significant. They build trust, and that is the leadership treasure that enables them to prosper.

Balboa, N. and Glaser, R. (2019) observed that

> Conversations are not just a way of sharing information; they actually trigger physical and emotional changes in the brain that either open you up to having healthy, trusting conversations or close you down so that you speak from fear, caution, and anxiety.[7]

Leaders that are aligned to the needs of the 2020s employee use conversations as their "HOW" of leading. They factor in two-way communication as a tool to intentionally give and build trust, because it's the essence of leading the 2020s workforce.

Challenge 3: Trusting others: "letting go"

Unleashing the potential of others is our most prized achievement as a leader. It is what enables employees to achieve great things. Already the 2020s are truly abundant with challenges that require this from leaders. A global pandemic, climate change, information overload, famine, drought, and wildfires that threaten our most basic needs. In time, it is employees that will find a cure for cancer, help reduce emissions, create alternative energy sources or ways to thrive in the face of environmental catastrophes.

The leaders' role is to create the conditions for employees to thrive, by letting go of behaviours, restrictions, or limits to team achievements.

When leaders fail to trust, they come up with all of the answers and they limit outcomes. This approach reduces employee thought and effort.

> Letting go requires leaders to step away from the feeling that they know or have all the answers.

Trust and success increase when leaders focus on creating conditions for others to succeed, not themselves. Moving towards a coaching presence, away from a commanding presence is central to this. Trusting in this way requires a specific set of leader skills and behaviours.

Controlling: holding on	Trusting: letting go
Shuts down employee brains	Opens minds: a bonding mechanism
Limits employee connection: "I am inferior"	Lifts employee connection: "I'm worthy"
Excludes contribution: "I've nothing to add"	Locks in contribution: "I have value to add"
Reduces ideas: leader solves	Increases ideas: employee solves
Employees feel excluded, limited.	Employees feel included, lifted.

So far, in this chapter, we have learnt WHY conversations and trusting are a better way to lead the current workforce. Now, we will explore exactly HOW leaders become more trusting so they can unleash potential in others.

Mastering trust: being more trusting of others

The net effect of multiple leaders trusting employees can be breathtaking. Here is a roadmap for leaders and teams to help master the power of trust. The map helps leaders evolve, build trust, and be more trusting of others.

Step 1: Involve

Real involvement (where leaders include, ask, listen, and take on the ways or words of others in decisions) fast tracks trust. When we have legitimate involvement in this way, it creates multiple benefits.

The obvious benefits are increased diversity in a team or business that exist in a range of voices and opinions. The covert benefit is the trust of those that feel legitimately involved. Inclusion adds a layer of respect and lifts a barrier that enhances belonging. It allows leaders to access greater effort and thinking.

> John Banfield, former CEO of BPAY Group Australia, recently shared how they lifted engagement with greater involvement and empowerment: "We eventually moved our engagement scores from 59% to 93% engagement in about four years. A big part of that has come from employees being empowered, accountable and aligned" (Matthews, P. 2020).[8]

Step 2: Insights

Involvement unveils deeper insights. And our 2020s' workforce is keen to share theirs. Trusting others to contribute using their knowledge is a vital skill for leaders.

> Daniel Goleman said that you build trust with employees when you *"honour those people by listening and responding in earnest"*.[9]

Unleashing knowledge, experiences, and ideas like this enables leaders to open minds and focuses the energy of those around them. When this happens, employees trust leaders more. The activity builds respect and encourages employees to repeat the behaviour, enabling greater sharing of insight, which in turn also drives up levels of trust.

Using insights in a business of 40,000 employees

I interviewed Michael Schneider, Managing Director of Australia's Bunnings chain of hardware stores. They are possibly one of Australia's most trusted and loved brands, with over 40,000 employees.

Throughout the pandemic, trusting their retail employees was critical to responding to the pandemic. By listening to employees, the business was able to gauge customer sentiment and build an effective pandemic response.

> *some of the recent actions we took during the pandemic came from leaders listening to the fear or confusion of team members on the front line about safety during the pandemic.*
>
> *some employees were scared senseless during the COVID19 crisis. They were dealing with lots of people who might have been infected. The voices from the front line have helped us realise some good learnings when it comes to customer and team safety in that respect.*
>
> (Matthews, P. 2020)[10]

Step 3: Influence

Applying the insights that employees share, allowing them to influence our decisions is a visible and valuable way to show that we can be trusted. Demonstrating that you have taken employee feedback or insight onboard, shows your employees that you are someone that cares about their views and experiences and that they matter. This behaviour removes barriers to trust.

Angela Tsoukatos, Executive Coach (Australia), recently shared her insights on this.

> *All perspectives matter. We all benefit from collective thinking.*
>
> *Be generous. Acknowledge others and the contribution they make. Drive out fear so that others feel like they can contribute and be open and honest.*
>
> (Matthews, P. 2020)[11]

Being influenced is a critical part of leading. If we cannot show that we are responsive to evidence, data, insights, and opinions, then we operate in a vacuum. We fail to evolve, and we lose relevance if we are not opened to influence.

Step 4: Impact

When we involve others, unveil their insights, and take these on board, our impact soars. The conversations we have lift us. Trust building in this manner lifts our results. It lifts our impact as individual leaders. It raises the roof on our results as a team.

> Trust creates an impact that enables you to access high-level benefits that old-school leadership styles cannot achieve.

Treasure it

As we move through a process of involvement to gaining insights, we achieve a deeper understanding of our people and ourselves. This is when trusting others starts to bring trust back to you as a leader.

When we use insights and allow others to influence our decisions, we unlock potential and greater learning. This builds collective impact. The trust we build doing this unites those around us. Eventually, this serves to unleash our potential and the potential of those working with us. And it becomes a cycle of continuous growth and reinforcement that deepens trust and consistently lifts results.

The trusting leader roadmap

Building trust, finding its treasure, can be a challenging and difficult voyage for leaders. Getting the balance right can be hard. It requires reflection, learning, and a switch in behaviours to align with the needs of those around us.

Whilst we have an understanding of what builds trust, we must invest time and effort in creating moments to display the behaviour of trusting others. When a leader eventually masters the power of trust, it's like cracking open a treasure chest of motivation, innovation, and accountability.

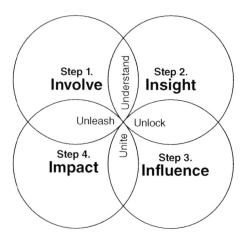

FIGURE 9.1: Leader Roadmap

Investing time involving others and listening and valuing their ideas and insights brings riches that extend far beyond those attainable using our own capabilities. By helping leaders to give their trust, my goal is that they embody behaviours that in turn build trust in them as leaders, leading to a lift in enterprise-wide performance.

My Trusting Leaders roadmap shows leaders how to master the power of trust, by trusting others. Trust is precious. It can take years to build. It can erode in seconds. We really should take the time to treasure it.

Follow-up questions: ask yourself

- How have recent changes lifted or limited trust for you?
- How can you change to harness more trust?
- How can you create more opportunities to be trusting of others, so they can contribute and succeed?
- How can you help other leaders evolve and lift trust?
- What lies ahead that might test trust in you? How can you prepare?

Notes

1 Goleman, D. (2015), How Leaders Build Trust. *LinkedIn*. Available at: https://www.linkedin.com/pulse/how-leaders-build-trust-daniel-goleman/
2 McLeod, Carolyn (2020), *Trust*. The Stanford Encyclopedia of Philosophy. Fall 2020 edition. Edward N. Zalta (Ed.). Available at: https://plato.stanford.edu/archives/fall2020/entries/trust/

3   Goleman, D. (2015), How Leaders Build Trust. *LinkedIn*. Available at: https://www.linkedin.com/pulse/how-leaders-build-trust-daniel-goleman/

4   Frei, F. and A. Morris (2020), Begin With Trust. *HBR*. Available at: https://hbr.org/2020/05/begin-with-trust

5   McCrindle, M. (2018), Generation Z/Alpha. *McCrindle*. Available at: www.McCrindle.com

6   Ghandi, V. (2018), Want to Improve Productivity? Hire Better Managers. *Gallup*. Available at: https://www.gallup.com/workplace/238103/improve-productivity-hire-better-managers.aspx

7   Balboa, N. and R. Glaser (2019), The Neuroscience of Conversations. *Psychology Today*. Available at: https://www.psychologytoday.com/au/blog/conversational-intelligence/201905/the-neuroscience-conversations

8   Matthews, P. (2020), *SWITCH: From Telling to Trusting With Powerful Leader Conversations*. Available at: www.paulmatthews.com.au/switch

9   Goleman, D. (2015), How Leaders Build Trust. *LinkedIn*. Available at: https://www.linkedin.com/pulse/how-leaders-build-trust-daniel-goleman/

10   Matthews, P. (2020), *SWITCH: From Telling to Trusting With Powerful Leader Conversations*. Available at: www.paulmatthews.com.au/switch

11   Ibid.

Further reading

Butler, M., A. Hagan et al. (2020), *What the Hell Do We Do Now? An Enterprise Guide to COVID-19 and Beyond*. Available at: https://www.amazon.com.au/What-Hell-Do-Now-enterprise-ebook/dp/B08JCFY1KH

Matthews, P. (2020), *SWITCH: From Telling to Trusting With Powerful Leader Conversations*. Paul Matthews. Available at: www.paulmatthews.com.au/switch

10

MASTERING THE POWER OF PRESENCE

Karen Glossop

Abstract

We experience presence as a mysterious quality that we assume people are just born with. When we are really dazzled, we call it charisma. However, presence can be learned and developed by anyone. In this chapter, I'll share insights from my training and experience from the world of the theatre, where actors make it their business to engage audiences and use the spotlight to their advantage. My ideas are illustrated with real-life examples. I'll also offer practical suggestions for how you can develop your own presence and use it to make the impact that you want.

Keywords: Presence, charisma, engagement, impact

Introduction – the enthralling power of presence

Throughout the ages, different cultures have reported the feeling of being enthralled by the quality of an individual's presence. As Freddy Mercury, the famous British singer, songwriter, and lead vocalist of the rock band Queen, once said, "The reason we're successful darling? My overall charisma, of course".[1]

There is something enigmatic about presence. It's not always easy to define. In the words of the former French President, Charles de Gaulle, "There can be no power without mystery. There must always be a 'something' which others cannot altogether fathom, which puzzles them, stirs them, and rivets their attention".[2]

DOI: 10.4324/9781003219293-13

To explain how the power of presence works, we often resort to stating what it isn't. It doesn't depend on the usual desirable attributes: social class, beauty, wealth, intelligence, physical strength, or even being tall. We all know presence when we see it, whether we're watching a president or a rock star, or perhaps an influencer in our local community. Sometimes, the most unexpected people have it.

New Zealand Māori use the word Mana for the supernatural authority that warriors embody.[3] The classical Greek word Χαρισμα – charisma – suggests that human beings are possessed by an external force or grace.[4,5] Or today, as armchair judges of pop talent TV shows, we might exclaim: "This person has the X Factor!" Presence seems such a mystery that it's tempting to give up trying to define it and conclude that some people are just born with it.

So how can we demystify presence, nurture the quality in ourselves, and learn to use it as a power to influence others?

Blossoming after the Tsunami

I met Ai, a young Japanese woman, when she signed up for my eight-week Presentation Skills course at City, University of London in the UK. She was an introverted, attentive student who enjoyed learning how to craft creative speeches.

By day, Ai worked in an administrative role at the London branch of a large Japanese bank. Outside of work time, Ai regularly volunteered for a charity. One of the charity's relief projects was called Nadeshiko, named after the Japanese Women's Football team. The project was a social enterprise, based on a partnership between London fashion designers and a group of older women in Higashi-Matsushima. These women had been manual workers in the fisheries until the 2011 tsunami destroyed their homes and their industry. The London team devised a range of designs that the Japanese women used as patterns for handcrafting beautiful accessories out of their tsunami-ruined kimonos. The profits from their handicrafts were used to rebuild the community. Ai showed me one of the flower-shaped brooches that were the product of this collaboration. The damaged silks had been given a stylish new life.

Ai was invited to speak at the Japanese Embassy in London about the project to audience of international dignitaries, including the Ambassador. She was nervous about public speaking, but she was even more intimidated by the news that her boss at the Bank would also be a guest at the event. She kept her own participation a secret from him.

In preparation, Ai had written a great script to tell this inspirational story, which she hoped would draw more people into the collaboration. The only problem was that Ai feared she didn't have the charisma to make the impact she wanted on the audience. Usually, Ai's demeanour was reserved. Because of a blend of her culture and her personality, Ai had chosen all through her life not to draw attention to herself. She realised that in this situation, she needed to take a different approach. She came to me for advice.

The solution would be to explore and practice new techniques. To begin with, Ai read her script without lifting her eyes from the page and stood with her feet glued together. Her voice was so soft it was barely audible. Ai and I worked together on technical aspects like her voice and her posture. I also encouraged her to connect with her emotions and not hide them. After a couple of rehearsals, Ai's desire to engage the audience became greater than her shyness.

I contacted Ai after the event to ask her how it had gone. "It was wonderful!" she told me.

> I really enjoyed it. So many people came up to me afterwards to tell me how well I'd spoken, and how it made them want to buy the kimono brooches and help in other ways. But the best part was when my boss at the Bank came over to congratulate me. He told me he had no idea I would be speaking that evening, and he couldn't believe that I was the same person who worked in the office quietly and efficiently processing invoices. He said he had never guessed that I had this secret life as a charismatic spokeswoman for a charity.

So how could Ai achieve such a transformation? How did she enhance her presence in front of the audience?

We say so much without words

I discovered the tools to manage my own presence through my drama school training, and I've developed them through my long career working in the theatre as an actor alongside talented performers. I've also learned from observing people who aren't professional actors, but who display the knack of managing well in the spotlight.

Drama schools equip people to understand the impact they make on others through how they stand, move, and engage with others through eye contact, timing, and space. Then, they train students to transform themselves, so that they can play a wide range of different characters on stage and screen. What is extraordinary is how much an audience decides to trust, respect, fear, love, or be moved by an actor before a single line is spoken. This feeling is based entirely on that actor's presence. If we really like someone's presence, we call it charisma. Audiences love actors like Jennifer Lawrence and Salman Khan, and watch their movies for their appearances as much as for the story itself.

In the theatre, we describe presence as the relationship you have between your own body and the space you occupy, and how you connect to the other people in the room. A tense body will always reveal your insecurities. For instance, gripping your hands over your groin, however instinctive this self-protective gesture may be, shows you feel exposed to attack. Feet pressed tightly together will undermine both your physical stability and the impression you make. Placing your feet very wide apart, as if you are riding an invisible horse, will suggest you are desperate to take up as much space as possible. Neither stance will give you flexibility to adjust in the moment.

Your posture will also affect your breathing and your voice. And if you can't be physically heard, your opinions and insights won't be either. No matter what words you use, you'll be weakening your case.

Sometimes, we don't realise what signals we're sending out. So, in my workshops, we take a playful approach to discovering how our physical presence is interpreted by other people. One of the games we play is acting out the same script in many different ways, so that although the words stay the same, and come out the same order, the scene can mean something completely different. An actor who says her lines punctuated by pauses, while she holds her gaze very still and direct, will make a different impact from one plays the scene with big gestures and speaking rapidly. We could even say that changing the quality of the presence changes the meaning of the story.

Interestingly, there doesn't seem to be a rigid code of "correct" non-verbal behaviour that you can learn by rote to make your presence compelling. It's more accurate to say that it's vital for the actor to physically relax and to have the courage to experiment with what works.

While actors learn these skills to entertain, I teach them to people in all walks of life so that they can be more effective communicators. Changing your presence can bring all sorts of further changes. It can make you feel more confident, or bring more energy to the conversation, or help grow the relationship between you and others.

The paradox is that, although presence is physical, it isn't superficial. It transcends conventional standards of attractiveness. Even historically ablest societies have recognised the magnetism of disabled figures such as the English poet, Lord Byron, and the Mexican painter, Frieda Kahlo.

It's also worth remembering that presence isn't a moral attribute. We don't have to like someone or agree with their values to admire their ability to hold their own in the spotlight. Donald Trump or Vladimir Putin may be controversial, but their power to fascinate is not.

You don't need to be a specific type of person to make a huge impact on others. If you want to connect with others and have the courage of your convictions, you are more than halfway to holding your audience in the palm of your hand. Different types of people have different strengths to draw on to make their unique brand of impact.

Extroverts benefit from feeding off audience feedback. They are open to improvising when the situation demands it. Their natural expressiveness helps people connect with them on an emotional level. No one is surprised by how comfortable an extrovert is in the spotlight. An extrovert's enjoyment can be contagious. They can be magnets for audiences' attention.

More unexpectedly, shy people can make the best actors. When introverts step into a role, they lend themselves wholeheartedly to the task of communicating, although they may find it more exhausting than extroverts do. Introverts respect the need for preparation, and they have a huge capacity to use their vulnerability as a means of bonding with audiences.[6]

Here are two contrasting figures with different styles and backgrounds, who could both be described as having a big presence on the world stage.

Usain Bolt

Many athletes win admiration and popularity for their talent on the field. Among these stars, Jamaican sprinter Usain Bolt stands out for his extraordinary achievements, such as eight Olympic Gold medals including three Golds back-to-back for the 200 m sprint, and 11 Gold medals at the World Championships.[7] However, his rapport with his global audience transcends the world of sports.

Usain Bolt, towering 1.96 m tall, nevertheless doesn't meet expectations of physical perfection and symmetry. He was born with scoliosis, a condition which curves his spine to the right.

No matter what the upcoming challenge, Usain Bolt always is relaxed in the spotlight. He lives in the present moment and engages in people around him. While other athletes are self-absorbed in their pre-race preparation, he winks or fist-bumps volunteers.

Usain Bolt's extrovert personality speaks through his body language. Before even reaching the finish line of the 200 m 2012 Olympics, he placed his fingers to lips. The message was clear: the doubters can shut up. And on being declared the winner, he performed five press ups to celebrate each of his Gold medals.

His famous pose is the Lightning Bolt. He stands at a diagonal, with his weight back on his slightly bent right leg. His right elbow is drawn into the side at shoulder height. He extends and raises his left arm up and to the side. The effect is to emulate the sudden energy of lightning. It exudes his self-confidence. The pose has become a real-life meme, copied by fans all over the world. Striking the Lightning Bolt allows them to embody his joy and repurpose it for themselves.

Usain Bolt's charisma is expansive enough to include everyone who wants to celebrate with him.

Greta Thunberg

The young Swedish climate activist Greta Thunberg has made a huge impact on global consciousness despite starting her campaigning at school age.[8]

Her small stature only heightens the contrast between her and the world politicians who must now share the world stage with her. She does not seek to disguise her physical vulnerabilities, including her Asperger's condition, which she has reframed as a gift. These very vulnerabilities are part of her appeal to audiences who feel inspired by her example, perhaps especially those who identify with her introversion. More than 11 million people now have gone on strike to protest inaction on climate change.

Greta Thunberg takes on the challenge speaking to mass rallies like an actor. She says:

Onstage is okay, because then I can go into another character.

Greta Thunberg is visibly driven by her sense of purpose. Her gaze is direct, at times almost fierce, as she challenges older adults to halt the environmental crisis by taking real actions. Her voice is high-pitched, but there is no hesitation in her delivery. Unlike Usain Bolt, she doesn't often smile at her audience, which emphasises her seriousness. She is open about her emotion, such as in her speech to the UN, in which her question "How dare you?" feels raw and real. Although her facial expression and tone mirror her feelings, she expresses her strong feelings clearly through crisp, clear diction not in an incoherent howl.

Enhance your presence

No one is born with presence. It's something we develop as we find our place in the world. If we don't ever take the risk to step into the spotlight, we may never discover our capacity to make a personal impact on others. Experience and incorporating simple techniques into our practice allow us to grow in confidence.

So what can *you* do to develop control over your own presence?

Shakespeare understood that the skills that actors use are in fact life skills for everyone:

> *All the world's a stage*
> *And all the men and women merely players*
> *They have their exits and their entrances*
> *And one man in his time plays many parts.*[9]

Your gaze, timing, posture, gesture, and use of space all send a message to others about who you are and what you stand for. The more intentional you are, the more control you will have over how others perceive you.

Preparation is everything. However, preparation for presence is different from the kind of preparation you might do for a written exam, because it involves your body as much as your mind.[10]

Learning to relax is your starting point. When you feel calmer, you'll have choices about what kind of energy you want to share – whether you want to be warm, intriguing, or challenging. This is why actors do warm-ups to get rid of the physical tension, which is a symptom of anxiety. Once you develop your own daily practice, you'll begin to be able to draw on these techniques in testing times if you integrate them into your life. You may even find that they transform how you move through the world and connect with others.

It isn't possible to *have* presence without *being* present. When you are in the middle of communicating, keep aware of yourself and your environment. Don't let your mind race ahead or stay stuck in a moment that has passed.

People sometimes take a self-limiting attitude to presence. "It's just not me", they say. "I don't want to be inauthentic". Presence isn't about faking it, but it is about amplifying who you are so that you can reach more people more memorably.

Explore:

Prepare by learning to relax:

- Develop a sense of awareness of your body and breathing. Start at your feet and work your way up to the top of your head. What can you identify as a physical habit? Is it helping you project the image you want, or not?
- Imagine that you are surrounded by an eggshell. This is your personal space. Are you shrinking into it like a raisin, or expanding beyond it, like a ripe Brie cheese?
- Practice a three-minute daily warm-up routine to free yourself from tension. Release tension from your neck, shoulders, jaw, knees, feet, and spine by stretching.
- Release your breath fully through your mouth five times in a row, breathing naturally in between. This will allow your in-breath to slow and deepen. Do this several times a day.

Be present:

- Use eye contact to connect with others. It will help you maintain your energy and your audience's attention. It will also help you project your voice.
- Don't lose self-awareness. Notice if you are holding your breath, constricting your shoulders, gripping with your feet or hands. Decide whether you want to be sending these signals or not.
- Keep aware of others. Listen and watch out for signals from your audience. But if they don't seem responsive, don't become down-hearted. Just change something. Vary your delivery or cross the stage. If you're seated, change your position – lean forward or lean back.
- Don't ignore the environment. If a loud drill starts to drown out your speech, don't struggle on. Acknowledge it and take a judgement call on whether to continue. Being flexible is more effective than staying rigid.

Amplify:

- Experiment by going over the top in rehearsal or role play of high-stakes meetings. Commit totally to whatever you are doing – speaking, listening, gesturing, or being still. People are often surprised when they get the feedback that too much is just enough from the audience's point of view.
- Harness the power of your voice. This may mean speaking more loudly, but it will also mean holding moments of stillness and silence – the pause. Breath support will give you the oomph to sustain your energy all the way to the end of your sentence.
- Bring energy to whatever you're doing. This means not holding back. It doesn't mean forcing it. This is why you need to start relaxed.

Summary

Presence is essential for anyone who wants to be persuasive. Having presence gives you the right to be noticed and your opinions to be heard. Without personal presence, it's difficult to sell even great ideas.

No one will have exactly the same presence as you. If you choose to assert your presence, you will access the unique power of your own personality and gain the opportunity to win over the world.

Most of all, give yourself permission to be greater than your fears. Your vulnerability, if you harness it rather than feel shamed by it, can help other people connect with you on the deepest level.

Be willing to tap into all the different versions of yourself that you can possibly be. Then you can choose to be you at your charismatic best.

Follow-up actions

- Let go of self-limiting beliefs that you don't have the personality to make an impact on others.
- Use the aforementioned suggestions to create your own relaxation practice. Remember that self-awareness is useful, but harsh self-criticism will block you.
- Keep focused on your audience and your ideas.

- Take up the opportunities to be in the spotlight that come your way. If you don't take a risk, you'll never know what you're capable of. Start with small challenges and then build to bigger ones.

Notes

1 Jackson, Laura (2011), *Freddie Mercury: The Biography*. Hachette Digital.
2 de Gaulle, Charles (1960), *The Edge of the Sword*, trans. Gerard Hopkins. Faber & Faber.
3 New Zealand Māori Concept of Mana. Available at: http://www.manashuzou.co.nz/about-mana-shochu/the-meaning-of-mana.aspx; https://www.nzgeo.com/stories/the-meaning-of-mana/
4 Greek Concept of Charisma. Available at: https://www.merriam-webster.com/dictionary/charisma
5 See Charisma in Business. Available at: https://www.psychologytoday.com/gb/basics/charisma; https://hbr.org/2012/06/learning-charisma-2
6 See Vulnerabilty, Brené Brown. Available at: https://www.ted.com/talks/brene_brown_the_power_of_vulnerability?language=en
7 Usain Bolt. Available at: https://www.linkedin.com/pulse/leadership-secrets-usain-bolt-greg-pritchard; https://www.youtube.com/watch?v=93dCOo2aHto; https://www.youtube.com/watch?v=4zyHXavtpes
8 Greta Thunberg. Available at: https://fridaysforfuture.org/; https://www.youtube.com/watch?v=KAJsdgTPJpU; https://www.bbc.co.uk/programmes/p099f58d; https://www.bbc.co.uk/programmes/p090xz9z
9 Shakespeare, William (1926), *As You Like It*. Sir Arthur Quiller-Couch and John Dover Wilson (Eds.). Cambridge University Press.
10 Body Language and Presence, Amy Cuddy. Available at: https://www.ted.com/talks/amy_cuddy_your_body_language_may_shape_who_you_are?language=en

Further reading

1 Cain, Susan (2012), *Quiet: The Power of Introverts in a World That Can't Stop Talking*. UK: Penguin.
2 Johnstone, Keith (1979), *Impro: Improvisation and the Theatre*. UK: Methuen.
3 Rodenburg, Pasty (1992), *The Right to Speak*. UK: Routledge.
4 Anderson, Chris (2016), *TED Talks – The Official TED Guide to Public Speaking*. UK: Headline Publishing Group.

11

MASTERING THE POWER OF STORYTELLING

Gabrielle Dolan

Abstract

One of the most powerful skills we should master when it comes to leadership, communication, and influence is the skill of storytelling. As humans, we are hardwired to communicate through stories. We are not hardwired to communicate through PowerPoint slides and bullet points.

Stories are like the gift that keeps giving. They allow us to communicate our message more effectively, strengthen the connection, and trust when it comes to our relationship with people.

This chapter first explores why storytelling is such a powerful communication and influential skill. It explores the four types of stories you need to look for and the various situations you can share stories. It also provides practical advice on the five keys to mastering the art of storytelling.

Keywords: Storytelling, influence, trust, communication

Discovering the power of stories

The power of stories has been with us throughout the history of mankind. As Lord Tyrion Lannister, the fictional character from the TV series, Game of Thrones, wisely stated, *"What unites people? Armies? Gold? Flags? Stories. There is nothing in the world more powerful than a good story. Nothing can stop it. No enemy can defeat it"*.[1]

DOI: 10.4324/9781003219293-14

I first discovered the power of stories while working in leadership roles at a major bank. I noticed that when I shared a story to communicate a message, it had better retention and outcomes with my audience. On reflection, I realised that the leaders I found inspiring and consequently wanted to work with, were sharing stories with success. What's more, I observed that brilliant speakers were also brilliant storytellers.

It was in 2005 that I started to read books about storytelling in business. To enhance my understanding of the topic further, I studied both *Squirrel Inc.* and *The Leaders Guide to Storytelling* by Steve Denning. In addition, other influential titles such as *The Story Factor* by Annette Simmons and *Wake Me Up When the Data Is Over* by Lori Silverman.

It is my belief that one of the best ways to learn something is to teach it. So, I started combining all the insights I was reading about storytelling alongside my own expertise and experience. In time, I was running my own business-training people on effective communication and influence in business.

Sharing stories with success

Over the last 15 years, I have seen people share stories with success in a variety of ways. Business Storytelling can be used to:

- lead and influence people
- ensure your presentations are more impactful
- sell yourself or a product
- make a great and lasting impression in a job interview
- demonstrate your personal values
- teach, coach or mentor people

Storytelling is truly one of the most powerful and versatile skills you can learn, and it can be applied in both your professional and personal life. It is just like any skill that you study, you will get better at it if you put in the time and effort to do so. Moreover, I think that you are never too young to start learning how to use stories with success.

When it comes to business, we tend to focus on logic alone. We have been taught, perhaps all our career, that business communication is driven by data – to provide the pertinent facts and figures. You may have been told by managers in the past to "*just show me the facts*" or that business should not be personal and you should avoid showing any emotion.

Yet as humans, we are emotional beings. While logic has its place in business, most of the time, it informs but does not influence or inspire. Bestselling author, Dale Carnegie, put it well when he said;

"*When dealing with people, let us remember we are not dealing with creatures of logic. We are dealing with creatures of emotion*"[2] – Dale Carnegie (1888–1955), author, lecturer, and course developer. The reason stories are one of the most powerful ways to communicate and engage people, because they:

- provoke emotions that engage and interest people
- make people feel a connection towards the storyteller
- help build trust and credibility
- influence people into making a decision
- help people understand and remember messages better, and for longer

Trust is critical to a positive organisational culture.

> In my research I've found that building a culture of trust is what makes a meaningful difference. Employees in high-trust organizations are more productive, have more energy at work, collaborate better with their colleagues, and stay with their employers longer than people working at low-trust companies.[3]
>
> (Paul J. Zak [1962–present], American neuro-economist)

A powerful example

When it comes to sharing stories in the workplace or business environment, most people will stick to anecdotes about previous work they have completed or stories about clients. While this can be valuable, the most underutilised yet powerful stories you can share are those relating to something personal. For that reason, the masterful storyteller will share a personal story to communicate a business message.

Take, for example, the following story from Anne Bennett. I worked with Anne several years ago when she wanted to share a personal story with her team around integrity and doing the right thing.

This is the story she shared:

> My dad was an elite swimmer when he was young, and at 16 years old he was in the backstroke finals to make it into the 1964 Tokyo Olympic Games team for Australia.

Dad flew out of the blocks and was out in front of all his competitors, but as he approached his turn at 50 metres, he missed the wall. Knowing he hadn't made the touch, he swam back, touched the wall, and kept racing.

Dad came in seventh that day and missed out on making the Olympic squad. After finishing, the judges told him that they hadn't seen the missed touch (it was well before technology recorded this) and if he had kept going, he would have come first and potentially broken a world record.

Dad would always tell my sister and me that he has never regretted that split-moment decision and, even though the judges didn't see the missed touch, he knew he had missed it and he knew turning back was the right thing to do. For me, doing the right thing is a lifelong lesson shown to me by my dad and the integrity he showed that day.

When I think of integrity, I think of my dad. We will often be faced with situations in business where we have to decide if we go back and touch the wall or not. It is at these times I always ask myself what my dad would do.

Anne's story showed her team that integrity is important to her. Integrity is what her parents expect of her, it is what she expects of herself and therefore what she expects of the people in her team. Anne's example demonstrates how you can use a story to show a personal value. Not only has she used this story when new people join her team or when she has started in a new position, but she has also used it in presentations and job interviews.

Utilising storytelling

Job interviews offer an important opportunity to utilise storytelling. The interview format and structure naturally lend itself to sharing stories. While many hopeful candidates focus on sharing business-related stories that demonstrate skills, they miss a vital opportunity to share their personal values. It goes without saying that it is important to share stories of what you have achieved in business. Just don't underestimate the power of sharing a personal story to demonstrate your values. Sharing a personal story in a job interview also provides you with the opportunity to humanise yourself and bring your resume to life. If the job you are applying for requires effective communication, then sharing an appropriate personal story will demonstrate your skills in this area.

Presentations also provide another opportunity where you can share personal stories. Whether it is a presentation on stage to hundreds of people or a meeting with a few colleagues, a well-constructed personal story will help you connect and engage with your audience. During a job interview, we are fully aware that we are auditioning for a role and it is just as crucial to approach every public speaking engagement in a similar way.

One of the key skills of any public speaker is the ability to tell a good story. Subsequently, it is vital to think about how you can share a story to get your key message across in a way that is both engaging and memorable. Consider how to start with a personal story to immediately capture your audience's attention and set up the context of your presentation.

The four types of stories

From my 15 years of storytelling training in business, I have realised that there are four types of stories you can share. They are stories of:

1. Triumph
2. Tragedy
3. Tension
4. Transition

Triumph stories

These are stories of achievement – the moments in your career and personal life that you are especially proud of. Triumph comes in all shapes and sizes and isn't just about winning . . . it could be about having the courage to try, regardless of the outcome.

Triumph stories should not just be about you, they should also include how you have helped other people succeed. To make sure you don't look like you are bragging, triumph stories should include a good dose of vulnerability and humility. This could involve sharing your fears at the time and identifying any challenges you overcame along the way.

Tragedy stories

Like triumph stories, these stories vary according to your perspective of what you consider a tragedy. Some examples may truly be about tragic circumstances, while others may be stories of regret.

Stories of regret may be when you didn't have the courage to do something. This could be going for a promotion or taking that overseas assignment. The regret could be about not asking the love of your life out on a date or feeling like you didn't spend enough time with your parents when they were older.

Try to focus not only on the tragedy but also more importantly on what you learnt from it.

Tension stories

These are stories of conflict that are driven by your values, loyalties, or obligations.

Tension stories that compromised your values might create conflict, because you were forced to choose between two different beliefs. Or it could recount a time when you did not stay true to your values. Ironically, sharing stories of when you did not uphold one of your values, and the regrets you have about that, demonstrates greater credibility than you may think.

Regardless of what you are torn about, don't just focus on the decision you made. Make sure that these stories focus on your inner struggles and the internal or external tension the event caused.

Transition stories

These stories are about key transitions in your life. If work-related, they might include events such as changing jobs, companies, industries, or careers. Non-work-related stories, on the other hand, may include moving countries, getting divorced, going back to study, or having children.

The most powerful transition stories take the audience through what you were thinking and feeling at the time. Highlighting the anxiety you felt when you made the decision is crucial, as is outlining your fears or level of excitement.

The key to being a good storyteller in business is to have a variety of these four types of stories prepared and ready to share for different business situations.

Five key factors to mastering storytelling

When it comes to sharing stories in business, there are several factors to consider. I've listed my top five for you here.

Be clear on your message

Ensure that you are clear on what message you are trying to communicate through your story. Also make sure that you only have one message in your story. If you try to communicate too many messages in the one story, it will lose impact and could be confusing to your audience.

Be succinct

It does not matter how exciting you think your story is, in business, your audience will be thinking (and sometimes saying) "Get to the point". Ensure that your stories in business go no longer than 2 minutes. People can always ask you for more information.

Use language that is real

The power of stories occurs when people feel and visualise something when you share your story. I often see people in business using corporate jargon or safe, professional words that do not elicit an emotional or sensory experience with their audience. Avoid jargon and use words that trigger feelings.

Be truthful

Your stories must be true. It is not worth the backlash to your credibility to make up stories or pass other people's stories off as your own. Telling inauthentic stories in business is perhaps the single biggest mistake you can make with storytelling, as it can do irreversible damage to your brand.

Prepare and practice

Ensure that you prepare your stories by writing them down as you would say them, then practise, practise, and practise some more. Time yourself to ensure that they are not going too long and seek feedback from someone you trust.

Summary

Storytelling is a powerful communication and influence tool that can be used in all aspects of your life. If you invest time in practising the relevant skills that have been listed earlier, you will become better at using stories to connect and engage your audience with your message. In the words of Steve Jobs: "*The most powerful person in the world is the storyteller*"[4] – widely attributed to Steve Jobs (1955–2011), industrial designer, investor, and co-founder of Apple.

Follow-up actions

When I ask people to reflect on their stories, they often respond with, "I don't have any stories to share". However, we all have stories! The first step to mastering storytelling is to uncover your own stories.

In my training, I use the following two approaches for finding stories.

Approach 1: Finding work-related stories

To find different examples of the four types of stories that are related to a work situation, grab a piece of paper and divide it into five columns. Label each column (left to right) as follows:

1 job
2 triumph
3 tragedy
4 tension
5 transition

List all the jobs you've ever had in the first column, starting with your very first job and moving through to your current role. Don't leave out any job, no matter how small or insignificant it feels now, and include any work experience or a casual job you had for a short time when you were young. I had a casual job working in Woolworths for two weeks when I was 17, and I have so many stories from that short experience.

For each role, now think carefully about specific events that stand out for you in relation to the four types of stories. You are like a metal detector for stories. Don't dismiss it too quickly by thinking something like, "*That was boring, nothing happened there*" or "*I was only in that job for three months*". The memories will be hidden just below the surface, so you need to be patient and thorough when investigating.

Some questions that can get your memories jogging:

- How did you come to take on or leave the role?
- Was there anything significant in that process?

- Did the role involve moving locations?
- Was taking the role or leaving it a big decision at the time?
- Why did you leave?

These questions could end up providing good transition or tension stories.

- What success did you have in that role?
- What achievements did you or your team enjoy that you are particularly proud of? Did you win any awards?
- Did you struggle with one aspect of the role or one person in your team which you worked through?

Asking yourself these questions can bring up potential triumph stories you could use.

Do you have any regrets from that job that could form tragedy stories?

- Did you take a course of action or make a decision that ended up being the wrong call and something you regret?
- Was a strong relationship with one of your peers or clients destroyed that you wish hadn't been?
- Did something happen to one of your colleagues that had a devastating impact on you, which you still think about today?
- Did you learn a valuable lesson from a mistake?

Remember that tragedy stories don't always have to be about significant loss; they can be about regret and the lessons you learnt.

Approach 2: Finding non-work-related stories

Now, it's time to find some personal stories you could use. With a fresh sheet of paper, once again divide it into five columns, this time with the following labels:

1   experience
2   triumph
3   tragedy

4   tension
5   transition

Next, think through your past, from your earliest memories to your most recent and write down the significant events that have happened in your life. Experiences that are significant can vary from person to person. The fact that you remember these experiences probably indicates that they are significant to you.

Try not to analyse the experiences that emerge; just write them down. Even though you have added them to your table, it doesn't mean you will necessarily share them. One of the key rules of storytelling in business is that you as the storyteller determine what stories you share and with whom. So, you may be willing to share a particular story with your team or in a one-on-one coaching conversation, but not necessarily with a client or on stage to 500 people.

Once you have lots of different work- and non-work-related events and memories, put a tick in one of the four columns to indicate what type of story it may be: triumph, tragedy, tension, and/or transition. You'll likely find one story could be more than one type of story.

The next time you would like to share a story to communicate a business message, simply look over your list, and choose something that matches what you want to communicate.

Once you experience the power of stories, you will start to notice many different experiences that you can add to your collection. Things will just happen to you as you go about your life and you'll naturally start to see how you might be able to use them in a business setting.

Notes

1   The Iron Throne (2019), Game of Thrones, Series 8, episode 6. HBO, 19 May.
2   Carnegie, Dale (1936), *How to Win Friends and Influence People*. USA: Simon & Schuster.
3   Zak, P.J. (2017), The Neuroscience of Trust, Management Behaviours That Foster Employee Engagement. *Harvard Business Review*. Available at: https://hbr.org/2017/01/the-neuroscience-of-trust
4   Direct source unknown, widely attributed to Steve Jobs.

Further reading

• Denning, Stephen (2005), *The Leaders Guide to Storytelling*. USA: Jossey-Bass.
• Denning, Steve (2011), Leadership Storytelling. *Ted Talk*. Available at: https://www.youtube.com/watch?v=RipHYzhKCuI

- Dolan, Gabrielle (2017), *Stories for Work: The Essential Guide to Business Storytelling*. USA: John Wiley & Sons.
- Dolan, Gabrielle (2021), *Magnetic Stories: Connect With Customers and Engage Employees With Brand Storytelling*. Doolan: John Wiley & Sons.
- Hasson, Uri (2016), This Is Your Brain on Communication. *Ted Talk*. Available at: https://www.youtube.com/watch?v=FDhlOovaGrI
- Silverman, Lori (2006), *Wake Me Up When the Data Is Over*. Doolan: John Wiley & Sons.
- Simmons, Annette (2001), *The Story Factor*. UK: Basic Books.

PART IV

Strategising, thinking, and decision-making

12

MASTERING THE POWER OF STRATEGISING

Josef Bruckschlögl

Abstract

As a business leader or entrepreneur, mastering the power of strategising should be your personal goal, since you are constantly striving to outperform your competitors and make positive impact on society. Your customers, employees, shareholders, and other stakeholders expect you to deliver great results. The most important key to your success is the bridge between your organisation and the outside world of customers, suppliers, distributors, and regulators – this bridge is called the strategy. The success of your organisation depends on how effective the strategy of your business is and how efficient is its execution. In this chapter, I have described how I have been on a journey to master the science and art of strategising to lead my business.

Keywords: Strategy, strategising, leadership, sustainable growth, commercial and social impact

Introduction

> *"Never let the future disturb you. You will meet it, if you have to, with the same weapons of reason which today arm you against the present."*
>
> Marcus Aurelius Antonius, Roman Emperor, 121–180 AD[1]

"Are you interested in building an e-commerce platform to sell our company's products and services?" the Chief Marketing Officer of my employer, the Austrian telecommunications company, asked me in the year 2000.

DOI: 10.4324/9781003219293-16

I had recently finished university education and lacked practical skills for this important assignment. However, I understood that if I succeeded in completing this project, it would have a major impact on the company and on my personal career.

E-Commerce was quite a new thing back then. Hardly anybody in Europe had sold telecommunication services online. It was the first time in my career that I was intensely exposed to the challenge of strategising in a commercial context without any example in the market to learn from.

The process of strategising in an organisation (called crafting strategy) is a complex discipline. There is no single definition of strategy and strategising. For the purpose of sharing with you my insights about strategising, I will say strategy is a bundle of choices that a leader and his or her team make in the short-, medium-, and long-term interests of the business, its stakeholders, and society at large. Correspondingly, I will define strategising as deliberate or emergent processes for making and implementing these choices.

The strategy provides a bridge between the external context and the organisation in order to achieve its goals. Strategising is the process of building this bridge. In my journey as a strategist, mastering the science and art of strategising is an ongoing process. I have to constantly learn to cope with new challenges. I always tell myself that one can never craft a perfect strategy for business no matter how smart one may be. As long as my organisation using fair and honest choices performs better than the competitors, then it is fine.

Why master the power of strategising?

It is necessary to put things in context, and as a leader, it is your responsibility to know and explain to employees and other stakeholders why you are doing what you are doing. It gives a sense of meaning and direction to all parties and invokes their commitment. It provides pathways to employees and business partners to mount their actions. In an organisation, you have many different departments, which often exist and act in "silos" resulting in weak alignment and poor performance. Therefore, it is necessary to provide an umbrella to all the departments to "break the walls" and come together to work as a well-oiled machine. Strategising process and strategy helps in this integration process.

A highly participative strategising process promotes dialogues and helps the organisation to respond to the emerging reality. It also creates "buy-in" and ownership which is necessary for execution of the strategy. Everybody feels involved and give their best ideas. During the execution phase, the employees in different departments provide valuable feedback to the leaders to take corrective actions in order to stay the course.[2]

I first came across the word "strategy" when I was studying for my master's programme in media economics and telecommunication at St Polten University in Austria. The lessons on how business leaders impact the present and future of their businesses by making strategy choices were very inspiring and thought provoking. They sowed the seeds of my role first as a business line manager, then as consultant and as chief executive officer in the telecom-services industry.

How did I master the process of strategising?

It started when I joined a course on strategy at the University. The strategy class was vibrant with intense discussions on real company case studies. In the course, I learnt many tools and techniques to analyse business situations. I gained confidence in making decisions as if I were running business organisations. As a business leader, I have been regularly attending industry conferences to learn what other business leaders are doing. I have been attending executive education programmes to learn new tools and techniques for strategising or to validate the strategising approaches that I use in running my business.

One of my preferred methods of learning is one-to-one conversations with CEOs of diverse companies. I have also been selectively reading about the professional journeys of several business leaders who have created enormous value for their stakeholders. The story of the success of Dietrich Mateschitz, the co-founder of Red Bull, is fascinating. Red Bull's headquarter is only a few kilometres from my hometown and the company and its leaders managed to establish a new product category of energy drinks in Europe and finally across the globe by adopting a product already available in Asia. Thanks to their innovative marketing approach focusing on extreme sports like mountain biking, surfing, or skateboarding – and sponsoring athletes in this segment – they managed to penetrate the market and build a globally recognised brand extremely efficiently and at a rather low cost.

In the last three years, besides running my organisation, KWAK Telecom Ltd., I have been teaching young graduates in universities in Austria. This is hugely beneficial: it allows me to be in touch with young people and to learn about their values, aspirations and indeed their preferences as consumers. Their curiosity challenges me to diversify my own knowledge of the strategy discipline.

On a daily basis, all the deep conversations that I have with our employees, business partners, and clients also serve to teach me very important insights for strategising.[3]

Strategising – my first lessons

The ten most important lessons about strategising in business that I learnt in university (1996–2000) and while attending the prestigious Oxford Advanced Management and Leadership Programme in 2014 are:

1. Strategising in an organisation is planning your actions in advance for today and tomorrow. The objective of these actions is it to outmanoeuvre and outperform your competitors.
2. Strategising involves a step-by-step analysis of the external and internal context of the organisation. This is followed by the determination of how we are going to compete and what markets we will serve to achieve our objective.
3. Strategising involves preparing a detailed strategic plan comprising time bound actions that everyone in the organisation should implement.
4. The strategic plan serves as the basis for setting up the tasks and key performance indicators for the departments and employees to guide their actions and measure their performance.
5. An important aspect of strategising is to determine how the performance of the organisation will be measured using a Balanced Scorecard framework.
6. Strategising involves making choices at many different levels in an organisation: for example, corporate-level strategy to seek synergies across multiple business units; business-unit-level strategy to highlight how a business is going to compete in the marketplace; functional-level strategies to highlight how different functions such as technology marketing, finance, human resources, and operations will be organised and orchestrate the implementation of the strategic plan.
7. Strategising starts with a deep understanding of the vision, mission, goals, and objectives of the business.
8. Strategising involves an understanding of five forces as identified by Professor Michael Porter.[4] These forces are how buyers, suppliers, competitors, and the threat of new entrants and of product substitution will influence and shape the competitive context.

9. Strategising involves deciding how the organisation will build and exploit its capabilities to outsmart its competitors.

10. Strategising can include disrupting the market to race ahead of competitors by launching innovative new products and services.

These lessons prepared me to master the science and art of strategising.

Am I a master strategist who never fails? No: I would never be able to claim this kind of reputation! While we are strategising, we are always playing with risks. The reality is that CEOs have to navigate through business environments which are constantly evolving and with increasing ambiguity and uncertainty. There are events that are beyond the control of organisations and that impact the organisation both positively and negatively, for example, the rapid shift in media consumption. TV and other classic media used to be the major driver in promoting our businesses, but, within a short period of time, internet, applications, and social media became the most relevant source for the payment services we offer.

As a business leader, I feel like a child playing with a Lego set trying to assemble my favourite dumper truck. The only problem is that there are some pieces that are missing and there are others, which are constantly changing their colours and shapes! How do I assemble the truck? Strategising in practice for me is like solving a jigsaw puzzle and that is what inspires me to spend hours with my team and stakeholders making strategies to steer the businesses.

Strategising – my world of practice

As CEO of a medium-sized company in telecom-based financial services, my team and I strategise and implement a range of decisions for achieving our business objectives and making a positive impact on the lives of our partners and users.

Simple as it may sound, it is not. Every day is a constant battle to cope with a rapidly changing business environment: that is when the priorities shift from planning for the future to achieving superior performance today and tomorrow. In my industry, the technology changes very fast, and there is high rate of product and service innovations. As a result, product and service life cycles are short, and consumer preferences continuously change.

To illustrate this constant technological change, think of your smartphone and the continuous improvement in its performance through added features like face recognition, augmented reality, or integrated payment functionalities. It is obvious that as a telecom company we have to adopt our strategy in quick succession to take advantage of changing technological opportunities and client expectations. So how do we strategise in a rapidly changing environment? We are in a race against time in grabbing opportunities.

As a deliberate choice, we keep the scope of our products and services narrow. We offer new features in our products and services to existing clients and also seek new customers. While pricing our products we have to cope with many competitors who offer many choices to buyers. So, we have to match the expectations of our clients to grab our share of the market.

When studying, I used to think that a good strategy based on detailed analysis would enable my team to control and dominate in the market. The reality it is very different. Both technology and consumers are highly unpredictable – while they create new opportunities for growth, they also exert extreme pressures on our thought processes and resources. So, we have to find a trade-off between trying to be extremely innovative versus quickly following the emerging demand trends.[5]

In the early phase of my career, I learnt a very important lesson – if you are too early with innovations in the market, there is no guarantee that you will succeed. However, if you are too late in the market then you are guaranteed to fail! I have experienced a lesson of being too early when I was E-Commerce director of Telekom Austria back in the year 2001. We had developed a 3D online shop where users had the possibility to explore our product and service offerings in a virtual reality environment. The problem was that back then the penetration of broadband internet was rather weak, and our futuristic e-shop demanded plenty of bandwidth to perform and a huge plug-in that had to be initially downloaded to be able to use the shop. As you might imagine, this initiative was not a success, and we took the shop offline a couple of weeks after launch. Timing is an essential aspect of strategy![6]

Organisational culture also plays a role. While we may not have deep control over the markets, we do enjoy latitude within our company to grow a strong culture which helps us to create and share value with our employees and partners. This is important for our success. Our employees, partners and customers remain loyal to our products and services. Working together with partners, we learn a lot and that helps in improving our response time – a measure of agility.

As an important aspect of our strategy, we nurture the competencies of individual managers and promote collaboration and teamwork for deep alignment. We train them in appropriate behaviours so that our business partners can connect and trust them.

We follow an organic growth strategy meaning growing around our core products, services, and markets. We do not pursue an abstract vision; our vision is realistic and evolves around our organisation's capabilities and the emerging needs of our existing and new customers. In terms of our values, our aim is to compete fairly by making ethical choices in order to build and protect the reputation of the company. We encourage our employees to treat all partners and clients with dignity and respect. These elements of strategy in our organisation are as important as product innovations.

An important cornerstone of our strategy is balancing commercial gains and the social impact of our organisation. We take pride when we see that our services are making positive impact on the lives of people by enhancing their livelihood and quality of life. In my current role as CEO of KWAK Telecom, I really enjoy seeing when our payment services based on a telecoms infrastructure enable the creation of new businesses and jobs in unbanked areas like parts of sub-Saharan Africa. Combining commercial success and social impact is not just a joyful experience. It is also a driver in creating an organisation's purpose and therefore the motivation of its team.

What lessons have I learnt as a strategist?

As I mentioned before, I learn new lessons every day. I would like to share some of the most important ones.

1. Strategy is a dynamic and not static choice, and therefore, I have to be in strategising mode continuously. A rigid plan does not work in fast-changing environments.
2. Strategy is highly dependent on external and internal influences and limitations, and I have to be realistic. In our business, we are in a highly competitive environment, and the fee structure of our payment service is easy to compare with those of our competitors. Therefore, the competitors' market prices are a massive influencer on our own market behaviour and our service strategy. Internal limitations such as cash availability, access to talent and the technological abilities of staff impact our strategy choices. As a leader I must take into account all the external influences and internal limitations or constraints to craft a realistic strategy.

3. While strategising, I have to make product and service and market choices and at the same time decide on actions that will help in building a strong culture and an agile organisation. Our agility helps us to seize emerging opportunities before it is too late. Approximately 18 months ago, we tested our agility by offering services outside our core business and markets. We launched applications for facilitating charity donations. Within one year, this new opportunity has become a vital line of business, and we were able to aggregate significant donations for institutions like the Austrian firefighters.

4. I am not always able to set a long-term vision as I learnt in the classroom. I focus on making correct choices in a series of steps on ongoing basis. This helps me to achieve sustainable growth in our business.

5. The execution of strategy is always a bumpy road and plans can go wrong without any pre warning. There could be many reasons for things going wrong and it hurts in a medium-sized business like ours. In 2019, we took the decision at KWAK Telecom to grow the company not only just organically but also by acquiring other companies in Asia. As we were making progress, I got the first indications of the coming COVID-19 pandemic from our staff in China. Soon the restrictions on travel, lock downs, and shaky markets followed and delayed the progress. This was inevitable, and we took a pragmatic view. We decided to pause, and as soon as the situation stabilises, we will pursue our new growth strategy.

6. I always remind myself and my leadership team that the timing of our actions is critical. An opportunity lost can never be regained.

7. My people, suppliers, partners, and clients are key elements of our success. It is a must for us to take care of them.

8. Finally, the strategising processes and strategy should be understood and adopted by all stakeholders. This helps in removing doubts in the minds of people and in execution.

Mastering the power of strategising – my suggestions

Based on my knowledge and experience, I will prescribe the following directions:

- **Build strong relationships!** Strategising is not a one-man act; it is essentially collective work. Learn to surround yourself with diverse sets of people and **listen** to them. This will broaden your perspective about what is happening around you and what is in the best interest of our organisation.

- **Encourage teamwork!** When we deal with strategy, it's never about a sprint but always a marathon. It's impossible for an individual leader to anticipate the opportunities and threats of complicated environments better than an informed team.
- **Develop your sensemaking and analytical and judgemental skills!** Strategising is complex, and you will need many different ways to comprehend the world and make choices.
- **Try to connect dots and generate patterns!** The picture of the world does not come ready made. Thousands of related and unrelated events are happening around you. You need to connect these and develop several coherent pictures of the world.
- **Learn to frame problems realistically and creatively!** Problem statements don't come readymade. You have to frame the problems so that you can develop comprehensive, creative, and relevant strategies and actions.
- **Learn to present your ideas to others in an authentic way!** Remember that people will cooperate and align towards a common direction and goal when you are respectful, transparent, and inspiring. They will trust you as a leader.[7]
- **Value the importance of speed and timing!** Markets are very dynamic because consumer preferences are constantly changing. Make sense of changing trends and respond quickly!
- **Learn to be a learner!** Learn from other strategists what they are doing and why. Read new ideas and concepts about strategy. Keep your curiosity alive all the time.
- **Deliver results!** Remember that what really counts is your organisation's ability to deliver better results than the competing firms. Your people, strategising skills, strategy, and organisation's capabilities will help you to achieve results.

Summary

Strategising is not an exact science. It is a dynamic process involving interplay of analytical skills, sensemaking, judgement, risk taking, timing, teamwork, and collaboration. Strategists have to constantly sense the changing world, make strategic choices, and implement these choices to serve the interests of customers, employees, shareholders, and other stakeholders. The leadership team has to create enabling culture and encourage teamwork. For sustained success, the leaders, employees, and organisation as a whole have to have a strong learning mentality. Mastering the strategising processes is a continuous journey and it never ends.

Follow-up actions

As a next step, review the strategising processes in your organisation by asking these questions:

1   What is your role in deciding the strategy of your business? Do you involve your customers, employees, and business partners in the strategising process? How deep is their involvement?
2   Do the strategising process and the strategy of business in your organisation provide clear direction and shared goals to your employees and business partners? Do they feel inspired? Are they committed to implement actions? Do they support each other and work as team?
3   Are you continuously processing emerging trends and performance data and information? Are you able to quickly respond to changes and adjust your business strategy?
4   What are some of the critical gaps in your strategising processes? What actions will you initiate to make the strategising process and strategy more effective?

Notes

1   Aurelius, M. (2001), *Meditations*, trans. M. Casaubon. USA: Project Gutenberg, eBook No. 2680, The Seventh Book, VI.
2   Dalio, R. (2017), *Principles*. Illustrated edition. USA: Simon & Schuster.
3   Senge, P.M. (2006), *The Fifth Discipline the Art & Practice of the Learning Organisation*. Revised and updated edition. USA: Doubleday.
4   Porter, M.E. (2008), The Five Competitive Forces That Shape Strategy. *Harvard Business Review*, 57(1), 57–71.
5   Grove, A.S. (1996), *Only the Paranoid Survive*. 1st edition. USA: Doubleday Business.
6   Christensen, C. (2016), *The Innovator's Dilemma: When New Technologies Cause Great Firms to Fail (Management of Innovation and Change)*. Reprint edition. USA: Harvard Business Review Press.
7   Eiler, T. and A. Austin (2016), *Aligned to Achieve*. USA: John Wiley & Sons.

Further reading

Chan Kim, W. and R. Mauborgne (2015), *Blue Ocean Strategy*. Expanded edition. USA: Harvard Business Review Press.

Von Clausewitz, C. (2008), *On War*. Abridged edition. UK: Oxford World Classics.

Kahneman, D. (2021), *Thinking Fast and Slow*. UK: Penguin.

Sun Tzu (2015), *The Art of War*. 2015 edition. USA: Chiron Academic Press.

Thaler, R.H. (2016), *Misbehaving: The Making of Behavioural Economics*. Reprint edition. UK: W.W. Norton & Company.

Thiel, P. (2015), *From Zero to One*. UK: Blake Masters, Virgin Books.

13

MASTERING THE POWER OF ANALYTICAL THINKING

Prasad Ramakrishnan

Abstract

In this chapter, I have shared my experiences, and those of others, in the use of analytical thinking. Learning from these, I have suggested a systematic way in which you can master the power of analytical thinking.

The basic steps include clearly defining an opportunity, engaging the right people who can support you, deep analysis of relevant data, developing and trying out potential solutions, and using the lessons learned to fully achieve the opportunity. I have included examples of how fast evolving technology solutions are increasing the speed of both data analysis and creation of new opportunities.

Analytical thinking today, with the profusion of tools such as digital analytics and artificial intelligence, is an expertise that is highly valued by employers across industries globally. I have suggested references that can provide examples, along with ideas for enhancing your skills in this area.

Keywords: Defining opportunity, digital analytics tools, artificial intelligence, learning by doing

Introduction

In early 2004, working with the Ford Motor Company, my family and I moved to the seaside city of Salvador, Brazil. We were excitedly looking forward to the experience of living in this vibrant South American culture – a first in our lives. Leading a team that was launching one of Ford's most

DOI: 10.4324/9781003219293-17

modern operations in the world was a dream come true. The first few months were exhilarating – a whirlwind of change, new experiences, and new relationships. One day at work, I was reflecting on the projects ahead, when a couple of key team members dropped into my office unannounced. They were very dejected and seemed hesitant to talk to me. Something told me that my honeymoon period was about to end.

After decades of successes and setbacks in the South American market, a group of seasoned Ford leaders had devised and implemented a radical project to turbo charge Ford's future in the Brazilian market. After intense, exhausting work over several years, they created in the arid shrublands of northeastern Brazil, a modern centre for the design, engineering, supply chain, and manufacturing of cars. After successfully launching the initial products, it was time to scale up operations to the facility's full potential. But the size and scope of what had to be accomplished over the next months seemed insurmountable – which is what a couple of my managers wanted, reluctantly, to discuss with me.

The power of analytical thinking

It was my responsibility to help this team to accomplish their goal. My prior work experiences had taught me the importance of clearly defining objectives and ensuring that the right people were on board. They had also underlined the importance of gathering relevant information and deeply understanding the patterns that data, and the behaviour of people, were indicating and piloting and testing solutions before heading into full implementation. But this was for me a new culture, in a new location with a team I was just beginning to understand. So, I started by first confirming my full confidence in the team, my commitment to immerse myself deeply to help the team succeed, and my desire to understand and learn from their experiences. I hoped that they saw me as more confident than I was feeling at that moment.

We gathered several key leaders together very early the next day and began by talking about how we ideally defined success, assuming no obstacles and full resources. We also considered obstacles, the steps needed to get there, and the skills and capabilities required. This generated questions we could not yet answer.

We agreed to gather the information required for further discussion. Everyone became quiet. Suddenly, after a few moments of total silence, the floodgate of frustrations broke open and the group started to candidly talk about their worries, the obstacles they could see and, the lack of sufficient resources. They expressed an overwhelming fear of committing to a project to be delivered with timing they saw as impossible.

It had already been a long and tiring day in the meeting. However, the tone of the dialogue changed for the better. The more experienced in the group shared how they had worked through difficult prior projects. The thinkers in the group started connecting relevant data to open questions. The team started to develop a plan of critical actions. They made a list of what could go wrong and what could be done to avoid it.

For example, we needed to hire many qualified personnel to add a third operations shift in the plant and launch a new vehicle. Could we find enough qualified people in the neighboring areas? How could we train new employees effectively on complex operations before the target deadline? The team listed each potential obstacle on an Excel spreadsheet and created a Project Management Plan of Action. They analysed specific data, such as the quantity and profile of potential employees in the region, to highlight those with the desired skills.

Based on this analysis, they made decisions, such as where to prioritise the employee search and how to attract and hire potential job seekers. They used a project management template to create a detailed plan for recruiting and training employees. This was only one example – there were many more issues the team had to resolve. The way in which they used information for each issue was increasing their confidence in finding a smart way forward. The sun had set and the group was exhausted. But they were also energised at having a tangible plan of action on paper.

In the months ahead, we implemented the actions. In some cases, a solution that looked good on paper failed when implemented. The new data were analysed to identify the reasons for the failure and what should be done differently. This learning was used to modify the initial plan and adopt a revised plan. This process was repeated – guided by the data from each repetition. Eventually, after months of continued efforts, the project was successful. In retrospect, one of the contributing factors in our success was the analytical thinking approach, which I would summarise as:

- Clearly **define the objectives** of the project;
- **Engage the people** with required competencies and expertise;
- **Identify, collect, and analyse** the relevant data;
- Based on detailed analyses, **map a plan of action**;
- **Test the plan** and analyse the outcomes;
- **Adjust the plan** based on the lessons learned;

- Continue to **repeat this process** until successful project closure;
- Learn from each experience and **refine the approach**.

I will conclude with the wise words of Carl Sagan: *"Knowing a great deal is not the same as being smart; intelligence is not information alone but also judgment, the manner in which information is collected and used" (Carl Sagan [1934–1996], an American astronomer, planetary scientist, author, and science communicator).*[1]

Digital enablers enhance analytical thinking

Are there tools for enhancing the analytical thinking skills of individuals and teams? For example, various sensors fitted in your automobile engine continuously collect and process data to monitor the performance of the engine. The performance data in the hands of the service engineer in the garage are very useful for diagnosing problems. It saves time and costs.

These days, we are using applications based on Artificial Intelligence (AI) to analyse large amounts of data, determine patterns, and use this information to perform intelligent tasks. For example, when you use an internet service to reserve a flight ticket or a hotel room, the information you provide is automatically analysed and compared with all available options (processing a huge amount of data almost instantaneously), pick the ones closest to your requirement (software analytical thinking), and enable you to confirm and pay for it (safe transfer of credit card and other confidential information) using other connected applications.

At the organisation level, the speed and scope of technology developments in Data Analytics and AI have provided more ways to rapidly extract solutions from data patterns in fields such as medicine and finance. The German biotech company Evotec, partnering with the AI design platform of UK-based company Exscientia, was able to reduce drug discovery time from 4–5 years to 8 months.[2] They did this by using analytics to sort through properties of millions of small molecules to identity the 10 or 20, and finally the best drug candidate for clinical trials.

The Royal Bank of Canada "built a private AI cloud for enhancing banking services".[3] Such smart AI applications have enabled faster delivery of new solutions such as digital assistant-based customer service and faster fraud detection.

A study by American Management Association and i4CP in 2013 found that

> organizations with fully developed analytics skills – the ability to organize, analyse, and communicate data that can be applied to their human

capital and not just to the other elements of their businesses – will continue to be the top performers in the years to come.[4]

This is great news for those who are looking to change jobs or start a new career.

Integrating digital tools and analytical thinking

I am currently the Chief Operating Officer of Motiv Power Systems, a Silicon Valley Electric Vehicle leader in the medium-duty commercial truck business, headquartered near San Francisco, California. While preparing this chapter, I asked Jim Castelaz, our Founder and Chief Technology Officer, how he had combined digital tools and analytical thinking to start a company. He defines analytical thinking as arriving at learning and decisions by identifying patterns in complex information. Jim created Motiv to "Free Fleets from Fossil Fuel" when he saw the emergence of electric vehicles (EVs) during 2006–2009.

Two major hurdles in the migration from fossil fuel-based fleets to EVs were range anxiety and suitable charge infrastructure. These are, respectively, the drivers' fear of running out of energy and being stranded on the road before going the full distance to reach their destination; and the availability of equipment that provides electrical energy to charge an electric vehicle. Local people- and goods-moving vehicles have planned routes and depots where they were kept each night. Jim figured out how these vehicles could overcome the hurdle of range anxiety and charge infrastructure. He saw the shift in complexity from the mechanical to the software domain that comes with going electric. He aligned others around a vision and company that would be a software-first approach to electric trucks in an industry where software was usually an afterthought.

Jim said, "*the real challenge of starting a company involves contrarian analytical thinking – seeing the patterns others don't always see and then aligning others to your vision*".

Analytical thinking for social impact

In her book, *The Intergalactic Design Guide*, Cheryl Heller outlines an analytical process of harnessing the creative potential of Social Design, which she defines as:

> *It's the creation of new social conditions intended to increase human agency, creativity, equity, resilience, and our connection to nature. It is essentially the same process used to develop innovative products and services but applied at a larger scale.*

She provides numerous examples of social design, such as Spring Health, which offers safe affordable drinking water to over 150,000 poor people in 250 villages in rural India.[5]

Explore:

Steps of the social design process

    Heller, C. *"The Intergalactic Design Guide – Harnessing the Creative Potential of Social Design"*. Island Press (2018). Chapter 4, Pages 50–67.[6]

From the various examples described, we can define analytical thinking as the ability to identify and extract key information patterns from data, and systematically use deep analysis, judgement, and intelligence to develop potential solutions for an opportunity or problem.

NASA's success in creating a mini helicopter to fly on Mars[7,8]

On April 19, 2021, the National Aeronautics and Space Administration (NASA) successfully flew a mini helicopter, Ingenuity, on Mars. This was the first powered controlled flight to be achieved on another world. After reviewing publicly available reference material, here is how I would summarise the analytical thinking approach in this project.

1. **Define the objective and boundaries**. Ingenuity is a technology demonstration to prove controlled powered aerial flight, for the first time, on a planet besides earth. Once proven, this would greatly increase the range of exploration on other planets beyond ground-based vehicles such as the Perseverance Rover on Mars. Some examples of boundaries of this objective include:

    a. Ingenuity is designed to fly only very short distances and heights after reaching Mars.

    b. Ingenuity will not fly between planets such as from Earth to Mars. Its interstellar transportation will need to be through other means – such as being attached to the Perseverance Rover.

2. **Build upon relevant prior work done by others.** The Ingenuity team took advantage of prior research work developed by others.

For example, a theoretical proof related to flying on Mars[9],[10] enabled a practical starting place for conceiving this project and provided encouragement and reasons to believe that the objective was achievable.

3. **Identify challenges and opportunities.** Successfully achieving this objective creates the opportunity for developing further advanced flying vehicles to support future robotic and human missions to Mars. However, some challenges for Ingenuity to overcome on Mars include:

    a. Operating autonomously given the 3- to 22-minute time lag in transmission of robotic commands over hundreds of millions of miles from Earth to Mars;

    b. Performing under very different conditions from Earth such as one-third lower gravity and very low atmospheric density 1% of that on Earth;

    c. Little prior information on the impact of these differences on flight dynamics on Mars;

    d. Surviving extremely cold night temperatures;

    e. The impossibility of fully replicating the conditions for testing on Earth;

    f. Ingenuity must work the very first time in the Martian environment.

4. **Collaborate with organisations and key people who can help you.** The Ingenuity team collaborated with many organisations to successfully develop and execute the mission. Some examples:

    a. Jet Propulsion Lab in Pasadena California (JPL) built the Ingenuity helicopter and managed the mission;

    b. Several NASA departments (e.g. NASA Ames Research Center) provided flight performance analysis and technical assistance;

    c. The separate Perseverance Rover project provided safe transportation for the mini helicopter from Earth to Mars.

5. **Complete design of the concept and parts.** JPL and AeroVironment developed and published a conceptual design for a scout helicopter to accompany a rover. The project required the design, development, and fabrication of the rotor system, the landing gear system, and all other structures integrated into the helicopter.[11] Taking into consideration the challenges, such as those stated earlier, the team used tough and radiation resistant, off-the-shelf consumer and commercial hardware, Linux-based software, and light components and large hi-speed

rotor blades for the rarefied Mars atmosphere. This was done with help from several organisations such as:

    a.   AeroVironment Inc., Qualcomm, and SolAero provided design assistance and major vehicle components;

    b.   Lockheed Martin Space designed and manufactured the Mars Helicopter Delivery system.

6.   **Through prototyping and simulations, formulate initial solutions** that could be tried as a potential way to develop an optimal solution (the best possible for a given set of boundary constraints) instead of a perfect solution (e.g. the ideal solution for all possible conditions). Examples include:

    a.   Full-scale prototype flown in a simulated Mars atmosphere in a JPL environment chamber.[12] The conditions on Mars were used as the criterion for setting up the simulated prototype testing. The results of these were in turn criteria for selecting an optimal solution.

    b.   Testing of individual sub-systems. For example, Qualcomm first completed extensive hardware testing of their Snapdragon 801 processor, which subsequently passed JPL's Martian simulation tests.

    c.   These actions helped the team to create the Ingenuity helicopter that subsequently flew on Mars.

7.   **Select relevant data to be collected and analysed.** The Ingenuity team developed specific requirements and performed tests under simulated conditions. They analysed the data, with the help of digital analytical tools, to ensure that each subsystem and the overall mini helicopter would work. For example, the low density of the Martian atmosphere reduced the lifting force and efficiency of the helicopter rotor. After sufficient data analysis, a model was created for effective performance operation of the rotor.

8.   **Implement proof of concept (final optimal solution).** The optimal solution, of the actual Ingenuity helicopter having to work the first time it arrived on Mars, was the proof of concept of this technology demonstration. Having more flights in addition to the initial objectives provided further learnings for an improved future solution. The team had to successfully achieve several specific objectives to arrive at the specific mission of initial flights, and then go beyond. For example:

a. Ingenuity, as a passenger on the Perseverance Rover, travelled from Earth and landed safely on Mars;
b. Ingenuity separated from the Rover and became an independent object on the surface;
c. It was able to autonomously stay warm in the intensely cold Martian nights;
d. It autonomously charged itself with its solar panel;
e. Ingenuity communicated with the Rover – and Earth;
f. It performed three flights within 30 Mars days for up to 90 seconds to distances of 980 feet, and an altitude of up to 15 feet.

Successfully achieving these objectives enabled Ingenuity, from April to September 2021, to go beyond the initial charter by completing 13 flights with a maximum duration of 169.5 seconds, distance of ~2051 feet and altitude of ~39 feet.[13] This was an iterative process with relevant data being collected and analysed after each flight.[14]

The analytical thinking that ensured thorough planning for all contingencies, while leaving room for last minute creativity after the first three flights, enabled the team to successfully exceed all mission expectations.

NASA's Ingenuity is a good example of analytical thinking across teams from different organisations to solve complex challenges and navigate through "never done before" opportunities.

Emotions and cognitive biases in analytical thinking

Luca Sambucci is Head of Artificial Intelligence at SNGLR Group and has been a cybersecurity expert for more than 30 years. At first glance, these appear to be very cerebral topics with no apparent role for emotions. I asked him how he balanced feelings with analytical thinking. Luca considers analytical thinking as the ability of breaking down a thought process, a situation, or a decision in all its constituent parts. This includes the most elusive ones like emotions, mental states, cognitive biases, habits; all parts accounted for, figuratively laid down on a table, properly identified, measured, and with all their dependencies and interactions evident.

When he needs to think analytically about a situation or a decision, he imagines himself as a scientist writing down in a notebook what he does and feels. His intimate knowledge of himself allows an understanding of what he's thinking and feeling, while this estrangement role play allows him to observe his emotions without being judgemental about them. This enables him to recognise biases, inconsistencies, logical fallacies, just as a scientist would see them and scribble them in a notebook.

Luca said,

> and layer after layer I remove feelings, biases, uncertainties, habits, memories, fantasies, fears, till I lay down in front of me all the peels of that onion that was once my problem, my decision, my situation, in all its factuality as well as its emotional baggage.

Luca credits analytical thinking for helping him know himself better, recognising his weaknesses, discovering new strengths, identifying his emotions, and continuously nudging him to become a better version of himself.

Learning from failures in analytical thinking

Jérôme Zürcher is Founder of LastingImpact.AI. After a career building analytics functions at large corporations, he now helps traditional small and medium enterprises (SMEs) to use Artificial Intelligence in their business.

He told me that he considers analytical thinking like applying the scientific method to problem-solving. When Jérôme started pitching his AI Transformation services to individual SME executive managers, the initial response was enthusiastic: most grasped the significant value potential of deploying AI across their business. However, the early excitement soon fizzled out as the executives' attention got diverted to putting out fires in their businesses and addressing other operational priorities. Jérôme was not getting enough paid engagements to sustain his business.

After researching possible reasons for this, he constructed the hypothesis that there wasn't enough leadership alignment at the executive management level around AI adoption. He started talking directly to SME investors and found that some, the Private Equity (PE) funds, willing to commit to turning traditional companies into data-driven businesses from the top down.

Jérôme said,

> my pitch-to-engagement conversion rate went from near-zero when talking to SMEs, to above 50% with PE funds. I ended up delivering the exact service I had envisioned from the start, supporting the AI Transformation of SMEs, but was only able to do so after figuring out that I needed to talk to their Private Equity owners.

Jérôme's most important learning was the realisation that it was not easy to succeed in this transition until he analysed and learned from early failures.

The power of analytical thinking lies in its simplicity

During our conversation, Dietmar Roettger said, *"for me, the power of analytical thinking lies in its simplicity and broad applicability. Be it in complex job environments or at home"*.

In addition to a distinguished global career in the energy industry, Dietmar teaches Innovation and Change Management to technology students at the Swiss Federal Institute of Technology (ETH) in Zurich. He is also an active mentor and start-up advisor. He defines analytical thinking as the ability to break down complexity into manageable items and leveraging data to enable sharp focus, as the foundation to create meaningful actions and/or decisions.

Dietmar was asked to lead a global quality transformation for a high-tech company to dramatically strengthen customer experiences and improve the company's balance sheet. He questioned leaders, peers, and teams about where to improve, why change was needed, what would be the impact, and how they could succeed in implementing the change. This enabled the creation of an aligned approach across the organisation. Most importantly, it provided data to answer the aforementioned questions, and after detailed analysis, select ten focus areas. The complex task was broken down into meaningful and manageable actions, which were subsequently accomplished.

Mastering the power of analytical thinking

Before I sum up, I would like to share some simple and practical approaches to master the power of analytical thinking.

- Participate in problem-solving discussions with peers – this could be at work, in your community or an organisation in which you may decide to be a volunteer;
- Read business case studies and analyse what you could have done differently to resolve issues highlighted in the case studies;
- Participate in competitions. For example, to develop a business plan for a new product concept;
- Read about, and take learnings from, how inventors worked to create new products, ideas, or services;

- Use various procedures and tools at your work. Learn tools such as mind mapping to broaden your ability to see patterns;
- Use reverse mentoring to learn from people who may be junior to you in experience but have deep skills in a specific area. For example, people with strong analytical skills in designing digital technology-based products or services;
- Refine your analytical thinking skills by seeking feedback or by subjecting yourself to questioning by design experts. Suppose you have built a prototype of a low-cost bicycle. Ask a design expert to cross-examine you about the safety and comfort features of the prototype. Collect all the feedback given by the expert and modify your design. Repeat this process until you reach an optimal design with better safety and comfort.

Develop a low-cost bicycle

Use the analytical approach to design and test a low-cost and "safe-to-ride" bicycle. The code name of this bicycle is "FunX".

- Identify the potential users of FunX.
- Collect information about the preferences of the users of FunX.
- Analyse the information and map preference patterns of the users of FunX.
- List the design features of FunX to satisfy the users' preferences.
- Based on the design features, build and test a prototype of FunX.
- Use test data to improve the design of FunX.
- Reflect on your analytical approach for designing and testing FunX. What lessons did you learn?

Summary

Analytical thinking is a valuable and teachable skill that has become even more powerful and applicable with the creation of digital tools supported by rapid technology transformations. This is a skill set that enables unprecedented disruption and creation of new products and services. It is highly valued by organisations today. Many opportunities are available to self-teach oneself the skills required. Be bold and pick an interesting problem to solve. Do it and learn by doing. Good luck!

Notes

1 Sagan, C. (1980), *Cosmos*. USA: Penguin Random House LLC.
2 Savage, N. (2021), *Tapping into the Drug Discovery Potential of AI*. Biopharma Dealmakers – a Nature Research Publication, May 27. Available at: https://www.nature.com/articles/d43747-021-00045-7
3 Levitt, Kevin (2021), *How AI Is Powering the Future of Financial Services*. July 16. Available at: https://www.finextra.com/the-long-read/231/how-ai-is-powering-the-future-of-financial-services
4 American Management Association, January 24, 2019. Available at: https://www.amanet.org/articles/companies-see-need-to-build-analytical-skills-in-their-organizations-a/
5 Heller, C. (2018), *The Intergalactic Design Guide – Harnessing the Creative Potential of Social Design*. USA: Island Press, Chapter 10, pp. 147–165.
6 Ibid., Chapter 4, pp. 50–67.
7 Ackerman, E. (2021), How NASA Designed a Helicopter That Could Fly Autonomously on Mars. *IEEE Spectrum*, February 17. Available at: https://spectrum.ieee.org/nasa-designed-perseverance-helicopter-rover-fly-autonomously-mars
8 Klotz, I. (2020), NASA's Ingenuity – the First Ever Off-world Helicopter – Is Set for a "Wright Brothers Moment" on Mars. *Scientific American*, July 27. Available at: https://www.scientificamerican.com/article/nasas-ingenuity-the-first-ever-off-world-helicopter-is-set-for-a-wright-brothers-moment-on-mars/
9 Balaram, J. and P.T. Tokumaru (2014), *Rotorcrafts for Mars Exploration*. 11th International Planetary Probe Workshop, Pasadena, CA. LPI Contribution No. 1795, id.8087. June 16–20. 2014LPICo1795.8087B.
10 Koning, W.J.F., W. Johnson and B.G. Allan (2018), *Generation of Mars Helicopter Rotor Model for Comprehensive Analyses*. NASA. Available at: https://web.archive.org/web/20200101170950/https://rotorcraft.arc.nasa.gov/Publications/files/Koning_2018_TechMx.pdf
11 Pipenberg, B.T., M. Keennon, J. Tyler, B. Hibbs, S. Langberg, J. Balaram, H.F. Grip and J. Pempejian (2019), *Design and Fabrication of the Mars Helicopter Rotor, Airframe, and Landing Gear Systems*. American Institute of Aeronautics and Astronautics (AIAA), SciTech Forum Conference, January 7–11, San Diego, CA.
12 Balaram, J., T. Canham, C. Duncan, M. Golombek, H.F. Grip, W. Johnson, J. Maki, A. Quon, R. Stern and D. Zhu (2018), *Mars Helicopter Technology Demonstrator*. American Institute of Aeronautics and Astronautics (AIAA) SciTech Forum Conference, January 8–12, Kissimmee, FL.
13 NASA Mars Exploration Program Website (2021), *NASA's Ingenuity Helicopter to Begin New Demonstration Phase*. April 30. Available at: https://mars.nasa.gov/news/8936/nasas-ingenuity-helicopter-to-begin-new-demonstration-phase/
14 NASA Mars Exploration Program Website (2021), *NASA's Helicopter Tech Demo Flight Log*. September. Available at: https://mars.nasa.gov/technology/helicopter/#Flight-Log

Further reading

Agile Lean Life. *How to Improve Your Analytical Skills to Make Smarter Life Decisions*. Available at: https://agileleanlife.com/analytical-skills/
Cote, C. (2021), *4 Ways to Increase Your Analytical Skills*. 7 January. Available at: https://online.hbs.edu/blog/post/how-to-improve-analytical-skills
Jordan, J. and M. Sorell (2019), Why Reverse Mentoring Works and How to Do It Right. *Harvard Business Review*, October 3. Available at: https://hbr.org/2019/10/why-reverse-mentoring-works-and-how-to-do-it-right
MindMapping.com. *How to Make a Mind Map*. Available at: https://www.mindmapping.com/
TalentBridge (2017), *7 Steps to Improve Your Analytical Thinking Skills*. October 19. Available at: https://talentbridge.com/blog/7-steps-to-improve-your-analytical-thinking-skills/

14

MASTERING THE POWER OF CREATIVE THINKING

Anshul Sonak

Abstract

Creative thinking is one of the human skills through which we visualise new perspectives, adopt new ways to solve problems, and design innovative solutions. Creative thinking facilitates new pathways for progress and prosperity of humankind.

In this chapter, I will discuss my experiences in promoting creative thinking and nurturing creative thinking skills of young people. We partner with government agencies and educational institutions to deliver technology and creative thinking skill programmes in countries around the world.

In recent years, scores of young people are using digital technologies including artificial intelligence for developing creative solutions for solving day-to-day problems faced by communities.

Creative thinking skills can be learnt by anyone. Based on my experience and research evidence, I will discuss practical ways to master the power of creative thinking.

Keywords: Curiosity, creativity, experimenting, learning

Introduction

Albert Einstein's famous equation $E = mc^2$ (energy equals mass times the speed of light squared) is a great example of creative thinking in science. In 1905, he became the first scientist to propose the equivalence of energy and

DOI: 10.4324/9781003219293-18

mass. The equation is at work in every aspect of our life. For example, when a small mass of coal burns in a steam engine, it creates energy, which moves the railcars.

My other favourite example of creative thinking is the double-helix structure of DNA proposed by Francis Crick and James Watson in 1953. They were the first scientists to visualise the double-helix structure of DNA. Their pathbreaking discovery has since then contributed to our understanding of the importance of DNA to life and health.

In these examples, the scientific data were already there, and it was the creative thinking skills of these scientists, which enabled them to make these discoveries. They visualised patterns and relationships, which no other scientist before them had seen.

In common parlance, we describe creative thinking using different terms and expressions, for example, *thinking out of the box, connecting the dots, proposing a new interpretation, or developing an innovative solution*. In each of these expressions, the underlying meaning is that the thought or the innovative solution is original and has not been proposed by anyone before.

For defining creative thinking, I don't believe that there are any rules as long as our thoughts are fresh and pathbreaking. The meaning of creative thinking depends on the purpose of the thinker and the context of thinking. I define creative thinking as a mechanism to develop new solutions for improving peoples' quality of life.

Creative thinking is an essential skill

Creative thinking skills are essential to your success in your job and life. They give you and your organisation an edge to develop innovative products and services to stay ahead of competitors.

In its Future of Jobs Report 2020, the World Economic Forum has identified critical thinking and analysis, creativity, and originality amongst the top ten skills.[1] Creative thinking is increasingly playing a critical role in our life and work. It enables us to adapt to changes taking place in our context. Creative thinking can help in enhancing resilience to cope with new challenges that we face in our jobs and careers. In organisations, creative thinking skills of employees play a significant role in developing innovative products and services. Innovation is a key to winning in markets by staying ahead of competitors.

The global landscape of competition in business is a brutal place. Many companies, for example, Kodak, Nokia, and Blackberry lost their leading positions to competitors. These competitors outsmarted these companies by taking advantage of innovative digital technologies and products.

As the competition heats up, the life span of business organisations has been shrinking. With disruptive innovations adding fuel to fire in the marketplace, it is imperative for organisations to embark on fast innovation tracks by building a culture of creative thinking.

The days of steady and lifelong jobs and career are also coming to an end. *The average number of jobs in the lifetime of an individual was 12.4, according to a longitudinal survey by the Bureau of Labour Statistics, USA.*[2] That means, we need to continuously learn, unlearn, and relearn new skills to remain employable or relevant in a dynamic job market. With the introduction of digital solutions, many traditional jobs like that of a librarian and accountant are changing or disappearing. We need to continuously upgrade our skills. Sharpening creative thinking skills will help us in improving our chances for coping with change in our workplaces, careers, and jobs.

Creative thinking and technology

My work at Intel involves building awareness about the potential of digital technologies amongst students, educators, and policymakers with the aim of bringing positive change in the society. We inspire them to adopt new technologies to develop creative solutions for helping people and communities.

We design and implement digital readiness programmes for people, regardless of their location, gender, ethnicity, and technology knowledge or access.[23] The purpose of these digital readiness programmes is to prepare people for the digital economy. We aim to educate them to master these technologies, enhance their trust in new technologies, and help them to identify new opportunities for responsible use of emerging technologies such as artificial intelligence (AI).

As part of our digital readiness programmes, I lead technology education and skilling programmes for the younger generation. These programmes are implemented under the umbrella of local governments, universities, colleges, and schools in several countries around the world. To ensure the success of these programmes, we need to understand what people need from technology and how they will benefit by using it.

I recently met a group of high school students from India, who had attended our programme on Artificial Intelligence (AI) skills. Inspired by their learning experience, these students built an AI-based solution to democratise citizens' grievance redressal processes. I was not surprised when they told me that in their community if the water supply is disrupted, they didn't know where and how to lodge a complaint and follow-up for getting the water supply restored.

Following a creative thinking roadmap, these young innovators built an AI-based handwriting scanner as a complaint-registering tool in multiple languages. It empowered members of the community to register complaints and follow-up with the appropriate local government agency whenever there was disruption of water or electricity supply or sewage disposal.

This is a great innovation by young students! They used their newly learnt AI skills to build a solution that helped to improve the quality of life of the people in the community. The successful demonstration of the AI-based tool for registering complaints with the government agencies convinced everyone in the community that digital technologies can be trusted and have the potential to improve quality of life.

From the innovative solutions developed by students who have participated in our digital readiness programmes, we have ourselves learnt many valuable lessons:

- To demystify and democratise the applications of emerging technologies such as AI, we need to encourage people to solve problems they face in their daily life.
- Young students are naturally conversant with problems that their communities face. They are impatient to solve these problems to improve the quality of life.
- Young students are excited when they learn the potential of new technologies in solving their problems. They feel encouraged to think creatively.
- Whenever a technology assists in resolving daily problems, communities begin to trust the technology and the government agencies responsible for providing essential public services.

We used these lessons to redesign our AI-skilling programmes to encourage young students to solve real-world problems creatively. For example, we launched "Impact Festivals" to encourage students to showcase their problem-solving skills and real-world innovations. These programmes are now adopted by many countries where we provide technology-skilling capabilities and opportunities in partnerships with local governments and academic institutions (see note 3 above).[3]

To master the power of creative thinking and technology, it is useful to be aware of the creative thinking process. My suggestions to aspiring innovators are as follows:

- Be sensitive to the problems your community is facing.
- Choose a critical problem and inspire your team to solve it.
- Talk to various parties who are part of the problem and identify possible causes of the problem.
- Brainstorm and generate creative ways to address and eliminate the causes of the problem.
- Talk to your teachers and experts and learn how digital technologies can assist in implementing your creative ideas to eliminate the causes of the problem.
- Simulate and test the feasibility of your ideas by including all parties involved.
- Use a set of criteria to select an optimal solution.
- Implement the optimal solution by involving all parties.
- Gather feedback, learn, and continuously improve the solution.

By following this or a similar process of creative thinking and application of digital technologies, anyone can solve real-world problems and bring happiness to people.

Buying cabbage when the price is low

In South Korea, I talked to the students in a high school who wanted to build an application to predict the prices of cabbage, which is vital for making kimchi, a staple food in Korean cuisine. Knowing the prices in advance can help them in managing their daily home budget, because they will buy cabbage when the prices are lower.

For the students with limited or no experience in data analytics and cabbage cultivation, this was an ambitious project. Designing this application was not straightforward.

During the design-thinking workshop, we discovered that the students needed continuous support from their teachers; and they needed access to open data for cabbage cultivation like rain records, past pricing patterns, soil, and temperature records. While the students were trained in data analysis skills, their teachers were not.

We quickly built a separate training programme for teachers so that they could coach the students. We encouraged the local community to help the students and got officials to provide open data for the last few years on rain, temperature, price pattern, etc.

With the support of the teachers, the students built a data-based model for predicting cabbage prices that helped their parents and communities to plan the buying by avoiding days when prices go up. And the school provided access to the wider community by hosting the model on the school website.

This indeed was a brilliant piece of creative thinking by young students.

Automated clothesline

In an Indonesian island, I spoke with two sisters who, after attending our digital-skilling programme, created a clothesline. It was no ordinary clothesline – it would automatically stretch outdoors when the sun was shining and would spring back indoors when it was raining. The sisters invented this automated clothesline by using a combination of simple sensors to detect rain, the mobile phone, AI-based software, a set of pulleys, and a small electric motor.

I wondered what inspired the sisters to develop this creative solution? They told me that they wanted to help their mother who would wash clothes and hang these outdoors before going to work. The tropical weather on the island made it extremely difficult to predict when it would rain. Whenever it rained, it ruined the washed clothes and their mother's hard work would go to waste. On learning about the basics of the Internet of Things technology and sensors, the sisters were ready to apply their knowledge and solve the problem their mother had faced all these years.

This is another great example of creative thinking triggered by feelings of empathy for mothers and a sense of responsibility to help them.

Inspiring lessons

In the last two decades, I have met hundreds of young people who have designed and developed creative solutions by successfully combining their creative thinking skills and knowledge of digital technologies. Their stories have taught me many lessons. The important ones are as follows:

- *Young people have strong instincts to think creatively and build innovative solutions.* They have curiosity, dreams, and new ideas.
- *Young people are sensitive to problems in their communities.* They are impatient to solve these problems. They care about quality of life in their communities.

- *Young people are quick learners.* They have an open mind and welcome and trust new technologies. They are very quick to appreciate how technology can help in solving problems faced by people.
- *Technology is a great enabler in the hands of young people.* It can help them to analyse complex data. It can give them reach and access to agencies for help. It can help young people to realise the fruits of their creative thinking in solving real-life problems.

These lessons are important and give me hope. I was born and brought up in a remote village in Central India. In the village, we did not have clean running water. The electricity supply was erratic. The social services in the region were appalling. We suffered from all kinds of inequalities. I am happy that the journey for social change has picked up pace with the help of new technologies. It gives hope to billions of people!

Creative thinkers

A question that has intrigued me is – are there special characteristics or habits of creative thinkers? Since my schooldays, I have read books about people who have made scientific discoveries. In my work life, I have met many innovators, and I have noticed that these creative thinkers follow routines, which anybody can learn.

Creative thinkers are curious people. When they observe an event or phenomenon, they want to know why it happens the way it does. Legend has it; when Sir Issac Newton saw the apple falling from the tree, he wanted to know why the apple always falls towards earth. His assertion that a force is pulling the apple downwards laid the foundations of the concept of gravitational pull.

Creative thinkers are not constrained by orthodox views. They use imagination to conceive new perspectives. Albert Einstein proposed the interchangeability of mass and energy – a completely radical idea at that time.

Creative thinkers liberate their thinking from known constraints – they step outside the box to design new ideas to overcome the constraints. Two recent examples come to my mind. The first is the development and extremely successful demonstration flights of the rotorcraft Ingenuity in the rarefied atmosphere of Mars by NASA scientists and engineers. Another example is the successful development of vaccine to limit the transmission of the COVID-19 virus. The teams of scientists and virologists at Oxford University, for instance, developed the vaccine in less than one year compared to the several years it had taken to develop a vaccine in the past. In these examples, the teams defied conventional thinking and overcame known constraints.

Many creative thinkers spend enormous time to gain deep insights in a discipline to advance the frontiers of knowledge and develop new products. They have a strong dedication to solving problems faced by humanity. A recent example is the successful development of the malaria vaccine. It took several years of sustained scientific research by thousands of experts and scientists to understand the complex nature of the disease. In the end, their persistence paid off and they have successfully developed a vaccine to fight the scourge of malaria.

In the business world, there are many pioneers, who are famous for introducing breakthrough products and services. Walt Disney pioneered animated cartoon films. The Japanese engineer, Taiichi Ohno, developed the lean manufacturing philosophy behind the Toyota Production System. Elon Musk founded SpaceX, which has transformed the aerospace industry by successfully developing reusable rockets.[4]

These pioneers and inventors are simply dissatisfied with the status quo. They question the underlying assumptions that encourage the status quo. They have a strong urge to improve the existing ways of doing things.

Accepting serial failures is another interesting characteristic of innovators. They regard every failure as a learning opportunity.

Creative thinking in organisations

Francesca Gino (2018)[5] advocates promoting a culture of asking questions in organisations. She argues that curiosity increases creativity and innovation in organisations. Creativity is the bedrock of organisational strategy. It enables organisations to design and launch innovative products and services to gain advantage over their competitors.[6]

Encouraging creative thinking and innovation in organisations

Earlier I mentioned that innovation is the key to success of an organisation in a hypercompetitive environment. The big question is how organisations can create culture that encourages creative thinking and innovation. It is challenging, because organisations are always in a state of momentum, and it is not easy to steer them away from their well-trodden tracks. Innovative solutions are associated with a perceived risk of market failure. The leaders and their organisations need to orchestrate change towards culture of innovation. Based on my conversations with Professor Lalit Johri, co-editor of this book, and other colleagues, I have identified a menu of actions for creating the culture of creative thinking and innovations.

1. **Be a champion innovator in the industry**. This is a powerful vision and a commitment. It inspires everyone in the organisation and invokes a culture of innovation. It serves to inform how our organisation is competing and maintaining its leadership in the sector. ZARA is amongst the world's largest retailer of clothing brands. One of the reasons for its astounding success is the high frequency of introducing latest high-quality and trendy clothing lines at affordable price. Zara has redefined the notion of creativity and innovation in a sector where leading brands use to take months to launch collection. Zara does it in weeks!

2. **Organise for promoting innovation**. Creative thinking and innovation require a degree of professional and administrative freedom. An established bureaucratic structure in an organisation can stifle creative thinking. To encourage innovation, many organisations use dedicated structures. For example, Samsung has concentrated its R&D capabilities for innovation in Global R&D Centres and AI-dedicated Centres as part of a global R&D network. The Samsung Design Innovation Centre in San Francisco oversees the end-to-end process of product design and development. Nestlé has built a network of independent R&D centres in several countries around the world to develop innovative products for people and pets. NASA uses dedicated project organisation for specific missions – recent examples are the Mars 2020 Perseverance Rover project and the earlier Mars Helicopter Ingenuity project.

3. **Involve potential customers and experts in product–service innovation processes.** In the event of a failure, many innovation projects involve financial and reputation risks. Early engagement of customers and experts helps in collecting valuable feedback and do mid-course correction before it is too late.

4. **Collaborate with other organisations.** This can include, if advantageous, your competitors who have complementary assets and competencies to develop innovative products. For instance, in the late 1970s, two competitors Philips and Sony came together to develop the compact disc jointly. Such collaborations not only resolve technical challenges in the development process but also reduce time to market the innovation. In the automobile sector, leading manufacturers of vehicles

fallback on eco-systems comprising suppliers of knowledge, hardware, and services to co-develop innovative products.

5. **Train in order to nurture creative thinking mindsets and skills**. Onarheim and Friis-Olivarius have used principles of neuroscience of creativity to teach creativity in business schools in Canada and Denmark. Their Applied NeuroCreativity (ANC) programme is designed to help trainees eliminate cognitive barriers in creative thinking.[7]

6. **Nurture an entrepreneurial culture and provoke "design activists" in the organisation.** To unleash the creative instincts of employees give them time, space, tools, and resources. Encourage them to experiment with new ideas.

7. **Listen to the contrarian views of "rebel thinkers" in the organisation.** Give them access to the leadership team. Appoint sponsors who will support them through the entire cycle of innovation from idea to prototype to commercialisation.

Mastering the power of creative thinking

To master the power of creative thinking, you should focus on yourself, your context, and your agenda.

1. **Inculcate a strong urge to make a positive difference**. Focus on solving real-world problems affecting your community. When you solve real-world problems, you alleviate pain and suffering. It makes people happy. It will boost your self-confidence.

2. **Gather diverse knowledge from different fields**. A multidisciplinary approach facilitates creative thinking. It enables you to analyse a problem from different angles.

3. **Believe in yourself.** Self-confidence fuels the urge to think creatively.

4. **Go to free thinking environments.** Spend time away from the four walls of your office. A liberating environment triggers creative thinking.

5. **Create a curiosity group.** Form a circle of friends to discuss contemporary challenges and develop team projects to solve problems. Curiosity stimulates creative thinking. Never stop asking questions about intriguing subjects and events.

6. **Try new ideas without fear of failure.** Reflecting on successive failures will deepen your learning. Develop a passion for creating new ideas and inventing new products.

7. **Believe in the power of teamwork.** Learn to collaborate. Increasingly, we work in multicultural teams and improve your cross-cultural skills to help to create a vibrant team.

8. **Pursue your hobbies**. Play or watch your favourite sport, solve puzzles, play board games, watch movies, or go to theatre.

9. **Diversify your interests and seek new experiences**. Visit new places and meet new people. This will help in broadening your perspectives, which is essential for creative thinking.

10. **Be agile and alert.** Pay attention to your health. Eat nourishing food and do regular exercise. Wellness improves cognitive activities.

11. **Never stop learning.** As we make progress, we encounter new problems. We have to continuously learn, unlearn, and relearn to solve emerging problems. Connect with your teachers and experts and discuss your new ideas and projects. Attend seminars to gather new ideas or test your own ideas.

12. **Develop a vision for your creative pursuits.** Creative thinking is a journey with many ups and downs. Your vision will provide you the inspiration and direction to endure.

To promote creative thinking and innovation, many countries have adopted national programmes.

In Korea, a national network of *Centres for Creative Economy and Innovation* is supporting startups.

Ireland promotes innovative research projects as part of *Creative Ireland Programme*. The *National Creativity Fund* provides funding support for research and community programmes.

DesignSingapore Council has created *School of X* where people from all walks of life come to solve business and community problems using design thinking.

Explore:

School of X
   https://www.designsingapore.org/initiatives/school-of-x.html

---

Summary

Creative thinking is the fountain head of human evolution and progress. Creative thinking mindsets and skills play very important roles in the success of individuals, teams, organisations, communities, and countries. The emerging digital technologies are enabling people and organisations to develop innovative solutions to solve the problems of society. Many countries and organisations are implementing programmes to encourage creativity and innovation. Let's be part of the innovation revolution by mastering the power of creativity.

Personal Action Plan

1 List your limiting beliefs that prevent you from creative thinking.
2 List the organisational barriers that you face in creative thinking at work.
3 Develop your personal action plan to enhance and apply your creative thinking skills.

Notes

1 World Economic Forum (2020), *The Future of Jobs Report 2020*. October. Available at: https://www.weforum.org/reports/the-future-of-jobs-report-2020
2 Bureau of Labour and Statistics, U.S. Department of Labour News Release (2021), *Number of Jobs, Labour Market Experience, Marital Status and Health: Results from a National Longitudinal Survey*. August 31. Available at: https://www.bls.gov/news.release/nlsoy.nr0. htm
3 Intel® Digital Readiness Programs. Available at: www.intel.com/digitalreadiness
4 Hollinger, P. (2015), Business Pioneers in Industry. *Financial Times*, March 31. Available at: https://www.ft.com/content/c18fd2c6-cc99-11e4-b5a5-00144feab7de
5 Gino, F. (2018), The Business Case of Curiosity. *Harvard Business Review*, September–October. Available at: https://hbr.org/2018/09/the-business-case-for-curiosity
6 Brandenburger, A. (2019), Strategy Needs Creativity. *Harvard Business Review*, March–April.
7 Onarheim, B. and M. Friis-Olivarius (2013), Applying the Neuroscience of Creativity to Creativity Training. *Frontiers in Human Neuroscience*, October 16. Available at: https://www.frontiersin.org/articles/10.3389/fnhum.2013.00656/full

Further reading

Dobelli, R. (2013), *The Art of Thinking Clearly*. UK: Harper Collins.
Grant, A. (2017), *Originals*. UK: Penguin Books.
Judkins, R. (2016), *The Art of Creative Thinking*. UK: Sceptre Books.
Pease, A. and B. Pease (2017), *The Answer*. UK: Seven Dials, Orion Books.

15

MASTERING THE POWER OF SENSEMAKING

Sunil Deshmukh

Abstract

We live in an uncertain world where our context changes constantly and rapidly. The change is often sudden and caused by unexpected events. The leaders face questions about what caused the change, its implications for our organization, the new opportunities and threats, and how to navigate the fast-changing landscape in our industry. These are difficult questions because of the complexity and ambiguity of rapid change. The leaders have to cope with incomplete information. Instead of using step-by-step analytical thinking processes, they have to make sense of the emerging context to take business decisions. This chapter will explore the nature of sensemaking and how to master this critical leadership skill.

Keywords: Uncertainty, ambiguity, judgement, intuition

Introduction

"Common sense in an uncommon degree is what the world calls wisdom". This quote from Samuel Taylor Coleridge (Taylor Coleridge, 2012),[1] an English poet, philosopher, and theologian, is appropriate to start the discussion on mastering the power of sensemaking. Indeed, in our complex business environment, the act of sensemaking on decision-makers is an excellent asset of any organization. It is a rare skill and merits serious attention from business leaders at all levels in an organization.

DOI: 10.4324/9781003219293-19

During the 1990s, the market environment in India was changing rapidly as the government adopted liberal policies to reduce or remove market barriers. Most of the industry sectors were thrown open to foreign companies. Many foreign companies launched their consumer products in India due to observing the growing middle-class consumers. At that time, I worked with an Australian brewery company in India. We launched one of our lager beer brands in the premium segment, and it was projected as mild beer. The Indian consumers responded favourably, and our market share grew rapidly. In a short time, our lager beer brand ranked number one in the premium segment in Western India.

With two years of sustained growth behind us, we started thinking big and decided to expand our presence in the Indian market. The market research showed that the demand for strong beer (alcohol content more than 5 per cent) in India grew faster than the demand for mild beer. The logical choice was to launch another beer brand in the premium segment; hence, we launched a strong beer variant in the Indian market alongside our successful mild lager beer brand in the premium segment. As a foreign company, we did not want to compete in the low-price segment, which many local brands dominated.

In the subsequent months, we discovered that our strong beer variant was not doing as well as the mild lager beer. The premium image of our lager beer was also adversely affected, and our market share started declining. It was a significant setback for our company. We soon discovered that the Indian consumers perceived a strong beer as a "non-premium domestic product", and they did not think that our strong beer was a premium product and rejected it. We had failed to "*sense*" the perceptions of the Indian consumers and made a wrong decision to position our strong beer variant next to our mild lager beer in the premium category. Several other foreign companies in different product categories also experienced market failures, because they failed to understand the complex behaviour of Indian consumers.

Sensemaking is a critical skill in decision-making under uncertainty and was first recognized by Karl Weick, an organizational psychologist (Weick, 1995).[2] Weick compared sensemaking to map-making (Ancona, 2011).[3] "*While preparing a good map, we depend upon where we look, what factors we chose to focus upon, the terrain, etc. Hence sensemaking is more than an act of analysis, it's an act of creativity*".

In a complex and ambiguous business environment, the sensemaking skills of business leaders are critical. These skills are valuable in interpreting the changes taking place in the environment and framing the emerging threats and opportunities. Sensemaking based on sound executive judgement and intuition combined with analytical thinking plays a vital role in making strategic and operational decisions. Sensemaking skills can help in visualizing and extrapolating evolving situations. It is a continuous process of interpreting and reinterpreting unfolding situations. A leadership team that can make sense of the future before it happens can win the competition race – known as a first-mover advantage.

Sensemaking is a critical skill

Making sense of what is happening around us is critical for living beings and organizations. What we make of a situation drives our responses and helps us navigate through the situation to achieve our objectives.

We make sense of people, events, and situations based on information and intuition. Sometimes when we meet a person for the first time, we may not trust that person instantly. We consciously and subconsciously watch for signs and clues that help us "make sense of the person" and whether we should trust them. When we are visiting a new city for the first time, we make sense of the safe places to go. In a strategic planning meeting, the CEO makes sense of the executives' diverse views and takes appropriate decisions to steer the business.

In an ideal world, when we have comprehensive information and tools to analyse the information, we make decisions confidently. However, we don't live in a perfect world. Many events happen without any warning and impact positively or negatively. The fundamental question facing business leaders is how to interpret rapid changes in the environment to make good decisions. This chapter will explore some aspects of sensemaking that I have learned during my professional career as a business executive.

During the 16th and 17th centuries, the great explorers depended on their sensemaking skills to navigate safely towards remote destinations. They did not possess accurate maps and precision instruments to stay on course. They relied on the positions of the stars at night-time, watched the movement of the sun during daytime, observed the direction and the speed of the wind to sail; they had to remain alert and make sense of the changing weather conditions day and night. Their safety and success depended on how good they were in sensing the weather and the direction.

We have heard the story of how Sir Isaac Newton sensed the presence of the force of gravity by seeing an apple fall from the tree. Whether the "falling apple" episode is true or not, he sensed that the only way a static object will move is when a force is applied. In other words, he sensed that "the force of gravity was pulling the apple towards the ground". There are many other stories of how scientific discoveries have been made based on curiosity and sensemaking.

My favourite example of a great act of sensemaking is Mahatma Gandhi's strong belief in non-violence to oppose India's oppressive British colonial rule. The British were powerful and exercised control over the people of India through an organized machine comprised of civil servants, police force, judiciary, and military personnel. On the other hand, Mahatma Gandhi stood up for the powerless people of India. He was trained as a lawyer and was far removed from weapons and violence to oppose the colonial power. He was against colonial rulers and sensed that non-violence and non-cooperation were effective strategies for countering British rule in India. He garnered the support of millions of people all over India to join him in India's struggle for independence. Mahatma Gandhi's choice of non-violence teaches us how our beliefs and values impact our sensemaking behaviour.

There are examples of companies who have paid a heavy price in the business world, because the leadership failed to sense the impact of changes in the business environment. Nokia failed to exploit the growing popularity of smartphones, and Kodak failed to take advantage of digital technologies in photography. Ironically, the engineers in Kodak and Nokia had developed a prototype of a digital smartphone and a digital camera way ahead of competitors. Unfortunately, the leadership teams in these companies failed to read and sense the benefits of digital technologies and changing consumer preferences, for good sensemaking leaders require a broader vision to look beyond the obvious and strong will to challenge the status quo.

Since the onset of the COVID-19 pandemic, we have witnessed the failure of political leadership, public health agencies, health experts, and citizens to predict the transmission pattern of the virus and its catastrophic impact on society. Unfortunately, several million people have died, and the world's economies have collapsed. The only exception in this tragic story has been the rapid development of vaccines to protect human beings. The vaccine development teams sensed the potentially devastating effect of Coronavirus, and using scientific knowledge and tools, they produced the vaccine and gave the gift of life to millions of people.

Navigating the fast-changing environments

I was born and raised in India. My career as a business executive has followed the path India took in the early 1990s, shedding its legacy of socialism and carving its way to a more liberal direction for economic growth and prosperity. The economic policies of the country began to change rapidly. New competitors entered the Indian market, and new technologies were disrupting the businesses of the 1960s vintage. Global brands started invading the consumer market; the consumers' preferences were changing. The whole business environment in India was highly dynamic, posing numerous challenges to existing and new businesses. It was the "wait, watch, sense, and act" approach for many new entrants. Challenging, the companies did not want to miss riding on the wave of growing optimism in India. There were opportunities for the businesses to grow and make profits to make sense of the unfolding business environment. As the new market order emerged, it was difficult comprehending the evolving trends to make timely decisions. In many industries, historical data was not very helpful for making decisions.

Taking long-term business decisions in a stable and slowly changing environment was relatively familiar to most of India. We analysed historical data, combined with market research, and made decisions. However, the fast-changing business environment in India posed new challenges in decision-making. The new investment decisions, acquisition of new technologies, or launching new products were inherently risky because of the unknowns of rapid change. It was a constant battle to make sense of the future and navigate in an imperfect information environment.

In the late 1990s, I worked with a joint venture company in the tire industry. We were introducing state-of-the-art radial tires in India. We sensed that the radial tires would be expensive, and the buyers would take time to adopt the new technology and product concept. The market scenario looked uncertain. It was a pioneering project, and the cost of setting up a greenfield radial tire plant was prohibitive. There was a considerable risk in further escalating the cost of production and the price of tires. Defying the logic of the competition, two fiercely competing companies, Goodyear and Ceat, formed a joint venture company to share the manufacturing plant set up costs and moved fast in entering the market. In this case, we sensed the looming uncertainty. We followed an unorthodox strategy to keep the costs low by setting up a joint venture between two competing companies, to manufacture radial tires in India.

With the entry of foreign companies in India, the consumers were getting exposed to a plethora of new consumer products and brands. The aspiring consumer classes were quick to adopt these foreign brands. The consumers in urban and rural India started buying automobiles, mobile phones, fast food, and personal care products. The concept of Western fast food was catching up, thanks to the enthusiastic response of India's middle class.

The changes in the marketplace were fast, and historical data were of limited use in crafting business strategies. We approached big decisions as if we were solving jigsaw puzzles. Imagine children playing with Lego pieces, assembling different things without reference pictures. They connect the pieces based on their common sense, creativity, and judgement.

During rapid economic change, we made many decisions based on common sense, intuition, and prudence. McDonald entered India in the mid-1990s. We did extensive market research in India and found that 60 per cent of the "potential" customers were vegetarians. It was logical to conclude that the company would develop and launch vegetarian burgers to attract a broader segment of consumers. However, there was a challenge in winning the trust of "vegetarian consumers"; we sensed that they would not eat vegetarian burgers prepared in the same kitchen where chicken or fish burgers were being prepared. McDonald decided to have two separate kitchens. It was the first food chain in India to follow the strategy of having a separate vegetarian kitchen. The local and foreign competitors found it difficult to emulate this strategy because it required significant resources and time to adopt new processes and standards.

Recent research has shown that sensemaking helped small businesses in enhancing the resilience of these companies during the COVID-19 pandemic. The leaders in these companies sensed the new patterns of demand and quickly adapted new product lines (Sarkar and Clegg, 2021).[4]

Sensemaking process

Throughout my executive career, working in the fast-changing and often uncertain business environment in India, the Middle East, and South-East Asia, sensemaking has been a constant feature of decision-making. My executive teams followed an iterative approach against a rigid step-by-step process. The iterative approach was largely unstructured and based on interactions with people inside and outside the companies. We combined analysis and subjective judgement to make sense of the business situations we faced. Our risk management decisions were in the form of a series of medium-term actions with the flexibility to reset and adapt when the unexpected happened. The main features of our sensemaking-based decision-making approach were:

- Engaging with people at different levels in the government, industry, and our companies to exchange views and likely scenarios

- Tapping multiple sources of information both inside and outside the companies
- Sifting "good" and "bad" information
- Reorganizing good information to identify patterns.
- Negotiating and integrating diverse perspectives and opinions of the team members
- Extrapolating, making assumptions, and building likely scenarios about the immediate future
- Taking and validating our decisions by engaging with diverse sets of people in the industry
- Resetting and refining our assumptions and scenarios as the situation evolved

Though not so well organized as presented earlier, these steps helped give us the confidence to make business decisions. We took many big investment decisions that proved successful in the growing economy.

The S-type and H-type executives

You might be wondering, "how can I nurture my sensemaking skills". Professor Lalit Johri, co-editor of this book, and I have pondered on this question, and we have categorized executives as S-type and H-type. The S-type executives are good at sensemaking, whereas H-type executives make decisions based on hard-core evidence.[5]

The S-type executives that I have worked with enjoyed the fast movements in the market and were very confident in making decisions. These executives stood out amongst other executives in how they interpreted and drew meaning from mixed trends in the consumer markets. Over a period, I observed their behaviour and interests.

They were forward-looking: The S-type executives preferred to talk about the future trends in the technology and markets. They enjoyed writing "back of the envelope" plans for the future. They spent less time looking at the historical data.

They were open-minded: The S-type executives were good at asking questions and were patient listeners, and they considered the perspectives of staff from different departments. They were outstanding in building relationships with suppliers, agents, retailers, and customers and listened to their opinions. They interacted with executives working with our competitors. They read business magazines looking for the latest information on different subjects.

They were comfortable working with limited information. We needed demand forecasts to invest in our production capacity for meeting growing demand. The S-type executives were sound in extrapolating future demand for our products based on limited historical data and a sense of how consumer preferences will fuel future demands.

They were good at visualizing multiple scenarios. The S-type executives visualized fast-changing business trends by drawing inferences in multiple time horizons ranging from short term to long term. The socio-economic structure of the Indian consumer market is quite complex. The S-type executives were able to develop insights about the overall consumer market and different social and economic classes in different time horizons.

They were energetic risk-takers. The S-type executives were enthusiastic and motivated to perform better than their colleagues. They were the first to rise in accepting high-risk assignments to satisfy their hunger to do difficult things and enjoyed taking on challenging projects.

They exercised their intuition and imagination. The S-type executives were driven by instinct and creativity instead of spending too much time analysing limited historical data and making too many assumptions. They were good at reading weak market signals, and they exhibited courage and confidence to make decisions and convince their colleagues in the company. At the same time, they were flexible enough to adapt when their assumptions were proved wrong.

They were actively connected with the world. The S-type executives were active outside their companies. They regularly participated in the industry associations and attended seminars and conferences. They were also associated with social organizations, sponsored community projects, and gave lectures in schools and colleges.

They had culturally rich experiences. These executives had worked in fast-changing industries in many countries with rich cultures before joining the organizations that I was leading. The exposure to diverse cultures seems to have sharpened their spirit of discovery and sensemaking skills. Their knowledge about the anthropological and cultural roots of people in different countries helped understand people from different walks of life.

Unlike the S-type executives, the H-type executives firmly believed in hard-core evidence and logical analysis. They were influenced by history and the need for a status quo. They had a fixed rule book and did not encourage out-of-box thinking. They worked under performance pressures to meet time-bound targets. They were overconfident, rigid, and unwilling to unlearn and relearn. To some extent, the organization's culture of maintaining the status quo, paranoia and fear of failure, and emphasis on decision-making based on complex financial data and market research data also discouraged H-type executives from abstract thinking and sensemaking. Sometimes, the H-type executives played an essential role as challengers and assisted the team by asking realistic questions.

Mastering the power of sensemaking

There are many political, economic, natural and ecological, cultural and social, and technological factors shaping our lives and work environment. To master the power of sensemaking, it is necessary to make appropriate decisions. When you make good sense of the evolving context, your decisions will have better chances of achieving your goals.

Sensemaking is a journey and is a process. One can't expect to be an expert in sensemaking quickly. Mastering the power of sensemaking does not mean that you would acquire skills for making correct decisions all the time. Improving sensemaking skills will only equip you with a higher probability of dealing with uncertainty. To build sensemaking skills, I would suggest the following:

Develop a 360-degree view of the business environment. Draw a list of key trends and monitor these trends regularly. Gather correct information from authentic sources. In the age of social media, there is much fake information circulated by people with vested interests. Be wary of information from unknown sources.

Build an active network of stakeholders for debates and discussions. People with diverse interests, expertise, and deep insights can help you map the future. Seek their views in cracking complex and perplexing information. Their expert views provide critical lenses for organizing information.

Interpret information using different lenses. Your beliefs and the purpose, vision, and values of your organization are lenses for interpreting information and building scenarios. Use your imagination to build "rational" assumptions and choices.

Involve employees from different levels in the organization. To examine and validate the assumptions and decisions made by the leadership team, involve employees and ask them to examine the decisions critically.

Address doubts and disagreement. Use influencing and negotiating skills to convince the stakeholders.

Develop an inspiring narrative about the future. To invoke high levels of participation, build an inspiring story about the future and highlight how the organization and employees will benefit. However, don't brush the risks under the carpet. Discuss with employees how the organization will deal with these.

Be flexible when the reality is at variance with expectations. Respond promptly when the facts are at variance with expectations because of unforeseen events and trends.

In the latter part of my executive career, I started a Future HR Manager mentoring programme for our HR team responsible for recruiting fresh graduates from university campuses in India. The programme's objective was to instil sensemaking skills in our HR managers.

Historically, we used a series of tests to assess the applicants' quantitative, language, reasoning, and analytical skills for selecting fresh graduates in our management trainee scheme. Although we had no problem in the recruitment process, we found that there was a high turnover of these graduates within the few months after recruitment. The trainees selected from Tier-1 cities in India constantly chased other job options and quickly switched jobs. They did not have any purpose except to earn a higher salary. They were also very rigid in their thinking. The trainee recruits from Tier-2 and Tier-3 cities and towns from middle- and low-income family backgrounds were relatively more loyal and were inclined to build their career in our organization. They had strong values of honesty, integrity, commitment, and loyalty. They believed in hard work and wanted to prove to their family and friends that they could rise to higher positions in a large organization. We found that these trainees were keen to learn and quickly adopted the culture of our organization.

On the basis of this trend, we decided to focus on recruiting fresh graduates from smaller cities and towns. We discontinued the tests used in the recruitment. We encouraged our HR managers to use their sensemaking skills to select graduates with solid values who would be loyal to our organization and grow with it. The *Future HR Managers* mentoring programme and the new recruitment process and criteria were successful. Later, we designed a mentoring programme for developing sensemaking skills in our marketing and sales executives.

> **Reflect:**
>
> 1 Is sensemaking a common practice for analysing business trends in your organization?
> 2 Discuss and map a recent decision-making situation in your organization when you and your team adopted a sensemaking approach.
> 3 Discuss how you and your team can improve sensemaking skills.

Summary

Sensemaking is a critical leadership skill useful for comprehending changing contexts. Combined with analytical thinking, sensemaking is widely used in business organizations to navigate a fast-changing environment. During my business career, my fellow colleagues and I have adopted the sensemaking approach to solve many puzzling business situations. Recent research has shown that sensemaking has helped small businesses in enhancing the resilience of these companies during the COVID-19 pandemic. It is an essential leadership skill that can be learned.

Notes

1 Taylor Coleridge, Samuel (2012), *The Complete Works of Samuel Taylor Coleridge: With an Introductory Essay Upon His Philosophical and Theological Opinions*, Volume 5 Paperback. Calcutta, India: Saraswati Press, August 31.
2 Weick, K.E. (1995), *Sensemaking in Organisations. (Foundations for Organisational Science)*. Thousand Oaks, London, New Delhi: Sage Publications, p. 4.
3 Ancona, D.G. (2011), Sensemaking: Framing and Acting in the Unknown. In S. Snook, N. Nohria, and R. Khurana (Eds.), *The Handbook for Teaching Leadership: Knowing, Doing, and Being*. Thousand Oaks, CA: Sage Publications, pp. 3–20.
4 Sarkar, S. and S.R. Clegg (2021), Resilience in a Time of Contagion: Lessons From Small Business During the COVID-19 Pandemic. *Journal of Change Management*, 21(2), 242–267. doi:10.1080/14697017.2021.1917495.
5 Discussions with Professor Lalit Johri, August 2021.

Further reading

Ancona, D., M. Williams and G. Gerlach (2020), The Overlooked Key to Leading Through Chaos. *MIT Sloan Management Review*, 62(1). September. Reprint 62125.
Likierman, A. (2020), The Elements of Good Judgment. *Harvard Business Review*, January–February. Reprint R2001H.

PART V

Mentoring and development

16

MASTERING THE POWER OF MENTORING

Victoria Wall

Abstract

This chapter explores the potential of mentoring in building positive and reciprocal working relationships to benefit mentors, mentees, and the organisations they work in.

Victoria Wall, Executive Coach, Leadership Consultant, and Founder of VWA Consulting, shares concepts from her mentoring training workshops, along with reflections on her own career journey and the impact mentoring has on her.

Using evidence-based research and data insights, Victoria references inspiring, historical leaders to bring to life the power of mentoring and how others may harness its potential.

Citing key new trends and outlining views of the future for mentoring, Victoria provides key practical tips on how to be an effective mentor, find a suitable mentor, and nurture mentoring relationships in an uncertain and complex world.

Keywords: Mentoring, mentor, mentee, personal development

Introduction

The great American poet and civil rights activist, Maya Angelou (1928–2014), once said, "*I've learned that people will forget what you said, people will forget what you did, but people will never forget how you made them feel*".[1] How right she was.

DOI: 10.4324/9781003219293-21

Fuel your passion

In my final year at university, I decided on a career path oriented towards helping people. Human Resources sounded good to me. I conveyed this to the college's career advisor, and his suggestion was . . . to join the army and become a cook!

If he was listening to me, he wasn't hearing. His lack of focus and understanding left me shocked, disillusioned and frustrated. It also provided the inspiration I needed to fuel the passion within me to provide guidance to young people and to help them identify the skills that would enable them to make the right career choices and realise their potential. The careers advisor proved to be an enormous help, but it was accidental. This gave me the ambition to help others make the right career choices by setting up my first business.

It has been said that there's a mentor behind every successful person. Richard Branson, the founder of Virgin Group, asked the entrepreneur Sir Freddie Laker to be his mentor when he was struggling to get his airline business off the ground. "*It's always good to have a helping hand at the start*", he said, "*I wouldn't have got anywhere in the airline industry without the mentorship of Sir Freddie Laker*".[2]

We are all mentors

I believe that mentoring sits at the heart of our personal and professional relationships. We are *all* mentors. And if we want to learn and improve our lives, we should all strive to be mentees.

With friends and family members we listen, support, guide, and advise based on the "internal frame of reference" that comes from our life experiences. Mentoring in the professional environment is exactly the same. A mentor is a trusted "professional friend" who cares about our success and development. They commit to a long-term relationship to help and support the mentee with their career goals and objectives.

By definition,

> *A mentor is a more experienced and knowledgeable person who teaches and* nurtures *the development of a less experienced and knowledgeable person. In an organizational setting, a mentor influences the personal and professional growth of a mentee.*[3]

A meaningful relationship in your life

When asked to reflect on significant mentors in my life, I focus on two relationships.

My late father, Thomas Wall, remains "my inner motivation". His optimism and belief in my ability to "have a go" and take risks gave me the courage to set up my business at the age of 24, with little experience. Throughout my 20s, everything was a new challenge, and Thomas was my sounding board – caring, non-judgemental, and encouraging.

Oprah Winfrey said of her mentor, Maya Angelou, *"she was there for me always, guiding me through some of the most important years of my life"*.[4] Thomas was that person for me, and 25 years after his passing he continues to be a presence in my "inner dialogue", exemplifying the true power of mentoring.

If you explore meaningful mentoring relationships in history, you will find that many leaders cite more experienced and knowledgeable people in their fields of work. A substantial number reference a parent, teacher, or colleague as being influential.

To explore this further, I recently took a sample of my coaching clients★ and my employees, in the 25–39 age group, and asked them "who has been a significant mentor in your life?"

These are the findings

Colleagues (peer who they learnt from)	25.5%
Senior Colleague (Manager/Director)	52%
Teacher	1.5%
Family friend	1.5%
Mother	10%
Father	8%
Sibling	1.5%

★A UK sample of educated professionals aged 25–39 working in professional services, finance, media, technology, and pharmaceutical sectors

While senior managers remain the most common mentor group, it is interesting to note that peer-to-peer mentoring is popular for skills training, dealing with organisational challenges, and problem-solving, while younger people can strengthen our grasp on technological development and innovation.

In recent years, my daughters have become significant mentors for me. Taking time to understand their perspectives on life, and embracing their ability to challenge my thinking, has enabled me to learn from them and keep an open mind.

Adjusting to future social, political, digital, and environmental challenges is vital for me to remain connected to the generation that will lead us into the future. Today, most businesses are experiencing some form of transformational change, driven by a need to understand how to effectively use data and artificial intelligence to successfully lead and future proof our organisations.[5] To achieve this, leaders need to listen and learn from their younger colleagues. This is known as reverse mentoring, an initiative where older executives are paired with and mentored by younger employees on topics such as technology, social media, and current trends.[6]

Reflect:

Who has been an influential figure in your life?

A learning partnership

> "*Tell me and I will forget. Teach me and I may remember. Involve me and I learn*".
>
> Benjamin Franklin (1706–1790), American writer, scientist, statesman, and political philosopher[7]

The central theme to mentoring is the "learning relationship".[8] It enables individuals to take charge of their own development, realise their potential, and achieve results. While mentoring is traditionally described as "*as transfer of skill or knowledge from a more experienced to a less experienced person through learning dialogue and role modelling*",[9] I strongly believe that mentoring is a mutually beneficial partnership.

A learning relationship can span beyond two people, with one mentor being an immediate manager or pre-assigned mentor and the rest of your "developmental network" being comprised of peers, organisational leaders, family members, and junior members of staff with specific technical expertise – all being valuable mentors.[10]

Working as Search Consultant in the early part of my career enabled me to develop my business acumen and acquire knowledge of what drives people. I was already practising the "art of mentoring", albeit subconsciously, but everyone I met helped me make deposits into my accumulated knowledge bank, from which I could draw on to mentor others. Professional training, further study in the field of occupational psychology, and a growing interest in developing talented leaders resulted in me becoming an Executive Coach and Leadership Consultant.

I believe that the fundamental powers of being both a mentor and a mentee are the ability to "actively listen" without judgement, to empathise, and to ask insightful questions. The sooner we learn how to listen properly, question effectively, and suspend judgement in our daily lives, the better equipped we will be to give and receive feedback, and to reflect, with purpose, on our strengths and weaknesses.

Providing this level of emotional support, by asking mentees "how they are feeling", more than once in a conversation, can enable them to openly share their current state of mind. Additionally, paying attention to the "whole person", whilst sharing your own experiences, can help provide empathy and strengthen ties in the relationship.[11]

This is especially important in today's context, with recent studies suggesting that over half of young people have reported an increase in loneliness and depressive symptoms following the start of the Coronavirus pandemic.[12]

Reflect:

Think of a piece of advice or feedback you have recently received that you have acted upon? Who gave you that advice? Why did you accept it?

Finding a mentor

> *"In order to be a mentor, and an effective one, one must care. You must care . . . know what you know and care about the person, care about what you know, and care about the person you're sharing with".*
> *Maya Angelou, (1928–2014), American poet and civil rights activist*[13]

As mentioned, the traditional scenario has seen a focus on senior employees mentoring a junior within the same organisation, but this doesn't have to be the case. The aim is to find a mentor who can share relatable experiences that can be learned from, with career objectives in mind.

Reflecting on what you want to gain from the mentoring relationship is the first step and requires you to identify the specific objectives you would like to discuss.[14] For example, if you are focused on finding a mentor to advise and support you in finding a new job, you might want help with the following:

Example objectives

- To identify potential and build self-confidence
- To manage a professional transition
- To recover from redundancy or difficult professional situations
- To identify a new career path and make a transition
- To deepen knowledge and technical skills within your profession

Once your objectives have been decided, spend time researching who you admire and identify why you resonate with them.[15] Reflect on your own levels of self-confidence and evaluate if your potential mentor has the right intentions, and won't project their idea of success onto you. As suggested by Robbins, a mentor that is trustworthy, motivating, respectful, and honest is a key for a flourishing mentoring relationship.[16]

Research cited by Phan outlines the importance of bridging the gap between thinking about the importance of having a mentor and being proactive to begin the process of finding one.[17] Evidence suggests that spontaneous social interactions that spark creativity and collaborative efforts are less likely to occur within a hybrid-working world.[18] Don't be afraid to reach out to potential mentors to ask for a short alignment call.

In an initial email, you could share what you admire about them, your own experiences, and outline your intentions and expectations from a future relationship. By asking questions about life beyond work, sharing desires for growth, and being appreciative for their time, you can set the tone for a meaningful and reciprocal mentoring relationship.

Suggested steps to begin a mentor–mentee relationship

1   Reflect on what you want from a mentoring relationship
2   Identify who would make an effective mentor for you
3   Send a short email introducing yourself and aligning your expectations
4   Begin a potential relationship through a no obligation virtual or in-person "coffee chat"

> **Reflect:**
>
> What are the key topics you would like to focus on in a mentoring discussion?

What does a powerful mentor do?

> *"The delicate balance of mentoring someone is not creating them in your own image, but giving them the opportunity to create themselves".*
>
> Steven Spielberg, (1946–present), American screen writer, film director, and producer.[19]

One of the first questions I ask a mentee is, "what is your purpose?" I need to understand the "why", just as much as the "what". An impactful, empathetic mentor will guide a mentee towards making the connection between their career goals and their purpose in life.

A good mentor will:

- Act as a role model
- Share experience(s)
- Be available and reliable
- Support the achievement of objectives
- Challenge assumptions
- Be a trusted sounding board
- Give guidance and impartial advice
- Give constructive and sensitive feedback
- Summarise discussions
- Identify and introduce new opportunities
- Offer career advice and make development recommendations

I asked a highly successful CEO and friend, "what makes you a good mentor?" He answered, "*I help people believe the parachute will open for them. I enable people to take risks*" (Tech CEO, Private Sector).

> **Reflect:**
>
> Think of a time when you have helped someone believe that they can make a leap, and that the parachute will open for them?

Inspirational mentoring relationships

There are many famous examples of successful mentoring relationships – in business, politics, and the arts and beyond.

In the early days of setting up Facebook, Steve Jobs mentored Mark Zuckerberg. They shared stories on how to manage and grow their businesses, with the common goal of impacting the world. When Steve passed away, Mark posted on his Facebook page, "Steve, thank you for being a mentor and friend. Thanks for showing that what you build can change the world. I will miss you".[20]

I also love the story of Mother Teresa's mentoring relationship with Father Michael van der Peet, which began in Rome, when they were waiting to catch a bus.[21] Their constant exchange of ideas led to them inspiring each other to dedicate their lives to charitable and spiritual works.

My personal list of mentoring stories is lengthy, with the common theme of helping people realise their potential. But the most impactful and memorable experiences relate to being a role model to ambitious, high-performing women embarking on motherhood. A significant life change can result in highly successful people dealing with identity issues, imposter syndrome, and lack of confidence. Sharing my own experience of having two children and running two businesses in a still male-dominated world, I hope I have inspired as much as I have received inspiration.

An organisation I work closely with is mothers2mothers (www.m2m.org) which is a wonderful example of peer-to-peer mentoring. Through training and employment, m2m unlocks the power of HIV-positive women to become change makers in sub-Saharan Africa.

A mothers2mothers Mentor Mother explained that I could still be healthy, and thanks to her support, my boy was born HIV-free. Becoming a Mentor Mother changed everything. I used my knowledge to educate my family about HIV, who treated me like a human again

Wilbroda Awuor Akuro, an m2m
Community Mentor Mother in Nairobi, Kenya

Reflect:

Thinking about these examples, what type of mentor would inspire you?

Setting up a successful mentoring process

At the start, there will be several unspoken expectations and assumptions between the mentor and the mentee. To achieve success for both parties, key principles need to be established.

Mentoring principles[22]

- A broad range of topics can be discussed
- It is an open-ended process with no fixed timelines
- It is based on sharing wisdom and experience
- Establish a relationship framework based on both parties' values
- Agree clear objectives
- At regular intervals re-evaluate mentee and mentor expectations

Trust and understanding are crucial in the professional friendship that constitutes the mentoring relationship. Mutual respect, open communication, and equality are essential.[23]

The impact of mentoring

Mentoring can have beneficial psychological and performance benefits for mentors, mentees, and the organisations that they work for.

What are the benefits of being a mentor?

Over 30 years of academic research has suggested that being a mentor is associated with a range of improved career outcomes, including higher levels of compensation, faster promotion cycles, increased feelings of organisational commitment, and a higher belief in one's career advancement.[24] Mentors can also benefit in the following ways:[25],[26]

- An opportunity to develop "coaching" skills
- Broadening of one's own perspective and developing empathy
- Contributing to growth and the retention of staff
- The satisfaction of helping others
- Developing analytical skills and leadership qualities
- Staying up to date with technology, trends and processes
- Being rewarded for developing talent
- Feeling rejuvenated with a sense of purpose
- Lower levels of anxiety through learning coping mechanisms from others

How will you benefit as a mentee?

On a psychological level, mentees can benefit through connecting to their deeper human motivations, building career momentum, and working towards true psychosocial maturation.[27] On a practical level, mentees can benefit by having:[28],[29]

- A "sounding board" to test ideas
- A different perspective on career-related challenges
- Experiential insight and support
- A role model to learn from
- Increased levels of resilience
- Increased engagement to job role and industry
- Develop career attributes including social capital, exposure, and visibility
- Encouragement and motivation to make career transitions
- Specific knowledge about the organisation working for
- Industry knowledge and skills guidance
- Networking opportunities and career advice

What are the organisational benefits of having a mentoring programme?

By developing a culture of learning, organisations can improve their productivity and leadership outlook through the encouragement of mentoring relationships across their business. Over the long term, the benefits on an individual level will have positive repercussions for the organisation, such as follows[30],[31]:

- Reduced staff turnover
- Building of talent pipeline
- Meaningful and deeper connections across the business
- Increased trust
- Cascading of knowledge across the organisation
- Wider development of supervision and leadership skills
- A culture of celebration
- Greater managerial effectiveness

> **Reflect:**
>
> How do you think mentoring could broaden your perspective as a mentor or mentee?

The future of mentoring

By 2025, 75% of the global workforce will be composed of Millennials.[32] As at every point in human history, they will have to adapt to the impact of technology and shifting social landscapes by drawing on their support systems and networks. We now live in a social sharing culture that lends itself well to the concept of mentoring, with many organisations implementing digital mentoring programmes to create an informal support culture, using cloud-based packages and apps.[33]

The emergence of new virtual norms triggered by the disruptive nature of the coronavirus pandemic has further reduced the barriers between working and personal life activities for individuals. Whilst reducing the ability for spontaneous interactions to occur in a physical capacity, this evolution in working practices has provided the opportunity for an increase in novel methods to cultivate effective mentoring relationships in a virtual manner.[34]

Specifically, the proliferation of technological platforms suitable for communication purposes has diminished barriers around time, location, and budget, increasing the flexibility of mentoring relationships.[35] Mentoring over online channels, termed as "telementoring", allows for a boundaryless partnership, with Scigliano noting its ability to bring about more personalised, deeper levels of learning, whereby the whole globe becomes a classroom to those involved in the mentoring relationship.[36]

Mentoring within a remote context can help to build equitable relationships, with the lack of physical context reducing any social biases that may occur during in-person interaction.[37] Additionally, the digitalisation of mentoring allows individuals to proactively seek out "virtual mentors", consuming asynchronous content such as webinars, podcasts, and books as a method of continuous growth.[38]

This also allows for anonymous mentoring to thrive, with reduced barriers allowing for all personalities and backgrounds to have the comfort and ease of connecting with others as needed, without the perceptions of stigma or judgement from others.[39]

Social media tools have also been suggested as a method to leverage the power of imagery and video content in tracking successes as they happen. This allows for an engaged, relevant audience to share progress as it happens, even potentially adding their own knowledge and experiences to the narrative.

Mentors can utilise the increasing range of platforms to personalise communications with their mentees. Individuals may have different preferences for communication, so creating a bespoke plan for how and where mentoring exchanges take place can set the scene for both parties working together.[40]

On both sides of the relationship, mentoring enables the individual to become more self-aware – professionally and personally – focusing on identity, achievements to date, and future career paths.

The power and impact that come from mentoring another person are one of the greatest gifts a human being can bestow and another can receive. There is no better feeling than to know that you have inspired someone to navigate the future with confidence and integrity, and to make the world a better place for themselves and those around them.

> *When you've worked hard, and done well, and walked through that doorway of opportunity, you do not slam it shut behind you. You reach back.*
> Michelle Obama (2012), an American attorney and author and served as the First Lady of the United States from 2009 to 2017[41]

Summary

Having worked as Executive Coach and Leadership Development Consultant for over 23 years, I have seen how mentoring sits at the heart of human development, allowing people to become full-rounded, authentic, happy, and healthy human beings.

Mentoring has formed the foundation of my coaching style and made me aware of the importance of surrounding yourself in both your personal and professional life with people who lead by example and provide you with key insights to help you progress.

Being mentored goes beyond achieving career ambitions – mentors can help people to develop their emotional skills and well-being and empowering them to become more comfortable in their own skin and return to their equilibrium in challenging times.

Mentoring others can help develop your active listening, sense of empathy, and ability to ask insightful questions – lifelong skills enabling others to take charge of their journeys and achieve their goals.

The evolution of technological platforms has created a boundaryless world of mentoring across time and space – I have recently seen this first-hand as an Executive Coach supporting leaders living and working in five different continents!

Finding a mentor, you can trust and feel safe which provides the foundations of a reciprocal relationship focused on meaning and purpose with a view to making the world a better place for the next generation.

With benefits for mentors, mentees, and organisations, mentoring will continue to evolve, inspiring the future of work.

Practical exercise: preparing to be a powerful mentor

What does mentoring mean to me?

What topics and experiences am I comfortable sharing as a mentor?

What do I envisage a mentee would like to explore and learn from me?

Which characteristics of being a "good mentor" will be challenging for me to practice?

Which skills or techniques in the *The Power of You* have inspired me to be a good mentor?

Notes

1 Tunstall, E.D. (2014), *How Maya Angelou Made Me Feel*. Available at: https://theconversation.com/how-maya-angelou-made-me-feel-27328

2 Onzain, M. (2017), *What Entrepreneurs Can Learn from These 4 Mentorship Stories*. Available at: https://tech.co/news/entrepreneurs-learn-mentorship-stories-2017-02

3 Hart, W.E. (2009), Nurturing Relationships Provide Many Benefits. *Leadership in Action*, 17–19.

4 Littleton, C. (2014), *Oprah Winfrey on Maya Angelou: "She Will Always Be the Rainbow in My Clouds"*. Available at: https://uk.finance.yahoo.com/news/oprah-winfrey-maya-angelou-she-always-rainbow-clouds-172736541.html

5 Pencheva, I., M. Esteve and S.J. Mikhaylov (2020), *Big Data and AI – A Transformational Shift for Government: So, What Next for Research?* doi:10.1177/0952076718780537.

6 Techopedia (2011), *Reverse Mentoring*. Available at: https://www.techopedia.com/definition/28107/reverse-mentoring

7 European Mentoring & Coaching Council (2018), *EMCC Competence Framework*. Available at: https://emccpoland.org/wp-content/uploads/2018/02/EMCC-quality-glossary-v2.pdf

8 Garvey, B. and G. Alred (2003), *An Introduction to the Symposium on Mentoring: Issues and Prospects*. doi:10.1080/0306988031000086125.

9 European Mentoring & Coaching Council (2018), *EMCC Competence Framework*. Available at: https://emccpoland.org/wp-content/uploads/2018/02/EMCC-quality-glossary-v2.pdf

10 Kram, K.E. and M.C. Higgins (2009), *A New Mindset on Mentoring: Creating Developmental Networks at Work*. Available at: https://www.bumc.bu.edu/facdev-medicine/files/2009/12/Kram-Higgins_A-New-Mindset-on-Mentoring.pdf

11 Fessell, D.P., V. Chopra and S. Saint (2020), *Mentoring During a Crisis*. Available at: https://hbr.org/2020/10/mentoring-during-a-crisis

12 Tu, M. and M. Li (2021), *What Great Mentorship Looks Like in a Hybrid Workplace*. Available at: https://hbr.org/2021/05/what-great-mentorship-looks-like-in-a-hybrid-workplace

13 Harvard T.H. Chan School of Public Health (2021), *Maya Angelou*. Available at: https://sites.sph.harvard.edu/wmy/celebrities/maya-angelou/

14 Thorndyke, L.E., M.E. Gusic and R.J. Milner (2008), *Functional Mentoring: A Practical Approach With Multilevel Outcomes*. doi:10.1002/chp.178.

15 Sastry, A. and A. Tagle (2020), *The Right Mentor Can Change Your Career. Here's How to Find One*. Available at: https://www.npr.org/2019/10/25/773158390/how-to-find-a-mentor-and-make-it-work?t=1627999906092

16 Robbins, T. (2021), *Finding a Mentor*. Available at: https://www.tonyrobbins.com/personal-growth/how-to-get-a-mentor/

17 Phan, J.T. (2021), *What's the Right Way to Find a Mentor?* https://hbr.org/2021/03/whats-the-right-way-to-find-a-mentor

18 Microsoft (2021), *The New Future of Work*. Available at: https://www.microsoft.com/en-us/research/uploads/prod/2021/01/NewFutureOfWorkReport.pdf

19 University of Nebraska (2021), *Information for Mentors*. Available at: https://www.unmc.edu/academicaffairs/faculty/mentoring/mentors/index.html

20 Umoh, R. (2017), *Why You Should Find a Great Mentor If You Want to Be Successful*. Available at: https://www.cnbc.com/2017/09/11/why-you-should-find-a-great-mentor-if-you-want-to-be-successful.html

21 Uhland, S. (2017), *Famous Mentors and Mentees That became Very Successful*. Available at: https://suzzanneuhland.wordpress.com/tag/father-michael-van-der-peet/

22 Conway, C. (1995), *Mentoring Managers in Organisations*. doi:10.1108/eb010639.

23 Thakral, A. (2015), *Four Things I Learned About Mentorship From Former CEO of AstraZeneca David Brennan*. Available at: https://glginsights.com/news/four-things-i-learned-about-mentorship-from-former-ceo-of-astrazeneca-david-brennan-by-anshul-thakral-gm-of-glg-life-sciences/

24 Bidwell, L. (2021), *Why Mentors Matter: A Summary of 30 Years of Research*. Available at: https://www.sap.com/uk/insights/hr/why-mentors-matter.html

25 Health and Social Care Board (2014), *Coaching and Mentoring in Social Work – A Review of the Evidence*. Available at: http://hscboard.hscni.net/download/PUBLICATIONS/SOCIAL-WORK-STRATEGY/Coaching_and_Mentoring_in_Social_Work-Review_of_the_Evidence.pdf

26 Roulet, T. and M. Gill (2019), *Stressed at Work? Mentoring a Colleague Could Help*. Available at: https://hbr.org/2019/03/stressed-at-work-mentoring-a-colleague-could-help

27 Health and Social Care Board (2014), *Coaching and Mentoring in Social Work – A Review of the Evidence*. Available at: http://hscboard.hscni.net/download/PUBLICATIONS/SOCIAL-WORK-STRATEGY/Coaching_and_Mentoring_in_Social_Work-Review_of_the_Evidence.pdf

28 Ibid.

29 Tu, M. and M. Li (2021), *What Great Mentorship Looks Like in a Hybrid Workplace*. Available at: https://hbr.org/2021/05/what-great-mentorship-looks-like-in-a-hybrid-workplace

30 Health and Social Care Board (2014), *Coaching and Mentoring in Social Work – A Review of the Evidence*. Available at: http://hscboard.hscni.net/download/PUBLICATIONS/SOCIAL-WORK-STRATEGY/Coaching_and_Mentoring_in_Social_Work-Review_of_the_Evidence.pdf

31 Tu, M. and M. Li (2021), *What Great Mentorship Looks Like in a Hybrid Workplace*. Available at: https://hbr.org/2021/05/what-great-mentorship-looks-like-in-a-hybrid-workplace

32 EY (2017), *The Future of Work Is Changing: Will Your Workforce Be Ready?* Available at: https://www.ey.com/Publication/vwLUAssets/ey-the-future-of-work-is-changing-will-your-workforce-be-ready/$FILE/ey-the-future-of-work-is-changing-will-your-workforce-be-ready.pdf: ey.com

33 Biro, M.M. (2017), *Make 2017 the Year to Get Serious About Mentoring*. Available at: https://www.forbes.com/sites/meghanbiro/2017/01/27/make-2017-the-year-to-get-serious-about-mentoring

34 Tu, M. and M. Li (2021), *What Great Mentorship Looks Like in a Hybrid Workplace*. Available at: https://hbr.org/2021/05/what-great-mentorship-looks-like-in-a-hybrid-workplace

35 Abdelrahman, N., B.J. Irby, R. Lara-Alecio, F. Tong, Z. Chen and J. Koch (2021), *Virtual Mentoring and Coaching: The Perceptions of Female Principal Candidates*. Available at: https://issuu.com/tasanet/docs/jtwse-2021

36 Scigliano, D. (2010), *Telementoring: Taking Learning Global*. Available at: https://conference.pixel-online.net/FOE/files/foe/ed0010/FP/6596-ICT4603-FP-FOE10.pdf

37 Tu, M. and M. Li (2021), *What Great Mentorship Looks Like in a Hybrid Workplace*. Available at: https://hbr.org/2021/05/what-great-mentorship-looks-like-in-a-hybrid-workplace

38 Open University. (2021), *Exploring Career Mentoring and Coaching*. Available at: https://www.open.edu/openlearn/ocw/mod/oucontent/view.php?id=74756&section=5.1

39 Meister, J.C. and K. Willyerd (2010), *Mentoring Millennials*. Available at: https://hbr.org/2010/05/mentoring-millennials

40 Tu, M. and M. Li (2021), *What Great Mentorship Looks Like in a Hybrid Workplace*. Available at: https://hbr.org/2021/05/what-great-mentorship-looks-like-in-a-hybrid-workplace

41 Weinger, M. (2012), *Michelle Obama's 10 Most Memorable Lines*. Available at: https://www.politico.com/story/2012/09/michelle-obamas-10-moving-lines-080715

Further reading

Connor, M. and J. Pokora (2017), *Coaching and Mentoring at Work*. 3rd edition. London: Open University Press.

Cranwell-Ward, J., P. Bossons and S. Gover (2004), *Mentoring – A Henley Review of Best Practice*. London: Palgrave Macmillan.

Morrissey, H. (2018), *A Good Time to Be a Girl*. London: William Collins.

Szgzyglak, G. (2016), *How to Be a Brilliant Mentor*. Harlow: Pearson.

17

MASTERING THE POWER OF PEOPLE DEVELOPMENT

Shawn D. Mathis

Abstract

This chapter explores essential ideas to understand how to master the power of people development – simple, enduring principles shape conversations for success in assisting others to achieve their best in life. People development is a noble thought and action leading to the evolution of a person, community, and society. The process of people development centers on knowledge and action. A six-step process to develop others is described in practical terms of application in helping others reach their best potential. Practical examples are shared from a business dedicated to professional development and a healthcare leader who has devoted his life to helping others. Eastern philosophies – Confucian and Ancient Indian – and Western thought during the Italian Renaissance are explored, providing examples of how we arrived at modern thinking about people development. Concepts for mastering the power of people development are explored as enduring ideas. The life of the mind is at the heart of being good at the work of people development.

Keywords: Development, teacher, student, mentor, knowledge, experience

Introduction

There are few things in life that can be more rewarding than people development. As the great leader Nelson Mandela (1918–2013) said at the

DOI: 10.4324/9781003219293-22

acknowledgement ceremony for FCB Harlow Butler in Johannesburg in 2004, "*There can be no greater gift than that of giving one's time and energy to helping others without expecting anything in return*".[1]

The journey of development, whether for personal or professional reasons, is about knowledge and action. Determining career choice is a time of learning about opportunities and deciding which path to follow, all with a certain level of unknowing and uncertainty. The process of people development encourages one-to-one conversations with those whom you trust, admire, and want to gain knowledge from and who will help you move into action. Both mentor and student are learners. In my own experience, I learn from each interaction with those I mentor. Great joy comes from educating others and learning from them as well.

As a young person, I recall thinking about what I wanted to become in my professional life. During my time of early career decisions, the Internet became available to the world. I was 28 years old, having grown up in a predigital age. As I look back, my task was to determine how to function and grow in a time of great transition in how the world operates. The opportunity was to navigate those decisions with a pre-Internet mindset while learning about professional opportunities emerging in the digital age.

Decisions such as career choices are best made in conversation. As a person learns about available opportunities, it is challenging to make well-founded decisions without conversations with trusted advisors, friends, family, mentors, teachers, and others. In retrospect, there were occasions when a decision led to multiple opportunities. Often, a single choice charts the course for many years to come. Anchoring our knowledge in good, healthy conversations can lower the risk of mediocre decisions.

What is people development?

People development is a noble thought and action. The result is the evolution of a person, community, and society. Development is a thought process focused on behaviors to help a person reach full potential. Embracing potential is to remember what knowledge has been forgotten and to apply what one has forgotten to apply. Since both mentor and student are learners, people development is a mutual effort to learn. I speak mainly from the developer (mentor) rather than the student (mentee) perspective throughout this chapter.

A mentor can help validate a hypothesis of right and wrong. Confirmation of thought comes from discussion and experience, which is the process of validation. Encourage the learner to explore their doubts and strengthen their resolve to act with knowledge. The goal is to get people to use the knowledge that they have been made aware of through conversation. Always think of ways to apply what has been learned for the benefit of society.

The work of people development is about applying knowledge for bigger purposes. In business, the teacher (manager) helps the student (team member) learn how to give their best to the organization. Even if a person is the best in their profession, a mentor can help them learn. Companies that focus on people development are dedicated to attracting and retaining the best talent. Thriving companies have regular, thoughtful discussions about how to help develop their team members. Genuine engagement in people development builds healthy, thriving organizations.

Process in people development

The process of people development centers on knowledge gathering and a call to action. Knowledge gathering occurs when an individual is introduced to a new idea. Action occurs when knowledge leads to activity.

For the mentor, the six-stage process of people development includes:

1. Build a foundation of trust with those whom you want to help in personal growth.
2. Inspire others by sharing your life experiences.
3. Encourage the student to be ready to act upon what has been learned with an appreciation for life experience lessons.
4. Urge an awareness of learning moments for possible life-changing discussions.
5. Create circumstances to act upon the new knowledge learned from conversations. In the process of people development, action is essential. Otherwise, development is only in terms of knowledge gathering.
6. Mentor the student to reflect on what has been learned by asking and what new lessons have you learned? How do you define what you have learned from the teacher?

A trust-based conversation where experiences are shared encourages the student to act upon what is learned. Be aware of opportunities for teaching moments. Mentor the student to actively reflect on what has been learned. These six steps are the complete process of people development.

Online versus face-to-face mentoring

Learning and mentoring are the same in my way of thinking about education. Nothing we discover in an exchange with another human being occurs without a sense of one learning from another. Think of learning as mutual mentoring, whether reading a book or speaking in person or a form of online interaction.

Former ways of learning. Throughout my academic and professional career, I have experienced both online and face-to-face learning. When I first entered the university as a student, online education did not exist. The professor lectured the students who interacted with the teacher and with one another. Much of the learning experience was through reading hardcopy textbooks, traveling to libraries for access to essential books and journals, and preparing for in-person classroom lectures and discussion. Examinations were administered with printed tests answered in longhand writing. One of my favorite activities is to study old books in libraries throughout the world. I reminisce fondly of those former ways of doing education.

Adapting to new ways of learning. After completing the master's degree in the early 1990s, I was not engaged in university education for nearly 20 years. My entry back into education was through a pre-recorded postgraduate-level course at Harvard University, the opposite of all educational experiences I have had in the past. I listened online to the history course taught by Dr. Niall Ferguson. I chose the course, because Dr. Ferguson is one of my favorite authors. I was happy that I could study online without the weekly travel from Nashville, Tennessee, to Cambridge, Massachusetts, and could have the occasion to study with an admired thinker at a world-class university.

I diligently read all hardcopy assignments (not yet all digital), did my best to digest the material, and completed the course. I was amazed at how much I learned, having not spoken to any student or professor in person. The study was very much asynchronous learning, but I learned a lot. This seminal experience led to the conclusion that I could engage in advanced academic study sitting at a computer in my home. Since then, all formal education activities I have been personally involved in, whether as a student or healthcare and business professor in the university setting, have included online resources as a foundational structure to the learning process.

Helping others experience the best of online learning. I have worked as an executive in online healthcare learning for over 20 years. In that time, I have created two companies solely focused on the nursing profession.

One of those companies, OnSomble™, provides behavior diagnostics and education for professional nurses engaging sophisticated software algorithms to help the nurse experience a more targeted educational experience, all in an online environment. I recall that questions continued until 2015 about whether online education could be as valuable as in-person education.

COVID-19 changed the way mentoring occurs. As the grip of COVID-19 became tighter on the world, and the world shut down, what emerged in late 2020 was an interest in discerning how nursing professionals could continue their education through online resources. What moved slowly for the previous 20 years seemed to have a tectonic shift during a single year, the year 2021. In the shutdown of the world, a mindset shift occurred, which I think of as the Zoom transition. With the advent of Zoom meetings becoming as common as the use of the mobile phone in daily life, the atmosphere of education changed. And with that change, the idea of mentoring transitioned along with this mindset shift.

The widespread adoption of online learning has changed the world of education. The world of mentoring has changed in parallel with the academic and professional ways of learning that have occurred worldwide. Four observations that I have taken note of related to the question of in-person and online mentoring in a world that has experienced COVID-19 include:

- **Online mentoring is as accepted, if not preferred, as in-person interaction with the student.** My preference is to engage online resources as a first step in the journey and reserve the in-person meetings for more special interactions, such as deeper conceptual conversations or celebrating success over a cup of coffee with a mentee.
- **The monologue teacher lecturing another person has transitioned to a culture of interaction.** Both teacher and student collaborate in learning.
- **Learning is literally at your fingertips on a keyboard.** Resources are available online, complementing the physical resources – libraries, hardcopy books, journals, etc. As a destination for study, libraries remain an essential and abiding aspect of education, having evolved to embrace a new way of teaching that includes online learning.
- **Yet a great joy remains in the in-person experience.** There is a joy experienced in holding a book in my hands. I take pleasure in contemplating thoughts on the page of a book. Nothing is more enjoyable than sitting in a library such as the Bodleian at Oxford with a book in hand.

- **Online mentoring mirrors the ways of online education.** Online resources are now the backbone of learning, whether formal education or informal mentoring. The in-person time with others is reserved for more significant social interaction and idea exchange, thus deepening the overall experience.

OnSomble™, a company that engages in the professional development of nurses

Many years ago, I partnered with healthcare leaders in the USA to develop a process for helping nurses learn more about daily professional behaviors required to best care for patients. The reason I chose the nursing profession is that the nurse is the frontline caregiver to the patient. In a world of billions of people, the number of nurses to care for the world population is only in the low millions of caregivers. First, I engaged in research, which resulted in two books that I wrote to help me better understand the world nurse shortage crisis.[2] I wanted to reconcile what seemed to be an unsolvable problem. How can a world with so many people have meaningful healthcare with so few nurses?

The goal was large-scale adoption of behavior assessments and education technology delivered to many nurses to encourage better one-to-one patient care. To do so would require considerable technology infrastructure, essential theoretical frameworks, and relationships with healthcare organization leaders and managers to empower nurses to understand how their behaviors influence patient outcomes.

The Dreyfus Skill Acquisition model was chosen as the theoretical framework to measure the knowledge and action of nurses in their work.[3] The Dreyfus model grew out of many years of research to determine if common stages exist through which a person evolved as thinking matures. Learning how to play the game of chess, pilot an airplane, and learn a new language was studied to understand how skill acquisition occurs. The research conclusion was that all three – playing chess, flying a plane, and learning language – evolved through the same five stages – novice, advanced beginner, competent, proficient, and expert.

Each of the five stages included ever-increasing skills in knowledge, standard of work, autonomy, decision, and perception of context.[4] The novice person only knows facts and has minimal experience. The expert knows many facts and has years of experience. The transition is from a basic understanding of facts to the expert thinker who seemingly makes complex decisions without appearing to think through all the details.[5]

The decision was made to engage the Dreyfus model – novice, advanced beginner, competent, proficient, and expert – to measure a nurse's professional behaviors – leadership, decision-making, communication, and practice – in a 360° peer feedback cycle among the supervisor, nurse, and peer with a 21-behavior clinician assessment. Behavior experts developed the assessment, and third-party experts tested the model for scientific validity. I concluded that a large-scale effort was needed to provide professional development resources for nurses (people development) through technology.

After many years of software development and forming relationships with healthcare organizations worldwide, OnSomble™, a company I created in 2007, provides a proprietary Software-as-a-service solution called OnRole™. We work with many healthcare organizations and thousands of nurses to offer behavioral assessments and education in an adaptive-learning software environment. Our system was developed to teach nurses to discern professional behaviors and perform their daily work better. That is our platform to empower nurses to better care for patients.

Challenges faced in developing people have been to help nurses become comfortable with providing candid feedback about one another in the 360° assessment. Often, nurses are concerned that they might offend someone or feel like they are not being optimistic about the other person. The self-assessment is a challenge, because some nurses think negatively about themselves, resulting in unreasonably low self-assessment scores. At times, a person might have an overinflated perception of their behaviors, resulting in a higher self-assessment score that is not realistic. Through online behavior assessments and micro-learning education modules, we work with the nurses to help them provide more balanced self and peer assessments.

A lesson to learn is that actual people development is a process. The process of people development may include the use of technology. Technology is readily available for your use: smartphones, the Internet, virtual meetings with tools such as Zoom, and so many easy-to-use, low-cost solutions. The key is to teach people who want to learn. Help those that are interested in developing their skills and behaviors.

I encourage you to engage in the art of people development. You don't have to build a technology company to be involved in people development. You could follow a simple process to try a small experiment instead of thinking big about thousands of nurses. Think of an alternative approach of mentoring, running small classes, face-to-face conversations. You can do this kind of work in any organization with which you are affiliated.

OnRole™ is a solution delivered to the client solely through the Software-as-a-service platform, which was the intent from the beginning. In early 2020, we were uncertain what effect COVID-19 would have on our business, as was the situation with many companies worldwide. We learned that we were positioned well for a client base that migrated more fully to online assessments and education. OnSomble™ was not required to move entirely online, because we were already fully online.

We were required to unlearn the pre-pandemic ways of conducting business with organizations that were not online as completely as our company. Our clients moved more fully online so that we are now better aligned than we ever have been in the past. Our challenge has been to assist clients in learning how to function in a digital environment. The lesson learned is that change is a constant that never ceases. We are continuing to evolve our understanding of how we can better help nurses learn and actively engage their knowledge in a situation such as a pandemic.

Explore:

OnSomble™ – Our mission is to help caregivers thrive
    https://www.youtube.com/watch?v=E3N_Gkc-QXI&ab_
    channel=OnSomble

People development at Providence St. Joseph Health

Dr. Sylvain ("Syl") Trepanier, System Chief Nursing Officer at Providence St. Joseph Health in Renton, Washington, USA, is responsible for leading a team of 48,000 nurses across 52 hospitals.[6] One of his responsibilities is to grow the Providence Nursing Institute, a professional development programme for nurses.

Through the years, I have observed with admiration Syl's leadership wisdom and effective management of people. He leads from deeply held principles related to the whole person, not simply a bottom-line driven corporate objective. He has a caring heart for others, and he is a high-performance executive. He accomplishes so much without sacrificing an essential idea, that is, of people development.

Syl has served at the vital center of providing care to those in need due to the COVID-19 crisis. His compassion and kindness towards others did not wane even amid very complicated life-threatening circumstances for both his team and the patients they serve. Syl shared a few of his experiences with me in an interview on mastering the power of people development.[7]

Question: What is the essential thought in people development?

Syl: The development of others is the most important priority of any leader. I constantly remind myself that we are nothing without our people. The people we serve are the soul of the organization. Hence, we must prioritize them, invest in them, support them, and inspire them in their development. We can only do so by first showing up with intent and ensuring that we develop a meaningful relationship that will foster trust. Only when they trust us will we be able to inspire them and support their development. Developing others takes time. Leaders must be deliberate, and both the leader and the person need to be ready and open to it.

Question: What benefits have you seen when you focus on developing others?

Syl: I have seen so many benefits when you focus on the development of others. I recall a time when someone new came on the team. This individual had many years of experience, reported to various leaders in her career, and shared with me that I was the first leader engaged in her development and career path. Aside from being a feel-good moment for both the mentor and the mentee, we noticed a much higher level of engagement and performance. The team achieved excellent outcomes that benefited the leader, the team, the patients, and the organization. Never underestimate the power of supporting the people.

Question: Do you ever look back on your experiences and think about what you could have done better?

Syl: One of the most critical moments of growth for me is related to the biggest mistake I made as a new executive. I allowed myself to be bullied by others in making a decision that I knew in my heart was wrong. I was forced to terminate the employment of a nurse due to a series of unforeseen circumstances. I recognized, after the fact, that I had a choice. I could have stuck to my core values and opted not to terminate employment. At the time, I did not recognize that I was being bullied into carrying someone else's values.

I share this story to highlight the importance of staying grounded and connected to your core values. Your value as a leader and those of others and the organization you serve will clash at times. That tension is healthy to a certain point. That said, I would argue that one cannot sustain fulfillment and joy in the work when others are constantly challenging your values. When you reach that threshold, you must stay true to your core values, which may mean different paths for leaders. The lesson here in developing others is first to know yourself and ensure you assist everyone in connecting with the organization's mission, vision, and values.

Lessons learned from Syl:

- Lead from deeply held principles while performing well in your organization. Principles and performance are to be congruent with one another.
- Developing others is the highest priority of a leader.
- Always remember that people are the soul of the organization.
- Mentor those on your team who seek to be taught.
- Never underestimate the power of supporting people on your team.
- Learn from your mistakes.
- Stand by your core values. Stay grounded and remain connected with who you are as a person.

Explore:

Providence Nursing Institute
  https://www.providence.org/business/nursing-institute

People development in Eastern and Western philosophies

Eastern and Western philosophies alike are dedicated to the education of the mind, body, and soul. In Confucian philosophy, "experience is a learning tool for self-cultivation to obtain knowledge which is used to correct and guide one's moral behavior and thought for harmony".[8]

Ancient Indian education is based upon the Gurukula system of the family (kula) and Guru (teacher). The student is immersed in years of training with their spiritual advisor, the Guru. The student leaves their own family and becomes a part of the Guru's family to be "subjected to rigorous discipline", being taught to "work hard; never sit idle; never lose temper; never speak untruth".[9]

The Renaissance education was a matter of learning the ways of the Greco-Roman classical thinkers to transfer the classical mind into their present situation, which was the advent of modern Western philosophy.

Confucian philosophy

- Experience is fundamental to personal development. Learning is engaged as a tool for growth.
- To gain knowledge, the learner focuses on their personal development.
- Knowledge is a measure to improve behavior and govern moral thinking and actions.
- Harmony of knowledge, moral behavior, and virtuous thought are the end goal of Confucian education.

Ancient Indian education

- The Guru–student family experience is fundamental to personal development. The life setting is engaged as a method for growth.
- To gain knowledge, the student is for years under the tutelage of the spiritual advisor.
- Rigorous discipline is required as a source of gaining knowledge through experience.
- Education grounded in family and experiential learning has as the end goal the development of the whole being.

Classical thought

- Studying classical works of the ancient Greeks and Romans was the curriculum to be learned in Renaissance Italy.
- The learner focused on knowledge gathering and then applying what was learned in their modern times.
- The human was the center of all learning and happiness was the highest moral goal to be achieved.

Confucian philosophy, Ancient Indian education, and Classical thought represent ideas of people development from Eastern and Western perspectives. The three ways of thinking each base their views on:

- Experiential knowledge gathered through the teacher–student relationship.
- Active application of the principles in daily life.

- Interaction between the teacher and student is essential.
- Encouragement to act on what is learned.
- Adherence to discipline in study and practice.
- Helping develop the mind of the student.

Concepts for mastering the power of people development

The enduring ideas – faithful, virtuous, humane, and excellent – are deeply held beliefs common among those who desire to help develop others.

- ***Seek the faithful.*** People development has an integrity factor. The person who would help others seeks to be true to the facts or faithful to that which is intellectually correct.
- ***Seek the virtuous.*** People development has a goodness factor. The person who would help others seeks a higher moral standard.
- ***Seek the humane.*** People development has a compassion factor. The person who would help others is kindhearted and benevolent towards others.
- ***Seek the excellent.*** People development has an exceptional factor. The person who would help others seeks that which is of the highest quality in others.

To do something well, to be good at anything, requires an enormous time and energy commitment. In a sense, mastering anything is a matter of focusing the mind on what one determines to accomplish. Learning the power of people development requires no less a commitment.

A commitment to people development includes:

A desire to influence others for the better. Be a positive guide to help others. Help the student learn something new or recall forgotten knowledge. Influence thinking that results in better outcomes. Nurture your desire to influence the betterment of the person, community, and society.

Being available to others as an investment of time. Being social, we seek interaction with others as natural to our existence. We learn. We teach. We exchange. At times, a mere transaction of information; occasionally, transformational thoughts. Some are complex, others are simple. People share. How and what we share informs how and what we learn.

An openness to learning in the moment. One can learn in isolation, even on a long walk in the forest, through contemplative moments. The mind receives information more rapidly than we even pause to comprehend. All-day. Every day. The mind passively receives much of the data received throughout life. We experience life through the constant flow of information obtained through the senses into the mind.

The decision to actively learn. Not all learning is merely sensory. There is a form of learning through active engagement of the mind. Not passive, rather active. Here, knowledge acquisition is a decision. To read a book is a decision to input the information on the page into your mind. To study a concept is an on-purpose effort to gain more knowledge, to learn. The active learner decides to engage in better understanding the nuances of thought.

Influence as a passive form of teaching. One can teach others without knowing what is being taught, whether by a misplaced comment or poorly chosen behavior. Perhaps the lesson taught is a good life lesson. Passive teaching appears in the influence one has on another person.

The interplay of teacher and learner. A skilled teacher calls upon the art and science of information transference. Neither active learning nor active teaching is an accidental occurrence. Both are learned behaviors. The interplay of teacher and learner is at the center of mastering the power of people development. Teaching in isolation is not a practical method since developing others involves dyadic interaction (one-to-one relationships). A remarkable exchange occurs when one person shares with another.

Student participation in episodes of exchange. With isolation removed and interaction engaged, information begins to flow, resulting in the illumination of new ideas or the confirmation of well-placed thoughts. Here, one no longer relies on isolated learning moments; instead, the student participates in episodes of exchange – one person with another.

Transferring ideas from one person to another. Consider any book you have read. Envision the author's effort and time to write the manuscript resulting in the book. The physical act of writing each word ultimately results in thousands upon thousands of words arranged to share comprehensive and straightforward thoughts. Years of contemplative thinking and continued writing go into creating great books.

Exploring the written works of teachers from long ago. The words of a book teach others long after the death of the author. The author's work remains within the boundaries of the book until a willing reader appears. Ideas sit silently within the book's covers until someone decides to pull the book off the shelf, open the work, and begin reading the words.

The life of the mind. Words are carefully arranged on the page of the book to share the mind of the author. When the person opens the book to read, the words come to life, and the author's ideas transfer as active concepts into the reader's mind: as if spoken from the author to the reader, the teacher to the student. This symbiotic relationship – the author and reader – is, in many ways, parallel to that of the teacher and student.

Similarly, the teacher's mind is full and ready to be pulled from the mind's bookshelf for the learner's study. Mastering the power of people development is about transferring ideas from one mind to another. The unique relationship between teacher and student is one of information transfer. One has information to share; the other desires to hear the announcement of thought.

Mastering the power of people development emerges through the life of the mind

To master the power of people development is to master human interaction. The mentor and student learn together through an ongoing interest in the discussion topics. Personal interaction requires a genuine interest in seeking to understand others. Pithy sayings and witty remarks do not capture the idea of mentoring others for growth. Being a confidante is not about how clever one can be rather how thoughtful one is concerning others. The power of people development resides in understanding what it takes to help develop others.

Whether the novice student or expert teacher, all would do well to seek counsel from trusted advisors. Keep the mind open to new ideas. Be willing to unlearn and relearn a better way. People development begins with self-development, an active journey that provides fertile soil to be a teacher of others.

After teaching the lesson, the teacher will take the students to the science lab, helping them apply the theory taught in class. The students do the experiment themselves, which is a form of action. In these exercises, the student learns new lessons the teacher may not have taught.

The open mind. Mastering the power of people development requires an open mind. The teacher's mind is full of life experience and studied thought. The student is a follower. Without the ability to follow, one cannot learn. An open-minded person can learn from the teacher, which is a matter of capacity, willingness, and learning. The open mind is a learning mind ready to receive rather than always desiring to impart thought. Quintilian concludes that "precocious intellects rarely produce sound fruit".[10] Clement of Alexandria quotes Heraclitus, "Much learning does not teach intelligence".[11]

The curious mind. The human mind naturally has an eagerness to search for answers. The astute teacher understands this as part of human nature, while the student may only have an elementary understanding of the mind's desire to seek answers. The teacher's role is to help the student learn how to engage the curious mind. Curiosity undeveloped remains a mere fascination. Clement of Alexandria states, "Clarity contributes to the transmission of truth".[12] Cicero rightly observes, "The distinctive faculty of man is his eager desire to investigate the truth".[13]

The cultivated mind. The cultivated mind seeks that which is humane. As a seed planted matures, the mind cultivated creates mighty oak trees of intellect. Isocrates asserts, "The cultivation of the mind is the noblest and worthiest of pursuit".[14] The cultivated, educated mind sees humanity from the most elementary letters of an alphabet and basic words of language to the most complex reasoning of grammar, logic, rhetoric (the trivium) and number, geometry, music, and science (the quadrivium).

The educated mind. The human mind searches to know. That knowing, in time, forms the foundation of one's education. Erasmus opines that "a sound education contributes . . . to wisdom" and "a proper and conscientious instruction is the well-spring of all moral goodness".[15] Jerome notes, "The very rudiments and first beginnings of knowledge sound differently in the mouth of an educated man and of an uneducated man".[16] Education is not limited to the classroom, nor does the education process culminate only in a certificate or diploma; rather, the mind's education never ceases.

The humane mind. To be human is to be a part of humanity. One can be human without being humane. To be humane is to be aware of and sensitive to humanity's needs, desires, and ways. The humane mind is compassionate, benevolent, and kind towards others. A humane teacher will share a message of what is true and good and beautiful on the earth.

Summary

Keep in mind that people development is about knowledge and action. Knowledge is transferred from one person to another in a variety of methods. Often, the mentor and student learn together by applying (doing) what one or both have learned (thinking) through life experience. The person who would master the power of people development is first a person who wants to better society by helping others to be the very best that their potential allows. This is the first and foremost purpose for engaging in people development. There is great worth in the simple idea of knowledge gathering or learning. However, knowledge gathering coupled with action to cause good to occur is the best combination. What better situation could exist than knowing and acting in a manner to make the world a better place for all. We all can contribute to this in every act of kindness given to others.

Simple exercises to experiment with mastering the power of people development

Choose a teacher who can help you learn how to master the power of people development. Ask your mentor to explore with you the success and failures experienced along their life's journey of helping others in their development.

Actively engage in people development by allowing yourself to be in the mentor's role. Encourage teacher–student interaction. Be aware of your role in helping the student gather knowledge and guide them towards a call to action to apply what has been learned. Keep in mind the need for study and practice in the discipline of people development.

Notes

1 Mandela, N. (2004), *Address by Nelson Mandela at the Acknowledgement Ceremony of FCB Harlow Butler, Johannesburg*. Available at: http://www.mandela.gov.za/mandela_speeches/2004/040227_butler.htm

2 Mathis, S. (2008), *Solving the Global Nurse Shortage: Social Media and the Cultural Transformation of Nursing*. Nashville, TN: Cumberland Publishing Group and Mathis, S. (2010), *Republic of Nurses: Solving the World Nurse Shortage Through a Global Nurse Community*. Nashville, TN: Cumberland Publishing Group.

3 Dreyfus, S. and H. Dreyfus (1980), *A Five-Stage Model of Mental Activities Involved in Directed Skill Acquisition.* University of California Berkeley.
4 Honken, N. (2013), Dreyfus Five-Stage Model of Adult Skills Acquisition Applied to Engineering Lifelong Learning. *American Society for Engineering Education*, 9.
5 Dreyfus, H. and S. Dreyfus (1986), Why Expert Systems Do Not Exhibit Expertise. *IEEE*, 86–90.
6 Bean, Mackenzie (2021), *People are the Priority, Says Providence CNO Dr. Sylvain Trepanier.* October 21. Available at: https://www.beckershospitalreview.com/nursing/people-are-the-priority-says-providence-cno-dr-sylvain-trepanier.html
7 Trepanier, S. Interview. By Shawn D. Mathis. October 24, 2021.
8 Chuang, S. (2007), The Influence of Confucian Philosophy on Adult Learners Who Come From Confucian Influenced Societies. *Louisiana State University*, 4.
9 Kachappilly, Kurian (2003), *Gurukula: An Exposition of the Ancient Indian Education System.* p. 7. pdf available from https://www.academia.edu>Gurukala Re
10 Quintilian in Gamble, R. (Ed.) (2012), *The Great Tradition.* 3rd edition. Wilmington: ISI Books, p. 116.
11 Clement of Alexandria in Gamble, R. (Ed.) (2012), *The Great Tradition.* 3rd edition. Wilmington: ISI Books, p. 173.
12 Ibid.
13 Cicero in Gamble, R. (Ed.) (2012), *The Great Tradition.* 3rd edition. Wilmington: ISI Books, p. 84.
14 Isocrates in Gamble, R. (Ed.) (2012), *The Great Tradition.* 3rd edition. Wilmington: ISI Books, p. 53.
15 Erasmus in Gamble, R. (Ed.) (2012), *The Great Tradition.* 3rd edition. Wilmington: ISI Books, p. 361.
16 Jerome in Gamble, R. (Ed.) (2012), *The Great Tradition.* 3rd edition. Wilmington: ISI Books, p. 212.

Further reading

Schall, J. (2006), *The Life of the Mind.* Wilmington: Intercollegiate Studies Institute.
Sertillanges, A.G. (1998), *The Intellectual Life: Its Spirit, Conditions, Methods.* Washington, DC: Catholic University Press.

PART VI
Mental resilience

18

MASTERING THE POWER OF MENTAL FITNESS

Mark O'Brien

Abstract

Unleashing the Power of You will never be realised without the mental fitness required to achieve your vision and goals. Building great mental fitness is a pre-requisite for performing to the best of your abilities as you strive for a noble purpose – one that will provide you meaning and leave your unique mark on the world.

Cultivating the discipline to keep "Turning Up" when faced with adversity is a super-power that anyone can develop by focusing on strategies that build mental fitness. Examining the story of how inspiring leaders have built their own mental fitness is a helpful way to evaluate, and adjust, your own powerful narrative – one that will act as a compass as you navigate a life of meaning and service.

Keywords: Resilience, mental fitness, performance, purpose

Introduction

> *"Do the thing and you will have the power"*.[1]
> *Ralph Waldo Emerson (1803–1882), an American essayist, philosopher,*
> *abolitionist, and poet*

It is not hard to find advice on the key role physical fitness plays in your chances of experiencing good physical health. Likewise, philosophy, science, and religious traditions offer guidance on how you increase the likelihood of

DOI: 10.4324/9781003219293-24

experiencing good mental health. But just as pursuing physical fitness won't guarantee an illness-free life, and having great mental fitness doesn't mean that you will automatically avoid the psychological pain inherent in the ups and downs of life, mental illness, or a paralysing existential crisis. However, any vision you have – or goals you set – to unleash the Power of You will never be realised without the mental fitness required to achieve them. And Emerson suggests that creative capacity arise from action – even in the face of doubt and uncertainty. Building great mental fitness is a pre-requisite for performing to the best of your abilities as you strive for a noble purpose – one that will provide you meaning and enable you to leave your unique mark on the world.

Definition

Mental Fitness is the changeable capacity to utilise resources and skills to psychologically adapt to environmental challenges or advantages to meet psychological needs.[2]

Most people, if asked, can identify the key steps an elite athlete takes to attain peak physical fitness. But for most of us, it's not as easy to compile a similar list for mental fitness. In my view, the aforementioned definition holds important truths about mental fitness, emphasising the critical ability to develop sufficient control over our thoughts and emotions so that are capable of responding in the most effective way to change – whether we perceive that change as "good" or "bad".

In my professional life, I have had the privilege of reading and studying great thinkers and researchers on how to acquire the mental fitness necessary for high performance. And on paper, it looks quite straight forward – even easy. There are no shortage of academic publications or helpful books on how to increase your happiness and resilience. But while our "conscious" brain can learn the "what" of mental fitness, our "unconscious" brain can easily sabotage our chances of success by processes we are completely unaware of.

In my younger years, I often castigated myself for my "weakness" at not being able to fully understand and master the unhelpful behaviours and attitudes, seemingly out of conscious control, that I knew would not bring me happiness or success. I know as a doctor that such attitudes and behaviours

TABLE 18.1 A Conceptual Model of Measuring Mental Fitness

Strength
- Self-efficacy
- Positive affect
- Social support
- Emotional management

Flexibility
- Mindfulness
- Acceptance
- Psychological flexibility

Endurance
- Resiliency
- Meaning
- Purpose
- Autonomy

arise from cultural, family and religious/philosophical influences in early life, personality, "disposition" and defensive responses to hurts and rejections – to name but a few. I believed at that time that fully understanding these factors in myself would somehow turn me into an enlightened being! Please don't misunderstand me; deepening self-understanding is important, but it doesn't magically predestine personal fulfilment or success. And so, my purpose in this chapter is not to drown you in mental well-being research on the "what". That's easy to access. Rather, I would like to reflect on the "how". What does one do to master the challenge of building mental fitness to have impact?

The evolutionary challenge

One of my favourite lines in presentations to medical colleagues is:

> *Despite our brains having amazing computational "hardware", our software is still Human 1.0 – and there hasn't been a significant upgrade in 40,000 years!*

In my view, a key to understanding mental fitness is to fully recognise the limitations that we, as primates, have in understanding that how and why we act. However, research has shown we are quite exceptional in retrospectively creating narratives (mostly inaccurate) that we tell ourselves and others about why we acted. For example, studies have shown that individuals tend to under-estimate the impact of luck and good fortune and over-estimate their own ability, agency, and talents in any success they have achieved.[3]

I believe luck has played a critical role in my life. I had loving parents, was born into a stable country, received a good education, and married my best friend. Acknowledging the role of luck, in my view, is too infrequent in "self-help" and motivational texts and is profoundly disrespectful to those who have suffered great misfortune. Attaining mental fitness is harder for those not blessed with a dollop of good luck.

The importance of overcoming challenges

But there is a paradox here. Many successful people attribute the attainment of their mental fitness to lessons internalised in overcoming difficulties and challenges in their past. And the research agrees with them. Like an athlete refusing to work against resistance to gain strength, too much "good luck" can predispose to mental laziness and underachievement.

For me, the straining against the grief of losing two younger brothers in tragic circumstances along with the inevitable disappointments inherent in a long personal, professional, and business life have done more to strengthen my mental fitness than anything else. And like hard physical training, it can hurt!

The psychologist, Paula Robinson, has proposed a model (Table 18.1) that, while designed as a conceptual framework for measuring mental fitness, also provides helpful clues on taking a holistic approach to building mental fitness.[4] It draws heavily on a comparative analysis with physical fitness emphasising Strength, Flexibility, and Endurance. This resonates with my own discernment of key characteristics in those who have achieved much.

- The ability to tolerate and overcome a greater level of psychological stress than others (Strength)
- The ability to "move on" when the psychological comfort of familiarity no longer serves their personal, or the common, good (Flexibility)
- The ability to master their feelings of frustration – and even futility – and keep going when success appears more distant than they had hoped (Endurance)

Further information on this model, and its application, can be found at https://www.positivepsychologyinstitute.com.au

But for me, like attaining physical fitness, what really counts is "turning up" to continue the work of using your talents for a noble purpose – despite what thoughts maybe running around in your head. The best vision, supported by the best plan to get physically fit, counts for nothing if you don't actually go for that run or pick up those weights. The highest levels of motivation are obtained from the experience of doing the work – not succumbing to procrastination waiting for inspiration to magically appear. The increased levels of mental fitness I believe I enjoy at this stage of my life are more attributable to the fact that I have become progressively less fearful of failure, less concerned about whether my efforts will be futile, less pensive about whether it is the right time to take risk – and more concerned about the level of my commitment to keep "turning up" to do the work.

Of course, I try to keep up a meditation practice, work to gain self-knowledge, spend time with friends and family, attempt to build my emotional intelligence and attend to my physical fitness –with varying degrees of success! Each of these research-based strategies will add to my mental well-being. But, more than anything else, I keep "turning up" to undertake the work that I feel is important for me to do, with a greater understanding that overcoming any resistance I encounter makes me stronger. And in doing so, I am constantly challenged to reflect and adjust, to the extent I am capable, my attitudes and behaviours to maximise the contribution I can make.

Attaining mental fitness requires recognising that resisting change for the better, avoiding the discomfort of risk taking, and an obsessive craving for certainty and predictability are the physical fitness equivalents of lying in bed, eating ice cream, and watching streaming TV services – not a recipe for high performance and success. Once you start taking purposeful, committed action, your chances of success increase no matter how bad your luck and no matter how many think you will fail.

Mental fitness improves performance

As a medical doctor, I am well aware of the profound impact that the philosophical ideas, enunciated by René Descartes and commonly referred to as "Cartesian Duality", have had on western medical thinking. In short, in this paradigm the "mind" and "body" are seen as two separate – and poorly linked – entities. At its worst, this has led to research on both "entities" never being joined up!

In the last decade, there has been a plethora of studies confirming what should have been blindingly obvious – at least in my view. The healthier your body, the healthier your mind is likely to be! The purpose of this chapter is not to dazzle you with the sheer volume of this research but to alert you to the fact that keeping moving during the day, eating well, getting sufficient sleep, ceasing smoking, avoiding excessive alcohol and other drug ingestion, taking regular aerobic exercise, and keeping your weight in the heathy range all make a major contribution to mental fitness. The cellular processes in brain cells are basically the same as cells in other parts of your body. So, it's hardly surprising that the research shows that what keeps any organ healthy will keep our most evolved organ, the brain, healthy too.

Not all studies that hit the public media have great statistical "power". That's why doctors can sometimes be a little sceptical of "amazing findings". For me, one of the most recent studies with strong scientific "power" worth paying attention to at the time of writing (2021) is a prospective study of 150,000 people in the United Kingdom showing those with low levels of cardiovascular and physical strength fitness were likely to develop a range of mental illnesses over a seven-year period at a staggering one and a half to twice the rate of those with high levels.[5]

Examples of those who have mastered mental fitness

1. Nelson Mandela

I have had the privilege of twice visiting the jail on Robbin Island where Nelson Mandela, leader of the African National Congress and first president of an apartheid-free South Africa, languished for decades. While smashing rocks and digging lime (the lime would damage his eyes so that he suffered poor vision for the rest of his life), he and his colleagues educated each other, formed a "shadow cabinet" and planned the policies and programmes they would implement should the apartheid regime fall and they assume leadership.

To me, Mandela and his colleagues demonstrated almost superhuman mental fitness. How futile their cause must have appeared at times? How easy it would have been for them to succumb to bitterness and abandon hope? Yet day after day, on that windswept island in the Western Cape, they did what their values and talents demanded on the *chance* that one day they would be given the opportunity to make a powerful contribution to their country. On my second visit, looking back across the sea at Cape Town and imagining what that great man must have been thinking as he took in the same view, I felt that I internalised my understanding of how to build mental fitness to achieve a noble purpose more than from any text I had read or speaker I had listened to. Mandela to me represents the pinnacle of mental fitness- an extraordinary human who just kept "turning up" day after day to do the work dictated by his values – and in the process laying the preconditions for greater equality in South Africa.

2. Robert (Bob) James Lee Hawke

In 2019, Australia mourned the death of our 23rd, and some would argue greatest, Prime Minister. The outpouring of emotion from both sides of the political spectrum spoke of the enormous gratitude my country felt for having had such a gifted leader – a man who took Australia from a place where many of the brightest and best felt that they needed to leave to fulfil their potential to one where the brightest and best proudly call home.

Bob Hawke had a fierce intellect, and luck played an important part in his life, being blessed with an extraordinary affability, which connected him to people from all walks of life. From an early age, he reported feeling destined to achieve greatness. He rose quickly though the powerful Australian Trade Union movement in the turbulent late 1970s and, using his extraordinary negotiation skills, resolved disputes that would have otherwise paralysed the country. He seemed divinely touched to assume the highest office in the land.

However, I include the story of Bob Hawke deliberately in this chapter because of its moral complexity – and because on our journey to mental fitness each of us wrestles with the primal drives and contradictions, that while inherent to our evolutionary success story as a species, hold the potential to derail us as we seek to act with a higher societal purpose.

Bob Hawke was a self-acknowledged alcoholic and stories of his serial infidelities offended many – and were blamed for the breakdown of his marriage to his much loved and admired first wife. Subsequent to his death, his daughter made allegations that he failed to protect her – allegations which appear difficult to test due apparently to lack of corroborating evidence or, of course, his ability to respond to.

Many who recognised his potential doubted that it may be realised. So his announcement in 1980 that he had "quit" alcohol was understandably met with some disbelief and derision. Yet he was not to have another drink until many years after he had served as Australian Prime Minister from 1983 to 1991.

As a doctor, I've seen the enormous struggle necessary to give up the "demon drink". Bob Hawke's continued abstinence demonstrated extraordinary mental fitness. Ceasing alcohol abuse is an hour-by-hour, day-by-day determination to be true to your pledge to regain self-mastery. How easy it would have been to relapse as he strode the world stage – or justify a drink on the stress of his job. In interviews, he disclosed he knew that if he was to transform the country his drinking had to stop. Knowing "what" to do was the easy part.

Bob Hawke's day-by-day "turning up" to the struggle with his addiction is an extraordinary example of how great mental fitness is built – and made him one of Australia's greatest political leaders. In documenting my great admiration for the mental fitness demonstrated by him, I ponder also on the frailty of the human condition and the battle between the "monster and the saint" that Richard Holloway so eloquently describes rages inside each of us.[6]

3. Anne Frank

Achieving mental fitness can occur at any age. I remember reading the diary of Anne Frank as a teenager 40 years ago and being inspired by the values and determination of this incredible young woman hiding from the Nazi regime in an attic in the streets of Amsterdam.

The following extracts from her diary, written in 1944 less than a year before her death, speaks eloquently of the need to "turn up" to build mental fitness – irrespective of what circumstances you find yourself in.

> *I finally realized that I must do my schoolwork to keep from being ignorant, to get on in life, to become a journalist, because that's what I want! I know I can write . . ., but it remains to be seen whether I really have talent.*
>
> *I want to be useful or bring enjoyment to all people, even those I've never met. I want to go on living even after my death! And that's why I'm so grateful to God for having given me this gift, which I can use to develop myself and to express all that's inside me.*[7]

What I find so inspiring is her understanding of the need to take action consistent with her values and talents to fulfil a noble purpose – even when success seems unlikely or the future uncertain. For whatever reason, I too felt this strongly after the death of a brother in my early thirties. Anne understood that death might have been only one house search or betrayal away yet, at a very young age, grasped that to build her mental fitness to make a contribution to the world required "turning up" every day to write her story. Not every person's efforts to make their unique contribution results in transformational success or public acknowledgement. Anne Frank's life ended in the most pitiable of circumstances caused by unspeakable evil. Yet today the world is richer for this young woman who took seriously her need to do what her values and talents demanded – leaving a legacy of incalculable value.

Important concepts

Resilience

The ability to weather the ups and downs of life and recover from challenge and disappointment is built by facing adversity with courage, reflecting on one's response to a challenge to learn lessons for the future, and respecting the need for a time of recovery to maximise the chances of "bouncing back".

Mindfulness

The ability to pay attention to what is happening in each moment – in our external environment, in others, and in ourselves – so that our actions are not purely pre-determined by the biases and scars of the past nor the fears and pre-occupations of the future.

Emotional intelligence

The capacity to make conscious, identify and name, and then choose the healthiest and the most life-affirming response to the mixture of emotions that our brain generates in response to the way we understand and perceive the world, others and ourselves.

Cognitive biases

The unconscious errors in thinking our brain makes in its attempt to reduce the "hard" work of collecting data and interpreting facts free from pre-judgement and poorly informed opinion. Creating practices and strategies to negate cognitive biases is an essential element of the mental fitness required to make great judgements.

Some simple mental fitness strategies to improve your ability to thrive as a leader

- Understand that stress is inevitable – so seek to ensure that the stress you choose to take on derives from creating something of value and worth

- Focus on discerning truth and removing bias so that you see the world as it really is – then live your life in that truth and reality
- Plan "time in the desert" so that you can listen to your heart and discern what is significant, and creates meaning, for you
- Develop a personal mission statement
- Create a plan on how you advance your move from success to significance in this decade of your life
- Review your calendar and consider whether your time is spent wisely in light of your discernment of what matters to you
- Learn to manage difference in opinions by listening and then building bridges – rather than perceiving different viewpoints as a battleground

I finish my short reflections on mental fitness with a quote that I return to again and again in my personal life when plagued by "Imposter Syndrome" or near-paralysed by procrastination or doubt. I hope it speaks to you of the need to keep "Turning Up" to life as powerfully as it does to me.

> *It is not the critic who counts; not the man who points out how the strong man stumbles, or where the doer of deeds could have done them better. The credit belongs to the man who is actually in the arena, whose face is marred by dust and sweat and blood; who strives valiantly; who errs, who comes short again and again, because there is no effort without error and shortcoming; but who does actually strive to do the deeds; who knows great enthusiasms, the great devotions; who spends himself in a worthy cause; who at the best knows in the end the triumph of high achievement, and who at the worst, if he fails, at least fails while daring greatly, so that his place shall never be with those cold and timid souls who neither know victory nor defeat.*[8]
>
> *Theodore Roosevelt (1858–1919), an American statesman*
> *and 26th President of United States*

Reflect:

What noble purpose, consistent with my values, would benefit from my unique combination of personality, talents, and lived experiences?

Summary

While tragedy and loss, bad luck, and personal inadequacies can seem enormous barriers to unleashing the Power of You, building mental fitness by straining against adversity and challenge is the common path taken by exceptional individuals who live authentic lives and make a contribution of value unique to their talents. Resources to learn about the "what" of building mental fitness and well-being are freely available and are a valuable aid in the journey of self-improvement. However, knowledge and understanding do not always translate into action. Strong unconscious forces can easily derail the best vision and goals. Unleashing the Power of You arises from a commitment to "turn up" in the face of challenge to apply your unique talents and insights to a noble purpose aimed at making a contribution to others and the world.

Explore:

The Positive Psychology Institute www.positivepsychologyinstitute.com.au

    Positive Psychology Centre
        www.ppc.sas.upenn.ed
    Mindfulness-Based Stress Reduction
        www.umassmed.edu/cfm/
    Headspace
        https://headspace.org.au/

Notes

1   Emerson, R.W. *Attributed*. Available at: www.goodreads.com/quotes/9971512-the-law-of-nature-is-do-the-thing-and-you

2   Robinson, P., L.G. Oades and P. Caputi (2015), Conceptualising and Measuring Mental Fitness: A Delphi Study. *International Journal of Wellbeing*, 5(1), 53–73.

3   Biondo, A. and A. Rapisarda (2018), Talent vs Luck: The Role of Randomness in Success and Failure. *Advances in Complex Systems*, 21, 1180500145.

4   Robinson, P.L., L.G. Oades and P. Caputi (2014), *Conceptualising and Measuring Mental Fitness*. Ph.D. Thesis, University of Wollongong: Australia, p. 48.

5   Kandola, A., D. Osborn, et al. (2020), Individual and Combined Associations Between Cardiorespiratory Fitness and Grip Strength With Common Mental Disorders: A Prospective Cohort Study in the UK Biobank. *BMC Medicine*, 18, 303.

6   Holloway, R. (2009), *Between The Monster and The Saint: Reflections on the Human Condition*. Canongate Books.

7   Frank, A. (1952), *The Diary of Anne Frank*. Bantam Publishers, p. 184.

8   Roosevelt, R. (1910), *The Man in the Arena. Speech, Sorbonne University*. Theodore Roosevelt Center at Dickinson State University.

Further reading

- Mandela, N. (1985), *A Long Walk to Freedom: The Autobiography of Nelson Mandela*. UK: Time Warner Books.
- Frank, A. (1952), *The Diary of Anne Frank*. USA: Bantam Publishers.
- D'Alpuget, B. (2010), *Hawke: The Prime Minister*. Australia: Melbourne University Press.
- Holloway, R. (2009), *Between the Monster and the Saint: Reflections on the Human Condition*. UK: Canongate Books.
- Brown, B. (2017), *Rising Strong: How the Ability to Reset Transforms the Way We Live, Love, Parent, and Lead*. USA: Random House.

19

MASTERING THE POWER OF SELF-CONFIDENCE

Chloe Phillips Harris

Abstract

What is self-confidence, and how do you get it?

With enough self-confidence, you are able to achieve anything you put your mind to. Although life can be filled with challenges and roadblocks, these experiences are actually opportunities for increased confidence and success. This chapter explores techniques to increase your own self-confidence and personal stories that you can seek inspiration from.

Keywords: Self-confidence, confidence, challenges, experiences

Introduction

This chapter is about self-confidence, an attribute that can help you to achieve anything that you put your mind to. What then, is "self-confidence"? The *Oxford Concise Dictionary* describes self-confidence as "*a feeling of trust in one's abilities, qualities, and judgement*".[1]

As the famous Austrian poet and novelist, Rainer Maria Rilke (1875–1926), wrote:

> Be patient toward all that is unsolved in your heart and try to love the questions themselves like locked rooms and like books that are written in a very foreign tongue. . . . And the point is, to live everything. Live

DOI: 10.4324/9781003219293-25

the questions now. Perhaps you will find them gradually, without notic-
ing it, and live along some distant day into the answer.

(Letters to a Young Poet, p. 35)[2]

Personal experience

It was raining, the sky filled with unmoving light grey clouds that had stuck
themselves in amongst the surrounding hills – there was no hope of the wet
sky easing.

It was winter in New Zealand, the mud sucked at my boots and everything was dripping with water. For those of you who haven't experienced
mud, this is not the wet splashy kind. No, it sucks at your feet, threatening
to pull boots off and weighing you down with every step. Water was running
down my face, neck under my clothes, in my boots and it tickled. Trying to
itch just added more mud and discomfort. I stood miserable and looked at
the scene in front of me: my vehicle was stuck. Both wheels on one side at
least a foot lower than the other where they had sunk fast in the awful mud.
I'd tried putting it in four-wheel drive but there was no use and the more
I tried to drive it out the more the wheels dug in deeper.

I telephoned my dad; he was usually the one who could help with these
kinds of problems. "You'll just have to get it out yourself, I can't come. You
can figure it out". There was no point ringing my mother who was at least
two days away, at a sporting event with my brother. I was alone on the farm
in the rain and it was up to me to get unstuck. I had animals to feed, and if
I didn't get the car out, I couldn't go anywhere either.

It took hours. I got shovels and dug. I got rocks and put them either side
of the wheels. Then, I got in the driver's seat, turned the ignition, and put
the car in "Drive". I rocked it back and forth, from first gear to reverse and
back again, minute after minute slowly building up momentum until the
wheels gained traction on the rocks. I touched the accelerator and kept the
forward movement going. I didn't stop until I was out of the paddock, keeping my cool even as the truck slid sideways, fish tailing across the wet and
muddy ground.

That was over 15 years ago, but I still remember the moment of finally
reaching solid ground. I realised I could do things on my own, and although
it would have been nice to have help, I didn't need it. I have not pursued
a life of four-wheel driving, but it was moments like this throughout my
younger years that gave me confidence in myself for a variety of adventures
that have followed.

Many years later, I sat at the kitchen table, smiled, and looked directly down the lens of a camera while an interviewer asked me questions. I'd just led the first expedition of its kind across the Gobi Desert in winter. The temperature had been as low as −43 C and we'd crossed 300 km of wild remote areas on camels. I was nervous, but I was confident. I knew I could do this.

How did I go from stuck in the mud on a farm, to crossing a desert and finally sitting in the kitchen talking to TV cameras? It was all the usual stuff – hard work, patience, etc. – but most of all it was confidence in myself that I could do these things. When everyone said something was impossible, I had a quiet feeling in myself that it was possible and I would not be swayed.

Self-confidence is essential to success, innovation, and happiness. It also comes in many forms. In some people, it is the ability to stand in front of a room of peers and give a presentation. In others, the ability to dance on stage, to take a class outside their comfort zone, to enter a race, or to push oneself to accept new challenges.

For me, it is exactly as the dictionary describes: "a feeling of trust in one's abilities, qualities, and judgement".[3] It manifests itself in the small voice inside my head that says "you can do this, you can solve this" no matter what I face. Everyone in life will face insecurities; everyone will face critics and judgement in some form. This is why a belief in yourself is so important. It is that voice that I trust when faced by those who doubt or disagree with my plans or abilities.

Self-confidence to me is about knowing that you can figure out a solution, a way to overcome any challenge or task. It is believing that although some things in life are hard, they are not impossible, and you can achieve anything you want. There is always a way forward, and if you believe in yourself, you can find the solutions and pathways to success. If you don't believe in yourself, all you will see is the road-blocks and obstacles.

But how do you develop this innate ability to believe in yourself?

I think it comes down to three main points that you can build on:

1. Self-confidence is something you can build with experience.
2. Have a plan.
3. Develop positive self-talk.

1. Build experiences

Rainer Maria Rilke (1875–1926), poet and novelist, said *"perhaps all the dragons in our lives are princesses who are only waiting to see us act, just once, with beauty and courage. Perhaps everything that frightens us is, in its deepest essence, something helpless that wants our love" (Letters to a Young Poet, page 69).*[4] This resonated with me and led me to believe that not everyone is born with a lot of self-confidence. We all have doubts, fears, and insecurities that can stop us achieving great things. Luckily, self-confidence is something that you can grow and develop. If you don't have it now, it doesn't mean you never will. If self-confidence is defined as a trust in "yourself and your abilities", then like any trust between friends or in a leader it can take time to develop.

Like all examples of trust, there is an ongoing, building, shifting, and growing development. The trust starts small but the more you test it, and succeed, gradually the bigger that confidence grows.

Where do you start? Your self-confidence increases from experiences and having mastered particular activities. The day my father told me to get my own vehicle unstuck was the moment I remember, because it was one of those times my belief in myself grew. There were other times I got trucks out of the mud, fixed pipes, mended broken fences, and learnt how to make water pumps work as I was growing up. At the time I hated it, but every little victory added inches to my self-confidence. None of these tasks has specifically helped me in my career, but the confidence and ability to believe in myself have helped. I am still faced with challenges that are outside my skills, my schooling, or my background. Yet I no longer find this daunting because I'm building on so many previous experiences.

If you want to gain self-confidence, the more things you try and master the bigger the belief in yourself will grow. I believe that they do not have to be specific to your work, hobbies, or interests. Anything where you push outside your comfort zone and succeed in any task helps grow your self-confidence. Do this continuously, keeping setting yourself new tasks and ensure you achieve them.

It can start with the smallest task. For some people, it will be going to see a movie or change a tire on their own. For others, it may be solo traveling to a new country. I know for me there were steps in my career I found challenging. Sending my first sponsorship proposal or reaching out to experts in the field for advice and guidance was daunting. Although at first these tasks seemed scary, for having done it my confidence grew and I no longer hesitate to do any of these things.

I used to be terrified of parallel parking when I was in the city. So much so that I'd park my car blocks away to avoid it. The thought of having to manoeuvre my car on busy streets with people watching was terrifying to me. Yet one day, I realised that I was being ridiculous, I could drive a big truck through mud, hills, and rivers, yet I was letting a car park scare me. I found quiet streets and practised parking my car until I got it right. It was the tiniest thing, but it felt amazing to achieve. Then came the day I had to race from the countryside where I live into the city for a meeting and managed to place my car into a busy down-town car park. I sauntered into the office building ready to take on the world.

There are of course things you need to do specifically to grow your confidence in your chosen field job; practise these skills. The biggest mistake I see is people lacking the skills to do a task and so they hide the fact, hoping no one will notice. Having to hide a lack of knowledge or feeling ashamed is a big killer of self-confidence. This only ever holds them back. Do what it takes to master a skill, even if you have to break it down into smaller steps. Ask someone on the job to mentor you until you feel confident. Or, we are lucky enough to live in a day and age where the internet has an answer for everything; there is no excuse for not mastering small tasks. Seeking this knowledge and advice will help not only with your job or passion but also with your self-confidence as well.

The skills I learnt growing up didn't necessarily give me the experience to race horses across a foreign country or tackle a desert in the middle of winter. But when faced with new challenges I drew on what I could do and the confidence I had already established. I could train wild horses at home, I could fix things, I'd spent endless hours alone, I travelled a lot and knew how to take care of myself, what to pack and where I needed to ask advice. I had gotten myself out of so many tricky situations and overcome challenges before. Although I had fears, I also now had the self-confidence to know I could do these new things.

2. Have a plan

The path to self-confidence is helped greatly by having a plan. If you want to start a business, travel the world, dance on stage, or anything else that you may dream of but don't have the confidence to do now, then you need to make a plan of how to get there. Start small, build up to the dream.

First things first, why don't you feel confident in your abilities? What would help develop that confidence? So many people give up before they start because whatever it is they want to achieve seems to overwhelming.

I draw great confidence from having a plan. I don't always map it out on paper but I go over everything in my head: whether it's for an expedition to somewhere I've never been, or just having to do a presentation to a crowded room; I make a plan. It gives me a place to start, visualise the tasks to achieve, and it makes the big dreams seem possible.

Start with the big goal, whatever that may be, then work backwards

What is your big goal, what do you want to achieve? The big goal might be to run a marathon. But just saying this out loud is not enough.

Start with what skills do you have already that will help you? From there, what skills do you need to develop? These would be my first questions. Do you have the right equipment, the running shoes? No, then first how do you afford the shoes and where do you buy them? Then how much running do you need to do to be able to run this marathon, how long do you have to train for? Do you need a coach or running partner to keep you motivated, or is downloading a running plan off the internet enough? Asking these questions and then acting upon the answers will make the plan happen and bring the big goal closer to success.

For example, if you were starting from never having run before, you would have to buy the shoes first and then start with running just one kilometre. It could take you six months to get ready for just a five-kilometre race. But if you can do a five kilometre race, then your confidence in your ability to run a complete marathon is going to greatly increase. Ticking off every one of these steps along the way boosts confidence and makes the bigger goal seem more achievable. Finally, when you start that marathon you will have ticked off all the parts of your plan and feel confident in your ability to finish.

This example of running a marathon has a principle that can be applied to so many things. I have had to present presentations to where I did not feel confident in doing so. But I would make a plan and go over it many times in my head in the lead up. What was my message, what points did I need to get across, how did I get these across. If I could answer this myself then when it came time to stand in front of a room, I felt like I could do a good job.

Your plan needs to reveal the ways you're going to tackle problems or gain the skills to achieve the big goal. There were times when I couldn't answer the questions myself and the biggest step I learned was to ask for help. Finding the answers to create your plan is crucial to giving you the confidence and skills required, so you can achieve anything.

3. Develop positive self talk

In breaking out of self-doubt patterns, I reflect on the words of journalist/novelists Katty Kay (1964–present) and Claire Shipman (1962–present). *"The propensity to dwell on failure and mistakes, and an inability to shut out the outside world are, in his mind, the biggest psychological impediments for his female players, and they directly affect performance and confidence on the court"* (The Confidence Code, page 5).[5]

Develop a strong internal dialogue. Everyone gets nervous, everyone has doubts, but you must not let them rule you. Do not dwell on them. Since I was a young adult, every time I'm faced with a problem, my thought pattern goes: "You can do this. How can you make this work?"

I don't give myself the excuse of dwelling on insecurities. Those are pushed aside immediately. I consciously work on how to find the solution.

This is not something that magically happened. I actively worked on trying to find solutions or telling myself I was good enough until I had taught my brain not to dwell on insecurities or shortcomings.

I worked on it and acted on it until I believed it. It takes practise but it pays off. Overtime, I learned to shut the doubts that threatened to overcome me out. I went through plans in mind of how to overcome challenges. I went over the skills I was good at until it became habit to regularly install my self-confidence. I gave no room to the part of me that doubted and felt I wasn't good enough. All my energy went in to how to figure out the skills I needed to succeed.

It's not just about using positive self-talk. It's not good enough to have a track of endless positivity such as "I am great", going on repeat in your head. I actively list through the things I can do and how I'm going to do them. You need to teach yourself to mentally format solutions. With this skill, you will have the confidence to approach unfamiliar situations and overcome hurdles. With practice, you can teach yourself to think like this and will achieve great things.

Summary

To have self-confidence, you don't have to be the bravest, the loudest, or the smartest. You just have to have a quiet belief in yourself that you can do anything.

In life, there will always be people who doubt you, who don't believe in you, who will criticise. It is your job to believe in yourself and your dreams regardless of what others think or say.

Belief in myself and the confidence to chase my dreams is a skill I value above all others. It is something that has taken time to develop, but has allowed me to achieve so many of my dreams. I built self-confidence by trying and achieving new things. I made plans. I asked myself what skills I had and what I needed to do to reach my goal. Once plans were formulated, I kept to them and I refused to let doubts and fears guide me. I made my inner voice of belief louder than any of my own doubts or those of others.

I think these three things are so important for success in anything you want to achieve, and by working on them, it is obvious that the power of self-confidence is something anyone can master.

Follow-up actions

Start doing more. If you don't feel confident and don't have experience to draw on? Start creating experiences. Go on a walk by yourself, take a day hike. Take a class in something new. Learn how to change a tire.

Build your self-confidence by trying and achieving new things. They don't have to be huge, start with small steps. The more things you can do over a wide range of tasks the more you will start to believe in yourself.

Have a plan to reach your big goal. Ask questions and source the answers to them. Ask for help if you need to. Create smaller goals. Then, act upon those answers and work towards achieving the smaller goals. With every check point you tick off, your self-confidence will grow and you will have full trust in yourself to complete the big goal.

Notes

1   Oxford Online Dictionary (2021), *Self-confidence*. Available at: https://languages.oup. com/google-dictionary-en/. Accessed on: August 23, 2021.
2   Rilke, Rainer M. (1929), *Letters to a Young Poet*. p. 35. W. W. Norton & Company. Available at: https://www.goodreads.com/book/show/46199.Letters_to_a_Young_Poet. Accessed on: August 23, 2021.
3   Oxford Online Dictionary (2021).
4   Rilke, Rainer M. (1929), *Letters to a Young Poet*. p. 69. W. W. Norton & Company. Available at: https://www.goodreads.com/book/show/46199.Letters_to_a_Young_Poet. Accessed on: August 23, 2021.
5   Kay, Katty and Claire Shipman (2014), *The Confidence Code: The Science and Art of Self-Assurance. What Women Should Know*. Harper Business, p. 5.

Further reading

- Gillihan, Seth J. (2016), *Retrain Your Brain (Cognitive Behavioral Therapy in 7 Weeks: A Workbook for Managing Depression and Anxiety)*. USA: Althea Press.
- Harris, Russ (2011), *The Confidence Gap: A Guide to Overcoming Fear and Self-Doubt*. USA: Trumpeter.
- Markway, Barbara and Celia Ampel (2018), *The Self Confidence Workbook: A Guide to Overcoming Self-Doubt and Improving Self-Esteem*. USA: Althea Press.
- Phillips-Harris, Chloe (2019), *Fearless: The Life of Adventurer, Equestrian and Endurance Rider*. USA: Harper Collins.

Fearless is Chloe's own story of growing up, working with wild horses and riding the toughest horse race in the world, The Mongol Derby. The biography gives further examples of tasks overcome and is an inspiring read.

20

MASTERING THE POWER OF COURAGE TO TURN YOUR DREAMS TO REALITY

Avril McDonald

Abstract

We are all born artists with pure limitless creative potential – but as we grow, our creativity and innocent childhood dreams of who we wanted to become can be unintentionally shamed or emotionally beaten out of us by the cultural wounds of society, or educated out of us by the barriers of school systems. Reaching our creative potential personally and/or professionally therefore takes courage – the courage to listen to our hearts, to live our truth, to become aware of (and comfortable with) our own shadows, and to be vulnerable because courage cannot exist without vulnerability.

In this chapter, I share my own journey in learning what the power of courage can have in turning dreams and passions into a reality. I also share my practical strategies and recommendations to help you on your own brave journey – whatever that may be.

Keywords: Courage, journey, vulnerability, dreams

Introduction

Having the courage to overcome fear is one of our most important attributes and can hold the key to success. Courage has a huge effect on turning our dreams and passions into reality. As Professor Joseph Campbell so eloquently wrote,

> Where you stumble, their lies your treasure. The very cave you are afraid to enter turns out to be the source of what you are looking for.

DOI: 10.4324/9781003219293-26

The damned thing in the cave that was so dreaded has become the centre.[1]

Personal experience

What is courage?

Courage is not easy to define. As written in the Journal of Positive Psychology,

> Though numerous definitions of courage provide a rich foundation from which to build, we remain at a loss for an operational definition of this construct on which to base sound explicit theories. Even with all of the attempts to define courage, we have not advanced the domain to an agreed-upon conceptual definition.
>
> The Journal of Positive Psychology, 2007[2]

In pondering a lot about what my own definition of courage is, I think it's a very personal thing to define and we all have our own theories of what it means to have courage. For me, courage is facing (or being faced with) our fears, shadows or triggers and being kind and understanding to ourselves about whatever reactions we have to them. Ultimately for me personally, courage is when I face a fear and can find its gift in my own quest for self-actualisation.

Bringing dreams to life

One of the first things I was certain of as a child was that I was going to be an artist and performer. I was so certain, in fact, that I would boldly declare it with conviction to anyone who cared to listen.

Although I had found a lot of creative fulfilment in the careers that I had chosen, by the time I reached 40 and had two young children, I realised that I was not the artist and performer that I had dreamt I would become as a child. My heart was knocking to strive to reach my creative potential, to become the artist that I always wanted to be by turning my craft into my profession. I knew that this would take some courage. I had fears of failure, but I also knew deep inside of me, that not striving to reach my creative potential (and the regret that would bring), far outweighed my fear of failure.

What dream would you want to bring to life if you had no fear of failure? What do you think holds you back?

The science of achievement

Having grown up with anxiety disorders, I had discovered US Coach Anthony Robbins' work in my teens, which not only gave me strategies to manage my anxiety but also taught me what he defines as "The Science of Achievement" which is that you can achieve almost anything you want to in life.[3] You just need to find someone who is doing it well and ask them for their recipe and model their patterns and behaviours (because success leaves clues!).

I wanted to become a best-selling children's author and to create a global children's brand, which would give *all* children access to tools that help them manage tough emotions and reach their potential. No one ever just "knows" how to do all of this from the outset. I think that it's easy to have an illusion that others who achieve great success have some special talent or skill set in just "knowing" how to make their dreams come true, but in my experience, that is not typically the case.

What I have learnt is that those who achieve great success are usually very persistent and hardworking. They have a healthy attitude to what others perceive as "failure", and they are not afraid to ask for help. I needed to find the courage to believe in my dream and (be brave enough) to ask the right people to help me on my journey of transforming it into a reality.

Asking for help

It takes a certain amount of vulnerability to share a dream with others and to ask for help in bringing it to life. Hopes and dreams are like delicate seedlings; they need to be nurtured. One gust of wind can bring them down – the laughter or disbelief from others can shatter a precious dream in a second, even amongst the seemingly most confident people.

I found the courage to share my dreams and ask for help by looking inside my heart, becoming conscious of my deepest values, and following what was authentically true for me.

I intended to create something powerful and beautiful that served me creatively and served the world compassionately. I have learned that when you put forth a clear request that is authentic, passionate, and serves the world, others will (in most cases), want to help you bring it to life – enthusiasm and passion are delightfully contagious. Asking for help gives you the road signs you need to follow, and those "helpers" or mentors, can also give you the hope that you might need along the way during times when you will be tested or hit roadblocks.

Asking for help in my own journey

I had always known that I wanted to write my children's books in verse. For me, poetry speaks to the heart, and I feel that it is only through the heart that we can truly integrate our shadows and heal.

In my own journey in trying to get a publishing deal, I happened to ask a very successful children's author for his feedback on my work and for any help that he might give me in navigating the publishing journey. When he told me that he really liked my idea around stories for children that gave them emotional well-being strategies but didn't like my verse and "did I have to write in verse?", it totally deflated me and made me question my abilities as a writer.

After a day of feeling deflated, I knew in my heart that no matter what I simply had to write in verse, but I obviously needed to just get better at it! Within three days, (through some helpful industry contacts I had made along the way), I connected with a well-established published poet and asked if he would tutor me in my quest to become a children's author and write in verse. He liked my enthusiasm and passion for what I was trying to do and agreed to meet with me. After reading the work I had written, he very quickly decoded my natural poetry meter and showed me how to consistently write in that meter going forward. With his additional experience in the publishing industry as an editor, he then became my trusted poetry coach, editor (across every one of my books), and a delightful friend.

It would have been easy to give up based on one respected author's opinion had I seen his constructive criticism as a failure, but I now see it as one of the biggest gifts that I have been given in my journey and believe it was pivotal in the direction and success of my children's books.

There's no success without a healthy relationship with failure

My biggest childhood dream was to be a singer, songwriter, and performer so growing up, naturally all I ever dreamed of, was to get a recording contract with a large music label. That had never happened in the way I had envisioned, but after publishing my books and developing my children's brand, I saw the opportunity to fulfil my dream by creating a music destination for children with my characters and their world.

When I found myself sitting with the president of one of the largest global music labels and his marketing team, brainstorming the idea with the likes of some of the world's biggest musicians being a part of it, I had to pinch myself. We engaged in formal negotiations but then one Friday afternoon at 5 pm, the label suddenly pulled out of the deal. I was struck with a devastation and disappointment that I hadn't felt before in my journey.

My young daughter asked me what was wrong, and as told her, I started to cry which she had rarely seen me do. She knew how much it meant to me and asked what she could do to help. My partner and I had always agreed that we didn't want to ever ask our young children to get us alcoholic drinks from the fridge, but, on this occasion, I felt it justified an exception to the rule. I asked her to go and pour me a nice glass of wine.

My son also came in and asked if I was going to "give up" now. I told him that I was *never* going to give up on my dreams but that I felt very sad, and I would probably be sad for a few days and that I wanted to be on my own for a while and have a cry, but after that, I would come back stronger.

What I only realised later was that I was grieving the loss of a childhood dream, and even though this was the biggest disappointment I had felt in my journey, I had a strange inner excitement for the gift I knew I would be getting out of this moment of "death" and "chaos". It was like I had this wonderful new integrated understanding of the cycles in the hero's journey and a new healthy relationship with failure.

When one of my trusted mentors learnt of my disappointment over this deal, he reminded me that I had all the tools, networks, and ability to go and do it all myself which would also mean I would have full creative control and ownership over my creative intellectual property. So I did and I do! Sometimes we just need to be reminded of that.

What I've learnt thus far in my own journey is that every failure, every metaphoric "death", and every disappointment is where the real treasure lies. You are unlikely to have great success without failure and my roadblocks, disappointments, or closed doors have (in retrospect) shown me the way, made me stronger, and forced me to change or pivot where I needed to.

I've learnt to become comfortable with failure, comfortable sitting in the darkness, or weathering the storms, because I have seen for myself that this is where the most magical creative shifts or "eureka" moments have then happened. I am now reassured that the dark and chaos will pass, and I trust timing – the answers are not always clear, but if your vision is strong and true, your paths will eventually take you there. You might not arrive in the way you planned, and the destination might look vastly different to what you originally imagined, but with vulnerability, trust, and good intent, you will master the power of courage and reach your potential.

As Louisa May Alcott wrote in "Little Woman", "*I am not afraid of storms, for I am learning how to sail my ship*".[4]

Embracing our shadows

A big part of my journey of courage in transforming my dreams into a reality has been though learning about my own shadows or "blocks" and having the courage to acknowledge, embrace, and integrate them.

Many creatives (in particular) don't feel worthy of receiving money in exchange for their creative talents, and society hasn't always valued the creative arts as much as it has other industries. Some of us can feel a tremendous amount of guilt in following our passions.

Some of us may think that we are simply too old to follow our dreams; that our "ship has sailed". You are *never* too old to follow your dreams, and as John A. Shedd said; "*A ship is safe in harbour, but that's not what ships are built for*".[5]

I have learnt that the shadows, fears, or blocks I have had in my journey are best dealt with by having honest, vulnerable, and brave conversations. These can help to set up healthy boundaries, get your team on-board, and reveal any stories and assumptions you may have been telling yourself that are simply not true and are potentially holding you back.

As Paulo Coelho wrote in his inspiring book "The Alchemist" which is a fable about following your dreams, "*Don't give in to your fears. If you do, you won't be able to talk to your heart*" (Paulo Coelho).[6]

Examples of courage

Joseph Campbell

I have learnt a lot about healthy ways to deal with testing times and perceived failures in my own journey through the works of Joseph Campbell who was an American Professor of Literature, an author, and whose work covers many aspects of the human experience.

His most known work was his decoding of every great myth or story which he coined as "The Hero's Journey" or the "Monomyth".[7] Throughout time, there is only one myth, there is only one story, and we are all on our own "hero's journey".

Joseph was the author of "*The Hero With a Thousand Faces*"[8] which was an inspiration to many people around the world and a great influence on films like Stanley Kubrick's *A Space Odyssey* and George Lucas' *Star Wars*.

He also coined the phrase "Follow your bliss"; he believed from his own and others' experience that when you follow your bliss (following your deepest joy, creative passion, desire, or rapture), the universe will open doors for you where there were only walls.

He created a framework of the 11 stages of the hero's quest; from the call to adventure; to the crisis; finding the treasure; returning and transforming that are part of the natural "cycle" of life. Embracing and accepting this quest can help us make sense of our own challenges and find the courage to transform as the hero of our own journeys and "follow our bliss".

Reaching our pure creative potential and "following our bliss" take courage, but our courage is there to be found and we can often be surprised at how much courage we have.

What is your bliss? If you don't know, you can quite often find it by going back into your childhood memories and remembering what you wanted to be or what truly inspired you as a young child. Or it can be the dream you don't dare to tell.

Every "hero's journey" comes with elements of chaos, death, and re-birth. In order to transform and bring the new-found knowledge or the "elixir" back to the ordinary world from any hero's journey, one must enter the metaphorical "cave" and go through their darkness.

Brené Brown

I have gained amazing insight around having vulnerable conversations and understanding how damaging the stories we tell ourselves can be from Brené Brown, a research professor at the University of Houston. Brené has devoted her career studying vulnerability, shame, empathy, and courage.

Brené shot to global fame after her TED talk "The Power of Vulnerability" went viral and became one of the five most viewed TED talks in the world.[9] She talks about how we often combat our feelings of "not being enough" with pleasing, performing, and perfecting.

We can go through our lives thinking about whom we feel we are *supposed* to be and in doing this, we say yes to things we'd really like to say no to, and we say no to things that we would really love to say yes to.

She talks about how to have the courage to be imperfect, to be vulnerable and that courage cannot come without uncertainty, risk, and exposure. Courage and fear are not mutually exclusive! When things get uncomfortable, don't tap out of difficult conversations; instead, "rumble with vulnerability", have the tough conversations and find and speak your truth. This helps us to move away from the stories we make up in our mind that keep us stuck.

I have learnt in my own journey that we are often our own biggest critic, can think we are a fraudster and tend to hold ourselves back more than anyone else does. When we can change our inner thoughts and perceptions by questioning them and having honest, vulnerable conversations, we can find the courage to listen to and follow our heart.

When we stop holding ourselves back and bravely follow our hearts, our fear of success can be surprisingly as Marianne Williamson *wrote, "Our deepest fear is not that we are inadequate. Our deepest fear is that we are powerful beyond measure. It is our light, not our darkness that most frightens us"* (Marianne Williamson).[10]

Summary

We are all born with limitless creative potential, but in order to bring our dreams to life, we often need to push through our own limiting beliefs, find others who have successfully made the journey, and ask them for help on ours. By having brave, vulnerable conversations and getting comfortable with the darkness that the journey may bring from time to time, we can learn to see perceived failures, as the wonderful gifts they are in showing us the way to reaching our creative potential. We are all on our own "Hero's Journey" and there are great treasures to be found if we can master the power of courage.

Follow-up actions

- Write it down. Whether it's a childhood dream or a recent goal, write it down to make a plan from there.
- Recognise your fears. Recognising your fears will help you recognise where courage is needed.
- Reach out. Asking for help, advice, and mentorship will give you the tools you need for a greater chance of success in your journey. As I said before- success leaves clues!
- Embrace your shadows and your fears. Remember, these "dark" times are where the most success can grow.

Journal every step of your journey. When times get tough or when you are anxious about starting a new project, look back on the journal and you will see what amazing feats you have overcome before. Remind yourself of your courage.

Notes

1 Campbell, Joseph (1991), *A Joseph Campbell Companion: Reflections on the Art of Living (The Collected Works of Joseph Campbell)*. UK: Harper Perennial, p. 24.
2 Christopher, Rate R. et al. (2007), Implicit Theories of Courage. *The Journal of Positive Psychology*, 2(2), 80–98. doi:10.1080/17439760701228755.
3 Robbins, Anthony (2016), *The Science of Achievement*. Available at: https://www.youtube.com/watch?v=RngEEJHCkhc
4 Alcott, Louisa May (1868), *Little Woman*. Boston, MA: Roberts Brothers, p. 553.
5 Shedd, John A. (1928), *Salt From My Attic*. USA: Mosher Press.
6 Coelho, Paulo (1993), *The Alchemist*. USA: Harper Collins, p. 148.
7 Campbell, Joseph (1990), *The Hero's Journey*. USA: Harper Collins.
8 Campbell, Joseph (1949), *The Hero With a Thousand Faces*. USA; Pantheon Books.
9 Brown, Brené (2010), The Power of Vulnerability. *TedTalk*. Available at: https://www.ted.com/talks/brene_brown_the_power_of_vulnerability?language=en
10 Williamson, Marianne (1992), *A Return to Love: Reflections on the Principles of "A Course in Miracles"*. USA: Harper Collins, p. 190.

Further reading

Brown, Brené (2010), *The Gift of Imperfection*. USA: Simon & Schuster.
Brown, Brené (2012), *Daring Greatly*. USA: Penguin Putnam Inc.
Winfrey, Oprah (2017), Super Soul Sunday Conversations With Paulo Coelho, Part 1: What If the Universe Conspired in Your Favour? *Spotify*. Available at: https://open.spotify.com/episode/4gEHB1H7TrRjSWPcdVQRZX
Winkler, Matthew (2012), What Makes a Hero? *TED-Ed. YouTube*. Available at: https://www.youtube.com/watch?v=Hhk4N9A0oCA

21

MASTERING THE POWER OF CHALLENGING THE STATUS QUO

Mai Chen

Abstract

Every society needs people with the courage of their convictions to challenge the status quo (objectively) for the betterment of society.

In this chapter, I share my insights from 30+ years of experience in the practice of public law – challenging the status quo on behalf of my clients, and advising on better access to justice for culturally, linguistically, and ethnically diverse individuals and communities.

I illustrate my ideas with real-life examples and offer practical suggestions to develop your own capacity to successfully challenge the status quo for the better.

Keywords: Power, challenge, change, status quo

Introduction

Meeting the challenge of change for the betterment of society is critical to the future of mankind. As the famous American Minister, Nobel Peace Prize Laureate and Activist, Martin Luther King Jr., wrote in his book, *Where Do We Go from Here: Chaos or Community? "Today, our very survival depends on our ability to stay awake, to adjust to new ideas, to remain vigilant and to face the challenge of change"*.[1]

But making change is not easy. It requires creativity. But the Maltese physician, psychologist, and writer Edward de Bono wrote, *"Creativity involves*

DOI: 10.4324/9781003219293-27

breaking out of established patterns in order to look at things in a different way"[2] We need to look for new and different ways of doing things. *"There's a way to do it better: find it"*, said the great inventor, Thomas Edison.[3]

Humans are hardwired to maintain the status quo (which the Oxford English Dictionary defines as "the existing state of affairs, especially regarding social or political issues") – in psychology, the "status quo bias" means that people prefer things to stay the way they are – even if change would benefit them. So leaders hoping to challenge or disrupt the status quo must be highly skilled and practiced at doing so. They must also have the courage of their conviction, as challenging the status quo does not often make you popular – even if ultimately you will be proved right.

> *Being able to effectively challenge the status quo – to convince others that "the existing state of affairs" is no longer fit for purpose or ethically right (if it ever was) – is an essential leadership quality in our volatile, uncertain, complex, and ambiguous world.*
>
> *Bennett and Lemoine*[4]

So, what is the **special power** that allows you to set in motion forces that will unseat the status quo and replace it with a new equilibrium? First, you have to see how the status quo could be different. You can change the world if you can see clearly how it could be different. Not everyone can see it, but many will catch on once you describe it to them. Secondly, you have to know how to generate a wave of momentum or be able to see a wave forming and get ahead of it and ride it. Thirdly, you need to be able to advocate and persuade others to see what you see. Fourthly, you need to be able to implement and turn a vision of possibility into a practical reality.

When these steps are achieved, the results can be both startling and enduring. As Thomas Kuhn pointed out in his famous theory of "paradigm shifts", before Darwin, anyone comparing a human face to a monkey's face would be struck by the differences, but after Darwin, they would be struck by the similarities.[5]

My career has been defined by challenging the status quo. My second eldest sister and I are the first lawyers in the family. In my early years as a lawyer, I chaired a tri-departmental government review on the Policy of Excluding Women from Combat, and recommended changes to that status quo of exclusion in the Human Rights Act, in favour of inclusion for qualified candidates of any gender. Nowadays the inclusion of women soldiers in combat units is broadly accepted as the norm.

In my current law practice, I assist clients to challenge the status quo in the form of unfair policies, laws, and regulations. Chen Palmer was the first Public Law Specialist firm in Australasia and one of the first boutique law firms. As Adjunct Professor at the University of Auckland School of Law, I have mainly researched and written on law, policy, and constitutional reform. As a director of the board on the Bank of New Zealand, I have most recently focused not only on the need to increase diverse thinking capability to respond successfully to the huge disruption caused by technological change but also on the need to drive a more customer focused conduct culture, especially in the tone from the top.

And as Chair of the Superdiversity Institute for Law, Policy and Business, I have focused on making visible the status quo invisibility of how people not born in New Zealand (culturally, linguistically, and ethnically diverse, or "CALD") are transforming our country. Our biggest city, Auckland, is now the fourth most superdiverse city in the world (25% or more of the population not born in the country) with implications for every part of society, business, law and policy.

I attribute my diverse thinking ability to emigrating with my family from Taiwan to the South Island of New Zealand when I was a child. We were only the second Taiwanese family in the whole island and my father was an Olympics gymnastics coach, so we grew up on campus and spent most of our childhood in the pool or gymnasium or track and field competing in sport. The closest I came to a court in those days was the netball or basketball court! This unique background has helped me to master the power of challenging the status quo, and I share here what I have learnt on the journey.

Principle 1: you have to be able to see how the status quo could be different

I have always said that if I can see it, then I can do it. Challenging the status quo always starts with an idea or vision in my head. If it gets so strong that it takes over from the status quo – as if I am already living in that new reality – then I am usually galvanised and feel compelled to make it happen. If I cannot see it, then I cannot do it. I do not know where to start. I cannot lead others there when I cannot see the pathway myself. So clarity of vision is essential to start.

Where does that vision come from? Diverse thinking is an essential requirement for being able to effectively challenge the status quo. Diverse thinking is having a different viewpoint from the norm; seeing the same dots but joining them in a different way to see risks and problems and problem-solving in a different way; viewing issues through different lenses. Diverse thinking may come from having different demographic factors from others, such as gender, ethnicity, different cultural background, age, disability, or sexuality. But diverse thinking can also come from professional training and personal experiences, how you were raised and in what circumstances.

My Dad, who studies Nobel Prize winners, tells me that 60 per cent came from disadvantaged backgrounds. Research by David Pratt (2008) notes that "when they speak of prison and exile, communism and fascism, war and terrorism", Nobel Prize winners speak with "the voice of experience", and that the discoveries of Nobel laureates were achieved "with pain and effort. Pratt (2008) also writes that Nobel laureates often seem to have suffered more than their share of difficulties – several having lost one or both parents in childhood, and a sizeable majority having grown up in poverty.[6]

Diverse thinking can help you to identify gaps which no one else has seen – to see what is invisible to others. I saw that superdiversity creates more challenges and issues that need to be managed and redressed if New Zealand is to maximise the diversity dividend, maintain racial harmony, prevent racism from growing, and to prevent culturally, linguistically, and ethnically diverse peoples from becoming marginalised and unhappy.

Principle 2: understand the "why" of challenging the status quo

There has to be a good reason for challenging the status quo, because, otherwise, you will not be able to clearly articulate why to others who need to buy in and help you, nor will you be able to persevere while travelling on what will inevitably be a difficult and long road. In my research on diverse thinking in boardrooms, I have found that those who challenge without a clear reason tend to be ignored (Chen, 2018).[7]

As one of my research participants noted: "A problem Boards frequently encounter is that Directors feel compelled to offer an opinion, even if they do not have anything to add". Directors should consider the acronym W.A.I.T. – "Why Am I Talking?"! In other words, Directors should think more and make sure that they offer the highest order comment they can in order to maximise the value of everyone around the table. Directors should also be reluctant to position themselves with expertise over and above what they actually have. It undermines credibility and makes it harder to offer diverse ideas when they do have merit" (Chen, 2018).[8]

Understanding your "why" means that you must have overcome your own doubts about the need to achieve change before you can convince others. For many years, I saw the need to make visible the contributions that migrants made to New Zealand to combat the unmitigated diet of negative news stories. I also saw the discrimination faced by migrants, supported by research done for the *Superdiversity Stocktake* about the migrant effect – 27% less salary – and Asian clerks being the most over-qualified for their jobs.[9] But I wanted to gain a reputation as a sound lawyer for all New Zealanders before I started my work on superdiversity. So it was 25 years post-admission to the bar before I moved to Auckland and established the Superdiversity Institute, New Zealand Asian Leaders (NZAL), and Super-DIVERSE Women.

New Zealand Asian Leaders was established in 2013 to allow Asian leaders to connect, inspire, and grow Asian leaders across New Zealand. SuperDI-VERSE Women is an organisation for ethnic women to enjoy peer support and increase the visibility of their unique intersectional discrimination issues (the double disadvantage they experience) and their achievements despite that. I have also now established New Zealand Asian Lawyers, to mentor lawyers of Asian ethnicity in New Zealand, to help them succeed and to contribute to the profession, and to provide expertise on issues concerning Asians and the law.

The Superdiversity Institute for Law, Policy, and Business is mainstreaming superdiversity in those three areas, as reflected in the reports listed at the end of this chapter. Government and business are now beginning to understand the importance of incorporating a Superdiversity Framework on these areas.

Principle 3: delivery is as important as content – and timing is everything

Those seeking to challenge the status quo should remember that delivery is as important as content. It is not enough to be right – you have to be able to persuade others to see what you see and understand why that is right way to go. You therefore must be thoughtful about how to challenge in a way that is most effective with the particular group of people you need to get over the line.

This thoughtfulness also includes being strategic about timing. There is a balance to be struck between "seizing the moment" and being opportunistic, and being careful and considered. Sometimes, challenging when the time is not right can damage your case and strengthen support for the status quo.

But other times, faster is better. Just getting it done and implemented before opposition can form means that people can see your alternative vision in practice, and that makes it easier for them to understand the need for change while realising that their resistance to change was based on unfounded fears.

Sometimes you need to "dip your toe in the water" – it's the only way to see whether it is cold or warm for challenging the status quo! I was not sure about writing the *Diverse Thinking Capability Audit of New Zealand Boardrooms*.[10] But I tried it and found that everyone wanted to talk about it. Fifteen interviews turned into 65 and subsequent articles and another report on diverse thinking for not for profit organisations followed (Centre for Social Impact, 2019; Chen and Erakovic, 2019).[11]

Remember, it is not the shots you missed that you regret, it's the ones you never took. Or, as Wayne Gretzky put it, you miss 100% of the shots you don't take. I am now getting audits for the boards I am on that measure the diverse thinking ability of directors and the boards, for the first time. That is now becoming part of the status quo.

Sometimes, it is not until one person does something different, that others have sufficient faith and confidence to know it can be done. Back in 1954, Roger Bannister ran a mile in under 4 minutes, despite scientists saying that it could not be done. Shortly after . . . thousands of others did the same.

Principle 4: collaborate and involve others, especially stakeholders

As iron sharpens iron, so we sharpen one another (Proverbs 27:17).[12] Sometimes, you have half the vision and it takes two or three or a group of you to have the whole vision and to challenge the status quo.

Every challenge needs supporters – people who do not have the vision at the outset but can see it when you describe it or are prepared to trust your instincts are right, and to follow and help. You will need to inspire others to come on the journey with you. Do not take people on the journey who suck energy from you and eat up resources. Do cherish those who can really help you. As Oprah Winfrey wrote "passion is energy",[13] and being a passionate leader with people who understand and support the vision is essential. When you have your next vision of the status quo that needs challenging, you need to leave behind disciples who will continue the previous work.

Stakeholder buy-in is also essential. I never challenge the status quo unless I can get other major players to support the project financially or in kind. If you cannot sell them the vision and get them to buy in and have skin in the game, then you should not start. You either refine your pitch or abandon it. It is especially important to get those who will benefit the most from your work to buy in because if they cannot understand the why, then no one can.

For example, for the *Superdiversity Stocktake*, Peter Hughes, who was then CEO of the New Zealand Ministry of Education (MOE), approved $5,000 of funding support from the Ministry, but he also agreed to allow the Super-diversity Institute to audit his department against the Superdiversity Frame-work. I was able to tell other departments that MOE was being audited with the agreement of the CEO and that encouraged other CEOs of government agencies to follow and allow me to do likewise. In total, the *Superdiversity Stocktake* includes an audit of 32 New Zealand public agencies.

The value of change often goes beyond narrow self-interests. Changing the status quo can, and should, make many people better off. New Zealand public agencies who have supported the work of the Superdiversity Institute have included the Human Rights Commission, the Ministry for Women, the Office of Ethnic Communities, the Accident Compensation Corporation, the Ministry of Business, Innovation, and Employment, and WorkSafe, and many private companies have also provided support, and not-for-profit entities including the New Zealand Law Foundation and the Borrin Foundation.

Principle 5: if you are prepared to challenge, practice, and be prepared to implement

Mastering the power of challenging the status quo is not just in voicing the vision or idea – it is also understanding **how** to make it happen and how to ensure that changes are not reversed. Change requires vision **combined** with the ability to take action and know how to do that. Ideas are only one point, and implementation is nine! If you only have vision, you cannot effectively challenge the status quo.

Practice does make you better. Malcolm Gladwell's theory that 10,000 hours of "deliberate practice" is needed to master a skill holds true for the skill of challenging the status quo too – you need to keep practis-ing (Gladwell, 2011).[14] My experience is that challenging the status quo never gets easier. But the more you do it, the more experienced you get at knowing how to do it successfully, and the likely barriers you will need to overcome.

Principle 6: courage and the importance of hope

Back yourself. If you don't believe in yourself, then why should anyone else? Challenging the status quo is hard. It requires courage of conviction, a spirit of endeavour and perseverance, resilience in the face of resistance, and self-sacrifice. You will work long hours, be uncomfortable, and face stress and the risk of failure. You have to be able to encourage and resource yourself, and to surround yourself with others who can and will support you. Adrenaline will take you some of the way – but resilience, perseverance, and personal conviction are required to sustainably cross the finish line.

The ultimate kill-switch for those with power to challenge the status quo is a loss of hope. Having any hope of success taken away is the only time when I have not been able to keep challenging. It totally undermines your resilience and you feel as if any purpose has gone and the road map ends in an insurmountable brick wall. You must safeguard yourself against those who want to snuff the candle of hope out and be that brick wall.

Principle 7: derive inspiration and guidance from other countries

Auckland, New Zealand, is now the fourth most superdiverse city in the world, so there are other superdiverse countries with lessons to teach us about the gaps that laws, regulations, policies, and practices need to fill. Research is critical to not reinventing the wheel. Adaption, to New Zealand circumstances, of measures adopted in comparable OECD or superdiverse countries often shines the light on the best way to effectively challenge the status quo.

The problem is that sometimes the Superdiversity Institute's research has actually found a gap that no superdiverse country is successfully filling or has even identified. For example, in research done for WorkSafe (New Zealand's health and safety regulator) and ACC (the New Zealand Crown entity responsible for administering the country's universal no-fault accidental injury scheme) on health and safety of CALD, we discovered that other superdiverse countries either were behind New Zealand or were reactive and ad hoc.

Canada was the most advanced in its strategic thinking and use of targeted interventions to improve the health and safety of ethnically, culturally and linguistically diverse workers and the United States also had a number of useful tools, tactics and strategies (largely directed towards the large Hispanic workforce). In the United States, demographic projections are showing that very soon there will be no majority ethnic group – by 2044, more than half of all Americans are projected to belong to a minority group according to Colby and Ortman (2015).[15]

Principle 8: stay open

To master the power of challenging the status quo, you have to stay "match fit". The mind needs to be open (and uncluttered) to understand what you see. There are many ways you can do this – meditation, self-reflection, wide reading, and leveraging broad networks.

Summary

Our ability to challenge the status quo depends on:

- Seeing a better way to do things
- Articulating why that is a better way
- Delivering that message effectively
- Collaborating with supporters and stakeholders
- Implementing the change at a practical level
- Having courage and maintaining hope that change is possible
- Deriving inspiration and guidance from others who have been there before
- Looking after yourself so that all these other things are possible.

"Mastering" anything is not a simple magical formula – otherwise, everyone could do it. There is a formula, but it is more about how to create and maintain the mindset that drives everything else. Open eyes see; open minds understand – both are needed. The magic is to understand that you have to work on both at the same time and to understand the difference.

Mastering the power of challenging the status quo

- Consider whether you are a diverse thinker – First, work out what personal and professional experiences or qualities make you a diverse thinker. Then, consider your track record of sharing diverse thoughts – are you courageous enough to challenge the status quo? Also, are you persuasive? Or do you need to build your EQ?

- Understand what you see that no one else has seen, and that you care about – make a list.
- Find out who else sees the same gaps you do, so that you can collaborate with them. Try and develop working relationships.
- Research the subject so you understand the best timing and strategy and leverage off what has already been done.
- Identify and learn from those who are expert at changing the status quo. Who can you speak to, get mentoring from, volunteer to work for?
- Identify supporters and people who can help you get work done (and not just talk about it).
- Keep practising – what/who best feeds your mind and thoughtfulness? Spend time on that, and pushing yourself out of your comfort zone.
- Stay open, uncluttered, and awake.

Reflect:

1   Do I have this superpower?
2   How do I grow my power to challenge the status quo?
3   What impacts would this superpower have on my leadership?
4   How would challenging the status quo make me more effective round the Board table?

Explore:

- *Diverse Thinking Capability Audit of New Zealand Boardrooms 2018*
- *Health and Safety regulators in a superdiverse context: review of challenges and lessons from United Kingdom, Canada and Australia*
- *The Diversity Matrix: Refreshing What Diversity Means for Law, Policy and Business in the 21st Century*
- *Superdiversity Stocktake: Implications for Business, Government and New Zealand*
- *Superdiversity, Democracy and New Zealand's Electoral and Referenda Laws*

These publications are all accessible from www.superdiversity.org:

- *National Cultures and its impact on the Workplace Health and Safety and Injury Prevention of Employers and Workers,* October 2019
- *Culturally and Linguistically Diverse Parties in the Courts: A Chinese Case Study,* November 2019
- *What is the Future for NGO Governance,* Research Report, *Centre* for Social Impact, August 2019

Notes

1 King Jr., M.L. (1967), *Where Do We Go From Here: Chaos or Community?* New York: Harper & Row Publishers.
2 De Bono, Edward (1971), *Lateral Thinking for Management: A Handbook.* Penguin, UK.
3 Edison, Thomas via Spielvogel, Carl (1957), Advertising: Promoting a Negative Quality. *New York Times.* Quote Page 46, Column 6. New York.
4 Bennett, N. and J.G. Lemoine (2014), What VUCA Really Means for You. *Harvard Business Review.* Available at: https://hbr.org/. Accessed on: June 28, 2021.
5 Kuhn, T. (1962), *The Structure of Scientific Revolutions.* Chicago: University of Chicago Press.
6 Pratt, D. (2008), *Nobel Wisdom: The 1000 Wisest Things Ever Said.* JR Books Limited.
7 Chen, M. (2018), *Diverse Thinking Capability Audit of New Zealand Boardrooms 2018.* Superdiversity Institute for Law, Policy and Business, posted 18 November 2021.
8 Ibid.
9 Chen, Mai (2015), *Superdiversity Stocktake: Implications for Business, Government and New Zealand.* Superdiversity Centre.
10 Chen, M. and L. Erakovic (2019), *Diverse Thinking in New Zealand Boardrooms: Looking Through Rose-Coloured Glasses.* Paper presented to EURAM Conference, Lisbon, June 26–28, 2019.
11 Chen, M. and L. Erakovic (2019), *Centre for Social Impact. "What Is the Future for NGO Governance?"* Research Report.
12 Giese, R. (2016), "Iron Sharpens Iron" as a Negative Image: Challenging the Common Interpretation of Proverbs 27:17. *Journal of Biblical Literature,* 135(1), 61–76. doi:10.15699/jbl.1344.2016.2997.
13 Winfrey, Oprah (2015), *Bloomberg Daybreak: Americas Oprah Winfrey: Passion Is Energy.* Available at: https://www.bloomberg.com/news/videos/2015-10-15/oprah-winfrey-passion-is-energy. Accessed on: August 23, 2021.
14 Gladwell, M. (2011), *Outliers: The Story of Success.* Back Bay Books.
15 Colby, S.L. and J.M. Ortman (2015), *Projections of the Size and Composition of the U.S. Population: 2014 to 2060.* U.S. Census Bureau. Available at: https://www.census.gov/. Accessed on: June 21, 2021.

PART VII
Diversity and inclusion

22

MASTERING THE POWER OF INCLUSIVE THINKING

Rebecca Oldfield

Abstract

Inclusive thinking should be part of every leader's toolkit. While it requires us to adapt our behaviours from those which are more instinctive, the benefits are substantial. Inclusive thinking can unlock talent, drive creative innovation, and lead individuals, teams, and organisations to higher performance. It simply requires us to open our minds to multiple diverse sources of ideas and insights, including what we might assume to be the least likely and the most obvious. It requires us to place ourselves in new and potentially uncomfortable situations, regularly exposing ourselves to different ideas and perspectives. And it requires us to have the courage to challenge our own biases, and those of others, and seek feedback on how our behaviours can build or inhibit a safe space for others to share their views. With step-by-step guidance on how to put inclusive thinking into practice in your situation, this chapter seeks to help readers understand the power of inclusive thinking, how to deploy it, and where and how to build a virtuous circle of inclusion and problem-solving which drives superior performance.

Keywords: Inclusion, innovation, bias, disruptive thinking

Introduction

Inclusive thinking is a powerful ideology for individuals, teams, and communities. It can unlock the most incredible opportunities in the classroom, the

DOI: 10.4324/9781003219293-29

workplace, around the dinner table, and help us solve the most complex of issues. As McKinsey & Company's Senior Partner, Bill Schaninger, has said, "*When you make it easy for people to bring all their skills and thoughtfulness to innovation and problem solving, they do better. It builds up social exchange. It builds up goodwill. It's a virtuous cycle*".[1]

Inclusive thinking is a willingness to explore all approaches and ideas, irrespective of where they come from, and even after you have found one which may be good enough. When we think inclusively, we give equal weight to the input and ideas from multiple, diverse sources, including the least likely and the most obvious. Learning to think this way profoundly changes the way we see the world, the actions we take, the impact we have, and the decisions we make.[2]

In the Dreamworks movie "Mr Peabody and Sherman" from 2014, the citizens of New York are threatened by a rift in the space–time continuum, caused by Mr. Peabody and Sherman's travels back in time. In the penultimate scene, geniuses and leaders from history gather to try to solve the problem, including Leonardo Da Vinci, Einstein, and even George Washington himself. While each has an idea, the solution comes instead from a young boy, Sherman, who with a characteristic lack of confidence, asks quietly what would happen if they flew to the future, not the past. His rationale is that they haven't tried this before and it might be cool! Building on his idea, the mathematicians agree that if Mr. Peabody and Sherman fly at incredible speed to the future in their time machine, they can mend the hole in the space-time continuum, saving New York, and humankind, forever! This is obviously fictional, but the lesson about where and how innovation starts is very real. It shows us that the best ideas often come from the least expected places, and that if we don't open our minds in an inclusive way, we will miss them.

Since graduating from university in 1999, I have worked for Infineum – a leading transportation additives company – in a variety of roles spanning different sectors of the business. In 2018, as the Global head of HR, I was keen to align our maternity leave provision in the US with other similar corporations, and also create greater consistency across our global affiliates. Due to prevailing legislation in the US, we had not been able to find a suitable path to the outcome we wanted, based on concerns about infringing rights of other employee groups. Unhappy with this outcome, I looked at the question again and reached out to as many people as I could, inside and outside our organisation, for inspiration.

The solution came from a source I had not originally expected: not from the multiple HR policy experts I consulted, but from an experienced member of the Legal Department, who suggested a solution that not only met my desired outcome for new mothers but also included additional benefits for fathers, same-sex couples, and adoptive parents around the world. It was even better than I had expected, and would not have been possible without the power of inclusive thinking: of exploring ideas beyond the obvious, extending my network and amplifying the voices of those who might not otherwise have been heard.

Inclusive thinking is essential for navigating our complex world

Inclusive thinking has helped me to innovate in a rapidly changing marketplace by harnessing ideas from every member of the team, irrespective of their age, background, role, or language ability. In Infineum, we use inclusive thinking routinely to solve critical operational issues, which could affect our ability to reliably supply customers. By seeking ideas from multiple people, we have been able to protect supply to our customers and, in many cases, improve the procedures on our plants for future production. We've also applied inclusive thinking to designing new working cultures and setting our corporate sustainability strategy – improving the solutions, and creating a broad feeling of ownership for the outcomes.

Exclusive thinking is detrimental to our growth

Our previous experiences and biases are often the greatest barrier to inclusive thinking, which is why children are more adept at thinking inclusively than adults. Training ourselves to think more inclusively has many benefits; by challenging our natural tendency to EXCLUDE information and ideas which we consider irrelevant, we can create better solutions to problems, unleash the creativity and potential of others, and foster greater harmony and well-being for all.

Like many worthwhile disciplines, inclusive thinking requires us to adapt our behaviours from those which are more instinctive. Our brains instinctively filter information based on past experience, causing us to focus our attention on specific information at the expense of all other information. This is exclusive thinking or thinking by deficit. For example, if we have been told that people walking in dark streets at night are dangerous, we will instinctively assume that the person walking towards us in a dark street at night presents danger, even when there is no conclusive evidence at that moment to support this. Our brains have evolved in this way to allow us to manage the vast amount of information we encounter, and to react quickly enough to this information to survive. However, in the modern world, exclusive thinking can have far-reaching, negative consequences on individuals, groups, families, companies and countries, limiting our ability to progress, to change lives for the better and to leverage the plethora of resources and capability available to us.

The most negative examples of exclusive thinking in our history are those in which the biases and assumptions of certain groups have denied whole communities the opportunity to access basic human rights and the chance to fulfil their potential, simply because of the way they look, or their religion or gender. Examples in the 20th century alone include the apartheid regime in South Africa and the Nazi doctrine in Germany. As a result, we have not only created immense human suffering at times but also limited our ability to innovate, denied society some of its greatest leaders, and expended energy in trying to force uniformity rather than recognising the superior power of difference. Yet when people open their minds to the views and ideas of others, look beyond challenges and see opportunities, think inclusively rather than exclusively, the positive consequences can be immense.

Why I believe in and encourage inclusive thinking

Companies fall in love with different ideas at different times, and a few years ago, in Infineum, we fell in love with the idea of reverse mentors. Actually, this turned out to be one of the best recommendations I have ever had in my career . . . my reverse mentor has helped me tap into ideas and guidance from parts of our organisation I would never have accessed before. My reverse mentor is a young graduate in Singapore, and his perspective on the world of work is very different from mine. Our regular commitment to share ideas is one of my most valuable opportunities for inclusive thinking; recently he counselled me on specific language to help make the case for disruptive change in our organisation. He coined the phrase "if it isn't uncomfortable, it isn't transformation", which I then used to prepare our employees for the expected rate and pace of change. His advice helped me land the message much more effectively than I would otherwise have done.

On a different scale, back in 2018, our HR team were committed to ensuring that we practiced inclusive thinking during performance evaluations.

While we had been screening performance appraisal outcomes for potential bias on factors such as gender and ethnicity, we decided to extend this further to categories like age. This led to a targeted education programme for our leaders to help us understand better the motivations and needs of colleagues across multiple age brackets. The outcomes from this effort are now being actively measured through our colleague engagement survey to ensure we can attract, motivate, and retain colleagues across the full span of working ages. With more than 10% of our employees being either younger than 25 or older than 60, it is critical that leaders understand how to engage and support diverse age ranges, and inclusive thinking is a key part of this commitment.

Most recently, I have learned the value of the "upside down" meetings as a way to harness inclusive thinking, amplify voices that I would not otherwise hear, and seek solutions to problems I could not solve within my immediate network. Eighteen months ago, in an effort to build collaboration and inclusion, I set up monthly engagement sessions for my global team. These started off as a top down initiative – I set the agenda based on what I believed would be pertinent to this wide group of employees. But it turned out that more often than not, I was wrong about what really mattered to this group – engagement in the sessions was low, and I rarely received any questions or learnings. So we turned the meeting upside down, and the agenda is now set and run by the team members who tell me what they would like to brainstorm and discuss. Letting go of this control, and coming to serve the group, rather than the other way round has massively increased the engagement and collaboration, and taught me much more about the issues my leaders and their teams are facing. From these upside down meetings, I have discovered some of the cultural barriers to change and to achieving profitable growth, and learnt that meaningful development opportunities are the single biggest lever to drive greater motivation and engagement in my team. As a result, I now have a quarterly dedicated session to Diversity, Development, and Engagement to address this lever on our performance.

Each of these examples is quite different, but in all of them, I have been able to explore diverse ideas and approaches, and give equal weight to every possible voice. This inclusive approach to problem-solving has helped me unlock growth opportunities, improve engagement, and drive transformational change. I could never have achieved this without the insights and diversity of ideas from multiple sources, including the least likely and the most obvious.

Inclusive thinking can help us to innovate

Another example of how inclusive thinking can unlock innovation comes from a US hospital in which infection rates of the MRSA virus were unacceptably high, and efforts to reduce infection in patients had so far failed.[3] The managers in the hospital called together senior clinicians to brainstorm the problem, and the group concluded that the virus was being spread as a result of poor personal hygiene. As a result, the hospital added notices in all the washrooms in the hospital encouraging people to wash their hands. Nothing happened. The hospital took down the notices in the washrooms and replaced them with bigger notices asking people to wash their hands. Nothing happened. Then one day, a janitor in the hospital approached a supervisor with an observation. When emptying the trash cans in the hospital, he had noticed that, in some wards, the trash cans were full of disposable gloves, and in other wards, there were hardly any gloves. This led to an investigation which found that staff in some wards were carrying out their tasks without gloves, because there were no gloves of the right size. When managers ensured that gloves in the right size were available, the infection rates of MRSA fell by 70%. The supervisor in this story could so easily have dismissed the observation from the janitor, based on preconceptions about where the solution was most likely to come from. Instead, inclusive thinking, and a willingness to explore all approaches and ideas, led to an impactful and low-cost solution which saved lives.

Inclusive thinking is a route to creative problem-solving

Inclusive thinking can help us create commercial success. When we think inclusively, we actively seek out ideas from "unlikely" or unconventional sources, recognising that finding the best ideas and solutions is more important than being the one to solve the problem. This in turn can create a virtuous circle of creative ideas, a shared sense of achievement, and greater enthusiasm for solving further problems. Jungkiu Choi demonstrated this when he moved from Singapore to China to take on the role of Head of Commercial Banking at Standard Chartered.[4]

Jungkiu challenged the existing assumptions and beliefs about where the best ideas for improving the business would come from. Contrary to the behaviour of previous incumbents in his role, he sought out ideas and insights directly from employees working in the branches, challenging previously held norms that the managers knew best, and should instruct the branches how to improve their metrics. His willingness to explore all approaches and ideas, even those from seemingly unconventional sources, led to a huge improvement in engagement and motivation amongst the branch staff, which in turn increased customer satisfaction by 54% in two years. His application of inclusive thinking enhanced the experience of his customers, his employees, and his stakeholders.

Inclusive thinking helps unlock talent

Inclusive thinking can create access to great previously undiscovered talent. When we apply inclusive thinking to challenge societal norms, we can unlock talent and capability on a massive scale. Reshma Saujani became aware of the significant gender gap in computer science while visiting schools during her campaign for US Congress.

With only one in five computer science graduates being female, and that number declining rather than increasing, Reshma decided to start a movement with the aim of creating the largest pipeline of female engineers in the United States. Named "Girls who code" her non–profit organisation aims to redefine what a computer programmer looks like, and equip young women with the skills to participate and succeed in technology roles in the 21st century. Her all-female programmes and clubs suggest that the lack of female software engineers is not a result of a lack of capability, or even interest, but mostly from societal conditioning about what a typical computer programmer looks like. By addressing issues of confidence and gender stereotypes, and providing access to computer science training and guidance from major Tech companies, she is opening up a previously limited career path to girls across the US, and unlocking future talent and capability for the Tech world on a massive scale. Inclusive thinking can change perceptions in society, and gift us with potential innovators and leaders who would otherwise been overlooked.

Explore: Girls Who Code

https://www.girlswhocode.com/

Each of these examples illustrates the power of inclusive thinking. When I came across these examples, my first thought is how wonderful it must have made people feel (the janitor, or the Bank staff in China, or the girls in US schools) when their voices were heard and their ideas were sponsored. That opportunity to contribute probably changed their perceptions of themselves and their behaviour towards others, thus creating a virtuous circle (see the quote at the beginning of this chapter). Inclusive thinking can not only give us great solutions and talent, but it can also create safety, belonging, and shared respect across communities, which in turn drives bravery, curiosity, and deep fulfilment for individuals.

The time to start YOUR journey to Inclusive thinking is NOW – what have you got to lose?!

Studies on inclusive thinking

There have been many studies of teams and organisations, across multiple geographies, which present both causal and circumstantial evidence of inclusive thinking driving innovation, creativity, improved commercial results, and a sense of belonging for individuals.[5]

Specifically, the link between inclusive thinking and creativity has been studied by Li et al.,[6] who determined that an inclusive environment leads to less social categorisation, creating a safe space where ideas can be shared and innovation can thrive.

A separate study by Qi et al.[7] investigated the impact of inclusive leadership on innovative behaviour. The authors showed that when leaders practised inclusive thinking with employees, listening to their new ideas, technologies, and processes, those employees felt more valued and cared for by the organisation and, thus, increased their innovative behaviour.

Mastering the power of inclusive thinking

So how can you harness the power of inclusive thinking? Here are four steps you can take to expand your thinking process.

1.   Understand your own biases

   a.   Discuss this with peers or friends and explore what makes you react positively to some, and negatively to others. You may find it interesting to explore why you think this is.

2.   Develop strategies to mitigate the impact of your bias on your communications and decisions

   a.   In your group, or class, or company, who are the people you find easiest to deal with, and who are the most difficult? How does this impact the way in which you communicate and interact with them?

b. Try this: When you are about to speak with someone whom you consider to be more difficult to interact with, imagine you are about to talk to one of your "in-group". This will change your body language and your facial expression and improve the quality and impact of the interaction for all parties.

3. Seek out the people on the edge of your network, and create a safe space in which they can share their views and ideas with you

a. Explore how you can hear different views on how to solve problems and answer questions, and how can you create an environment to ensure these views are honest and authentic?

4. Invite people to your meetings and discussions who wouldn't normally attend. Ensure that they, and everyone else in the room, have the opportunity to share their views and be heard.

a. Give equal weight to every voice, irrespective of age, physical appearance, seniority, background, and education.

In 2018, Minouche Shafik, an Egyptian-born economist and the first female Director of the London School of Economics and Political Science, said that "Talent is spread evenly around the world, but opportunities are not".[8] Inclusive thinking can help us address this moral dilemma, and in the process, we can also create better solutions in business and at home, greater success for individuals and societies, and increased harmony within communities.

Summary

Multiple studies have confirmed the causal relationship between inclusive thinking and innovation, for teams and organisations, and for individuals in a variety of settings. This alone makes inclusive thinking a "must-have" skill for current and future leaders operating in a disruptive and uncertain world. By seeking multiple diverse views, and opening our minds to the seemingly un-orthodox and contrarian view, we can unlock talent, amplify our own understanding and experiences many, many times, and find creative solutions to the most complex problems. To obtain the full benefits of inclusive thinking, leaders need to do more than just listen to different perspectives, they need to create a safe space for people to share their authentic ideas – this is a key to unlocking the truly unexpected and most valuable insights. In this way, inclusive thinking doesn't just enable great innovation and unlock talent, but it creates belonging and purpose for multiple individuals, and engenders higher levels of courage and ownership within teams. It is a discipline to practice, practice, and practice, using one or more of the techniques described in this chapter. When you have mastered inclusive thinking, it will change the way you see the world, the actions you take, and the legacy you leave for others.

Follow-up actions

1   **Set up a personal Advisory Board**[9]**:** This is a group of people who will tell you about your potential biases and guide you away from exclusive thinking. They could be peers, or friends, or a combination of all of these. The most important thing is that they are honest with you, they interact with your regularly, and they are committed to helping you think more inclusively. Ask them to give you feedback on behaviours which inhibit inclusive thinking and be prepared to act on their input!

2   **Disrupt your own thinking:** Exposure to new and uncomfortable situations, combined with open-ended questions and deep listening, expands your horizons and challenges your preconceived ideas. *Set up regular curiosity conversations* with people (join an affinity group, or sit in a different place each week) to understand the world from different perspectives and to multiply your own experiences by those of many others.

3   **When you make key decisions, ask yourself:** Will your decision work for women, for people from ethnic minorities, for people of different religions and ages, for people with disabilities or caring responsibilities, for people from LGBTQ communities, or for people not like me. If you don't know how your decision will affect different people, ask and find out, don't assume.

4   **Create a safe space for people to tell you all their ideas –
    try this:** Ask yourself how often do people in your team say
    things like "I am worried". "I made a mistake". "I need help".
    "I don't understand". Then ask yourself, is it because they don't
    feel these things or because they don't feel safe sharing. Psycho-
    logical safety is a key component of inclusive thinking. To harness
    the benefits of inclusive thinking, you need to create a safe space
    for people to share: try connecting with people (their thoughts
    and feelings) on an individual level – when they see you are truly
    interested in them for who they are, they will be ready to share
    their insights and valuable ideas

Notes

1   Hancock, B. and B. Schaninger (2021), The Elusive Inclusive Workplace. *McKinsey Talks Talent Podcast*. Apple Podcasts.
2   Ellis, M. (2021), *How to Get Better Results With Inclusive Thinking*. Available at: https://www.diversily.com
3   Brafman, O. (2017), *An MRSA Story*. October. Available at: https://www.youtube.com/watch?v=bbfrtNCbs9U
4   Cable, D. (2018), How Humble Leadership Really Works. *Harvard Business Review*, April.
5   Green, M. and J. Young (2019), *Building Inclusive Workplaces: Assessing the Evidence*. CIPD Research Report, September.
6   Li, F.C.R., C.J. Lin, Y.H. Tien and C.M. Chen (2017), A Multilevel Model of Team Cultural Diversity and Creativity: The Role of Team Knowledge Sharing and Inclusive Climate. *Journal of Management and Organisation*, 24(5), 711–729.
7   Qi, L., B. Liu, X. Wei and Y. Hu (2019), Impact of Inclusive Leadership on Employee Innovative Behavior: Perceived Organizational Support as a Mediator. *PLoS ONE*, 14(2), e0212091. doi:10.1371/journal.pone.0212091.
8   Shafik, D.M. (2018), Interview with Kirsty Young, Dessert Island Discs. *BBC Radio 4*, February.
9   Bourke, C.J. and A. Titus (2020), The Key to Inclusive Leadership. *Harvard Business Review*, March.

Further reading

Bourke, J. (2021), *Which Two Heads Are Better Than One? How Diverse Teams Create Break-through Ideas and Make Smarter Decisions*. 2nd edition. Australian Institute of Company Directors.
Brafman, O. and M. Dempsey (2018), *Radical Inclusion: What the Post 9/11 World Should Have Taught Us About Leadership*. USA: Missionday.
Kahneman, D. (2012), *Thinking Fast and Slow*. London: Penguin.

23

MASTERING THE POWER OF DIVERSITY AND INCLUSION

James Burstall

Abstract

This chapter aims to show how to harness the power of diversity and inclusion (D&I) in mass communication, providing insights that all organisations can benefit from.

An in-depth, personal example is given by James Burstall, CEO of Argonon, a group of TV production companies.

Using his 30 years of experience in broadcasting, James outlines the need for change in society and especially the media industry, which has a privileged position of responsibility.

James details his efforts to bring change within his company and gives tips for overcoming challenges and promoting D&I.

He believes that putting D&I at the heart of a business makes it stronger, more profitable, and provides a competitive edge. Although quantifying ROI is difficult, this belief is corroborated to certain extent with research sources quoted in the references section.

Keywords: D&I, competitiveness, unconscious bias, listening

Introduction

D&I (diversity and inclusion) is quite the buzzword right now. Implemented correctly, it can future-proof your organisation, and boost innovation and your bottom line. I also believe that it's the right thing to do from a social justice standpoint.

DOI: 10.4324/9781003219293-30

In the U.S., only 56% of millennials in the country are white (Frey, 2018).[1] By 2050, 30% of people in the UK will be of mixed race (Sunak and Rajeswaran, 2014).[2]

But changing demographics across the world mean that it is something you cannot ignore if you want to keep a competitive edge. Younger people in particular want workplaces that are committed to reflecting the country's demographics and where they feel welcome and respected.

A total of 67% of job seekers consider workplace diversity an important factor, and more than 50% of current employees want their workplace to do more to increase diversity (www.glassdoor.com 2014).[3]

And yet 78% of employees say that they work at organisations that lack diversity in leadership positions (Hewlett et al., 2013).[4]

The bad old days

I started out in print journalism. It wasn't a very comfortable environment unless you were like everybody else. Some newspaper editors were racist. They were from another era and no longer relevant. I just couldn't stay there any longer. The environment didn't make me feel creative.

I moved into broadcasting in the 1990s when things were beginning to change, but minorities were still hardly represented. I learned my craft at 10 independent production companies – and also learned how *not* to do business. I witnessed prejudice and bullying and thought, there's got to be a better way.

Fresh vision

I set up Argonon to be a centre of excellence and the home for the most talented creative people and top entrepreneurs in the world. I also wanted to be part of a change in how programmes are made and who makes them.

TV has a loud and influential voice in society. It can change the way we speak and think. TV producers have a uniquely powerful position as we are in the living rooms and on the smartphones of millions of people all round the world, every day. This carries a lot of responsibility. It can be used for nefarious purposes, as recent world events have demonstrated – the rise of populism and fake news – and it can also be used to effect change.

I see it as my personal and professional responsibility to reflect and represent the diverse society we live in.

I have a committed personal and professional vision of what diversity and inclusion are and mean and have built this into the DNA of my company, in who we are and what we do.

On-screen diversity is an agenda point at all our board and casting meetings, with the aim of giving underrepresented groups greater visibility. This results in people appearing on our screens who reflect our society and who the audience can relate to, rather than using a narrower elite, as has traditionally been the case.

Challenges

Argonon's board was already diverse – one of its founding directors is Londoner Joey Attawia, the son of a white Irish mother and an African father. His grandmother was a freed slave from Sierra Leone. Despite this, not all the senior management were on board with the concept of promoting diversity at first. Some thought that it was just "political correctness" and a waste of money.

But then we won commissions to make two series from the BBC and Channel 4 precisely, because we the cast and content were more diverse. We were marked as a company for the future. Even the sceptics within my company could see how D&I could help the bottom line.

Culture wars

Make no mistake, we are in the middle of culture wars right now and are having to deal with identity politics. People will accuse you of only hiring people, because you are woke★.

★Woke
alert to injustice in society, especially racism
Oxford English Dictionary – 2017

You don't want a situation where people might think that colleagues only got the job because of who they are. You have to be very careful to ensure you always only hire the best person for the job. However, to increase diversity, you should spread the net wider during recruitment and go the extra mile to ensure that you have a wide range of skills and aptitudes in the shortlist. But you have to make sure no one is left behind.

White people can feel excluded because of the drive to multi-culturalism, but you need to bring them along too. This is why we encourage applicants who span socio-economic backgrounds that some politicians see as fertile ground to whip up a sense of victimhood. I'm particularly proud that Argonon has a 7:1 ratio of state school versus privately educated staff.

Instead of diversity weakening group cohesion, we find that people just get used to it and rub along fine. People see that they actually have more in common with each other. The world is mixed and becoming more so. London, where I live, is an incredibly diverse and cosmopolitan city and I love and embrace its vibrancy. You tend to find that where there are only a few minorities, you have a higher rate of hate crime.

Driving change

At Argonon, we put D&I into action both on screen and off screen.

On screen

As well as producing challenging programmes that tackle social issues head on, we also make programmes that are far more diverse and representative of audiences. This means that there is more engagement, because people recognise themselves in them.

For example:

- We cast older women presenters who would have found themselves on the scrapheap with other broadcasters.
- We ensure that there is a diverse cast of performers and panels in our hit show *The Masked Singer*.
- In *Secrets of Valley of the Kings*, we used an Egyptian female archaeologist, and a transgender historian in the series *Abandoned Engineering*.
- The series *Supercar, Superfam* centres around two Asian brothers from Essex.
- When casting contributors (ordinary people) in series like *House Hunters International*, *Cash in the Attic*, and *Nightmare Tenants*, we ensure that they include people of colour and those with visible and invisible disabilities.

In this way, we are gently showing people that we live in a diverse society. Ten or 20 years ago, none of this would have been possible.

Off screen

The only way you can authentically make diverse programming is by having a diverse production crew who understand what they are talking about. Therefore, off screen we also recruit to ensure the production crew also reflects society.

In 2016, we launched "Argonon for Everyone" to promote greater diversity within the group. It covered all areas from recruitment, casting, and promoting an open and inclusive culture at Argonon.

An inclusive culture is one in which a mix of people can go to work and feel confident in being themselves. Would you want to work somewhere you feel don't belong? No, you would leave, taking your fresh, beneficial ideas, perspectives, and skill sets with you.

Only recently, we hired a woman who had left one of our competitors, because the board had replaced four senior women with men over the last ten years and she felt she wasn't heard or appreciated. She was demoralised and says morale there is on the floor. That company is not doing well at the moment – and I'm not surprised. So, inclusion also improves retention.

> *If you haven't got the best talent you're not going to be the best, if you're not representing properly the available pool of talent then you're missing an opportunity.*
> *– Alex Wilmot-Sitwell, EMEA President at Bank of America Merrill Lynch – (Source: Financial Times 2017)*

In the UK, it is illegal to positively discriminate, so while you can have targets, you can't have quotas. We set targets for above the national average for D&I and hit or exceeded most of them by 2020.

- One in five Argonon staff identifies as black, Asian, and minority ethnic (BAME).
- Over 50% of our staff are female, many in senior leadership.
- Lesbian, gay, bisexual, transgender, and others (LGBT+) is significantly above the national average.
- We score below national average on hiring people with a disability and recognise there is work to be done here.

We also support staff with visible and invisible disabilities with training and therapy if required. Going the extra mile matters. There are also sound commercial reasons for promoting D&I. It not only benefits your staff but can also lead to higher revenues for your company (Gompers and Kovalli, 2018).[5]

External impetus for change

Like any other business, Argonon makes products for clients and their audiences. We are commissioned to make productions for broadcasters, who have their own target demographics, and are now pushing for more diversity.

> From April 2021, the BBC has set a mandatory target that 20% of off-screen talent must come from under-represented groups. These include those with a disability or from a BAME or disadvantaged socio-economic background.

Advertisers trying to reach growing markets also require more diversity in programming. Just look at the ubiquity of people of colour in advertising posters. Only a few years ago, they were noticeable by their absence.

Our clients all closely measure who watches our programmes by age, socio-economic group, and ethnicity. They do this to demonstrate their success in reaching key audiences for advertisers and sponsors who fund their programmes.

Demand for change is also coming from the public. In 2020, the COVID-19 pandemic and Black Lives Matter demonstrations further highlighted this. We have a huge problem with racism and prejudice in the world.

> A total of 84% of BAME Britons think that the UK is still very or somewhat racist, and more than half say that their career development has been affected because of their race (YouGov, 2020).[6]

We have a chronic problem in the media too: it is still neither diverse nor inclusive. It has historically been dominated by a small, nepotistic set of Oxbridge graduates in the UK.

We responded by launching a new Argonon Diversity Steering Group to address challenges with diversity, inclusion, and equality and put in place long-term initiatives and a campaign for positive change. Thirty-five people from across the group from all levels volunteered to take part, from the board to the receptionist, empowering everyone at Argonon to truly own D&I, and be part of that change. After consulting widely, the Steering Group came up with a plan to focus on four specific projects to implement in 2021.

1. *Schools:* Working with Speakers for Schools, our staff speak to children at school to help them understand that a career in the media is possible for them.
2. *Young adults:* Argonon has partnered with the UK screen sector trade body, Pact, to create two funded bursaries for entry-level interns, plus two training funds per intern.
3. *Management:* We set up a mentoring scheme in partnership with Screenskills to proactively develop staff at Argonon into leadership roles. It is also launching a buddying scheme to connect staff with those outside their immediate teams, to encourage partnerships, lateral thinking, and career development.
4. *USA:* Leopard USA, based in New York and LA, has allocated two funded bursaries for internships, working with the non-profit organisations Made in New York on the East Coast and Streetlights on the West Coast.

Partnership is a key in this process. This is an ongoing programme, which we are going to continue to fund. Managing diversity and developing a culture of inclusion are a continuous process, not a one-off initiative.

Examples of other companies around the world successfully promoting D&I policies

Sodexo

Employees worldwide: 460,000

A total of 55% of all staff members in Sodexo are women (2009; 17%) and 58% of board members are female. They have found that an optimal gender balance within an organisation increases employee engagement by 4%, gross profit by 23%, and brand image by 5%.

Marriott International

Employees worldwide: 174,000+

Named as one of the "World's Best Multinational Workplaces by Great Place to Work" and "Best Place to Work for LGBT Equality" on the HRC 2016 Corporate Equality Index, a widely recognised benchmark for diversity and inclusion.

How D&I leads to competitive edge and superior performance

McKinsey & Company compared the diversity among top management at 663 firms in ten countries with their financial performance and found that companies in the top quartile for ethnic diversity are 36% more likely to have financial returns above their respective national industry medians and 25% more likely to have above-average profitability than companies in the fourth quartile of gender diverse (Dixon-Fyle, 2020).[7]

A *Harvard Business Review* study found that companies with above-average diversity on their management teams in terms of migration, industry, career path, gender, education, and age also reported innovation revenue that was 19% higher than that of companies with below-average leadership diversity (Lorenzo and Reeves, 2018).[8]

Harvard Business Review also reported that more diverse companies are 45% likelier to report that their firm's market share grew over the previous year, and 70% likelier to report that the organisation captured a new market (Hewlett et al., 2018).[9]

A *Wall Street Journal* study found that the 20 most diverse S&P 500 companies had an average annual stock return of 10% over five years, versus 4.2% for the 20 least diverse companies and concluded: "Diverse and inclusive cultures are providing companies with a competitive edge over their peers" (Holger, 2019).[10]

Deloitte Partner of Consulting, Juliet Bourke, highlights the benefits of diversity of thinking and demographic diversity, citing findings that a diverse workforce can enhance innovation by 20% and spot risks, reducing them by 30% (Bourke, 2017).[11]

Five per cent of Fortune 1,000 companies are run by women, but they account for 7% of the total revenue on the list (Fairchild, 2014).[12]

How to master the power of diversity and inclusion: follow-up actions for your organisation

There is no one-size-fits-all approach to D&I. Every organisation needs to determine their own appropriate D&I strategy, but the following tips should help:

Prioritise inclusion

There are always more pressing concerns – allocate adequate resources for any positive action and show a fierce resolve to overcome difficulties and effect change.

Get everyone on board

Ensure leadership buy-in: do senior managers know why D&I is a priority? Do your line managers have appropriate guidelines and training, especially in unconscious bias?

Some people may feel that it's an issue that doesn't concern them. Help them understand how helping others feel included can benefit them, for example, in areas of mental health, well-being, or workplace safety.

Listen!

If senior management have the humility to listen to their staff, they may be surprised by what they hear from the ranks. They might find that people are leaving, because they don't feel that they are respected or have opportunities.

Create an open-door, listening environment. Give your employees appropriate channels to ensure that their voice is heard and take action based on their feedback.

Ask!

The very act of asking your employees about how you can improve inclusion can have a big impact on making people feel more acknowledged and welcomed when combined with simple, practical changes that may otherwise slip your mind e.g. food and drinks at company events, facilities for nursing mothers, and acknowledging religious holidays. Flexible working hours can also enable you to attract and retain a wider pool of talented people.

Inform!

Keep your people informed about diversity policies and practices via in-house media.

Check!

Examine your job specifications and recruitment process for bias.

Measure!

Use data on D&I to highlight where barriers exist and show the impact of initiatives.

Benchmark your progress against other organisations and look at what others are doing – e.g. the percentage of women and minorities in senior positions.

Partner!

Partner with community organisations at grassroots level and universities to increase the diversity of your workforce.

And finally

Ensure that your D&I programme avoids tokenism and goes beyond merely meeting compliance targets. Create true change and a sense of belonging, positively impacting your organisation.

Summary

The data are compelling that putting D&I at the heart of a business makes it stronger and more profitable and gives it a competitive edge. Treating people well benefits staff, society, and organisations, which is why it is a no-brainer for me. It is also the right thing to do.

D&I helps to recruit and retain talent. People want to work for employers with good employment practices and feel valued at work. If you are a member of an underrepresented group, you are going to feel more comfortable in a diverse and inclusive workforce.

A diverse workforce with different backgrounds, skills, experience, and knowledge can also increase innovation and creativity, developing new products or services, and opening up new market opportunities and broaden your customer base. A workforce that is happier because an open and inclusive workplace culture makes everyone feels valued and respected encourages people to perform better and this contributes to competitiveness. All this can lead to higher revenues.

And while we can't be certain that Argonon is making more money as a direct result of our D&I work, the signs are positive: we are profitable and growing, and we are doing considerably better than some of our competitors.

Notes

1 Frey, W.H. (2018), *The Millennial Generation: A Demographic Bridge to America's Diverse Future*. January. Available at: www.brookings.edu
2 Sunak, R. and S. Rajeswaran (2014), A Portrait of Modern Britain. *Policy Exchange*, May 6. Available at: www.policyexchange.org.uk
3 www.glassdoor.com (2014), What Job Seekers Really Think About Your Diversity and Inclusion Stats. *Glassdoor*, November 17.
4 Hewlett, S.A. et al. (2013/12), How Diversity Can Drive Innovation. *Harvard Business Review*. Available at: https://hbr.org
5 Gompers, P. and S. Kovvali (2018), The Other Diversity Dividend. *Harvard Business Review*, July–August 2018 issue, 72–77.
6 YouGov Poll (2020), www.yougov.co.uk, June 26.
7 Dixon-Fyle, S. et al. (2020), *Diversity Wins: How Inclusion Matters*. McKinsey & Company. May. Available at: www.mckinsey.com
8 Lorenzo, R. and M. Reeves (2018), How Diverse Leadership Teams Boost Innovation. *BCG*, January. Available at: www.bcg.com>publications
9 Hewlett, S.A. et al. (2013/12), How Diversity Can Drive Innovation. *Harvard Business Review*. Available at: https://hbr.org
10 Holger, D. (2019), The Business Case for More Diversity. *Wall Street Journal,* October 26.
11 Bourke, J. (2017), *Which Two Heads Are Better Than One? How Diverse Teams Create Breakthrough Ideas and Make Smarter Decisions*. Australian Institute of Company Directors.
12 Fairchild, C. (2014), Women CEOs in the Fortune 1000: By the Numbers. *Fortune*.

Further reading

Bourke, J. (2017), *Which Two Heads Are Better Than One? How Diverse Teams Create Breakthrough Ideas and Make Smarter Decisions*. Australian Institute of Company Directors.
Dutton, J. and M. Worline (2017), *Awakening Compassion at Work: The Quiet Power That Elevates Individuals and Organisations*. USA: Berrett-Koehler.
Frost, S. and D. Kalman (2016), *Inclusive Talent Management: How Business Can Thrive in an Age of Diversity*. UK: Kogan Page.

24

MASTERING THE POWER OF GENDER EQUALITY

Alina Nassar

Abstract

"Mastering the power of gender equality" seeks to educate the reader on the importance of true inclusion of women in the formal economy, in public and private leadership and, in general, in all areas of the nations' development to achieve global economic growth and equitable prosperity for all. The affirmations are grounded on the author's own research, on her own experience, and on data revealing the current situation and how advancing women would boost progress and growth across the world. The reading provides examples on how leaders can act collaboratively to reverse a historic inequality. Finally, this essay invites us all to become agents of change and pursue a world in which opportunities to thrive are available to all, regardless of gender.

Keywords: Gender diversity, inclusion, equal opportunity, women leaders

Introduction

The inclusion of women in all areas of our development is a noble aspiration. But, as Ban Ki-moon, the former Secretary General of the United Nations, has emphasised, "*The world will never realize 100 per cent of its goals if 50 per cent of its people cannot realize their full potential. When we unleash the power of women, we can secure the future for all*".[1]

DOI: 10.4324/9781003219293-31

From spectator to player

"There's more to life than being a passenger".[2]
Amelia Earhart (1897–disappeared in 1937), American aviation pioneer,
first woman to fly solo across the Atlantic Ocean

I was used to academic and industry events where attendance, panellists, and keynotes were predominantly male. My professional environment was not vastly different, although at law school most of the students were women.

I did not question the *status quo* at that time. Neither did I challenge many other inequalities that have historically held back women's full potential as professionals, citizens, and human beings; perhaps, I did not consider them reversible, and after all, I knew few women standing out in the profession or in politics.

The gift of maternity positioned me at a crossroad, struggling with the guilt of pursuing a career while raising a family. I had had access to excellent education and graduated in a profession that I did not want to abandon, but the organisations' structures and society's environment did not provide the conditions for a professional working mother to develop her full potential in both roles. Moreover, as a woman in two male-dominated fields – aviation and law – it just seemed "normal" to see very few women at conferences, all-men panels, mostly male teams, and women sacrificing career advancement because of its incompatibility with motherhood.

In Costa Rica, my homeland, women are the predominant providers of care and housework; women who have the resources would stay at home raising their children or step back by downshifting at work. Others – head of their households – would simply try to manage both worlds. Indeed, whether they stay at home, stay in the labour force, or rejoin it, women still bear the highest percentage of unpaid care work, in comparison to men.[3]

Today, women across the globe are underrepresented, discriminated against, and denied educational and professional opportunities. The COVID-19 pandemic during 2020 and 2021 unveiled the profound inequalities that women face and enlarged the global gender gap, evidencing poor and uneven progress in this area despite years of conversations around the topic.

Long ago, I decided to actively participate in the rally towards the equality and opportunities I envision for my daughters and the generations to come. Real and responsible leaders must walk the walk.

The case for gender equality

"As women gain rights, families flourish, and so do societies. That connection is built on a simple truth: Whenever you include a group that's been excluded, you benefit everyone. And when you're working globally to include women and girls, who are half of every population, you're working to benefit all members of every community. Gender equity lifts everyone".[4]

Melinda Gates, (1964-present), an American Philanthropist (The Moment of Lift: How Empowering Women Changes the World, 2019)

The conversation about gender equality has been around for decades. Whether social justice, a fundamental human right, or a strategic business decision, advancing towards gender equality has proved to be in the best interest of the communities.

In 2015, the United Nations' (UN's) member States adopted the Sustainable Development Goals (SDG), a *"universal call to action to end poverty, protect the planet and improve the lives and prospects of everyone, everywhere"*.[5] Goal Five is achieving Gender Equality as the *"necessary foundation for a peaceful, prosperous and sustainable world"*.[6] Indeed, pursuing and reaching gender equality have a powerful impact on several others of the SDGs. By providing women with equal access to health, education, formal jobs, equal pay, and leadership opportunities in the public and private sectors, we reduce poverty, mitigate hunger, enhance well-being, reduce inequalities, and create strong and bonded communities with reduced social confrontation.

Women represent half of the world's population and play an active role in the advancement of society. Their participation in the work force brings additional income for their families, improves living standards, and triggers economic growth. A nation cannot achieve prosperity for all if it ignores female potential.[7]

In business, the impact of women's leadership contributions is well documented and supported by data. Several studies have found a correlation between diverse and inclusive leadership and financial performance and value creation. A recent study[8] shows that companies in the top quartile for gender diversity are 25 per cent more likely to have financial returns above their respective national industry medians. The highest performing companies have more women in decision-making positions.[9]

Diverse and inclusive teams boost creative thinking and problem-solving capabilities. In a globalised world with accelerated changes of the consumer base, companies need diverse perspectives to come up with the innovation required to manage rapid market changes. Diverse companies have better chances to expand their customer base, grow new markets, and of surviving and overcoming crises. Businesses that embrace diversity also improve in talent attraction and retention; employees feel appreciated when they can bring their whole selves to work.

The data to support the case for gender equality are compelling. However, women still face unfairness, discrimination, and challenges in every aspect. In business environments, women face, for example, reduced pay compared to equally competent men[10] and exclusion from promotions, challenging assignments, and training. Women remain underrepresented in public and private leadership and have fewer opportunities to reach top positions.

Progress made in some areas is still limited, slow, uneven, and is constantly threatened. Changes in policies, ineffective inclusion programmes, financial crises, and global events unveil the fragility of the gains.[11] Technological advancements automating many jobs – that are today gender-specific and held mostly by women – are also a threat.

At the present rate of progress, it will take nearly a century to achieve parity.[12] Can humanity afford to wait this long?

Championing gender equality in our organisations

"Over the past decade, many companies around the world have incorporated I&D[13] into their visions and strategies. Increasingly, business leaders recognize that a diverse and inclusive employee base - with a range of approaches and perspectives - is an asset when competing in a fast-moving, globalized economy".[14]
McKinsey Company, Diversity Wins (2020)

The route to gender equality is specific for each company and society given history, culture, beliefs, and experiences shape the process. Regardless of these particularities, advancement is a collective effort that governments, corporations, and individuals must embrace with strong conviction as gender equality leads to prosperity.

Through the formulation of public policies, the role of governments is essential to close the gender gap, and leading nations blaze the trail (Iceland, Sweden, Norway, Finland, and New Zealand).[15] However, governmental actions and policies are not always a possible, immediate, or effective solution; they are not exempted from political interests, budget constraints, inappropriate implementation, and lack of transparency and accountability. As a result, it is our responsibility as business leaders to influence change from the inside of our organisations.

Need a business case? Truly diverse and inclusive companies are 70 per cent more likely to capture new markets[16], 87 per cent more likely to make better decisions[17],[18] and faster in deploying innovation. Companies recognised for their inclusive culture attract more talent and have reduced turnover rates because of employees' increased satisfaction.

Despite the evidence, organisations still face many challenges in implementing effective gender equality initiatives.

In dealing with this topic, I have found that first, ensuring that gender equality requires more than issuing a statement pledging to it or adding women to the payroll. It demands real involvement and transparent commitment from leadership to make gender equality a company's purpose and long-term strategy. Second, changing the organisational culture and biases require time, discipline, and continuity. Effective programmes are those containing metrics to measure quantitative and qualitative improvement, and to hold leaders accountable. Third, gender equality shall be the result of collective understanding, acceptance, and commitment, which can only be achieved by getting the different stakeholders involved in the creation and implementation of the initiatives.

Leading by example

Nassar Abogados is a law firm in Central America, which originated in San José, Costa Rica, in the early 1980s as a "boutique" in Transportation Law (Maritime, Aviation). Through the years, the company grew to provide a variety of services in different areas of law and expanded very rapidly in the decade of year 2000. Although the firm already had a diverse employee base, the growth experienced in jurisdictions, services, and clients demanded to attract more of the top talent. Guaranteeing gender equality would open the door to female professionals, bringing also more diversity into our team.

Partly because of this need and partly because of my own realisation of the necessities of a working mother, I took the job of promoting a gender equality programme. At first, I experienced resistance. People did not necessarily understand what "gender equality" and "same opportunities" meant and entailed, and therefore, some feared losing their privileges to a minority or to another group, and some resisted to change something that was working well for the majority.

"Diversity", "inclusion", and "gender equality" may now be common words in our business and social vocabulary, and everyone seems to agree that equally competent men and women should have the same opportunities.

However, what opportunities are developed and how they are made available to all are not necessarily a shared view, neither was it back then. The programme, therefore, could only begin by socialising these concepts with training from the experts and – most importantly – by listening to the different stakeholders' perspectives and expectations on the topic. Education and alignment were fundamental to a common foundation from where we could all build.

Establishing gender equality does not suggest positive discrimination; neither it is aimed at transferring power, privileges, or benefits to one group by taking them away from another. To the contrary, it means being treated equally to someone in the same situation and with the same competences. Education, again, is central to a successful implementation of a gender equality initiative.

Mastering the power of gender equality

In practical terms, how can a leader determine if an organisation is gender-equal? What does gender equality really mean for a company? Based on my experience, it means:

- That women are no longer "punished" professionally when they go on maternity leave or because of other "unpaid work", and that they can move up and across the organisation equally as men do.
    - In our case, among other measures, flexible schedules were introduced for working mothers beyond the mandatory maternity leaves, and fathers were also granted flexibility to take care of family obligations. Accordingly, mothers can continue to work part time or full time, and parents can look after their families and organise their schedules. This has resulted in increased employees' loyalty and fewer turnover rates when women become mothers, which at the same time saves the company the costs of hiring and training new personnel.
- As obvious as it may seem, it means women and men in the same position and with the same qualifications and competences are paid equally, receive the same opportunities for promotions, mentoring, training, attendance to industry, or professional events – in sum, the same treatment.
- That team leaders intentionally invite women to take on challenging projects, to perform on different roles to develop new skills, and to participate in the decision-making processes.

- Our teams include men and women, with different specialties and backgrounds. The result has been an innovative approach to problem-solving given the rich diversity of the analysis.
- That recruitment processes are assessed to determine the existence of any biases – in the drafting of the profiles, the interviewing, or the selection phase – that may be preventing female talent to join the organisation or to progress in it.
- That the leadership of the organisation should be gender balanced and organisations should be bold in appointing competent women into leadership positions. It plays a role in the organisation's ability to remain relevant and sends a clear message about leadership's commitment to equality. Moreover, it inspires other women within and outside the organisation.
- By the time I am writing this chapter, my firm has a little over 50 per cent females in leadership positions across the jurisdictions in which it operates.
- To continuously evaluate the programmes and initiatives to understand its effectiveness and improve them. Successful programmes are those created jointly with the population they target, and constantly examined for improvement.
    - The metrics should not only go beyond the number of women joining the organisation at entry levels but also include turnover rates (and reasons), promotions, training opportunities, teams' performance, and their integration, among others.
- Employees receive continuous education on the topic, are listened to, and invited to propose new ideas and participate in the drafting of the policies and implementation of the initiatives. That way, employees are immersed in a culture of merits, respect, and equality, so much that promoting gender equality turns into a personal choice more than another imposed company policy to comply with.

Mastering the power of gender equality has paid off for our company and for the individuals themselves. Some of our greatest talents are working mothers whom we would have lost in the absence of specific measures targeted at their retention after giving birth to a child. This has also built us a reputation that has attracted other capable individuals. Women's presence in business has been linked to corporations' improved performance, and when a company does well, prosperity spreads to all its stakeholders.

As business leaders, we have most of the responsibility for promoting gender equality within our organisations. But every individual has areas of influence in which small actions help to turn a company's culture into a more inclusive one. Regardless of a person's position, small daily actions can make a big difference to inject gender equality into the corporate veins. Mentoring and sponsoring women, inviting them to work meetings and asking for their opinions, introducing them to business partners and colleagues so they can expand their networks, organising networking events targeted at young female professionals, and standing up for someone when discriminated against by gender (or any other basis!) are all forms in which we make a difference.

The power of role models in women's empowerment

> "But a role model in the flesh provides more than inspiration; his or her very existence is confirmation of possibilities one may have every reason to doubt, saying, yes, someone like me can do this".[19]
>
> Sonia Sotomayor (1954-present), Associate Justice of the
> Supreme Court of the United States

I was a young female attorney in the male-dominated field of aviation, when, in 2004, I was introduced to an organisation that has had a profound impact in my professional development and has put me in some way where I am today. That year, I attended the annual conference of the International Aviation Women's Association (IAWA), a non-profit international organisation that promotes the advancement of women in aviation and aerospace.

There, and for the first time in my – to that date – short career, I met several women holding top positions. Contrary to my prior experience at professional events and meetings, IAWA's annual conference hosted hundreds of female leaders who discussed the most relevant industry issues, shared their experiences, and brought to the table perspectives that I hadn't come across before. I was in awe by their achievements but particularly impressed by listening to their stories, and how they were able to overcome every obstacle to reach their goals.

IAWA showed me that there was room in the industry for women to succeed and that moulded every step in my personal and professional journey, including my activism for equality. I was instantly hooked and aspired to become, one day, one of those women. I understood that advancing our companies and societies to gender equality requires a community of brave and influential agents of change.

Guided by IAWA's role models whom I looked up to, I had access to mentors who gave me advice on business and career development, to sponsors who opened doors for me. Through IAWA, I was able to study organisations' best practices for gender equality, the challenges faced, and the tangible benefits of promoting women's advancement. I was also able to witness gender inequalities and to advocate for change.

IAWA has had a powerful impact in the industry by raising awareness of the importance of gender equality, by giving female leaders international visibility and showing their success stories, and by engaging different stakeholders and leaders into the conversation and actions for a more equal industry. IAWA provides women with mentoring, scholarship, business, education, and networking opportunities without comparison to any other similar organisation in the industry. IAWA has advanced many women in the profession and has educated the aviation and aerospace community on the returns of implementing gender equality as a core value.

The secret? IAWA's members are women of achievement who serve as role models to other women. Their stories and the obstacles they have faced are no different from those of other women across the globe, but they have had the drive to fight those inequalities, to advocate for other women and to challenge and change their own companies' culture.

The importance of role models in achieving women's progress and gender equality should not be underestimated. In jobs and fields in which female participation is lower such as sciences, technology, engineering, and mathematics, leaders are responsible for publicly recognising role models and for telling their stories. The road to gender equality has many structural obstacles that are still to be cleared, but seeing someone succeeding boosts a woman's own confidence and unleashes her potential.

In 2019, (IAWA), Korn Ferry and five other global organisations[20] launched the first ever study on gender diversity in aviation and aerospace. The "Soaring through the Glass Ceiling Study" focused on the primary enablers and inhibitors of women's evolvement in aviation and aerospace, and best practices of champion organisations.

The Study found as one of the primary inhibitors for women's inclusion:

> lack of female executives or board members. If there are no, or few, female role models in leadership positions, it is far more challenging for women to see a path for themselves or other women to rise within their organizations.[21] Convergently, the two most important enablers

were "representation of women in leadership and women serving as role models", as well as business leaders' strong and visible commitment to diversity and inclusion.

In my case, female role models have been more than examples of a road-map to achievement. They have been my push to begin, the inspiration to move forward, the courage to try again and the realisation of "I can". Success leads to success.

Reflect:

1   Study the prevalence of gender inequality in organisations in your country. Identify what are the causes and what steps have been taken to encourage gender equality?
2   Analyse what policies and practices in your organisation result in gender inequality. Prepare an action plan to promote gender equality in your organisation.
3   Analyse what actions you can take to advocate for gender equality beyond your organisation.

Summary

Live inclusion, love diversity, and laugh when a girl can break the circle of poverty, when a woman advances in the profession.

The world has a historical debt with women whose fundamental rights have been denied, severed, or undervalued. Vindication of women's rights to live in societies where opportunities are equal is neither a gender fight nor an exclusive task for women.

Men and women, corporate leaders, and politicians must work together to ensure that existent gender inequalities are eliminated. It's an investment in the families, the companies, and the societies, in the well-being of our communities.

The absolute benefits of gender equality have been supported by conclusive data over the years – data which should continue to be gathered and analysed for improved initiatives and decision-making.

Achieving gender equality is the right thing to do. We must all play our part as agents of change. The time to make it happen is now. The world cannot continue to afford the price of inequalities, and every person has the power to make a difference.

Notes

1 United Nations Secretary-General's Message on International Women's Day, March 8, 2015. Available at: https://www.un.org/sg/en/content/sg/statement/2015-03-08/secretary-generals-message-international-womens-day-scroll-down. Accessed on: September 18, 2021.

2 This quote is widely attributed to Amelia Earhart – see for instance https://anchor.fm>episodes>There and https://www.goalcast.com>top-american-quotes-to-inspire-you-to-soar. She is believed to have made this quote to a journalist.

3 Costa Rica National Institute on Statistics and Census (2019). Available at: https://www.inec.cr/multimedia/8-de-marzo-dia-internacional-de-la-mujer-construyamos-equidad-avancemos-hacia-la-igualdad. Accessed on: September 6, 2020.

4 Gates, M. (2019), *The Moment of Lift - How Empowering Women Changes the World*. New York: Flatiron Books, p. 26.

5 Available at: https://www.un.org/sustainabledevelopment/development-agenda/. Accessed on: August 30, 2020.

6 Available at: https://www.un.org/sustainabledevelopment/gender-equality/. Accessed on: August 30, 2020.

7 Teow, J. et al. (2019), *Women in Work Index*. Available at: https://www.pwc.co.uk/economic-services/WIWI/pwc-women-in-work-2019-final-web.pdf. Accessed on: September 5, 2020.

8 Hunt, V. et al. (2020), *Diversity Wins: How Inclusion Matters*. Available at: https://www.mckinsey.com/~/media/McKinsey/Featured%20Insights/Diversity%20and%20Inclusion/Diversity%20wins%20How%20inclusion%20matters/Diversity-wins-How-inclusion-matters-vF.pdf. Accessed on: August 29, 2020.

9 Hunt, V. et al. (2018), *Delivering Through Diversity*. Available at: https://www.mckinsey.com/~/media/mckinsey/business%20functions/organization/our%20insights/delivering%20through%20diversity/delivering-through-diversity_full-report.ashx. Accessed on: August 29, 2020.

10 Equileap (2021), *Gender Equality Global Report & Ranking*. Available at: https://equileap.com/wp-content/uploads/2021/03/Global-Report-2021.pdf. Accessed on: March 14, 2021.

11 Madgavkar, A. et al. (2020), *COVID-19 and Gender Equality: Countering the Regressive Effects*. Available at: https://www.mckinsey.com/featured-insights/future-of-work/covid-19-and-gender-equality-countering-the-regressive-effects. Accessed on: August 29, 2020.

12 World Economic Forum (2020), *Global Gender Gap Report*. Available at: http://reports.weforum.org/global-gender-gap-report-2020/dataexplorer. Accessed on: August 30, 2020.

13 "I&D" stands for "inclusion" and "diversity" in the organizational arena. It is also referred to, indistinctively, as "D&I".

14 Hunt, V. et al. (2020), *Diversity Wins: How Inclusion Matters*. Available at: https://www.mckinsey.com/~/media/McKinsey/Featured%20Insights/Diversity%20and%20Inclusion/Diversity%20wins%20How%20inclusion%20matters/Diversity-wins-How-inclusion-matters-vF.pdf. Accessed on: August 29, 2020.

15 World Economic Forum (2020), *Global Gender Gap Report*. Available at: http://reports.weforum.org/global-gender-gap-report-2020/dataexplorer. Accessed on: August 30, 2020.

16 Hewlett, S. et al. (2013), *How Diversity Can Drive Innovation*. Available at: https://hbr.org/2013/12/how-diversity-can-drive-innovation. Accessed on: March 14, 2021.

17 Ferry, Korn. *The Importance of Inclusion in the Workplace*. Available at: https://www.kornferry.com/challenges/diversity-equity-and-inclusion/importance-of-inclusion-in-the-workplace. Accessed on: March 14, 2021.

18 Grech-Cumbo, B. *Want Higher Profits? Hire a Female CEO*. Available at: https://www.kornferry.com/insights/articles/women-ceo-cfo-stock-performance#:

~:text=Companies%20that%20appointed%20a%20woman,profit%20than%20their%20 sector%20average. Accessed on: March 14, 2021.

19 Sotomayor, S. (2013), *My Beloved World*. New York: Alfred A. Knopf, p. 178.
20 Soaring Through the Glass Ceiling Study (2019). Available at: https://infokf.korn-ferry.com/rs/494-VUC-482/images/Soaring_through_the_glass_ceiling_FINAL.pdf. Accessed on: August 31, 2020.
21 Ibid.

Further reading

Criado Perez, C. (2019), *Invisible Women – Data Bias in a World Designed for Men*. New York: Abrams Press.

Hunt, V. et al. (2015), *Why Diversity Matters*. Available at: https://www.mckinsey.com/~/ media/McKinsey/Business%20Functions/Organization/Our%20Insights/Why%20diver-sity%20matters/Why%20diversity%20matters.pdf

Polonskaia, A. et al. (2020), *The 5 Disciplines of Inclusive Leaders. Unleashing the Power of All of Us*. Available at: https://infokf.kornferry.com/inclusive-leader-discipline.html?utm_source= website&utm_medium=banner&utm_term=website&utm_content=whitepaper&utm_ campaign=20-05-Global-inclusiveleader

Scott, L. (2020), *The Double X Economy*. New York: Farrar, Strauss and Giroux.

Teow, J. et al. (2019), *Women in Work Index*. Available at: https://www.pwc.co.uk/economic-services/WIWI/pwc-women-in-work-2019-final-web.pdf. Accessed on: September 5, 2020.

PART VIII

Negotiating and collaborating

25

MASTERING THE POWER OF NEGOTIATIONS

Josef Bruckschlögl and J.R. Klein

Abstract

From the moment we are born, we are forced into negotiations. Our verbal arguments at that stage are rather limited. Crying makes parents aware that we need food, attention, or something else. Parents understand our motivation and will most likely satisfy us. Over time, our techniques of negotiating improve, and our arguments will become more sophisticated.

Strategies of negotiations range from collaborative to combative, and its impact ranges from compromise to catastrophe. The old model of thinking of negotiations as a competition, rather than a process finding understanding and balance of the negotiating parties' needs is still prevalent and frequently evident in senior management. Many times, it is about winning and not much more. At its worst, it is defined as unethical behavior. At its best, it should be a way to focus attention in conversation and come to an agreement that allows both parties to win. The key to effective negotiations is in its leadership. Leadership that understands that empathy, openness, and collaboration produce a sustainable outcome.

Effective negotiations recognise the personal interests of each party and facilitates discovering a common solution. Research tells us that it is possible to significantly improve negotiation skills through education, preparation, and practice. Effective negotiating power comes with a hidden benefit. Being a better negotiator is being a better leader.

Keywords: Interests, distributive, bargaining, problem-solving

DOI: 10.4324/9781003219293-33

Introduction

When we were asked to collaborate on the writing of this chapter, it was a confirmation of the relationship we have developed since we first met at the University of Oxford in 2014.

As a senior executive of a social impact finance firm in the U.S., my (J.R.) four-decade journey resulted in many experiences and learning. As we will note in this chapter, it was a career filled with negotiations. I stepped away from my executive position to launch J.R. Global, a company dedicated to strengthening local communities by focusing on leadership and systemic change.

I (Josef) have observed the evolution of greater negotiation powers in the development of my daughters. Over the years, they have emerged from an agressive argument of, "Father, I want this or that!" to a much more sophisticated one of, "Dad, before you decide, please let us tell you what we want and why".

At our first meeting in Oxford, we discovered that we shared extensive experience conducting complex negotiations. Since then, we have continued to exchange our experiences and educate each other to master the power of negotiations.

Negotiation is one of those words that move us to the edge of the chair or causes shivers to go up the spine. Most people's perception of negotiating is based on what we have heard, observed, or experienced and seems to be something to avoid. Its simplest definition is the interaction between two parties to agree on an issue of mutual interest.

According to this book's co-author, Prof. Lalit Johri, who taught negotiations in the Oxford Advanced Management and Leadership Programme, negotiations can be broadly described as transactional or transformational. He described his experience in negotiations to highlight the difference between these two.

> I was consulting with a plastics containers manufacturing company in India. As a pioneer in the packaging industry, the company was preparing to introduce food-grade bottles used in packaging edible oils (cooking oils) and carbonated drinks (fizzy drinks). With positive feedback from the food processing industry, the company started discussions with a Japanese company to import the moulds and the equipment for manufacturing food-grade containers, the first in India. The negotiations focused on importing equipment for a small scale plant to manufacture

small and medium-sized bottles. The Indian and the Japanese company viewed the negotiations as a one-off transaction and focussed on negotiating the purchase price of the equipment. As the two companies were wrapping up the price agreement, the Indian company figured out that the landed price of the equipment inflated the cost of final products to the point that it was too high for the potential buyers in the food processing industry in India. At this point, the negotiations were called off with the understanding that further investigations were required for a financially viable solution.

The Indian company conducted extensive market research amongst institutional and household buyers in the next six months. The results were encouraging. The "food grade" feature was a winner, and the only inhibiting factor was the high price of the containers. The answer was in scaling up manufacturing to gain economies of scale.

The Indian company approached the Japanese supplier with a medium-term strategy to introduce food grade containers in India. It proposed to import equipment to establish multiple plants over a period of time and a more comprehensive range of moulds for manufacturing a variety of bottles and jars to cater to the needs of the institutional buyers and household consumers. This time both parties looked at the big picture. The Indian company saw the potential to diversify into consumer product categories and scale up the production to reduce the cost. The Japanese company saw an attractive opportunity to enter the Indian market. It shifted its focus to selling a wider range of equipment to our company and other manufacturers of plastics containers in India.

By adopting a broader vision and expanding their respective negotiation frames, the two companies successfully negotiated a series of agreements to import several manufacturing plants. The two parties took advantage of the economies of scale, and containers' final cost went down. The Indian company successfully launched food grade bottles and jars in the institutional and consumer segments and expanded its operations across India. As the two companies expanded the scope of their collaboration, their relationship deepened, and the mutual trust grew stronger and stronger. It was a transformational experience for both companies. On reflection, in the initial stage of negotiations, the two parties were unsuccessful because they had limited objectives and adopted a transactional approach. As soon as they looked at the big picture, they found a financially variable solution.

Lalit highlighted two essential lessons from this experience. First, the under-lying vision in negotiations opens an array of new opportunities for the parties to seek higher mutual gains. Second, as the vision expands, the opportunities grow. The trust between parties strengthens to the point that their relationship evolves from a "buyer-seller" to "partners" who are willing to help each other transform and grow. The initial transactional approach restricted the choices, and one party was winning at the cost of the other, typically win-lose outcome. The transformational approach expanded both parties' potential gains, leading to win–win outcomes.

Everyone is a negotiator

We deal with formal negotiations throughout our professional and personal lives. Formal negotiations, whether in conversation with an employer about a job offer, deciding which teammates have what responsibility, thrashing out a contract with a supplier, hammering out a conflict with a co-worker, or arguing over who works the night shift, are deployed. Even though nego-tiating causes anxiety for most, the fact is that everyone regularly negotiates in everyday life.

When we leave work, the informal, less obvious negotiations begin. Life is filled to the brim with it. We wrangle over the price of a car, barter about the cost of food, how much time can the kids spend online, carpool days, persuading a toddler to eat creamed pea, deciding what television pro-gramme to watch, what restaurant to go to, and what to eat. We negotiate every day, every day, from the time we wake up to when we go to sleep. Life is a series of negotiations.

Human neurology is designed to deal with life by working out what our senses tell us and figuring out how to survive by making decisions. Some of those are pre-cognitive or involuntary but most call for negotiation. The brain says that we are hungry, hot or cold, comfortable or uncomfortable, out of breath, and tired or refreshed. The cognitive mind is always ready to negotiate.

Types of negotiations

What Lalit described as a transactional approach in the example of the Indian company is referred to as *distributive negotiations*. The parties engage in "hard bargaining" to maximise their interests. If one party dominates and claims the negotiable value, the other party loses. In the end, there is a definite winner and a definite loser.

The transformational approach pursued by the Indian and Japanese companies in the example is referred to as *integrative negotiations*. The parties share a vision, explore opportunities for creating and expanding negotiable value and then share value for mutual gains. In this scenario, the parties share expanded value based on "give and take" to reach a win-win agreement.

Another type of negotiation in which several parties negotiate on common interests or concerns is called multiparty negotiations. COP26 Conference held in Glasgow, Scotland during October–November 2021, at which Glasgow Climate Pact was adopted, is a fine example of multiparty negotiations.

In multiparty negotiations, the involved parties often have conflicting interests, and they resort to trade-offs to find a common solution. At COP26, there were significant differences between developing and developed countries on the issue of the volume of carbon emissions and greenhouse gases contributed by respective groups of countries. The developed countries insisted that developing economies must cut down the emissions. The developing countries were unwilling to do so and took the stand that they had to pursue industrialisation for economic growth and improve their people's living standards. The real problem was the lack of or poor standards and systems regulating emissions and substandard technologies and manufacturing processes by factories in developing countries. After several negotiations, it was agreed that developed countries would provide hundreds of billions of dollars annually to developing countries to curb greenhouse gases. The financial support will enable developing countries to acquire new technologies with a lower carbon footprint and pursue their interest (Harvard Law School, 2021).[6]

The process of negotiations

In preparation for negotiation, creating a mindset that increases the probability of achieving the most rewarding outcome for all parties is essential. It must involve thinking about the process of creating a "table" culture that is conducive to compromise and collaboration. It must be built on trust and sustainable long-term relationships. Satisfaction with the outcome of negotiation does not depend solely on how much of the objective was gained or lost. It also depends on whether the negotiation process was collegial and fair. The process cannot be left to chance to maximise satisfaction and build a strong working relationship.

It is essential to take the time to clarify issues to be discussed. Successful negotiators have a good understanding of what is on the "table" and how to share it based on their interests and the other party's interests. They discover the other party's interests ahead of time and confirm them at the table. This clarification leads to sharing relevant information and being aware of the range of acceptable offers on both sides of the table. The information shared in the initial exchange should be clear and concise, with all parties confirming the question.

Conversation and discussion should progress towards closing the gap between offers. This involves both parties asking for and giving concessions. Sessions should reiterate and document progress in a culture of transparency. BATNA ("best alternative to no agreement") is an extremely useful benchmark used by seasoned negotiators to compare successive offers made by the other party as a basis for accepting or rejecting proposals.

Effective negotiation solves problems by exploring new avenues that facilitate impasse resolution through trade-offs rather than quitting. Successful negotiators solve problems by expanding avenues for collaboration, creating additional value, and sharing value in mutually satisfying ways. They focus on building long-term relationships opening gates for higher-level collaborations on future ventures (Harvard Law School, 2021).[5]

In 2017 we (Josef and KWAK Telecom team) negotiated a partnership to provide micropayment service to a mobile operator in Western Samoa. It was an attractive business partnership for both parties. Our negotiations for delivering the service and revenue sharing proceeded smoothly with a clear focus on recognizing the mutual interests and benefits. As we were about to sign the partnership contract, the mobile operator, who had no experience offering financial services, raised two concerns. The first was the reputation risk in the event of a fraud that could harm their standing in the telecom community, and secondly, in the event of fraud or non-payment, who would cover the losses.

We recognized that these were genuine concerns and acknowledged the mobile operator's concerns. These concerns paved the way for seeking new solutions for mitigating the risks associated with fraud and non-payment. Fortunately, we had built software tools and procedures for risk management and fraud prevention which we offered at no extra cost to the mobile operator. As a backup, we also offered to cover the financial risk of fraud or non-payment for the first three months of operations, and we were prepared to increase this to six months if necessary, which was not even needed. The mobile operator accepted our offers, and we entered into a robust partnership. Over time, this partnership resulted in significant benefits for all the stakeholders.

In negotiating and concluding this successful partnership contract, my team and I learned many important lessons.

- Recognising and satisfying the interests of the mobile operator created a positive environment for successful negotiations.
- Listening and responding to the concerns of the other party helped us to earn the confidence and trust of the mobile operator.
- Most importantly, we recognised that we would benefit from the partnership if the mobile operator succeeded.

Negotiating skills

The negotiations we have with ourselves determine how we behave and impact our lives' quality, and they are the most important debates we ever have. Though developing the skills of communications, relationships, and influencing people are vital in business, learning to negotiate effectively with yourself is even more essential to success. The capacity to build strong relationships and experience the satisfaction of richer rewards comes from the same place.

Although there may be few or no "born" negotiators, there is a world full of people "born negotiating". The internalisation of this concept will change the image of negotiations from a contest between adversaries with winners and losers to an interactive conversation resulting in a beneficially satisfactory solution. In our daily internal negotiations, several inner voices are competing for attention. Some are nice, but others are adversarial and fire the debate. These differing voices have their own rules of engagement, styles, interests, motivations, and desired outcomes. Neurologists tell us that they represent different parts of the brain. This fundamental neurological commonality becomes the practice field for external negotiations (Fox, 2013).[4]

Though people are born negotiating, there are few natural-born negotiators. However, research tells us that it is possible to significantly improve negotiation skills through education, preparation, and practice. This formula hones the internal propensities and heightens the capacity to be sensitive to the language positions regarding what parties demand, styles, opportunities, alternatives, and if sharpened successfully to discover and identify common ground.

This approach focuses on solving problems. It includes the courageous wisdom to manage the process of what, why, how, and who. It involves creating an environment that is conducive to give and take. It establishes a courteous and constructive interaction that frames the win–win objectives and outcomes. Regardless of the differences in party's interests in terms of what they want and why, the understanding is that concessions will be made, and not all goals will be satisfied. A good negotiation leaves each party satisfied and trusting that the relationship is open to future interaction (Business Queensland, 2020).[2]

The problem-solving approach in negotiations is not new and was first presented by Roger Fisher and William Ury in the book *Getting to YES* (Fisher et al., 2011).[3] The strategy focuses on the underlying interests of all parties rather than positions. It motivates parties to build and maintain relationships even in disagreement, and it understands that the adversarial process results in opposite outcomes.

As it is sometimes difficult for people to get along with one another, the best strategy is to sit down together and talk out a solution, so it is with most negotiations. Negotiation recognises the personal interests of each party and facilitates discovering a common solution. This simple concept is like driving a car. If you have the right skills, it is easy, but you can make a real mess if not. Negotiation requires some essential skills to achieve positive outcomes.

Probably, the most significant challenge is being unprepared. There is some disagreement about who actually coined the phrase, "*failure to plan is planning to fail*", but it is true none the less. Thinking only about your interests and ignoring the interest and needs of the other party become a considerable disadvantage. This means defining the negotiation strategy, expected outcomes, and how they are valued. This is an acquired skill that will also have value in preparation and at the table.

The skill of valuing the other party from the experience and success of your business is vital. It involves the essential ancillary listening tool for discovery, understanding, and creatively recalibrating to keep the momentum moving forward. It also involves empathising when needed. It not only just understands what the other party wants but also respects why they want it. This means building a culture that is open and interactive. Everyone should have the opportunity to express their views without interruption. Without this skill mastery, the alternative gives way to emotion or lack of patience.

This culture-building skill is frequently about time or the lack thereof. If at all possible, negotiations should never be rushed. Managing the process may be more of an art than a skill, but it remains a necessary trait to develop. Building the perception of a place or process that freely shares information, invites creative thinking, and is open and receptive to sensible ideas is a proficiency worth developing.

One must develop the ability to see through uncertainty and understand the issue from the perspective of the other side of the table. It involves active listening, cross-cultural thinking, and controlling your emotions. An effective negotiator must never underestimate the other party. Even the most minor details are up for negotiation.

Learning how to become aware of the strategies and tactics of the other party is an acquired skill. Do not think that the other party has not prepared or is not as intelligent, skilled, or committed as you are. You must not only know your BATNA but also have a good idea of what the other party's BATNA is.

Many clever negotiators use tactics such as framing and anchoring to gain an advantage. These tactics influence other party's perceptions and sense of judgement during negotiations. As many people are risk-averse, a sales pitch framed as a remedy for mitigating personal risk usually invokes a positive response from the target customer. In price bargaining, a faint-hearted negotiator might give in to a high price offer because their thinking and sense of justice may be anchored in the initial offer made by the seller. It is important to develop skills to avoid traps set up by other parties by clever framing and anchoring (Bazerman, 2013).[1]

The final skills needed for effective negotiation are both art and science. It involves the preparation, practice, and pragmatism of identifying trade-offs that give away less important value and taking more critical importance when it is to your interest. At the center of these attributes is to deploy creativity and problem-solving and requires calculating the tangible and intangible values and benefits and the deal's risks. At the end of the day, as negotiation moves to the point of understanding and documents are signed, make sure they are written clearly in the letter and spirit of the agreement. Remember that all negotiations are the same in that they are all different. Each one provides a learning opportunity (Thompson, 2019).[8]

From our conversations with experts, we have learned that it is essential for cultural negotiations to include the acquisition of a deep knowledge of the emotional make-up of people from different countries. They also require building relationships with executives at different levels and departments in organisations. Business to business negotiations involve educating and helping the buyer to understand the short and long-term advantages of new technology solutions and assisting legacy suppliers with finding new buyers inside their network. Even simple things like giving feedback to suppliers that will improve products through joint initiatives provide mutual benefits.

The negotiation process should be open and interactive. Everyone should have the opportunity to express their views without interruption. Though agreement may not be present, the courtesy must listen first. The alternative is giving way to emotion or lack of patience. Rational thinking transforms emotion into passion and fosters a feedback loop of intuition, sensitivity, and transparency to understand the other party's values, needs, and limitations. Negotiation is about listening, learning, and responding. The strategy on both sides of the table leads to practical solutions.

Most negotiators, including highly skilled ones, experience several types of tensions during negotiations. For example, there is a constant choice between empathy versus ruthlessness, rational versus intuition, mutual trust versus professional distance, holistic goals versus contractual details, and objective success versus personal satisfaction (Harvard Law School, 2019).[7]

When and why negotiations fail

For 40 plus years, I worked in social impact financing. We (J.R. and Finance Fund team) had a programme that ran through a resource offered by the U.S. government. It was a somewhat complicated programme driven by the attractive offering of tax credits. Investors' returns came in the form of a credit against their tax payment. All the projects were in economically distressed communities. Community development entities (CDE) would apply for an allocation of tax credits and "sell" them to an investor in the form of an investment in a targeted community project. Because the tax credits were relatively small, the project investment was bifurcated into equity and debt investments. This facilitated leverage of other resources for projects.

In the first round of this programme, we were fortunate to be awarded a $10 million allocation, representing about $50 million in project capital. Most of the investors were banks that could handle debt and equity investments. The commonality of all awardees and investors was that nobody knew what they were doing, and it was the first time anyone had done a programme of this type. One of the projects we presented resulted in investment from a bank partner of $6 million. The project was underwritten, risks were assessed, decisions were made, and documents were executed. The understanding investors would discover the agreement's validity and that outcomes would be shared equally, whether good or bad. The CDE group provided operational service, counselling, and intervention during the seven-year term, but the project did not succeed despite those efforts.

The dissolution of the business negotiation involved the CDE team and the bank's negotiator, with no involvement in the project or any such project. The bank came in with a position, not a solution, to get all the money back from any CDE sources. The negotiation was challenging and sometimes frustrating, but in the end, our upfront agreement to equally split the outcome won the day.

Lessons learned from that experience were:

- Think about the end from the beginning. The process would have been different if it were not for the share and share-alike understanding.
- There is no substitute for preparation. Do your homework, know what expertise is needed, and know who does what. It also means strategising for an equitable solution and not a "win".
- Manage the process activities that involve controlling yourself. It is often more effective to keep your mouth shut and listen for the clues that can lead to a solution. No one benefits from an uncivil dialogue.
- Be as transparent as possible. Be flexible enough to understand the objectives of your negotiating partner.

In this example, there is another dynamic, the commercial aspect versus the social impact. In these circumstances, it is vital to discover the equation that links them and define a path of deeper understanding, which is the stage for the common goal of finding a solution. In our case, the reference point had already been defined in the share and share-alike agreement, which negated unilateral claims and moved the focus to argue the case. All of these change the psychology from problem highlighting to problem-solving.

One of the significant challenges is being sensitive to what is going on and keeping the game plan in mind. This means thoughtfully and rationally presenting a clear and understandable process. It also means avoiding last-minute changes that cause confusion and misunderstandings. Expectations should be delineated at the start of the procedure, and the process must stick to its knitting. The goals should be to stay in conversation together to the closing table and then sign an agreement in the presence of both parties.

There are also DNA challenges that intrinsically doom negotiations. Some organisations do not have cultures acclimated to negotiations, and they are often rigidly hierarchical and based on an old model where every good thing comes from the top. These companies are already feeling the pressure of change and the malady of not delegating autonomy and authority to negotiating agents.

Another of the principal reasons for failure is not knowing who the final voice is. In the old model, that may be someone outside of the negotiating process or discipline. The new model is more inclusive and sensitive to the value of voices in the organisation regardless of position or experience. It understands that there must be a place where the "buck" stops. It also understands the concept of power asymmetry with its risk imbalance and the significance of symmetry.

Being too rigid is one of the biggest challenges to effective negotiation, and it may lead to the inability to assess the value of an agreement. I (J.R.) made my way through undergraduate school by doing many jobs, including piano tuning. It is interesting how much piano tuning is like negotiations. The first step is tuning the base octave first to tune a piano. The base was the middle octave of the keyboard and began by first tuning one note, "A", to 440 Hz or frequency per second. Theoretically, the following "A" up one octave on the keyboard should have been tuned to 880 Hz, which is the perfect pitch for it. The curious thing is that the perfect pitch did not always sound right. The key to a well-tuned piano was to set the best relative pitch that resulted in a sound that complemented the whole instrument. This is precisely what happens in negotiation. Creating an instrument, an agreement that works well, has everything to do with not the rigidity of the structure but with the ability to be flexible enough to sound good together.

There should never be an excuse for the use of criticism, sarcasm, and derogatory remarks at the table. It is the biggest threat to effective negotiation. At its worst, it is defined as unethical behavior. It is identifiable in false promises, unfair or misleading information, and no holes barred competitive or winning at all cost bargaining. At its best, intimidation creates a dynamic, threatening, and fearful environment. This strategy relies on the nervous and anxious feeling accompanying negotiation, especially if the stakes are high. Its motive is to exacerbate the natural tendencies and cajole acceptance of a bad deal or accept an agreement too quickly.

Good negotiators are sensitive and understand the negative effect of hurtful behavior on relationships. If the lack of civility is a strategy, it should be moved to the barn. It has no place at the negotiating table. It is good to remember that people are at the table to do business and make profits. Therefore, common sense dictates that thinking, logic, sensitivity, and civility should take the day. Honesty, integrity, and transparency are fertile soil. Negotiation should not be a battle.

Mastering the power of negotiations

While working with people and our staff, we have been mentoring them in the art and science of negotiations. We help them think for themselves, help them build confidence in themselves, give them tools to handle failure, and, more importantly, handle successes. The mechanism to accomplish this was a simple set of objectives.

1. **Know your environment**. The first was to develop the skill to know both external and internal markets. Building knowledge of a place, people, priorities, and problems help to create relationships and have sensitivity to problem-solving.
2. **Build your self-confidence**. The second was to help people think for themselves. Giving people autonomy authority, allowing independent decision-making, and allowing them to make mistakes were essential for building their self-confidence.
3. **Master problem-solving skills**. Instilling the capacity to ask questions, seek common ground, and identify problems was the third piece of the puzzle. This ability also enables innovation, creativity, and initiative in discovering solutions. They were taught to be detectives, and they were asked to do this with resources at their disposal, internal and external.
4. **Capture your experiences and introspect.** They were coached into the idea that all this cries for documentation. I (J.R.) encourage building the habit of journaling. It served as a tool for not only capturing what happened but also creating opportunities for thoughtful introspection, contemplation, and stress management.
5. **Learning by doing**. Negotiating is a complex process, and to master the power of negotiations, you should know the various concepts discussed in this chapter and experience using these concepts in real

situations. Each time you conclude negotiations, you should reflect on the experience and ask how to improve your negotiation skills.

6. **Knowing the other party.** Being well-informed about the strengths, weaknesses, threats, and opportunities of your offer and how it fits your client's strategic and tactical demands is mandatory to navigate through negotiations. Also, your competitors and their potential propositions should be on your radar.

7. **Brainstorming and preparation.** Before negotiations with your business customers, you should brainstorm with your colleagues and prepare to arrive with your customers at a mutually satisfying agreement.

8. **Creating a goalsheet.** Negotiations can become a dynamic process, and we easily become intrigued to "win" and "succeed". Thereby, we frequently forget about our initial goals. To achieve strategic and tactical success that creates measurable and positive output, a written goal-sheet helps to keep focus and avoid being dragged away along the process.

9. **Participate in negotiation simulations.** Participating in negotiation simulations is an extremely effective way to practice and build your negotiation skills and confidence. You can arrange an annual negotiation simulation competition in your business organisation.

10. **Establishing stable feedback loops for steady improvement.** Make sure that the feedback of the negotiations – no matter if positive or negative outcome – are shared with those in your organisation who can profit and improve on this information. This will enhance a positive outcome in the next negotiation process and continuously help you develop your negotiation skills (Harvard Law School, 2021).[7]

Practice exercise

You have successfully developed and tested an AI-based golf analyser – GX100 – to provide feedback to the golf players and offer them advice on improving their game.

You have discussed with several professional golf players who feel that GX100 is an effective training solution. There are hundreds of golf training schools and academies around the world. If GX100 is accepted by these schools and academies for training golfers, then you will earn substantial revenue from the sales of GX100.

What will be your negotiation strategy with golf training schools and academies to have GX100 adopted for imparting training to golfers?

Summary

Mastering the power of negotiations is like mastering the power of any other skill or trait. It begins with our mindset and an internal decision. The purpose of negotiation is to discover solutions to a common problem in a way that mutually satisfies and builds trusted relationships. Life is a series of negotiations. Human neurology is designed to deal with life by making sense of what our senses tell us and figuring out how to survive by making decisions. The cognitive mind is always ready to negotiate.

Being a better negotiator is being a better leader. With practice, quality leadership becomes second nature. It is not arrogant or boastful but exudes an era of confidence and control, and it becomes who they are, not what they are.

Further reading

Fisher, R. (Author), W. L. Ury (Author) and B. Patton (Editor) (2011), *Getting to Yes: Negotiating Agreement Without Giving In*. 3rd edition. USA: Houghton Mifflin.
Haskins, G., M. Thomas and L. Johri (2018), *Kindness in Leadership*. UK: Routledge.
Thompson, L. (2020), *The Mind and Heart of the Negotiator*. 7th edition. UK: Pearson Education.

References

1 Bazerman, Max H. and Don A. Moore (2013), *Judgment in Managerial Decision Making*. USA: John Wiley & Sons.
2 Business Queensland (2020), *Managing Business Relationships, Negotiating Successfully*. Queensland Government, Business Queensland, May 27. Available at: https://www.business.qld.gov.au/running-business/marketing-sales/managing-relationships/negotiating
3 Fisher, R. (Author), W. L. Ury (Author) and B. Patton (Editor) (2011), *Getting to Yes: Negotiating Agreement Without Giving In*. 3rd edition. USA: Houghton Mifflin.
4 Fox, Erica A. (2013), The Most Important Negotiation in Your Life. *Harvard Business Review*, September 3. https://hbr.org/2013/09/the-most-important-negotiation
5 Harvard Law School (2021a), *What Is a Problem Solving Approach?* Program on Negotiation, Harvard Law School, November 22. Available at: https://www.pon.harvard.edu/tag/problem-solving-approach/

6 Harvard Law School (2021b), *What Are the Types of Negotiation?* Program on Negotiation, Harvard Law School, November 22. Available at: https://www.pon.harvard.edu/tag/types-of-negotiation/

7 Program on Negotiation Staff (2019), *10 Top Negotiation Examples.* Program on Negotiation, Harvard Law School, September 26. Available at: https://www.pon.harvard.edu/daily/negotiation-skills-daily/famous-negotiators-feature-in-top-negotiations-of-2012/

8 Thompson, Leigh (2019), *Mind and Heart of the Negotiator.* 7th edition. Pearson Education, January 1.

26

MASTERING THE POWER OF HUMAN COLLABORATION

Desiree Botica

Abstract

Working in collaboration with other people can seem difficult and daunting, as it can often be outside our normal way of doing things. However, as this chapter outlines, it can be one of the most effective and beneficial ways to work on a project. With a successful plan and process, human collaboration exposes the project to a vast level of ideas, opinions, and knowledge that we wouldn't have access to if working alone.

Keywords: Collaboration, team, goal, plan

Introduction

Working in collaboration can be one of the most beneficial ways of working on a project and critically important to organisational success. As Steve Jobs, the former Chair, CEO, and Co-founder of Apple Inc., once said, "*Great things in business are never done by one person. They're done by a team of people*" (Steve Jobs).[1]

Personal experience

To me, collaboration is working actively with others to achieve a common goal. Being an active member means not only participating in conversations, meetings, and interactions passively (i.e. only listening and learning) but also actively contributing your thoughts, ideas, and opinions to the group.

DOI: 10.4324/9781003219293-34

Early on in my career, I learnt that the key to success is working well with others. Every project I have been involved in, whether it is an internal project or external client-facing project, has required input from many people. Often, the team input needed is not what is directly required in our job description but was necessary to achieve the goal. The most satisfying and rewarding projects I have been involved in are those where everyone pulled together and did whatever was required to get the job done. To me, this is mastering the power of human collaboration, as it is true commitment to the end game.

When I reflect on these experiences, I see strong human connections being formed, a shared sense of achievement, and significant support for others. When everyone pulls together to get a challenging job done, there is a recognition amongst the team that they have produced something worthwhile. These experiences build strong bonds that stay with us, even long after the goal has been achieved.

What it takes to succeed

Through experience, I have learnt that the most important aspect of human collaboration is the ability of all members of the team to listen, value the contribution, and to explore ideas from others. This doesn't mean agreeing with everything or accepting all ideas and implementing them, but it does mean listening and giving fair consideration for the ideas of others. Without this level of acknowledgement, collaboration doesn't work, as the teams are not willing to put forward their ideas and won't give their all to achieving the end result.

In my role as Sysdoc CEO, I am responsible for effective delivery of our core management consulting services, which are most frequently used to support organisations which are undergoing business or digital transformation. Sysdoc provides the programme and project management, change management, business process design and development and end-user training and support. Without effective collaboration, Sysdoc cannot provide effective client delivery and we have learnt through experience that the most effective collaboration occurs when members of a team trust each other and have agreed the values and guiding principles that will govern the behaviour of the group.

I have seen this work particularly well with the Senior Leadership Team we have established at Sysdoc. We worked together at the outset to agree on our values, principles, and code of conduct for our team. What this meant is that we agreed up front on how we would work together, and what this would look like. We also discussed the impact of artificial harmony which is when the team agree with each other to keep the peace and that there is an absence of healthy challenge which is essential to ensure that the team is most effective and productive.

Collaboration has allowed me to challenge and be challenged. It has ensured that we are open to ideas from all members of the team – regardless of age, experience, ethnicity, gender, or role. This has created shared ownership for the outcome and collective successes. This collaborative approach has enabled us to adapt services to ensure that they are relevant and future proofed in the face of digital disruption. This principle has been applied to all aspects of the business including improvements in how we innovate, deliver our services, track and manage financial return and create a workplace culture that others want to be part of.

As is the case with many worthwhile disciplines, the power of collaboration requires us to adapt and to trust a new process. In many cases, this means to work against our natural state as we all have a tendency to revert to what is known. This is especially true when we are faced with a situation where we have been successful already by applying a certain approach. The idea of doing something different can be difficult to comprehend but the reward could be far greater if we were to adopt this more efficient approach.

In order to collaborate, we are required to be open to exploring the ideas of others, and in the case of a true collaborative approach, at times accepting the majority decision which may not be what we personally would have chosen as the course of action. Collaboration requires courage and a true commitment to working with others which often means that we must compromise.

Looking at past examples

It is essential to recognise that successful collaboration requires planning and bringing together a complimentary set of skills and personalities in order to achieve a successful outcome. In a 2013 article in Forbes, contributor Ruth Blatt wrote about why "supergroups" – bands comprised of independently successful artists – so rarely work out when such an assemblage of talent should otherwise predicate success. She wrote:

> The problem with the additive assumption underlying "supergroups" is that it does not account for the process losses that come from egos,

quirks, over-confidence, sense of entitlement, and the expectation to lead that stars bring to the team. And it doesn't account for the skills required to build synergy on the team. Talented individuals need other-focused people around them who will support them and put up with their quirks.[2]

In other words, Ruth Blatt is saying that great collaborations do not occur from just throwing equally talented individuals on a project, but rather the coming together of both talent and complementary personalities. Done right, the collective will stand to achieve more than any one individual.

There are innumerable inventions, discoveries, and innovations that have been made because of the combined effort and ideas of two or more people working together. Some successes have provided us with pleasurable outcomes and comfort while others are life-saving scientific discoveries that have prolonged life and changed the way we live our lives.

The Wright brothers gave us all wings. Wilbur and Orville Wright got their start fixing bicycles, but, in 1903, they developed the three-axis controls that made flying a fixed-wing aircraft possible. Their invention not only made airplanes a part of industry and trade but also opened the world to the kind of travel most people had only dreamed about. Their work together resulted in one of the formative inventions of the 20th century – and a completely different world.

The COVID-19 epidemic highlighted the importance and benefit of global collaboration. This was evident when a team of Chinese and Australian researchers published the first genome of the virus, and the genetic map was made freely available for access by researchers worldwide. The virus has since been sequenced in excess of 3,000 times, charting both the original genome and its mutations. The COVID-19 vaccine would not have been possible without this research.

Harry, Albert, Samuel, and Jack Warner were the four brothers who founded Warner Brothers, the famous motion-picture studio, and shortly thereafter introduced to the world the first genuine "talkie", changing film-going forever. Knowing their talents, they divided themselves across the different facets of the business, with Harry as president and in charge of the New York headquarters, Albert as treasurer and head of sales and distribution, and Sam and Jack leading the studio in Hollywood. Together they revolutionised cinema, popularising the gangster genre with films like *Little Caesar* (1931) and *Scarface* (1932) and producing some of the most notable movies to come out of the Golden Age of Hollywood, including *The Maltese Falcon* (1941), *Casablanca* (1942), and *A Streetcar Named Desire* (1951).

Coco Chanel, or Gabrielle Bonheur Chanel, was a French fashion designer and the founder of the Chanel brand. She is the only fashion designer listed on *Time* magazine's list of the 100 most influential people of the 20th century. Incredibly, Coco Chanel only owned 10% of her business! The rest was owned by her financier, Pierre Wertheimer. You may hear this and think that it reflects poorly on her business sense, but it's actually the opposite. By strategically partnering, Coco Chanel was able to: maintain exclusive creative control over her brand; leverage Wertheimer's expertise, American business connections, and capital; and become fabulously wealthy off someone else's seed money.

Steve Jobs and Steve Wozniak founded Apple in Cupertino, CA, in 1976. The two men were friends in high school, and remained in touch for years to come. They got on well, and both shared a desire to create personal computers. Wozniak created the Apple I, and Jobs had the foresight to know that selling the device was the best way to fund their company. Jobs and Wozniak were good friends, and their shared interests were a crucial element of their success. Their partnership only lasted a few years, but what they created was timeless. Collaborations should begin with a shared interest, and each party should have something useful to contribute.

The Human Genome Project officially kicked off in 1990, and biology hasn't been the same since. Thirteen years, 18 countries, and thousands of scientists later, the DNA of the human genome had been sequenced, giving us the genetic blueprint for an average person. Thanks to the ambition, dedication, and collaboration of those involved in the Human Genome Project, today a full human genome can be sequenced in a single day and at a fraction of the cost. It's completely revolutionised the way we understand the body, including our understanding of how individuals are affected by disease.

We often forget that good collaboration depends on people and requires planning, commitment, trust, and courage. High-impact collaboration is when everyone works together to achieve a shared goal in the most efficient and effective way possible.

The principles that underpin high-impact collaboration

Principle 1: build the A-Team

It is essential that you put together the right team to get the job done. The term, *the more, the merrier*, does not apply to collaboration. Remember, you are often better off with a small committed group who are highly engaged and committed to getting the job done than a cast of thousands. Stick with the minimum viable group in order to stay agile and maximise impact. It is also important to revisit the past example of Blatt's theory where she explains that great collaborations are the coming together of both talent *and* complementary personalities. The team must trust one another to put forward their ideas.

The approach we apply in Sysdoc is very simple. We firstly validate the problem statement with a small tight group and then establish who will lead. The lead has full control over how they collaborate and with whom. The extent and number of people involved is based on an assessment of what is required to deliver the best outcome and every requirement is different.

The impact of this approach is clear to our people from day 1, and they are proud to be part of the A-team selected to work on a requirement.

Principle 2: define clear roles

Collaboration is an active process, and everyone needs to know what is required of them to deliver success. If people are looking disengaged or confused, there's a good chance that they don't know why they're in the room, or what's expected of them. It is essential that the project owner gives every contributor clear ownership of an area from the beginning and then tracks and reports progress to completion.

The approach we apply in Sysdoc is to be very clear on who is doing what and who is accountable and responsible for the outcome, there can only be one lead, and this person is responsible for getting the job done. Lack of clarity results in no one taking responsibility, unclear expectations, and slow and often ineffective solutions. I have observed much greater success on our projects since applying a more structured approach and the team are more engaged and motivated knowing what they need to do and when.

Principle 3: establish a clear goal

Collaborative projects often start with a grand vision, but failure to keep this end goal at the forefront often results in people getting lost in the process. It is essential to maintain a view of what you are trying to achieve and why to ensure that you are on track for delivery of the optimal result.

In Sysdoc, we apply a design-thinking approach, which starts out with a short discovery session to validate the requirements and goal. This discovery session delivers clarity from the outset and involves all key stakeholders in the validation and confirmation of requirements. We often find that what our clients think that they need or want to solve their problem is actually not going to deliver the outcome that they require, this process guides them through the process of validation and gains collective agreement on what is actually required to solve the problem. The approach is positive and collaborative and at the end of the session all stakeholders are clear on the goal and agree on the outcome and approach required to solve the problem.

Principle 4: communicate the plan and process for delivery

Make sure everyone knows what the plan and process is for delivery. This is especially important where you have a large team and multiple stakeholders. Ensure that your plan and process include frequent checkpoints to make sure everything is on track and that there is provision for making changes along to accommodate unexpected findings or changes in priorities. Set expectations accordingly, and maintain a shared, living document that is simple enough for all stakeholders to understand and use.

This is very simple for us in Sysdoc, as we have established processes and ways of working which are included in all staff inductions. We also run a standard kick-off session for all new projects which reinforce and validates the process for delivery. This is followed up with a daily stand-up to check-in on progress, clear roadblocks and to ensure that everyone has what they need to deliver to the requirements. This approach ensures that there are no surprises along the way and we are successful in what we set out to achieve.

Principle 5: use the right tools

Despite the recent rise of collaboration and social media tools, most people still rely on email and Microsoft Excel to manage highly complex projects. The benefits of leveraging social technologies to collaborate effectively are huge. A recent McKinsey study, The Social Economy: Unlocking value and productivity through social technologies, makes the case that social technologies can aid collaboration and improve the productivity of highly skilled knowledge workers, managers, and professionals by 20 to 25 per cent.[3]

Effective collaboration tools mean that multiple people can access and edit the same document at the same time. Documents are stored in a single location for access by all team members. Communication can occur within a channel which means that gone are the days where we need to trawl through emails to locate the required information. Most of these tools are cloud-based, enabling collaborators to work simultaneously from anywhere and at any time.

As is the case with all consulting companies, Sysdoc is constantly bidding for new business and we have developed a templated, repeatable, scalable approach to bidding for new business. The first step is to select a bid lead, who is responsible for implementing our standard template and way of working to validate the requirement and setting up the bid in our system (Microsoft O365). All aspects of the bid are managed through Microsoft Teams including communication with the team, collaboration with stakeholder, and all aspects of delivery. Tasks are individually allocated to the team members which establishes clear expectations, timelines for delivery and responsibility from day one. The method is scalable and repeatable across any bid regardless of size and complexity.

Principle 6: track and measure success

Make sure that you have an established set of success criteria from the outset and an agreed way of measuring success. It is critical that you are able to establish what success looks like from the start and then be able to easily measure, report on, and articulate progress.

The discovery process we follow at Sysdoc ensures complete clarity upfront. We discuss and agree on what success looks like and we will measure success before the project starts. Progress is tracked through MS Teams and report back to the team via the daily stand-up. Reporting varies for each requirements and can include reporting via MS Teams, Power BI, or other tools for client requirements. Once again, reporting requirements are defined and agreed in the discovery session before the project starts.

Summary

Mastering the art of human collaboration is something we should all work on. The ability to collaborate effectively with other human beings cannot be underestimated and the possibilities of what can be achieved are endless and beyond comprehension. Bringing together different people who have a range of talents, genders, ethnicities, experiences, and views enables us to create something more than we could on our own.

No matter how good we think we are, we can always learn together. In the words of the Indian author and teacher of meditation, yoga, peace, and compassion, "*Collaboration is the essence of life. The wind, bees and flowers work together, to spread the pollen*" (Amit Ray).[4]

Follow-up actions

I encourage you to continue to explore and hone the skills that are necessary to ensure success. Although much of what is included in this chapter relates to the benefits of human collaboration in business, I cannot emphasise enough how equally important collaboration is in our personal lives.

It is important to have an efficient collaboration plan that instils trust and motivation within the team. This can be done by following the principles stated in this chapter.

Notes

1   Jobs, Steve (2011), *Steve Jobs: His Own Words and Wisdom.* Cupertino Silicon Valley Press.
2   Blatt, R. (2013), What Do Eric Clapton and Chickens Have in Common, and Why Supergroups Rarely Live Up to Expectations. *Forbes Magazine*, August 12.
3   Chui, M. et al. (2012), McKinsey Global Institute. Available at: https://www.mckinsey.com/industries/technology-media-and-telecommunications/our-insights/the-social-economy
4   Ray, A. (2015), *Mindfulness Living in the Moment - Living in the Breath.* USA: Inner Light Publishers.

Further reading

- Adobe Workfront (2018), *Collaboration Tips: 40 Tips to Get Your Team Communicating Like Pros.* Available at: https://www.workfront.com/blog/collaboration-tips-40-to-get-your-team-communicating-like-pros
- Collaboration is at the heart of leadership culture at Adidas – CEO Kasper Rorsted, You Tube, 2018. Available at: https://www.youtube.com/watch?v=DvuDl8b1H_s
- Kituyi, M. (2020), *COVID-19: Collaboration Is the Engine of Global Science – Especially for Developing Countries.* World Economic Forum. Available at: https://www.weforum.org/agenda/2020/05/global-science-collaboration-open-source-covid-19/
- Markova, D. and A. McArthur (2015), *Collaborative Intelligence: Thinking with People Who Think Differently.* USA: Random House.
- Sawyer, Keith (2017), *The Creative Power of Collaboration.* 2nd edition. Basic Books.
- Simon Sinek on How to Collaborate on Projects More Successfully (2014), *You Tube.* Available at: https://www.youtube.com/watch?v=AMG8ObDmbaM

27

MASTERING THE POWER OF COMMUNITY

Jensine Larsen

Abstract

Through hardships and challenges, we find that anything can be possible through the power and support of community. The encouragement and feeling of belonging that come with a community inspires and allows us to do the otherwise unthinkable and achieve great feats together.

To what extent can being part of a community benefit us and our goals? And how can we become a part of a community that will enable us to do this?

Keywords: Community, connect/connecting, building, support

Introduction

American author and political activist Helen Keller once wrote, "*Alone we can do so little; together, we can do so much*".[1]

My own life experience has shown this to be true. Through hardships and challenges, anything can be possible through the power and support of community.

As Margaret Wheatley, the American writer and teacher who has championed the creation of communities worthy of human habitation, has written, "*There is no power for change greater than a community discovering what it cares about*".[2]

DOI: 10.4324/9781003219293-35

Personal experience

I grew up on a farm in the rural United States Midwest, paralysingly shy. As a young girl, my parents home-schooled me in our old farmhouse, but I often gathered my storybooks and crossed through the tall grass field behind our weathered red barn. I would lay out a blanket, and page through international folk tales, historical fiction, and young girl superheroes. Surrounded by the clucking of chickens, I dreamt of far-away places. I felt safe and free when I was alone, engrossed in the pages of another world. But when I was in public spaces like weddings, potlucks, or classrooms, I shrunk into the walls, afraid to speak. I could barely ask where to find the bathroom, or correct people when they mispronounced my name. I felt my voice trapped, burning inside me.

Little did I know that one day I would build and connect to a vast, global community of women across 190 countries that would change my life. Ultimately, this supportive community would help me uncover my own purpose and voice. I hope my story can inspire you to build a community that will help you realise your dreams.

This journey began at 19 years old, when my yearning to see the world grew so strong, it overtook my fear of being with unknown people. I saved money from odd jobs and work on the family farm and left my confining small rural town. I travelled to a place I loved reading about – the Amazon forest. There, traveling along the waterways with local organisations, I encountered indigenous women whose children were dying as a result of oil contamination on their lands. They asked me, *"Please be our messenger, carry our stories back to your country"*. So, I became a journalist. From there, I continued to travel to the Burma–Thai border where I interviewed women fleeing ethnic cleansing and mass rape of a brutal dictatorship. They were at risk of becoming trafficked, but they were also organising and building visions of peace for their country. They *also* asked me to be their messenger.

One night on the Burma–Thai border, I was out on an outdoor balcony, lying on a bamboo mat on a hot, sticky night. I was tossing and turning, heavy and sick, filled with stories of suffering. I knew I could try to publish these stories, but the global media didn't care much about what was happening here. I couldn't erase the flame I saw inside these beautiful beings, with so much yearning and hope inside of them – but ultimately crushed and ignored. The world was spitting on this treasure for transforming the country.

Suddenly, in between sleeping and waking, I looked up and saw a globe against the dark sky. It was lit with these beautiful, pulsing blue lights, lights I knew came from women unlocking their voices, which in turn, activated more voices, creating a building pulse of healing light that encircled the globe. In my moment of despair, I realised that I had just been shown the way forward. I knew, at that moment, that I no longer wanted to merely be a messenger for women, but that we needed a safe, communication source where women everywhere could speak for themselves, in their own words. A place where they connect to not feel so alone and unite their energy for a better world.

When I returned home, even though I was terrified to start something I had no experience with, I realised that I could no longer keep this vision bottled inside. In the years to come, I founded World Pulse, building a global print magazine distributed across North America with mostly volunteer teams, publishing voices, and stories from women across the world. As the internet revolution grew, it became clear that, for greater impact, I had to take this vision online.

During these years, I had many dark days as a woman social entrepreneur learning new skills and a new industry. I was struggling to build this vision I had glimpsed, but I had no roadmap – no idea what I was doing. I was trying to figure out how to lead a team and board of directors, which I had never done before. When I tried to raise money, doors closed on me and I had to figure out how to crack open the windows. People were telling me that my vision was too big and that I needed to scale it back. For the first five years, I barely slept. I felt that I was carrying the weight of the world's women on my shoulders. I couldn't let them down.

I'll never forget the day, a few months after we launched the online community, I was up late working around 2 am and exhausted, afraid this would fail. Suddenly, a message popped up on my computer screen. It was one of our new members, a survivor of HIV/AIDS in Kenya who was doing community awareness programmes. *"Jensine, zoom off to bed"*. She wrote, *"You must rest. Don't worry, I am carrying the flame"*. I felt that this relief wash over me. I realised the great irony that I had been building something so other women didn't have to feel alone, and yet I was feeling terribly alone. *"Listen"*, she said. *"One day this will be the place where presidents will come to test the security and insecurity of the women and children"*. Here was someone who would not only shoulder this dream with me on the other side of the world – she probably had bigger visions than I had! I felt a surge of support and I knew at that moment I would never give up.

After that, something amazing happened. Little by little, more women started logging on and sharing their lived experiences. They came from worldwide locations: from the post-election upheaval in Kenya, to the militarised, misty mountain regions of Kashmir, and the maternity wards of the South Bronx. As more women brought their buried stories to the light, the community started connecting. They started commenting, telling each other that they believed in each other. With each encouraging word, previously unheard women started to bloom like flowers, believe in themselves, and create bigger change in their communities where they physically resided.

And then, more messages started pouring back to me.

From the United Emirates, a woman sent a private message thanking me saying, "*It is no exaggeration to say that connecting on World Pulse has unmuted my soul*".

When my new-born nephew fell sick with liver disease, women from Bangladesh and Spain sent me online messages of solidarity, "*We are with you and we are praying for his health*".

A hand-drawn card arrived in the mail from Nepal. It was from the 6-year-old daughter of one of our members. "Thank you for starting World Pulse, I want to be a journalist because my mom got her new job and start on World Pulse".

Another member from the US called to tell me that her high school students partnered with a woman leader in Uganda they met on World Pulse. They were now educating hundreds of rural girls who risked child marriage to school. The US students are connecting online during class to the Uganda students and finding their purpose.

I started to get emails from husbands and sons saying, "*Thank you, my wife and my mother is a different person because of her time she spends connecting on World Pulse*".

I got so many invitations to visit women in their countries. One day, I was getting a haircut and it dawned on me that I could travel to any country in the world and I would have friends who would open their doors for me.

The messages kept coming monthly, weekly, and daily. "Don't give up", they said over and over again. To me! One by one, like a vitamin drip of strength, these relationships have powered me forward, to take my shaking voice and knees to the microphone, to radio shows on the BCC, to global Ted conference, and the halls of the United Nations.

Today, World Pulse is an award-winning social network, pulsing with women logging on from more than 190 countries, speaking for themselves, lifting each other up, and in turn, impacting over 12 million more people in their communities as a result of their new movements, businesses, and projects. A safe online space where every woman can rise up and make a difference.

I log on to this online community daily and something magical is happening there. We are mourning together and raging together across borders, cultures, and languages, but we are equally sharing in the celebrations. At night we fall exhausted into each other's supportive virtual embrace because someone else is waking up strong for the new day on the other side of the world.

As I look into the future, I see now that information technology is becoming relationship technology. What matters is that we use it in a sacred way – and women can lead the transformation to build meaningful community. Instead of weapons of mass distraction, lets us use cell phones as instruments of massive connection and creation. As women, we can take the lead and we can heal the world more quickly. If we use technology to connect, share energy, talent, and treasure, we can solve world problems and make the world we want.

Along the way, I've discovered that having this global sisterhood has changed my life, given me strength, and helped me find my voice and purpose. This is available to you and millions more.

Above all, I know now that we are not alone in my visions. And connected we are more powerful than we have dared to imagine.

Examples of community

Many of the women I have met online have shown me the power of using online community to in turn build offline change in their own physical communities.

Neema namadamu, democratic republic of congo

Neema Namadamu was born with polio in the Democratic Republic of Congo, one of the most violent countries in the world for women. Her mother carried her on her back to school, since they could not afford crutches. With every step of growing up, she fought for education and to be valued in a society that considered her disposable. When she started accessing computers and found World Pulse – everything changed.

She typed out her dream for her country – to link women leaders across the vast, war-torn nation. People around the world started to support her vision with funds and volunteer time. Soon she launched a home-grown cyber-café for only women. She started training hundreds of women leaders of diverse ethnicities and with disabilities – many who never before had an email account – how to use the internet. As more women benefited, she ignited an inclusive movement of over 800 "Hero Women" who are using the power of technology to connect to the world and mobilise for change – even reaching their voices to the White House and influencing the appointment of a US Special Envoy to the region.

Neema knew early on that her community would be more successful if she gave more opportunities to those around her. "*Impact is not measured by whether or not you are amassing followers, but whether or not you are inspiring leadership*", she said, "*We don't want a world of leaders and followers, but leaders only – all of us together leading this world into the good of all that's possible*".[3]

She saw how connecting diverse people could benefit everyone. She built trust with local military officials, who use her centre for their personal emails and, in turn, provide protection for the centre. Nobel Peace Laureates visit her community and shine a spotlight for the world. Hundreds of supporters from Europe, the United States, and elsewhere connect with her community online and send donations and supplies.

As a result, women who previously were ignored in her region are now going on to run for office, getting appointed to judicial seats, speaking at international conferences, and gaining more economic opportunities.

When the rest of the world considered Congo a lost cause just as she herself had, Neema knew deep down that her community could lift itself up. "*We are not victims*", she says, "*We are liberators!*"

Kara Lozier, United States

> "*There are two ways of spreading light*", according to author Edith Wharton. "*To be the candle or the mirror that reflects it*".[4]

Kara has long silver hair and lives in a small town in rural Vermont with her husband and three sons. Although it is so safe that she doesn't need to lock her door at night, she still felt isolated – and wanted to be a part of something bigger. She joined World Pulse to satisfy that need, and as she started browsing the voices from around the world, she noticed a story from a young man in Afghanistan. Ali was a 24-year-old male women's rights activist. He had helped his younger sister to escape from an abusive, forced marriage, and developed a passion for women's rights activism. He abandoned his dreams of college so that he could support his family and allow his younger sisters to return to school. His story immediately touched her heart.

With three sons, Kara had strong feelings about the role of men in the women's rights movement. She replied to his story, and they began to exchange conversations weekly. Soon, they began to work together to make his dream a reality, searching for college scholarships, teaming up to help grow his organisation and help his sister heal from trauma. Kara's connection with Ali enabled her to impact hundreds of people in Afghanistan while sitting in her living room in Vermont. When he won a scholarship to the US thanks to her help, she met Ali face to face and held him in her arms at the airport. Today, she considers him her son.

Kara continued to make more connections – more than she could count! In Canada, the UK, Afghanistan, Indonesia, Bangladesh, Japan, and more. Steadily, she wove together a web of mutually supportive connections that became her extended global community. She helped storytellers, victims, and visionaries to lend their voices to the global dialogue. She helped activists partner with organisations in other countries and secure funding and mentorship opportunities for their bold initiatives. And, her international family grew!

Kara has now travelled the globe meeting her new friends and continuing to build these relationships that have given her new life. Breaking her isolation started with giving back – and being a mirror for others. "*I realized I could channel all of my strengths and passions to support the activists and visionaries who share my dream*", she says

> I am a mirror spreading the light of those unseen candles and hidden stories in my community. Together, we can spread light around the world until we reach a time when we all embrace our differences and treat each other with dignity and respect.[5]

Concepts

According to research referenced in a *Daily Mail* article, social isolation and loneliness can lead to increased blood pressure, higher cholesterol levels, and depression – even premature death.[6] Science is recognising that strong social ties are good for your health!

There are some common threads to building a strong community:

> **Take the first step**. Extending your hand first to connect can be hard, especially for those of us that are shy. But for the person on the other

end, it can make a welcome difference. Turn your focus away from how you are being perceived to extend your support to the person on the other end, what do they need? How are they feeling? Reaching out will help your community feel more seen and heard.

Increase the confidence of your community! Everyone around you, whether it be in your work, neighbourhood, or your social feeds, are just like you and me. They're likely having some self-doubt and questioning of themselves. When you verbally encouraging someone, it helps them see themselves through your eyes. And, they feel more accepted and recognised. Your boost could help them take a step that betters their life and warms your relationship.

Help them connect to others. You have the power to link members of your community who may have shared passions or complimentary needs – online or off. Don't be afraid to make a personal introduction. Include a little about how you think each person will benefit from knowing each other. Or, host an event – small or large – to bring people together.

Summary

With the concepts and personal experiences explained within this chapter, I hope that you can find some inspiration to reach out to a community around you- or even from far away. With easy access to the world web, the possibilities are vast. You have the power to build a community that will lift you and help you reach your dreams. A strong community around you can give you a greater sense of belonging and well-being. Communities are defined by having something in common, whether that be a place or shared purpose. But to grow and sustain itself, every community needs community builders – and you can be one.

Follow-up actions

Practical exercise: Your community building map and action plan.

Find one hour, a quiet place, and a piece of blank paper with your favourite pen.

Draw circles of the communities you are already part of – professional and personal. Then, think of the two to five communities you would like to be a part of if you aren't already. OR, star the ones you are already a part of but that you would like to be more connected to.

In at least one of the communities that you would like to grow (or more if you wish), write down one person that is a part of this community that you respect and would like to know better. Someone that would add good energy to your life.

- Take the first step – reach out online or in-person to say hello.
- Boost their confidence – Let them know how much you respect them and how you would like to be a part of this community or deepen your connections. Ask their advice on how to be more engaged in this community.
- Be helpful – Find out more about who they are and what they care about and do one thing. Be prepared to take on some tasks to be useful to the new community!
- Keep nurturing your new community connections – Keep your list in your wallet, or a place where you look all the time – refrigerator, calendar, or computer, keep this community top of mind.

Over time, by cultivating these new trusted relationships, you will open doors to more connections and belonging.

Explore:

- World Pulse. A safe global online community where every woman's voice can rise. Available at: https://www.worldpulse.com/
- Borrup, Tom (2006), *The Creative Community Builder's Handbook: How to Transform Communities Using Local Assets, Art, and Culture*. Fieldstone Alliance
- Richardson, Bailey (2019), *Get Together: How to Build a Community With Your People*. Stripe Press
- People & Company. *An Agency That Helps Organisations Build Communities*. Available at: https://www.people-and.com/

- *How to Build a Community Poster: The Poster Corp.* Available also from Syracuse Cultural Workers: https://syracuseculturalworkers. com/products/poster-how-to-build-community

Notes

1 Keller, Helen. Original quote: "Alone, we can do so little; together, we can do so much". Sourced via: Lash, P.J. (1980), *Helen and Teacher: The Story of Helen Keller and Anne Sullivan Macy.* USA: Amer Foundation for the Blind; The Wheatley publisher Berrett-Koehler.
2 Wheatley, M.J. (2009), *Turning to One another.* Berrett-Koehler Publishers.
3 Namadamu, Neema (2015), original quote "*Impact is not measured by whether or not you are amassing followers, but whether or not you are inspiring leadership. We don't want a world of leaders and followers, but leaders only – all of us together leading this world into the good of all that's possible.* Sourced via Hero Women Rising. Available at: *https://www.herowomenrising.org/people*
4 Wharton, Edith (1902), *Vesalius in Zante.* University of Northern Iowa.
5 Lozier, Kara, in conversation with Jensine Larsen.
6 Pickles, Kate (2018), You Can Die of Loneliness: Social Isolation Could Raise Chance of a Premature Death by 50%, Study Warns. *Daily Mail.* Available at: https://www. dailymail.co.uk/news/article-5547407/You-die-loneliness-Social-isolation-raise-chance-premature-death-50-study-says.html

28

MASTERING THE POWER OF PARTNERSHIPS

Marita Lintener

Abstract

Partnerships between organisations are playing a crucial role in fulfilling the development agenda of nations. Partnerships in business open doors for diversification and expansion in new areas of technology, products, services, and markets. The importance and the need for partnerships between organisations are growing, as we grapple with wicked problems and solve these problems by combining the competitive advantages of the partnering organisations. In this chapter, I will share my learnings on various stages of the partnership process from conceiving to negotiating and to operationalising partnerships.

Keywords: Collaboration, alliances, public–private partnerships

Introduction

One of the most remarkable stories of 2020 is the successful development of the vaccine Covishield for preventing the spread of Coronavirus COVID-19. Covishield is the product of a partnership between Oxford University and the British-Swedish multinational pharmaceutical and biotechnology company, AstraZeneca plc. The partners pooled their complementary capabilities to develop and launch the vaccine in a record time. Since its introduction, the vaccine has helped in limiting the spread of the Coronavirus and has saved millions of lives around the world. Covishield is a great demonstration of the power of partnerships in the service of mankind.

DOI: 10.4324/9781003219293-36

Another great example of the power of partnerships is the assembly and use of the International Space Station (ISS) for scientific research, technology development, space exploration, commerce, and education for the benefit of humankind. The ISS is the result of multi-agency collaboration involving space organisations of the USA, Russia, Japan, Europe, and Canada.

Partnerships between organisations help in solving complex problems. You must be wondering what is a partnership? It is a form of a collaborative relationship in which two or more organisations work together for a clear purpose. According to the UN Organisation,

> partnerships are voluntary and collaborative relationships between various parties, both public and non-public, in which all participants agree to work together to achieve a common purpose or undertake a specific task and as mutually agreed, to share risks and responsibilities, resources and benefits.

This definition highlights important characteristics of a partnership.[1]

My journey in the business world started in 1989, after I graduated with a master's degree in Economics from the University of Bonn. I started my career with international commercial companies in the transport and tourism sector, Lufthansa and Thomas Cook, and worked there for more than a decade. Working in partnerships with colleagues is essential in big companies – across the different divisions and departments globally and also between people with a different skill set. Externally you deal with diverse organisations and stakeholders as partners.

However, I only realised the real power of working in partnerships once I started my own consultancy company in 2004.

As a consultant, I help organisations when their projects are stalled or reach a "dead end". Historically, I observed that the projects were stalled because different stakeholders were unable to forge strong partnerships to collaborate around business processes to complete the projects and create value for stakeholders. In specific terms, lack of a culture of cooperation, poor communication, lack of mutual understanding, mistrust, and lack of goodwill impacted the projects adversely. In my role as a consultant and project manager, I acted as a mediator and trainer to build a culture for collaboration.

Inspired by my early experiences as a consultant, I have pursued higher education to enhance my skills as a coach and a mediator. In this chapter,

I share my learnings from these studies and from my consulting practice in different industries and suggest ways to master the power of partnerships.

Creating and implementing business partnerships

I was very fortunate in getting involved into the European aviation industry. It taught me many lessons. The aviation industry is set in a very complex ecosystem with large number of organisations. The key success factor in the aviation industry is the web of partnerships between and amongst these organisations to orchestrate business processes.

As part of the leadership team of a European airline group, I was tasked with negotiating and implementing a new pan-European partnership organisation mandated by the European Commission (EC), called SESAR Deployment Alliance (SDA).[2]

This major multinational alliance was created and operated jointly by three groups of actors – airlines, airports, and air traffic service providers. The purpose of the alliance was to modernise and increase the efficiency of the European airspace system. With more than 40 organisations representing these three groups, it took two years to set up a complex web of partnerships.[3]

Notwithstanding the technical complexities inherent in the aviation industry, the biggest challenge was to find strategic alignment amongst the three groups of actors each with very different ecosystems and individual interests. Some groups work strictly on the commercial principles dictated by competition while others operate as state-owned public services. For example, the airlines and airports "work and think" in commercial terms, whereas air navigation service providers are mostly part of the governmental sector and have a fundamentally different decision-making culture. With these inherent differences between these three groups of actors, building and operating partnerships were very complicated and challenging.

Fortunately, the EC had developed a framework for the development and the governance of partnerships in the aviation and transport sector, based on the idea that strategic goals in Europe can only be achieved if the stakeholders work together. This was possible with SDA managing the SESAR Deployment Manager as a private–public partnership (PPP). The PPP collaborates with other public agencies and individual organisations providing specialised services. In these partnerships, the aim is to align and to operate the partnership jointly, in order to achieve the goals of the partnership – despite diverging business interests among the involved partner organisations.[4] In the "Joint Stakeholder Declaration on the Future of the Single (digital) European Sky" of September 2019, the concept of partnership has been reconfirmed as the only feasible way in which a co-operative approach will work to make the "Single European Sky" a reality.[5]

During the span of my work and consulting experiences, I have learnt many important lessons that I would like to share.

1. Negotiating partnerships requires strong leadership from each of the involved parties. The leaders must be committed to achieve a sustainable partnership.

2. Create joint working teams at an early stage when developing the partnership. Work on team building from beginning, and throughout the partnership.

3. From the very beginning, focus on building long-term relationships and open communications.

4. Adopt a mutually agreed charter of shared common goals and principles for operationalising these goals in the early stages. Ensure that all parties demonstrate commitment to these goals and principles through actions.

5. Invest time in building deep mutual understanding about the motivations, constraints, perceptions, the business model, the strategy, the operational environment, and the overall ecosystem of all the potential parties in the partnership.

6. Create trust before drafting any formal contract/partnership agreement. Trust must grow during the negotiations. The higher the trust, the higher the chances for the long-term success of the partnership.

7. Stakeholder analysis is a key. Understand each stakeholder's needs, interests, hidden agendas, and reason for resistance. Besides commercial issues, analyse social and sustainability issues.

8. Notwithstanding any Letter of Intent (LOI) or pre-agreements, do not sign the partnership contract without agreement on the key matters of the operation of the partnership. The key issues must be explored, negotiated, and agreed during the planning and negotiation phase.

9. It is prudent to discuss what can go wrong during the partnership. Negotiate and agree on voting, exit options, and arbitration processes in the necessary detail as part of the formal agreement. Lawyers have the final word in drafting; however, the content has to be agreed upfront between the parties from a strategic perspective.

10. While taking staffing decisions, ensure broad diversity – for example gender, age, background, and skills.

11. Develop the business plan during the planning phase and review it regularly during the operational stages of the partnership. Risk management is part of the business planning process and execution phase.

12. Ensure proper monitoring of milestones, deliverables, risks, and your key performance indicators (KPIs). Follow the principles of project management and – if you are not an expert yourself – seek the guidance of an experienced project manager.

13. Discussion on potential problems and conflict resolution needs to take place before the partnership starts operating. Do not try to ignore problems, as they will not disappear. You never know which side of the partnership may end up in a conflict. This is why it is so important to agree upfront on the processes for fair solutions. Be aware, problems will occur in any case – from inside the partnership and/or from outside. The better you are prepared, the better you will steer your partnership through troubled times.

14. Adapt the organisational structures and methods to the size of your partnership. No over-engineering needed, however do not underestimate the complexity of growth and a growing organisation.

15. Seek expert advice and guidance if you feel you will need support.

16. Always keep an open mind.

17. Regularly perform lessons learned sessions. Even more important is "lessons implemented". Be open to all suggestions for improvements.

18. Consider working with a mentor or coach, in particular in situations you face difficult managerial and leadership challenges. Asking for support and ideas is a strength, not a weakness.

Network partnerships

I would like to share an example of a network organisation – the "Women in Transport" platform in the European Union that I have been associated with. Recognising the low number of female professionals in the transport sector, in 2017, the European Economic and Social Committee in co-operation with the European Commissioner for Transport, Ms. Violeta Bulc, launched the "EU Platform for Change", aimed at increasing diversity and equal opportunities in the transport sector. The platform aims to enable stakeholders from all transport sectors to highlight their specific initiatives in favour of gender equality and to exchange good practices.

The platform for change has already spread with many regional initiatives through partnerships. In 2019, the platform has been enhanced with the launch of the European Network of Ambassadors for Diversity in Transport. Many best practises and studies are shared on the platform and are regularly updated.[6]

Leading partnerships with social purpose

Based on my experiences in spreading the mission of the European Network of Ambassadors for Diversity in Transport through local partnerships and in my engagement with the International Aviation Women's Association (IAWA) dedicated to diversity in the global aviation sector, I would like to offer the following suggestions for building partnerships where social purpose is the driving force. Several suggestions I have already made for building business partnerships will be applicable here too.[7]

1. Persons who strongly believe in the value of social purpose should provide strong leadership to drive the idea from concept to reality.
2. The leadership initiatives may come from the grassroots or from the top. If you believe in your idea, go for it!
3. Strong commitment from the members forging the partnership is a prerequisite for success.
4. Work on the story of your partnership. A convincing purpose and how it will benefit the partnership organisation and its people will enable your partnership to grow.
5. Form teams by gathering people with strong commitment and diverse skills. Leverage the power of these teams to drive the growth of the partnership.
6. Gain early support from external stakeholders. Harvest their ideas, network contacts, support, resources, and funding.
7. Organise inspiring events to promote the purpose of your partnership. During the events, ensure sufficient time for interaction, exchange, and networking.
8. Pay early attention to funding options for meeting operational expenses and think creatively.
9. If you are the initiator of the partnership:

   Be aware that you will have to commit a significant amount of time to kick-start the idea.
   Spread the news!

Gain supporters who join you and support you, as soon as possible.

- Engage in a team effort. This is a must and helps in scale up. Positive teams are inspiring and bring many new ideas.

Public–private partnerships

To seek private capital and expertise, it is common for government agencies to enter in partnerships with private enterprises and social organisations. These are called public–private partnerships (PPPs). PPPs have been playing an important role as a special purpose vehicle for building infrastructure as part of national development agendas. Every year billions of dollars are invested in PPPs for building and operating seaports, airports, railways, mass transit systems, roadways, schools, hospitals, housing, communication networks, etc., to provide public services to people in order to improve their quality of life.

In recent years, we are witnessing an increasing role of PPPs in space exploration and health care. For example, NASA has forged PPPs to expand its capabilities and opportunities in space. The successful completion of NASA's SpaceX Demo-2 mission is the result of a PPP between NASA and SpaceX. The pathbreaking mission has opened new opportunities for cost-effective human space flights. In the health sector, one of the world's leading pharmaceutical companies, GlaxoSmithKline, as part of its open innovation strategy, has forged partnerships with government agencies, public universities, and research institutions to develop vaccines and pharmaceutical products in many countries.

Explore:

GlaxoSmithKline Partnerships
https://www.gsk.com/en-gb/research-and-development/partnerships/

PPPs offer benefits to both public and private organisations and create employment opportunities, through various stages of a public project – from design to development to operations and exit. I discussed them with Professor Lalit Johri, who taught leadership challenges in PPPs in the Oxford Advanced Management and Leadership Programme.

Professor Johri said,

PPPs offer multiple benefits to partnering organisations and other stakeholders. At a time, when many governments are facing budget constraints
and a resource crunch, PPPs are an effective solution for attracting private capital and expertise. The government can then prioritise and commit its limited financial resources to other essential public programmes.
Following a transparent bidding process the government can select the
best private party. In successful PPPs, there is the potential for mutual
learning thereby enhancing the project planning and implementation
skills of staff. In an ideal situation, the public gets a superior service
experience. As the PPP experience of a country matures and grows,
the regulatory and operating environment of the business improves with
greater private investment coming in the public projects.

There are advantages for private companies too, in the form of growth
opportunities in public services through long term concessions to operate the public project and tariff collections. Working with the government agencies as partners helps the private companies to build new
capabilities for delivering public services. Many private companies take
pride in providing public services. In a PPP, the partners share the risk
which is a significant benefit for both parties. There is empirical evidence about service cost reduction during the life cycle of PPP projects.

Reflecting on the success of PPPs, Professor Johri also emphasised the
crucial role of the leadership team.

The leaders have to cement strong working relationships amongst
the staff representing various government agencies, private and social
organisations, and regulators. Together they must develop a high performance culture and focus on delivering excellent services to end users.
For example, the overall satisfaction of the travellers at an airport is
the sum of the experiences they have at the hands of the airline staff;
the immigration, customs and the security staff; the baggage handlers; the
staff in restaurants, lounges, and shops; and the staff responsible for passenger amenities. In 2018, I was doing research on leadership challenges
in a midsized airport formed under a PPP agreement. The CEO of
the airport management company told me that the biggest challenge
they faced was that each agency in the airport focussed on their own

tasks unmindful of long delays and discomfort caused to the travellers. The CEO introduced consumer service quality assessment to provide feedback and to convince various agencies to improve their respective services. To facilitate coordination between different agencies the CEO established a joint consultative forum where agencies were invited to discuss and resolve problems affecting the service quality. The airport management company initiated research projects in collaboration with leading technology companies to develop digital scanning and facial recognition biometric devices to automate some of the services that were performed manually and were causing delays. The CEO established soft skills training and personal development programmes for the staff of various operating agencies. These programmes were extremely effective in nurturing courteous staff behaviour. To sum up: trust-based integration of partners and creating a uniform culture is the key to the success of public–private partnerships.[8]

Explore:

The Partnership Platform, Department of Economic and Social Affairs, UN Organisation
   https://sdgs.un.org/partnerships

Sometimes, the size of the public and private investments in infrastructure PPPs is very large, and correspondingly the risk is very high. If the project underperforms or fails, it results in a loss of taxpayers' money and the capital invested by the private parties. It is therefore important to explore the common causes of the failure of PPPs. Here again, I would like to cite Professor Johri:

The common causes of failures are, for example, misconceptions about PPPs on ideological grounds, or the high prices of the services. These invoke a lukewarm response from the public impacting the demand adversely. Sometimes, technical glitches, underestimating costs, unexpected cost escalation; and overestimating income threaten the viability of PPPs. Differences and conflicts between partners can also lead to an erosion of trust and a lack of collaboration. Poor corporate governance, for example, lack of transparency in information sharing, conflict of interests, budget escalation, and frequent changes in the leadership team can also contribute to failure. As well, the role of the regulators is crucial because frequent and ad hoc changes in the regulatory environment disturb business planning and the business model of the PPPs.[9]

Explore:

The Failure of Metronet
 https://webarchive.nationalarchives.gov.uk/ukgwa/2017020
  7052351/https://www.nao.org.uk/wp-content/uploads/2009/
  06/0809512es.pdf

Mastering the power of PPP projects

To create and operate successful PPP projects, Professor Johri and I suggest a step-by-step approach from the concept to operations stages.

- Ensure that the project is founded with a strong purpose and stakeholders' support.
- Make realistic assumptions about the external environment and analyse the scope and scale of the project to ensure its viability and sustainability.
- Develop contours of the partnership by clearly defining the resources, capabilities, and assets each partner will contribute.
- Develop the strategy of the project in terms of how the financial resources, capabilities, and assets of different partners will be integrated to fulfil the purpose and achieve the goals of the project.
- Make realistic forecasts of project income and costs.
- Clearly spell out the risk-sharing and income-sharing arrangements amongst partners.
- Design and adopt an efficient project organisation structure and clearly define the roles and responsibilities of the partners.
- Ensure a stable leadership team: this is a must for the success of the PPP project.
- Promote high standards of governance, regulatory compliance, and accountability in the project organisation. Prevent conflict of interests.
- Promote mutual respect and trust amongst the staff deputed by partners.
- Bridge differences in the organisation culture of the partners. Ensure that a uniform organisation culture evolves.

- Observe transparency in information sharing, financial matters, and performance monitoring.
- Within the project organisation, create room for research and development. Encourage innovation to improve processes, products, and services.
- Build consultation and conflict resolution mechanisms in the project organisation.

Reflect:

Multi-organisation partnerships

1   Select a multi-organisation partnership. Identify the challenges involved in aligning the diverse interests of the partnering organisations.
2   Develop a roadmap for aligning the interests of the partnering organisations.

Partnerships with social purpose

3   Design a partnership organisation with a deep social purpose.
4   Write a "compelling story" to inspire the partnering organisations.

Public–private partnerships

5   Select a newly proposed PPP project facing resistance from local communities. Identify the possible reasons for resistance.
6   Design strategies and actions on the part of PPP partners to build trust and enhance the community engagement in the project.

Summary

Partnerships enable public, private, and social organisations to collaborate for the purpose of social, scientific, technological, and economic gains. With multiple stakeholders having diverse interests, making partnership work poses many leadership challenges. With the advantage of accumulated knowledge and expertise, we have tools to resolve these challenges. At the fundamental level, the success of a partnership depends on building trust and strong relationships, pursuing a compelling purpose, alignment, logical strategy, fairness, transparency, and high standards of governance. Welcome to the world of partnerships!

Notes

1   What Is the UN's Definition of a Partnership? https://sustainabledevelopment.un.org/partnerships/about
2   Single European Sky Air Traffic Management Research Programme (SESAR). Available at: https://ec.europa.eu/transport/modes/air/sesar
3   SESAR Deployment Alliance. Available at: https://www.sesardeploymentmanager.eu/about/; https://ec.europa.eu/transport/modes/air/sesar/deployment_en
4   SESAR Deployment Manager. Available at: https://www.sesardeploymentmanager.eu/about/sesar-deployment-manager-function/
     https://www.sesardeploymentmanager.eu/about/modernising-europes-air-traffic-management/
5   Joint Stakeholder Declaration 2019. Available at: https://ec.europa.eu/transport/sites/transport/files/2019-09-high-level-conference-future-of-ses-declaration.pdf https://ec.europa.eu/transport/modes/air/events/2019-09-high-level-conference-future-of-ses_en
6   The Women in Transport EU Platform for Change. Available at: https://view.office-apps.live.com/op/view.aspx?src=https%3A%2F%2Fwww.eesc.europa.eu%2Fsites%2Fdefault%2Ffiles%2Ffiles%2Fannex_outline_platform.docx&wdOrigin=BROWSELINK; https://transport.ec.europa.eu/transport-themes/social-issues/women-transport/women-transport-eu-platform-change_en
7   International Aviation Women's Association (IAWA) Connect, Inspire and Lead. Available at: https://www.iawa.org
8   Discussions with Professor Lalit Johri, October 2021.
9   Ibid.

Further reading

Lewis, Mervyn K. (2021), *Rethinking Public Private Partnerships*. 1st edition. UK: Edward Elgar Publishing.

Osei-Kyei, Robert and Albert P.C. Chan (2021), *International Best Practices of Public-Private Partnership: Insights From Developed and Developing Economies*. 1st edition. Singapore: Springer Nature.

Zak, Paul J. (2018), *Trust Factor: The Science of Creating High-Performance Companies*. USA: HarperCollins Focus.

PART IX

Social and environmental impact

29

MASTERING THE POWER OF FREEDOM OF INFORMATION FOR SOCIAL JUSTICE

Amrita Johri and Anjali Bhardwaj

Abstract

Empowering people with the right to access information is a key to ensuring social justice.

In this chapter, we share our journey of how the Indian Right to Information Act has become a powerful tool for people, especially vulnerable and marginalised communities, in their pursuit to secure delivery of basic rights and services. We outline, through multiple examples, how the transparency law has been used to prevent capture of social welfare benefits and deliver social justice.

We also share examples from other countries and research findings that establish the positive cascading effects of transparency on social justice and equity.

Keywords: Freedom of information, transparency, accountability, social justice, right to know

Introduction

As James Madison (1751–1936), *fourth President of United States, hailed as the Father of the Constitution of the United States* wrote, "*A popular Government, without popular information, or the means of acquiring it, is but a Prologue to a Farce or a Tragedy; or, perhaps both*".[1] We applaud this statement. "*Without facts, you can't have the truth. Without truth, you can't have trust. If you don't have*

DOI: 10.4324/9781003219293-38

any of these things, you can't have a functioning democracy", stated Maria Ressa, Filipino-American journalist and 2021 Nobel Peace Prize recipient in an interview with NDTV.[2]

Sunita Devi and Zarina Begum, residents of low-income slum settlements in New Delhi, were amongst scores of people who were robbed of their share of subsidised food grains for years due to rampant corruption in the Public Distribution System in India. They were told that their share of subsidised rations was not provided by the government to their ration shop. When the Right to Information (RTI) law was enacted in India, Sunita and Zarina decided to enquire. They sought copies of the supply records of their ration shops.

The information they received showed that every month their share of grain was being supplied to the ration shop and the sales register revealed that the grain was being provided to "ghost" beneficiaries – people who did not actually exist, including many who were dead. They used the information to hold officials accountable – complaints about corruption were filed to the authorities and a public hearing was organised where the records were read out and hundreds of people publicly testified about the denial of rations and corruption in the distribution system. The officials and shopkeepers were penalised. Sunita, Zarina, and other residents of their slum communities, who were denied rations for years, started receiving their fair share of subsidised food grains. As a result of informed action, social justice was delivered.

It is globally acknowledged that it is behind the cloak of secrecy that corruption thrives. Corruption in turn breeds social injustice and inequality. In many developing countries, corruption is rampant not just in the highest echelons of power but manifests itself at every level of administration. This has grave consequences for ordinary citizens, especially the poor and marginalised, as they are unable to access even basic entitlements of food and social security benefits without paying bribes.

One of the most effective ways of combating corruption is to empower people with information. To ensure that entitlements and services under government welfare programmes reach the intended beneficiaries, people must know how and where public money is being spent in the efforts to ensure social justice.

Recognising the need for transparency in public administration, public access to information has been included as part of the United Nations' Sustainable Development Goals (SDGs).[3] Countries across the globe have adopted legislations enabling citizens to access information from governments. Sweden was the first country in the world to guarantee a statutory right to information in 1766. A global survey conducted in 2020 by UNESCO found that 127 nations have enacted right to information laws or similar provisions.[4]

Empowering people with the right to seek information

While organising anti-corruption campaigns like "Don't pay a Bribe" in the late 1990s, we realised that unless people like Zarina Begum and Sunita Devi were empowered with tools to hold the government accountable, it was impractical to expect them to not pay bribes and lose benefits of government programmes/schemes on which their families depended for survival. It was clear that of all the tools available to hold the government accountable, the most effective instrument was transparency. This prompted us to demand a strong transparency legislation as part of the national movement for the adoption of an effective information access law in India. In 2005, following a long and wide-spread public campaign involving people from different walks of life – lawyers, farmers, academics, social activists, unorganised sector workers, and journalists – the Right to Information (RTI) legislation was enacted.[5]

A vibrant culture of enquiry has been impelled by the enactment of the sunshine law in India. It has encouraged citizens' engagement in the process of governance and has been used to query governments about their policies, laws, actions, and even the conduct of public functionaries. With over six million information applications filed every year, the Indian RTI Act is the most extensively used transparency legislation globally.[6] People have been innovatively using the law to demand accountability from the government on a range of issues involving corruption and abuse of power. The law has empowered ordinary citizens in their struggle for social justice.

Satark Nagrik Sangathan (SNS)[7], a citizens' group we set up in 2003, builds capacities of citizens to access relevant information from governments. In collaboration with the National Campaign for Peoples' Right to Information, SNS was among the organisations at the forefront of the public campaign to demand a people-friendly, effective information access law in India. Since the enactment of the RTI Act in 2005, the group empowers people to use information obtained to hold public hearings, file informed petitions, and organise peaceful protests to hold the state accountable for delivering basic rights and entitlements, including minimum wages, pensions, healthcare, education, water supply, and sanitation.

Report cards on the performance of elected representatives

SNS uses the RTI Act for monitoring the performance of elected representatives in India by accessing information on how elected representatives have
performed in relation to their roles and responsibilities. We create "Report
Cards", which provide a snapshot of the performance of individual elected
representatives during their term. The report cards provide objective information on various parameters linked to the primary responsibilities of political representatives: performance in the legislature including attendance in
the sittings of the house and number of questions raised on issues of public
interest; performance in various legislative committees; and allocation of
development funds at their disposal.

Report cards are disseminated widely through the mainstream media and
by setting up information camps in different constituencies to create awareness among citizens about the roles and performance of their representatives. This information has enabled people to have an informed dialogue and
engagement with politicians they elect. In many places, report cards have
empowered people to demand social justice and collectively ensure that their
community development needs are addressed.

The residents of a slum in Malviya Nagar, a constituency in New Delhi,
afflicted with acute water shortage had to line up for hours at a community
tap to access water, and "water riots" were a regular occurrence. Every time
they approached their elected representative, they were told that there were
no funds to provide piped water supply to their homes. When they read the
Report Card containing information on how the local area development
funds at the disposal of the representative were spent, they found that nearly
70% of the funds were spent on constructing fountains in parks!

Hundreds of families in the area collectively approached the political representative with the information and asked for the basis on which the decision
was taken to allocate funds to construct fountains in a water scare constituency
where people struggled to get water to drink. As a result of informed public
pressure, the representative sanctioned funds for laying water pipes in the slums
in the constituency and for other pressing development needs of residents.[8]

In 2008, prior to the state-level elections in Delhi, the Jameel Poverty
Action Lab (J-PAL), a research group at the Massachusetts Institute of Technology (MIT), set up a project to evaluate the impact of disseminating
Report Cards prepared by SNS. The study[9] found that in constituencies
where the Report Cards were disseminated, the voter turnout increased

by 3.5%. Furthermore, voters recognised and rewarded better performers – the incumbent vote share increased by over seven per centage points for political representatives who regularly attended the meetings of the oversight committees.

Elected representatives in a democracy are supposed to work for, and on behalf of, people to ensure social justice. We have been campaigning for proactive disclosure of information regarding the functioning of elected representatives at the national and local levels in India.

As a result of petitions filed by SNS to the Central Information Commission of India, a live webcast of the Delhi Legislative Assembly proceedings was initiated to enable citizens to be informed about the working of their lawmakers. Similarly, the commission directed that details of the utilisation of development funds by the elected representatives be publicly disclosed on display boards in their electoral constituency. The information on these boards have empowered all residents to monitor the way in which their representatives prioritise and allocate funds. Wide dissemination of information about functioning of political representatives has created a pressure on incumbents to improve their performance. An analysis by SNS of the expenditure of development funds after boards were displayed shows that, since transparency has been infused into the system, money is being spent more judiciously to address the most pressing development needs of people. Instead of allocating funds for non-critical activities like installing decorations in parks, money is being invested in providing essential infrastructure like constructing toilets for girls in primary schools and repairs of primary health care centres.

Transparency during the pandemic

The COVID-19 pandemic has underlined the need for ensuring that citizens have real-time information about healthcare facilities and know how public money is being spent to help people cope with the crisis.

A humanitarian crisis unfolded in India due to the COVID-19 pandemic, with the poor having to face the double brunt of disease and economic destitution caused due to unplanned lockdowns. Millions of people have slipped into poverty, accumulating huge debts.[10] One such family is that of Gautam Giri, who lived in Delhi with his mother, wife, and an infant daughter. He lost his mother to COVID-19 despite spending large amounts of money in procuring oxygen and essential drugs for her treatment. The Delhi government notified its compensation policy for the next of kin of those who lost their lives to COVID-19. Steeped in debt, Gautam filed his application with the requisite documents. When he did not hear anything about it from the authorities for months, he worried that some loophole would be cited to deny him the compensation. According to documents filed in the Court,[11] there were scores of people like him waiting for their dues. After Gautam filed an information request with the help of SNS to find out the status of his application, things started to move. The public functionaries who had been unresponsive approached Gautam and he received the compensation due to him.

Our learnings

Several estimates suggest that, since the RTI Act was legislated in India, over 30 million information requests have been filed across the country.[12] Our experience has taught us that even with an effective law, accessing information is no mean task for citizens. Vested interests that benefit from corruption and the resulting social injustice work towards dissuading information seekers. The resistance to share information takes various forms – from stonewalling information requests to mystifying data and in many cases even threatening or attacking those who seek transparency. The pursuit of information requires commitment, patience, and perseverance. Information applications need to be carefully drafted and followed up using appropriate appellate mechanisms.

Obtaining information is only the first step towards seeking accountability and social justice. The information received often needs to be disseminated widely – we prepare pamphlets in local languages for wide dissemination in the affected communities to catalyse people into taking action. Street corner meetings and discussions are organised and community led social audits carried out. Information is also broadcast in collaboration with the media. Where records reveal inadequacy of resources, flaws in policy design or other gaps, petitions seeking appropriate reforms are filed. If there is evidence of corruption or wrongdoing, we mobilise and assist people and communities to take action by filing complaints to appropriate authorities, organising public campaigns, and approaching the courts.

International experience of using the freedom of information for social justice

International experience corroborates the fact that globally peoples' struggles for social justice, and the fight against corruption and abuse of power, are bolstered when citizens are armed with relevant facts and information.

After the 25-year-long civil war ended in Sri Lanka in 2009, the government announced a compensation scheme to help people rebuild their lives. In Koomankulam, a village located in the Northern Province of the country, scores of villagers applied for the scheme but either only received letters promising the compensation or nothing at all. After the enactment of the RTI Act in the country in 2016, villagers began using the law to inquire about the outcome of their applications under the compensation scheme. Soon, the compensation money started getting deposited in the bank accounts of the villagers. After struggling for years, the people of Koomankulam finally got justice through the exercise of their right to know.[13]

In Chiapas, Mexico's southernmost state, women from a local community used their right to information to ensure the delivery of healthcare and medical services in their area. For more than seven years after its inauguration in 2008, the Lázaro Cárdenas Health Center did not have any full-time doctors, medical facilities, or even medicines to serve the nearly 1,300 residents for whom it was designed. It was only when women from the community filed an information request that it came to light that money had been allocated to hire a doctor to attend to patients at the centre from Monday to Friday. Furthermore, they discovered that an additional budget was allocated for making medicines available at the centre. Using the information obtained, the community wrote a letter to the authorities highlighting the violation of their right to health and demanding quality service. A doctor was then assigned and the health centre finally became functional as a result of informed action by the community.[14]

The head of the United States' environmental regulatory body, the Environmental Protection Agency, resigned in 2018 following a string of revelations about alleged tampering with records and attempts to conceal communications and controversial meetings with industry representatives. Many of these facts came to light through information obtained by environmental groups in the US using the Freedom of Information Act.[15] Dogged enquiry by people concerned about climate change enabled them to monitor and hold to account the regulator responsible for protecting the environment.

> **Explore:**
>
> Global Right to Information Rating by Access Info Europe (AIE) and
> the Centre for Law and Democracy (CLD).
> (https://www.rti-rating.org/)

How transparency strengthens the delivery of social justice: theoretical underpinnings

Joseph Stiglitz, the recipient of the Nobel Prize for his contribution to the theory of information asymmetry, called attention to the adverse effects of secrecy.[16] He noted that secrecy hobbles the ability of citizens to participate meaningfully in democratic processes, creates a fertile ground on which special interests work, discourages public participation, and undermines the ability of the press to provide an effective check against the abuses of government. But the most adverse economic consequence, he argued, is associated with the corruption that follows from excessive secrecy.

Stiglitz likens the culture of secrecy to a virus, spreading from one part of the government to another. According to him, greater openness and freedom of information are essential parts of good governance and result in better, more efficient resource allocations. He recognises that while a culture of openness may not always guarantee that wise decisions are made, but it is a major step forward in the evolution of democratic processes – a true empowerment of individuals to participate meaningfully in governance.

In his various works, including "Development as Freedom" and "The Idea of Justice",[17] Amartya Sen establishes that capture of social welfare benefits can be prevented only when political systems are transparent and when there is a free flow of information. Opacity works to the benefit of those who monopolise scarce economic resources. Peoples' scrutiny serves the purpose of ensuring that socioeconomic benefits actually reach the underprivileged for whom they are meant. Sen compares the response of non-democratic regimes in critical situations such as famine, with the responses of democratic societies in similar situations, and argues that disasters like famines do not occur in societies where there is robust enquiry by the public and media.

To assess if transparency could be an effective strategy to combat everyday coercive corruption, researchers from Yale University set up a field experiment in the slum settlements of Delhi.[18] The experiment involved assisting people in applying for a food security card under the government-run programme to provide subsidised rations to people living below a certain income threshold. The applicants, mainly from the minority community and surviving on an income of about $1.50 per day, were organised into a control group and experimental groups – those who paid bribes to middlemen and those who used the RTI Act to track their application for the food security card. The researchers found that while only 21% of the people in the control group got their ration cards over the course of the year, 94% of those who used the RTI Act got their ration cards. From the group that paid a bribe, a similar number managed to get their cards made. The experiment showed that the RTI Act can be used effectively by most underprivileged citizens, concluding that *"recourse to the RTI Act is considerably more effective than standard application procedures and is almost as effective as bribery"*.[19]

Explore:

United Nations Convention Against Corruption
  https://www.unodc.org/documents/brussels/UN_Convention_
  Against_Corruption.pdf)

How to master the power of freedom of information for social justice

The ultimate goal of societies is to ensure human well-being and a life of dignity for all. Through this chapter, drawing on our own experiences and on international research, we have described how access to information can empower individuals and communities to participate in democratic processes and take informed action in their struggle for social justice. We share here some insights on how to exercise the right to information in a meaningful manner to address issues of social injustice.

- **Familiarise yourself** with the information access law or policy in your country.
- **Get involved** with campaigns taking up issues of social injustice like hunger, poverty, unemployment, lack of access to healthcare, environmental degradation, and discrimination.
- **Develop an understanding** of the causes of social injustice by engaging with affected communities/persons, and looking at relevant literature and talking to experts in the field.

- **Document the problems** being faced by affected communities and identify the information gaps.
- **Identify the relevant government agencies and policy framework** related to the issues you wish to access information about.
- **Build capacities of affected people and communities** about the importance of seeking relevant information and how it could strengthen their struggles for justice and accountability. Assist them in using the RTI law/policy.
- Based on information accessed, **develop campaign ideas** on how the information can be used in addressing the problems. This could include public dissemination of relevant facts and details through media, public meetings, pamphleteering, petitioning local authorities, and planning collective action.
- **Approach relevant legal institutions** in the country – oversight bodies or the courts **for redressal**.

Follow-up actions

1   Study the freedom of information law in your country.
2   Use the law to gain practical knowledge of the procedures and systems.
3   Explore with campaigns and groups taking up issues of social justice how accessing relevant information using the FOI law could meaningfully assist causes.
4   Identify the information gaps in collaboration with campaigns and groups and use the FOI law to obtain information.
5   Think of innovative means to use information obtained including approaching and petitioning various pillars of the society to strengthen delivery of social justice in your country.

Summary

Peoples' struggles for social justice, and the fight against corruption and abuse of power, are bolstered when citizens are armed with relevant facts and information. Opacity works to the benefit of those who monopolise scarce economic resources. Peoples' ability to access relevant information is a key to ensuring that socioeconomic benefits actually reach people, especially the disadvantaged and marginalised, for whom they are meant. Transparent societies, where there is robust enquiry by the public and media, fare better in delivering social justice and ensuring a life of dignity for people.

Notes

1 *The Writings of James Madison, 9 Vols.* (1900–1910). Gaillard Hunt (Ed.). New York: G. P. Putnam's Sons.
2 NDTV, Interview with Maria Ressa (2021), Without Facts, No Truth, No Democracy: Nobel Peace Winner Maria Ressa to NDTV - Full Transcript. *NDTV Website.* Available at: https://www.ndtv.com/people/without-facts-no-truth-no-democracy-nobel-peace-winner-maria-ressa-to-ndtv-full-transcript-2569031
3 UNESCO (2020), *From Promise to Practice: Access to Information for Sustainable Development.* Available at: https://en.unesco.org/sites/default/files/unesco_report_16102.pdf
4 Ibid.
5 Official Gazette Notification of the Right to Information Act (2005). Available at: https://rti.gov.in/rti-act.pdf
6 Johri, Amrita, Anjali Bhardwaj and Shekar Singh (2014), Peoples' Monitoring of the RTI Regime in India, 2011–2013. *RaaG & CES.*
7 www.snsindia.org
8 Denyer, Simon (2014), *Rogue Elephant: Harnessing the Power of India's Unruly Democracy.* London: Bloomsbury Press.
9 Pande, Rohini, Abhijit Banerjee, Selvan Kumar and Felix Su (2011), Do Informed Voters Make Better Choices? *Evidence for Policy Design (EPoD),* Harvard Kennedy School.
10 Azim Premji University (2021), *State of Working India 2021: One Year of Covid-19.* Centre for Sustainable Employment, Azim Premji University.
11 The Hindu (2021), Processing over 6,700 Applications for ex gratia to Kin of COVID Victims. *The Hindu,* September.
12 IANS (2019), More Than 3 Crore RTI Applications Filed So Far: Report. *Outlook India Magazine,* October.
13 Sri Lanka – Citizens Use the RTI Law to Retrieve Government Compensation. *Open Government Partnership.* Available at: https://www.opengovpartnership.org/stories/sri-lanka-citizens-use-the-rti-law-to-retrieve-government-compensation/
14 Cuando la información cura: Palenque, Chiapas. *Article 19,* April 2016. Available at: https://articulo19.org/video-cuando-la-informacion-cura-palenque-chiapas/ available in English- "Mexican Women Diagnose Healthcare Budget", FOI Impact: Success Stories- Freedominfo.org. Available at: http://www.freedominfo.org/2016/09/foia-impact-success-stories/
15 Holder, Emily (2018), New Pruitt Question: Where Are His Emails? *Politico,* June.
16 Stiglitz, Joseph E. (1999), Oxford Amnesty Lecture Oxford, U.K. January 1999. "On Liberty, the Right to Know, and Public Discourse: The Role of Transparency in Public Life".
17 Sen, Amartya (2000), *Development as Freedom.* New York: Anchor Books; Sen (2009), *The Idea of Justice.* Cambridge, MA: Belknap Press of Harvard University Press.
18 Peisakhin, Leonid and Paul Pinto (2010), Is Transparency an Effective Anti-Corruption Strategy? Evidence from a Field Experiment in India. *Regulation & Governance,* 4, 261–280.
19 Ibid.

Further reading

Tilting the Balance of Power – Adjudicating the RTI Act. *RaaG, SNS & Rajpal* (2017). Available at: http://snsindia.org/wp-content/uploads/2017/07/Adjudicating-the-RTI-Act-2nd-edition-2017.pdf
UNESCO & IPDC, *Briefing Note, Unpacking Indicator 16.10.2 Enhancing Public Access to Information through Agenda 2030 for Sustainable Development.* Available at: https://en.unesco.org/sites/default/files/unpacking_indicator16102.pdf

30

MASTERING THE POWER OF IMPACT INVESTING

Giles Gunesekera

Abstract

Impact investments are investments made with the intention to generate positive, measurable social and environmental impact alongside a financial return.

There has been increased interest and activity in impact investment as businesses, governments, and communities seek new solutions to enable an inclusive and sustainable society in the face of social and environmental challenges. We are neither using money in the most effective way possible nor are we taking a human-centred, ecosystem-based approach to solving problems . . . but this is changing. There is an even greater need for us as a global community to work together to achieve the UN Sustainable Development Goals.

The hope, and my personal belief, is that one-day impact investing will cease to exist. It will simply be investing; with social and environmental impact becoming an in-built, expected standard.

Keywords: Social impact, profit with purpose, sustainability, impact investing

Introduction

As the famous French poet, novelist, and dramatist, Victor Hugo wrote in his novel, *Les Misérables*, "*Nothing is more powerful than an idea whose time has come*".[1] Impact investment is a case in point: its time has come.

DOI: 10.4324/9781003219293-39

The term "Impact Investing" was coined by a group of investors who were brought together by the Rockefeller Foundation[2] in Bellagio, Italy, in 2007. Thus, a name was given to investments made with the intention of generating financial return along with social and/or environmental impact. The group recognised the immense power embedded in capital markets, and they wanted to direct it to have a positive social impact. There was frustration that businesses doing the most good in the world often could not get capital. In contrast, those companies damaging the environment and exploiting society didn't have to pay for the negative impacts they had on the planet. Impact investing became a new way of identifying organisations that were becoming financially successful by simultaneously solving social problems. History has now revealed what we always conceptually believed was possible – the most sustainable, impactful companies deliver better long-term performance.[3]

At the age of 16, I joined Amnesty International and found the work to be incredibly rewarding, as I was able to live the values of gratitude and service, taught by my parents. Working with communities whose human rights were abused and/or non-existent brought it home that I was lucky to be raised in a country like Australia. It was evident through this work that there was 50% of the population that consistently did not receive the same benefits as the other 50% – and that was women.

Our first project at Global Impact Initiative (GII) was destined to be about gender equality. I knew through research and experience that the essential items that helped girls become women were better health, education, nutrition, and social and economic empowerment. We needed a solution that incorporated and supported the needs of both women and girls. This was new territory, and while there was interest, much education, hard work, and creativity were needed to create the solution.

Impact investing is a way of bringing the great ideas that exist in the not-for-profit world with the abundance of capital that exists in the investment world.

Like my dreams of becoming a pilot, my personal path to impact investing has been protracted, but on reflection, inevitable. The path has been punctuated with many setbacks and ultimately breakthroughs. My obsession with flight and its ability to soar beyond human limits are a corollary for my journey in Mastering the Power of Impact Investing.

The beginning of my journey

I flew my first glider solo at 14 and my first powered aircraft solo at 16. That same year, I bought my first shares. Back then, I had my whole future laid out for me. My dream was to enter the Air Force and then retire to a cushy Commercial Pilot role. I studied the right subjects, got the marks I needed, passed all the physical, and psychological tests, only to fail the final hurdle – I discovered that I was short-sighted. In 1786, Robert Burns, the renowned Scottish poet and lyricist, appropriately wrote, "*The best laid schemes o' Mice and Men gang aft agley*" – in modern day English, "*The best laid plans of mice and men often go awry*"![4]

The inspiration that led me to purchase those first shares, re-oriented me on a path towards a career in investments. If the sky couldn't be my literal limit, I decided to make it a metaphoric one in growing wealth, for myself and others. I spent over 20 years working for global fund managers and building teams, products and systems, but I found myself continually looking for meaning in my life.

Parental influences

I was fortunate to be raised by parents who valued service to others. My father, a doctor, has served our local community as a General Practitioner for 45 years now. My mum worked for the charity, St. Vincent De Paul, and volunteered for Meals on Wheels; an international programme in Australia that delivered meals to those who couldn't afford their own. At the age of 7, I began delivering meals with my mum and learnt the value of service, respect, and humility. These lessons learnt of gratitude and service underpin my values to this day and have informed and guided my journey into impact investing.

My search for a meaning

My mum's generosity kept me grounded and inspired me to try to be of service to others. I applied that quality to my investment career and sought out positions to be of service; board positions and volunteering, on industry bodies and in the community. I was energised but also frustrated as I could see the quantities of capital that existed in the corporate world wasted on bad ideas and generation of profit for profit's sake. In contrast, I could see the great ideas that existed in the not-for-profit world receiving no capital, crippling their ability to serve. Impact Investing became the way that I would bring those two worlds together and bring purpose to money.

In 2013, I fulfilled a lifelong ambition and attended the Advanced Management and Leadership Programme at Oxford University. I was in a cohort of 35 people from different industries and countries – it was diversity on steroids! I saw the true value that diversity brings to the decision-making process when all views and opinions are considered in a respectful way. The Oxford experience emblazoned in me the need and passion for change. I was surrounded by brilliant people, all doing amazing things, who like me wanted and knew we had to do more.

Constructing impact investments

Life is determined by the quality of your questions and not the answers you give, and the Oxford experience highlighted the need for an ecosystem approach to solving problems and the importance of discussion and understanding.

Our stages in constructing impact investments first consider whether the impact can be scaled with a focus on accelerating social impact for marginalised groups. We will also assess which of the five Pillars of our organisation that the strategy falls under: Gender Equality, Indigenous Communities, Health, Affordable Housing, and Climate. We will only undertake work that falls under one or several of these categories. We have deliberately chosen these pillars as we know through research that there is an intersectionality between these pillars. Gender equality can be integrated and social impact can be maximised when working within and across these pillars. The viability and business case for impact is important, as we partner with people and organisations with aligned interests and values. We recognise that investment capital is not an issue and thus we want this capital to be deployed, replicated, and increased over time.

Our business model at GII also involves engaging investors before we launch solutions. Through presentations via conferences, seminars, and meetings on many continents and across a wide cross section of investors, the solutions that we see today (and in the future) are born. This approach ensures that when products are launched, we have a "captive" audience, and our impact strategies are fit for purpose. These activities have also enabled us to build our intellectual property, which has been a huge advantage especially as an "early starter" in the industry.

We have used these values in designing Affordable Housing projects in Australia, India, and Bangladesh. We have found that taking a human centred, community-based approach to problem-solving has been the most rewarding and appropriate model. The best decisions are made by those vulnerable people that see the need and solution before anyone else can. Implementing a human centred approach that asks the right questions combined with a team with a diversity of skills and backgrounds delivers compassionate, tailored made solutions.

Our team is made up of highly experienced professionals from across different geographies, backgrounds, and industries. The team and partners are deliberately selected for their diversity and applicable for our bespoke projects to maximise impact.

Impact investing around the world

Professor Muhammad Yunus' 1998 autobiography *Banker to the Poor*[5] remains one of the most influential books on creating impact for me. While teaching economics in famine ravaged Bangladesh in 1974, Yunus became increasingly uncomfortable with teaching abstract theories while people starved around him. Realising his economic education was incomplete; he decided to visit local villages and asked people what they needed, as opposed to the university model of telling. Yunus uncovered the power of credit in mind-bogglingly small amounts and realised that it was the answer. Through Microfinance lending women were able to access finance that helped them start a business, which in turn generated income and support for their family. Thousands of children have been able to access education as a result of the loan.

In 2006, this humble Professor of Economics and his groundbreaking, Grameen Bank, won the Nobel Peace Prize, for developing the concept of microfinance and creating "economic and social development from below". Professor Yunus' research and analysis showed that loaning money to women impacted children and communities much more than loaning money to men who mostly spent it on themselves! Microfinance has also brought less reputable operators into the ecosystem looking to take advantage of the poor. However, practice shows that sustainable and ethical lending helps to lower gender inequality and empower women. Professor Yunus has been hailed as the founder of the concept of social entrepreneurship, whose principles resemble impact investing.

Explore: Grameen Bank

https://grameenbank.org/
 Today Grameen Bank, the "Bank of the Village", has extended credit to millions of people. Grameen makes small loans to the poor, women and people with no creditworthiness.

LeapFrog investments – profit with purpose

An example of an innovative and early impact investor is LeapFrog Investments. They invest capital, people and knowledge in purpose-driven businesses, helping them to grow, achieve profitability, and have real social impact.

LeapFrog has been able to open the gates of the capital markets for high growth businesses by bringing capital and diversification to drive rapid impact on billions of lives. LeapFrog operates as a co-owner standing alongside its investors, co-investors, management, and local communities and provides operational experience and advisory support to partner companies.

LeapFrog has been a trailblazer in helping create the industry known as Impact Investing and its philosophy of "Profit with Purpose" is set to become the future of investing.

Explore: LeapFrog Investments

https://leapfroginvest.com/
   Profit with Purpose
   LeapFrog invests in extraordinary businesses in Asia and Africa, partnering with their leaders to achieve leaps of growth, profitability, and impact.

The micro-lending Grameen Bank established by Professor Yunus and the innovative business model of LeapFrog can be recognised as incredible breakthroughs in the fields of social entrepreneurship and impact investing. GII's business model has been inspired by both these revolutionary concepts that has driven impact on millions of lives through economic empowerment. Grameen Bank was successful not only in creating financial empowerment among rural women but also in bringing about social and financial consciousness in the community. GII, similarly, helps companies achieve their financial potential alongside participating in high-impact social change programmes.

The values of diversity, inclusion, and purpose are common threads of the three business models. These organisations have found an enormous opportunity set and then established a viable logic on which to serve their communities and help them grow and prosper. They have built trust and brought happiness to marginalised communities to create a movement. All organisations are aligned in their desire and need to see impact in the form of financial returns and social impact mainstreamed and scaled.

The impact investing landscape

In his speech to the UN General Assembly 1998 Kofi Annan, Ghanaian diplomat, former Secretary General of United Nations and co-winner of the 2001 Noble Peace Prize, stated *"without a dream you'll not get anywhere"*.[6]

There is a growing chorus of prominent voices calling for business to play a proactive role in addressing social and environmental challenges: Bill Gates calls for "creative capitalism", Tom Friedman calls for a "green economy", Al Gore calls for the "sustainable corporation" and Muhammad Yunus calls for "social business". There has been increased interest and activity in impact investment over recent years as businesses, governments, and communities seek new solutions to enable an inclusive and sustainable society in the face of social and environmental challenges.

Institutional investors as well as philanthropists, foundations, and charities have implemented impact investment strategies. These strategies aim to yield financial returns, as well as positive and measurable social and environmental impacts. Commercial financial returns are pursued by some while others consciously elect to accept reduced financial returns in the interest of impact. It is very clear that attitudes and perspectives around investment and wealth are shifting. The major social and environmental challenges of our time need solutions, and governments are financially limited in an era of low economic growth and ageing populations.

Impact investments position in the investment world

Global companies operate in a challenging cultural climate in which issues such as environmental degradation, inequality, resource scarcity, poverty, and consumer trust are impossible to ignore. With power, visibility, and influence on both national and international levels, corporations have an enormous capacity to bring about positive change through responsible leadership. Alongside NGOs and international institutions, global corporations are becoming increasingly capable of assuming responsibilities that were once the remit of governments.

Impact investing enables these businesses to act responsibly while still making profits and engaging shareholders and staff alike. In addition, investors need to be encouraged to refocus away from short-term earnings. Public policy and law can be designed to assist companies in addressing societal problems.

One of the major reasons for the growth in areas such as impact investing is that business has changed, as has how people lead and interact inside entities. Employees want to work for companies that have a socially established mission and engaged employees, customers, and stakeholders. Our work at Global Impact Initiative has found that new graduates are asking more questions about sustainability, volunteering, and recycling from their potential employers, rather than asking how their bonus will be calculated and when it will be paid.

The implementation of impact investing

> "*Sustainability is not about changing the world; it's about changing with the world*".
>
> *(Anonymous)*

There are a range of instruments being used to implement impact investing. The largest asset classes (by assets under management) are private debt, real assets, and private equity.

Impact investment categories (and some examples) can be classified as follows:

- Fixed Income (Green Bonds, Social Finance/Impact Bonds)
- Public Equities (ESG, Thematic, Impact)
- Real Assets (Renewables, Green Real Estate, Sustainable Agriculture, Climate, Circular Economy)
- Private Equity (Social Entrepreneurship, Seed Capital, Venture Capital)
- Alternatives (Credit, Hedge)

Considering investments by positive impact enables investors to compare the financial performance and social impact of companies, funds, or enterprises with their peers. Impact investments differ from traditional investments, because they have an identifiable, intentional strategy for creating social and environmental impact and because their intended financial return may be atypical according to standard risk-return calculations.

Impact investments and private equity

Impact investing has its roots in private equity. In its early days, impact investing followed a model where investment firms or family offices invested directly in a private, unlisted company. The investors would then identify a company in which they could take a controlling share and, further, offer management assistance and expertise to help the company grow. The aim was to boost the company's positive impact, as well as its profits, while keeping a close eye on the management of the business. The investors would eventually sell the business to realise a financial gain. Impact investing evolved, as the "owners" were able to create intentional and measurable impact by considering the social and environmental aspects of their investments.

This model has proven so successful that it's pushed beyond the boundary of private equity to influence all the major asset classes, such as listed equities, fixed income, and property investing.

Blended finance

Blended finance attracts commercial capital towards projects that contribute to sustainable development, while providing financial returns to investors. Blended finance brings capital from the public and private sectors together to help de-risk a strategy/transaction to scale finance for financial and social impact.

The global community is demanding that more resources be mobilised to end extreme poverty and mitigate the effects of climate change. Blended finance is an approach to mix different forms of capital in support of development. This strategy has emerged as an important solution to help raise resources for the Sustainable Development Goals in developing countries. It is important to consider the risks before scaling up using blended finance. Blended finance can contribute to faster economic growth, but to achieve this it is vital to get donors into alignment. The challenges ahead are more than governments alone can manage and thus we need to mobilise private-sector resources and expertise to help the world's poorest and most vulnerable people.

Explore: Blended Finance and Gender Equality

Gender inequality is one of the world's most pressing problems. The empowerment of Women and Girls across all facets of society is long overdue and has demonstrable positive financial and social impact characteristics. The following case study is a good example of Blended Finance in action across public, private, and NGO segments.

Global Impact Initiative (GII) has developed the world's first, actively managed Impact Investing strategy focused on Women and Girls. Through active management, investors receive a financial return while also driving social impact for women and girls. The ecosystem solution engages both the private and public sectors, enabling the fund to invest in companies that promote gender equality through policy and action. Organisations whose products or business practices are detrimental to society and incompatible with sustainability are excluded. These include companies that are involved in dealing Controversial weapons, Firearms, Military contracting, Thermal coal, Nuclear Power, Palm oil, Tobacco, Alcohol, Gambling, and Adult entertainment. A gender lens is then applied to the investment universe after these companies have been excluded.

Additionally, the fund provides grants and support to enterprises that provide health, nutrition, education, and social and economic empowerment to women and girls. The fund is monitored and is mapped to the UN Sustainable Development Goals. It focuses on key social impact metrics around infant mortality, girls' education, gender equality in the workforce, and more. The fund's plan is to utilise the abundant capital that is sitting in investment and retirement savings accounts for social purposes.

The fund is led by a majority female board and executive team. The partners have also been screened under a gender lens and, they operate and are led by the populations they seek to support. Those who are directly and indirectly affected by the issues the fund is trying to address are part of the fund's leadership and decision-making. The fund has been developed to support women, girls, trans, and intersex persons in their efforts to uphold their rights. There is a clear vision and articulated strategy to challenge and transform gendered power structures.

Social impact measurement – the secret sauce

The Global Impact Investing Network's definition of Impact investments is "investments made with the intention to generate positive, measurable, social, and environmental impact alongside a financial return".[7] Peter Drucker, Austrian-American management consultant, educator, and author, appositely said "You can't manage what you can't measure".[8] Impact measurement is not subjective or ambiguous. It needs to be independent, precise, verifiable, and focused on people. The beauty of impact measurement is that it is intentional, additional, and granular. Impact strategies can measure the difference that capital makes on individuals, marginalised groups, minorities, climate, and the community.

There are a range of frameworks available that investors can use to assess their impact, but there remains a lack of consistency in how to approach the issue. While for some, this remains a reason to not measure or engage, for others, it's an opportunity to innovate and show why and how they are measuring the social impact. Ban Ki Moon, South Korean politician and diplomat, in his speech at Stanford University in 2013 stated "There is no Plan B, because there is no Planet B".[9] The world can't wait for conferences, discussion papers, and focus groups.

The United Nations Sustainable Development Goals (UNSDGs)

The UNSDGs are a set of 17 goals, established by the United Nations in 2015. These goals are often referred to as the "World's To-do List" – irrefutable actions that need to take place for the planet to survive. The agenda and framework of the UN SDGs is focused on an ambitious but necessary deadline of 2030.

The power of the UNSDGs comes from their global focus. Individuals and companies can identify which of the goals they are aligned to achieve by shifting their strategy, products, and operations. Their beauty is that they are more than just 17 goals. They are made up of 169 targets and 230 deliverables, which are objective, actionable, and measurable. The UNSDGs are becoming the standard for impact measurement and the engagement from governments, corporates, investors, and the not-for-profit world to date has been inspiring. Specialist firms have sprung up to help stakeholders measure their impact via technology and intellectual property mechanisms. The SDG's and other impact frameworks enable impact to be intentional, actionable, and granular – the ability to go micro from these macro frameworks is a real and intended consequence.

Impact measurement can be applied to areas such as Gender Equality, Indigenous Communities, Health, Affordable Housing, and Climate. These and many other areas are important for the growth and improvement of communities and societies. The secret sauce and continued growth in impact investment lies in the ability to measure the impact on people, planet, and communities. Impact data can enable us to see if improvements are being made.

Explore: United Nations SDGs

https://sdgs.un.org/goals

The 2030 Agenda for Sustainable Development, adopted by all United Nations Member States in 2015, provides a shared blueprint for peace and prosperity for people and the planet, now and into the future. At its heart are the 17 Sustainable Development Goals (SDGs), which are an urgent call for action by all countries. This is the World's To Do list. They recognise that ending poverty and other deprivations must go hand in hand with strategies that improve health and education, reduce inequality, and spur economic growth – all while tackling climate change and working to preserve our oceans and forests.

The UN SDGs provide a quantitative and qualitative framework and importantly allow us to measure, map, and monitor progress to the UN SDGs.

Leadership skills for nurturing and leading

I have found that having a human centred approach to leading humans seems to work! We are born with two ears and one mouth and we should use it in that ratio. The power of compassion, active listening, and asking the right questions has never been more crucial and important.

I have always sought meaning and purpose in my life and having this clarity of purpose has also brought a clarity of thought to all parts of my life. Listening allows us to be more empathetic to convert those feelings to action. Enabling humans to oversee their own solutions, builds trust, high-quality relationships, and sustainable positive change.

Leading impact investing initiatives requires collaborative entrepreneurship and the discussion and sharing of ideas. Diversity and inclusion also help to drive sustainable and ethical ideas. Furthermore, for competent teams to successfully collaborate with one another, they must recognise the distinctive contributions of diverse disciplines. Impact investment aims to reimagine capitalism as a regenerative instrument for fulfilling human needs.

Resilience is a necessary muscle to build. In establishing our organisation, we have encountered poor suppliers, partners, and regulators who slowed the pace of our product development and social impact. We had to utilise our values of compassion, resilience, and persistence while always knowing that we were doing the right thing. We lived these values in developing and launching the world's first actively managed, impact fund for Women and Girls.

How an aspiring impact investor can master impact investing – the road to mastery!

The role to mastery involves conscience, character, and purpose.

It is important to understand that there is no "one-size-fits-all" approach to impact investing. Impact can be created and measured differently by different organisations and individuals. The first step taken by anyone hoping to create impact investments should be the identification of the social and/or environmental objectives that are desired. In the process of devising these goals and starting with the end in mind, one must ascertain if the goals are realistic, measurable and achievable. Once the social/environmental outcomes have been identified, the next step should be determining which products, services, or projects are capable of generating the desired impact. The next aspect to be considered is the scale of the impact. Creating deep and measurable positive impact for fewer people will be more worthwhile than creating superficial impact that has little impact. It is critical to ensure that any incremental changes are positive and that these are intentional, measurable, and actionable.

Investors who would like to get into impact investing can collaborate with others. Interaction and dialogue among investors and social entrepreneurs can help both parties gain a better understanding of the requirements and objectives of their potential partnership, which can also lead to co-investment. Creating allies can play a critical role in the creation of new inclusive entrepreneurs and projects. It is important for an impact investor to understand what drives them and then identify partners that have a shared value system.

It's helpful to imagine impact investing as a process or path. This path has steps that need to be followed progressively to enhance the alignment of values to the impact potential, in a manner that matures with one's desired outcomes. Addressing complex social and environmental issues is difficult and one must be patient, flexible, and willing to take long-term risks to ensure that the desired social impact is realised.

Investments that make money while also doing good are enticing, which is why the impact investing industry is flourishing. It is essential to keep revisiting one's approach to impact investing as priorities and risks will change over time.

Summary

The biggest challenge facing investors is finding investable deals and projects – capital is not the issue. In emerging markets and developing countries, numerous projects are available in areas like solar, wind, or hydro energy, circular economy (waste-to-energy conversion), and affordable housing. There is an opportunity for "traditional" impact investors in collaboration with international finance organisations, development banks, foundations, and governments to develop projects that contribute to the realisation of the UN Sustainable Development goals. The list of goals highlights the need for corporations, not-for-profits, and governments to work together to achieve them.

Change is difficult and takes time, but what helped me make bold choices in my career was revisiting my values. I have never been after a "quick fix solution" but instead have tried to create sustainable impact at scale. This entails taking a long-term approach and collaborating. There is an African proverb stating, "anyone that thinks they are too small to make a difference hasn't spent the night with a mosquito". Taking ownership of the problem and seeking a solution that enables a systemic change are the need of our time.

The hope, and my personal belief, is that one day impact investing will cease to exist, and it will simply be Investing; with Impact becoming an in-built, expected standard. We are seeing ecosystem changes taking place and investors acknowledging that sustainable businesses are profitable businesses.

Practical Exercise:

Review your investment portfolio and/or retirement savings account. Do you have exposure to investments or sectors, which don't align with your values? Are you comfortable with those sectors and exposures? If not, speak with your financial advisor, fund company, stockbroker, plan sponsor, or website – (https://www.responsiblereturns.com.au – to see what options you have. . . . You will have several!

Responsible Returns

A website that helps you find responsible or ethical banking, superannuation, and investment products matching your values and interests
  https://www.responsiblereturns.com.au

> **Reflect:**
>
> How many SDG's does your company/business plan to engage with?
> What can you do with your own capital to make a difference?
> What are your financial, social, and/or environmental objectives?
> What are the current and emerging trends in the impact sector?
> What barriers could you face while making impact investments?

Notes

1   Hugo, V. (1987), *Les Misérables*. UK: Penguin Books.
2   Rockefeller Philanthropy Advisors (2017), *Impact Investing: An Introduction*. Available at: https://www.rockpa.org/guide/impact-investing-introduction/
3   Responsible Investment Association Australasia (2021), *Responsible Investment Benchmark Report Australia*. Available at: https://responsibleinvestment.org/
4   Burns, Robert, Poem (1786), *To a Mouse*. Originally published July 31, verse 7.
5   Yunus, M. (1998), *Banker to the Poor: The Autobiography of Mohammad Yunus of the Grameen Bank by Mohammad Yunus*. UK: Aurum Press.
6   Annan, K. (1998), Speech to the UN General Assembly, September.
7   Global Impact Investing Network (GIIN). Available at: https://thegiin.org/impact-investing/
8   Drucker, P. (2006), *Effective Executive: The Definitive Guide to Getting the Right Things Done*. UK: HarperBusiness Essentials, January.
9   Ban Ki Moon (2013), Speech to Stanford University, January 18.

Further reading

Clark, C., J. Emerson and B. Thornley (2014), *Collaborative Capitalism and the Rise of Impact Investing*. USA: Wiley.
Cohen, R. (2020), *Impact: Reshaping Capitalism to Drive Real Change*. UK: Ebury Press.
Mobius, M., C. Hardenberg and G. Konieczny (2019), *Invest for Good: A Healthier World and a Wealthier You*. UK: Bloomsbury Publishing.
Rodin, J. and M. Brandenburg (2014), *The Power of Impact Investing: Putting Markets to Work for Profit and Global Good*. USA: Wharton School Press.

Videos and podcasts:

Good Future Podcast
Hosted by John Treadgold
https://johntreadgold.com/goodfuturepodcast/
Good Will Hunters Podcast
Hosted by Rachel Mason Nunn
https://goodwillhunterspodcast.com.au/
ImpactAlpha Podcast
Co-hosted by Monique Aiken
https://impactalpha.com/podcasts/
Social Impact Investment – Turn Your Money Into Real Change

By G8 Taskforce on Social Impact Investment
https://www.youtube.com/watch?v=1Bpe_dAOL2M
Mainstreaming Impact Investing
By World Economic Forum
https://www.youtube.com/watch?v=_dBydk09L9s

31

MASTERING THE POWER OF SOCIAL EQUITY

Marsha Marshall

Abstract

Every one of us wants and needs to be included in and valued by the world we live in. We want to be able to participate in the activities that interest and excite us. We want to have a home, a purpose, a job, and friends, to be included and loved. This is what social equity looks like.

But for many marginalised groups, it is not easy to achieve. For people living with disabilities, social equity is often out of reach. However, with an emphasis in our society on self-direction and empowerment, disabled people can have the power to make their own choices and create the life they want, intentionally and without paternalistic interference. This chapter describes what self-direction is and how it supports social equity.

Keywords: Social equity, self-direction, empowerment, disability

Introduction

Everyone wants and needs to be included and valued by the world we live in even if we are different in some way. But for many marginalised groups, segregation occurs instead, and social equity is hard to achieve. In the words of Desmond Tutu, South African Anglican Cleric and Theologian, "*Differences are not intended to separate, to alienate. We are different precisely in order to realise our need of one another*".[1]

DOI: 10.4324/9781003219293-40

All lives matter. As speaker, consultant and author Michael Kendrick wrote: *"When individuals matter to the formation of human history, as they clearly do, then no life is lived without some consequence for others".*[2]

This chapter draws particularly on my experience in working with the disabled. All the stories in this chapter are of real people, told with permission. All names have been changed to protect anonymity.

Imagine this:

You are a 15-year-old boy named Bobby, and you have Muscular Dystrophy which is progressive, causing muscle wasting and loss of function that worsens over time. This has meant that for the last 7 years you have lived your life in a wheelchair as your muscles weakened.

You are a high achiever with many friends you do "normal" things with, just like non-disabled people, like going to parties and sporting events. However, everything is harder for you – and you know it will only get more challenging with age.

Recently, your parents have sought help from disability agencies for everyday things like your morning and evening routines. As you grow, balancing your needs with their daily lives is increasingly complicated. Often carers don't arrive on time, which makes you late for school, or they don't turn up at all which makes your family stressed, because they must complete these tasks. This makes you feel like a burden.

Usually, it is a different carer each time, and usually they are older than your mother. Mostly you just want it to be over. You feel humiliated and worthless. It seems like your friends are inviting you to things less, because they do not know how to include you or want to deal with the extra time it takes for you to participate. All you want is a normal life where you can get a job, go flatting, and have an exciting social life, maybe even an intimate relationship. Sometimes, you are scared about what the future holds for you, because you are dependent on others, and it feels like you can't make your own choices.

You do not have equal access to things – everything is harder, and some things are impossible. Social equity is not a feature in your life. You know you can do anything – if only others could see it!

We will come back to Bobby's story more later.

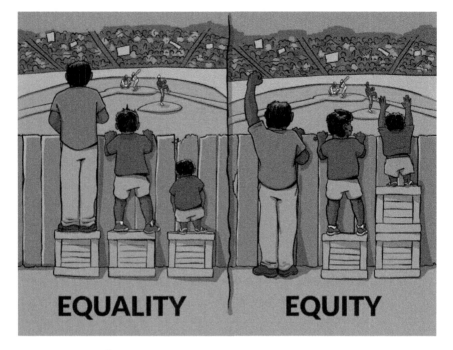

FIGURE 31.1:   Equality Versus Equity Diagram
Source: Reproduced with the permission of the Interaction Institute for Social Change
(2016)[3]

Equality versus equity

Equality means equal rights, opportunities, and advantages, regardless of characteristics, i.e., treating everyone the same. Inequalities occur when a group or population suffers exclusion from rights or opportunities, often simply by virtue of "different" characteristics.

But equality is different from equity. Equality is equal disbursement of resources amongst individuals. On the other hand, equity is disbursement of resources based on individual or group needs, to ensure an equal outcome overall. Sometimes taking an equal approach actually contributes to inequity, because not everyone is the same. Different people have different requirements to achieve the same thing. Equity challenges us to recognise and embrace difference, where equality is often based on "the same" for all.

Disability as an example of social inequity

I have seen the dramatic impact that disability has on social equity over my many years in this field, and I have also seen my own father disadvantaged by having Multiple Sclerosis (MS). I have seen people fundamentally restricted in their ability to participate in life by virtue of their disability. Conversely, I have also seen outstanding examples of transformation enabled by empowerment and self-direction. Paternalistic approaches prevent participation and social equity, whereas self-direction promotes it.

Statistics show that generally the disabled community exhibits poorer health, lower educational achievements, fewer economic opportunities, and higher poverty rates than people without disabilities.[4]

Paula Tseriero, Disability Rights Commissioner in New Zealand says, *"There are more than one billion people – or 1/6 of the world's population with a disability"*,[5] which implies that social inequity due to disability affects a large population globally. This inequity often leads to a breach of people's most basic human rights. To address this, The United Nations adopted the Convention for the Rights of People with Disabilities,[6] which aims to combat the social inequity and disadvantage that disabled people experience. Despite the specific focus on disability in this chapter, the relevance of these concepts can be applied across many marginalised or vulnerable groups like mental health, race, religion, gender, or poverty.

Why is social equity important?

So, why should we care? Social inequity impacts human rights, and the personal and emotional safety of people affected. Article 1 of the United Nations Universal Declaration of Human Rights (1948) states:

> *All human beings are born free and equal in dignity and rights. They are endowed with reason and conscience and should act towards each other in the spirit of brotherhood.*[7]

Social equity matters to society as a whole – not just to you and me as individuals. It contributes directly to the outcomes valued by everyone, to the communities we live in and lives we lead. Social equity promotes social cohesiveness within communities and people's ability to participate and contribute to economic and educational activities. It also promotes full citizenship, which strengthens rights, and promotes an inclusive and diverse society in which every person can make a valuable contribution.

Many people with disabilities are not able to participate in normal, inclusive environments or experiences, and spend their days intentionally excluded from everyday society. For example, some disabled people are placed in group homes to live together, special schools segregate disabled children to be educated together, and in sheltered workplaces, disabled people do menial jobs for little or no pay. These environments are not inherently wicked or evil. However, they can be resounding examples of social inequity which prevents people with disabilities from achieving the respect and experiences that many take for granted.

If something unfortunate were to happen to you – an accident, injury, or health problem – and it limited your independence or participation in life wouldn't you hope that society cared enough to include you, to help make your life good and equitable? That's why social equity is so important.

How can we promote social equity?

Now, we agree that social equity is important, how do we achieve it?

Looking at this issue through the lens of disability, promoting social equity starts by supporting people to be self-directed – to make their own choices and have individual control over their lives, as an abled person would. This means deciding how every day will go – from what time they get up, to the support they get and who delivers it. Self-direction means if you need assistance to have a shower or use the bathroom, you get to choose who sees you vulnerable.

The United Nations Convention on the Rights for People with Disabilities (CRPD) is based on empowering disabled people and moving the narrative from charity (doing for), to fully participating and self-determined citizens (doing with) in society. Supporting people with disabilities to make their own choices, to design and deliver their own supports, to have access to their community, and to have paid jobs and valued roles in society has transformational effects on their lives. This is simply because self-direction ensures that people have the power over the resources they require and promotes citizenship by strengthening and supporting people's most basic human rights.

Lillian's story

Lillian is a mother of six children, aged 6 months to 13 years. The family are refugees, having fled Iraq for a better life. They live in social housing and money is tight. Lillian's husband works two jobs to support them. They are Muslim and often experience discrimination and racism related to their culture and religion.

Their youngest boy named Tarrin was born with a disability and they have been referred to the children's home-care team for support. They have support hours each week to give Lillian time to care for her other children and have a break. A nurse from an agency attends three times a week to relieve Lillian and care for Tarrin, who needs specialist medical support.

Lillian has strong preferences around her son's care. The home-care team finds her challenging because she rings after every shift complaining about the care provided. The team implements detailed care plans and record keeping, reviewed weekly to reassure her. Despite this, Lillian continues to call, causing considerable disruption. A team member suggests this is likely due to a lack of control. Lillian has lost much of her personal control with the process of fleeing her homeland and now managing her son's disability. They suggested self-directed care, which would enable Lillian to manage the budget herself, find a support person she knows and trusts from within her own cultural and social circle.

This was considered a risk, because the family could potentially use the money for other family needs, instead of for Tarrin's care. Despite the risk, they tried it. Once Lillian could choose who came into her home to care for Tarrin, and how care was provided, calls from her stopped completely. Due to concerns about the use of the money, they checked on her regularly – and found that care was being provided by a family friend. She and Tarrin were both supported and happy.

The difference was control. Lillian could make the choices she wanted for her child's care, manage risk herself, and be trusted with the money. She was the master of outcomes for herself and her child.

We should ask, not tell

As illustrated in the aforementioned story – the most basic strategy of providing people with the opportunity to have autonomy over their actions, instead of prescribing things for them, has a tremendous impact. The "top-down" approach was simply not working. In Lillian's case, the home-care team did more for her by doing less, and by valuing her choices and role as a mother. A senior manager at a large disability support agency in New Zealand once asked me "What do you tell people about how to be self-directed?" My answer was that we don't tell – we ask. And the question is simple: what do you want your life to look like?

The answer is simple too – power belongs to the person receiving support, and questions should be asked, not unilaterally answered or prescribed. The person determines and owns the answers, and the system supports them to implement their own solution. This power allows people to determine how they live – who comes into their life and their home, and how they participate in their communities and social networks. It supports social equity by facilitating choice and control over everyday life, and beyond, to aspirations, purpose (for example, to have a job), personal relationships, and community contributions.

I believe this is a basic human right and should not be viewed as something we "allow" people to do, but as something, we must establish as the norm in society. Based on the principles of equity and human rights, self-direction should not be unique, in disability or in society.

In disability, self-direction empowers the individual receiving support and their family to have control over, and to design and deliver the support plans. While sometimes this can be complicated and intimidating for the person or their family, when the right support is put in place, it can enable and facilitate empowerment and their decision-making can create transformational success.

Mitchell's story

I met Mitchell in 2012, when he was 25. A disability advocate rang to see if my company could help. He had a progressive illness that was robbing him of mobility and strength. He was dependent on his powered wheelchair to get around, his speech was faint, and he only had movement in his hands, and head.

As a child, he was an adventurous Māori boy who loved his whānau (family), and playing with his friends on the marae (meeting house). When he began falling off his bike, it became clear that something was wrong, and his illness was diagnosed.

Mitchell's family was over-protective and preventing him from participating in everyday activities. He spent most days in his room – gaming, watching movies, or reading. He was depressed. He wanted what other young men his age wanted; a home of his own, friends, and a social life – and like Bobby, an intimate relationship.

We found Mitchell, a flat close to his whanau. However, the funding secured was not adequate for the 24-hour support he needed. Nonetheless, he was determined not to go into institutional care, or to stay with his family. Mitchell wanted to take control of his funding package and do it himself. My company supported him with the management of the money— such as doing payroll and taxes for the people he hired to support him.

To make it work, he had to be alone overnight, which terrified everyone. What if something happened while he was alone? But that was a risk he insisted on taking. Mitchell moved into his flat, kept his mobile phone on a lanyard around his neck at night with the emergency number programmed in, and everyone held their breath.

Mitchell hired young men his own age with similar interests to support him. He got a modified van through a local charity to access the community. He and his carers went to the pub on Friday night like most 25-year-olds. He made so many friends that he was always busy. His friends supported him on a volunteer basis, which helped extend his funding.

Mitchell even started speaking publicly about his story, about how important it is for society to recognise the issue of personal power and control, and how critical self-direction is for people with disabilities to achieve social equity. I never knew if he met a partner, but he was charismatic and charming, so probably.

The impact of risk

The concept of self-direction in disability is not new – active implementation of self-directed supports dates to the 1970s.[8] However, the uptake of this approach internationally has been slow. This is because the current models of health and disability are so deeply entrenched, they are difficult to change. It all comes down to risk, and how we limit risk.

But there is dignity in risk. People willingly choose to ride motorcycles, downhill ski, scuba dive, race cars, and any number of risky activities. The term "dignity of risk" first emerged in the 1970s in relation to the oppression of people with intellectual disabilities. Mitchell's story illustrates how critical it was for everyone to accept his choice to take a risk that enabled him to lead the life he wanted and promoted his individual dignity and social equity.

For entrenched health and disability systems, accepting risk and dignity in risk is difficult, because the systems are established to protect people by reducing risk through "duty of care".[9] Current health and disability systems are based on long-held beliefs related to duty of care, risk mitigation, accountability for safety, and stewardship for public funds. Transferring power to the individual is perceived as risky, because it impacts the perception of duty of care: particularly concerning personal safety and money. However, it makes no sense to attempt to protect disabled people from all risks. Aside from the fact that a risk-free life is boring, it is also restrictive, demeaning, and often breaches human rights and freedoms. More importantly though, this kind of overprotection does not deliver social equity, while the acceptance of some risk does. Accepting risk to facilitate empowerment is a fundamental shift in thinking, one that is necessary to promote social equity.

Additionally, the existing data on the outcomes of self-direction on social equity are limited. We need evidence to enable system changes around balancing risk with outcomes. Gathering data is critical to show the stories that quantifiably measure and illustrate impact, beyond the traditional anecdotal approach.

The growth in popularity for self-direction in disability offers hope that this trend will continue. There is greater hope that young people will have better, more equitable experiences and will shift the narrative towards self-direction as the norm.

My story

I was a new nursing school graduate with bright white duty booties and a crusader attitude. I got a job as a Neonatal Intensive Care Unit (NICU) nurse, and I knew everything. I was a high achiever with an attitude. However, being part of birth and death – sometimes at the same time – was a huge reality check.

One evening at the shift handover, the nurse for one of our most fragile babies reported that everything was stable. Unusual for this baby – he was born at 21 weeks, which left him with a long list of problems. Still, all vital signs, from measurements to drug levels, were stable. But according to the nurse, the baby's mum insisted something was wrong. That night the baby crashed requiring resuscitation yet again. Everyone had been diligent, and it all worked out, but it taught me an important lesson: Families always know, often before any other person or medical measure and we need to pay attention! This early experience in my career ignited my passion for self-direction and my personal and professional crusade to drive it authentically and honestly.

Since then, I have taken every opportunity to promote self-direction in my career, starting various programmes in health and disability with self-direction at the core. I was lucky to work in roles where I had influence and could drive the approach. My current company, Manawanui, is the pinnacle of this privilege; our mission is to support people like Mitchell to be self-directed, with ease.

Through my journey, I met Lillian, then I met Mitchell, and hundreds more like them, and of course, Bobby. These people taught me humility, respect, and the importance of valuing every person as unique, with their own life and needs. I have spent my professional and personal life supporting the concept of social equity as a human right. It drives me because every day I see the difference that social equity, self-direction, and empowerment make to all people, regardless of circumstance. When I lose track of what I think the best thing to do is – I stop, I listen, and I ask.

The rest is history, or in Bobby's case, the beginning.

Back to Bobby – his beginning

Bobby's parents taught him he could do anything he set his mind to, and to disregard people who didn't believe that. Luckily, he had strong character, good social skills, and self-confidence. However, over time, he required more support to do everyday things we take for granted. When he was 22 years old, the funding authority discussed placing Bobby in institutional care. This would have meant an aged care facility, because there was nothing else that could support him where he lived. Bobby and his parents refused.

They insisted on a self-directed package of funding for less money than facility care, that Bobby could manage himself. He wanted to employ support staff his own age who could help him get to university, parties, rugby games, and anything else he wanted to do. He wanted to be successful, have a job, and a partner. Anyone who underestimated his ability to do it was in for a shock.

Like Mitchell, Bobby hired people his age who became his friends. He managed all aspects of his support package including being a boss and managing the employment relationships. Bobby went flatting, and to university.

Bobby received not one, but two university degrees, took three overseas trips with his support team, excelled in his work, published two books, became a public speaker and life coach, and got a girlfriend.

He took control of his life – because he could, and should, because it is his right to do so.

Different but the same – critical concepts

I have discussed several concepts critical to achieving social equity. All these concepts are required to make social equity an authentic reality, even though they are applied to people in unique and different ways. These concepts are often difficult to implement due to their subjective nature.

The critical success factors are:

Inclusion – *"Nothing about us without us"* J. Charlton.[10] Inclusion in its purest sense means that disabled people are active participants, and engaged authentically in mainstream society, as opposed to being grouped separately for activities and roles.

Power – Authority is the sanctioned use of power. For a person to have authority over themselves, they must have the sanctioned use of power, instead of the traditional approach in which the system holds that power. Power facilitates authentic choices, and the ability to make one's own choice is the absolute definition of self-direction. This is a fundamental shift in thinking, requiring trust in the individual. That's what makes it the most challenging concept to master in achieving social equity.

Risk – The dignity of risk acknowledges that life experiences come with risk and that we must support people in experiencing success and failure throughout their lives. Accepting that everyone takes risks daily and that it is impossible to eliminate, or even mitigate, every risk is critical to self-direction, and ultimately to social equity.

Money: Socioeconomic status is often a singular source of social inequity. When a person is dependent on external resources simply to exist, as is often the case in marginalised populations, the social impact of money is dramatic. Therefore, control over the resources required to live well is also fundamental to both self-direction and social equity.

Citizenship – Social equity involves authentic participation in the community and society as a full citizen with valued roles. Duffy describes the seven keys to citizenship as love, life, home, freedom, help, purpose, and money. All these variables must be present for people to participate in society as full citizens, and therefore to have social equity.

Summary

Self-direction is essential to achieve social equity, and disability is a primary example of how it works to improve lives. But it really is more than that – self-direction is a basic human right that is fundamental to social equity across a variety of demographics, especially marginalised or disadvantaged populations.

Follow-up actions

I hope that these stories have inspired you to believe in the power of social equity, starting with empowering people to be self-directed. Here are some things you can do to promote social equity as a normal way of being:

- Set an example – listen, ask, never tell, and illustrate genuine value for others.
- Include disabled people and other marginalised groups in mainstream society and activities.
- Become an advocate – drive awareness campaigns.
- Get involved in community-building activities to actively build citizenship for all.
- Share the stories.

Most importantly, self-direction and social equity require direct engagement with the people affected. They should be at the centre of the conversation, directing everyone else around them. In disability, the phrase "nothing about us without us" is a common catchphrase that speaks to the importance of authentic engagement to achieve social equity.

Explore:

- Manawanui Support Limited. Available at: www.manawanui.org.nz
  - Manawanui is the pioneer and leading facilitator of Self-Directed Funding in New Zealand. Manawanui believes that self-direction is a human moral right. We are driven by this belief and support people to be as independent as possible using a self-directed approach.
- Citizen Network (2016) Available at: https://citizen-network.org/
  - Citizen Network was formed in 2016 to help make this process of global transformation real. We are all citizens; we are all equal and we all have a contribution to make. But this contribution can only be made through community – by working with others.
- Kendrick, Michael. Available at: https://www.kendrickconsulting.org
  - Michael Kendrick from the US is a speaker, advocate, educator, consultant, and author in self-direction, value-based leadership, service design, and reflective practice in the community services sector for over 30 years. He has published widely on issues related to self-direction and disability.
- International Initiative for Disability Leadership, Available at: https://www.iimhl.com/iidl-homepage
  - An international initiative bringing the disability sector together to enable learning and leadership to support each other to provide the best possible life opportunities for disabled people and their families.

Notes

1 Tutu, Desmond (2016), *Ten Pieces of Wisdom From Desmond Tutu to Inspire Change Makers*. Desmond Tutu Peace Foundation. Available at: http://www.tutufoundationusa.org/2016/01/03/ten-quotes-from-desmond-tutu-to-inspire-change-makers-in-2016/. Accessed on: August 23, 2021.
2 Kendrick, M. (1999), Formal Individualisation Systems : Their Potential & Limitations. *Crucial Times*, July; Services, K.C. (2011), Empowerment and Self Direction Relative to the Design and Governance of Personalized Service Arrangements. *Human Development, Disability, and Social Change*, 19, 57–68.
3 Interaction Institute for Social Change (2016), *Illustrating Equality vs. Equity*. Artist: Angus Maquire. Available at: http://interactioninstitute.org/illustrating-equality-vs-equity/

4 World Health Organisation (2011), *World Report on Disabilities*. Available at: https://
   www.who.int/publications/i/item/9789241564182. Accessed on: August 23, 2021.
5 Teseriero, Paula, Disability Rights Commissioner New Zealand, iCreate conference keynote address, 2019.
      United Nations (2006), Convention on the Rights of Persons with Disabilities and
   Optional Protocol. In *Development (Basingstoke)* (Vol. 49). doi:10.1057/palgrave.
   development.1100310.
6 The United Nations (2006), *Convention on the Rights of Persons with Disabilities (CRPD)*.
   Available at: https://www.un.org/development/desa/disabilities/convention-on-the-
   rights-of-persons-with-disabilities.html. Accessed on: August 23, 2021.
7 United Nations (1948), Universal Declaration of Human Rights. *Article 1*. Available at:
   https://www.un.org/en/about-us/universal-declaration-of-human-rights. Accessed on:
   August 23, 2021.
8 Breedlove, Lynn (2020), Self-Direction Worldwide: Contrasting Beliefs and Their
   Impact on Practice. *Citizen Network*. Available at: https://www.centreforwelfarereform.
   org/uploads/attachment/685/selfdirection-worldwide.pdf. Accessed on: August 23,
   2021.
9 New Zealand Nurse's Organisation (2016), *Fact Sheet: Understanding Duty of Care*.
   NZNO Policy, Regulation & Legal Fact Sheet. Available at: https://www.nzno.org.
   nz/LinkClick.aspx?fileticket=I1m5KZmr6-8%3D&tabid=109&portalid=0&mid=4918.
   Accessed on: August 23, 2021.
10 Charlton, J. (1998), *Nothing About Us Without Us: Disability Oppression and Empowerment*. University of California Press. Available at: http://www.jstor.org/stable/10.1525/j.
   ctt1pnqn9. Accessed on: August 23, 2021.

32

MASTERING THE POWER OF SUSTAINABILITY

Kishan Nanayakkara

Abstract

All life forms are subject to sustainability of nature. In recent decades, unchecked industrialisation and high consumption lifestyles have adversely impacted our environment. Our pursuit of economic growth based on questionable technologies has led to a rise in carbon emissions and climate change. In many parts of the world, there are signs of extinction of plant and animal life. If we do not act now, we may be heading towards catastrophic consequences. Fortunately, there are significant moves towards reducing carbon emissions. Our aim now is to contain the temperature rise to 1.5° by 2030. We have to collectively make difficult choices and adapt a sustainable way of life.

In this chapter, I will share my journey in the world of sustainability. What lessons I have learnt and how each one of us can make a contribution by adopting sustainability.

Keywords: Purpose, renewable energy, sustainability, sustainable development goals (SDGs)

Introduction

> "In this orange tree, there are many ripe oranges
> and branches hanging down
> Two oranges are enough for me and my sister
> We are not naughty children, who pick too many".
>
> *-Sri Lankan folk poem*

DOI: 10.4324/9781003219293-41

"In this orange tree" is a poem that kids of my generation have grown up with. We learnt it in the nursery, and it was probably our first classroom lesson on sustainability. It took me a further three decades to realise that the poem implied a message of sustainability. It is about the coexistence of life and nature; it is about responsible consumption, circularity, and renewal. These are primary concepts as we go on to learn about sustainability.

UCLA sustainability defines sustainability as "the balance between the environment, equity, and economy".[1] For sustainability, the three concepts, namely, conservation of environment, the nature of economic development, and fair distribution of the benefits of environment and economic development across a society have to be in equilibrium.

> *Every society clings to a myth by which it lives. Ours is the myth of economic growth.*
>
> *Tim Jackson*[2]

Tim Jackson, a British ecological economist, says, "People are persuaded to spend money we don't have, on things we don't need, to create impressions that won't last, on people we don't care about",[3] and unless we collectively respond to the call for a **new global deal for people and nature**,[4] this planet becoming an uninhabitable place is unavoidable.

Sustainability leadership: the spark matters

We all have a sustainability leader in us. The "new global deal for people and nature" demands us to create that spark within to bring out that leader in us. I discovered my deep-rooted passion for sustainability accidently.

After being a finance professional for over a decade, in early 2000, I joined a family-owned group of companies as its Director for Corporate Venture Funds. This was an unconventional role, and my responsibility was to identify new investment opportunities for the diversification and growth of the business. Despite the risk associated with investing in uncertain times, I took up the challenge as I felt it was essential for my career progression.

Although the role was centred on driving growth, the onus of making most out of it fell on me. In most cases, big growth plans can be shams, unless they are pursued aggressively and with strong commitment. The family-owned business was highly diversified mainly in related product categories. However, I approached my new role with an open mind to seek growth by diversifying in unrelated business areas.

As I set out in my new role, I was talked into a small hydropower generation project "deal". I went to see this project. My first sight of a small hydropower station, functional in the splendour of serene rural wilderness enthralled me. I felt it was an engineering masterpiece built for the coexistence of humans and nature. It was using flowing-water based on a concept called "run-of-the-river" without a large manmade dam built across it.

Since the engineering structure of the hydropower station was small, its environmental impact was correspondingly less. It instantly sparked the "sustainability leader" in me and I wished if I could develop one small hydropower station myself, no matter what the financial returns would be. It was an emotional wish without any strong financial calculations.

The power and appeal of sustainability can be extremely compelling. The thought of sustainability is very inspiring and resonates with one's conscience and concern for the survival of nature and humanity. It connects with the soul!

However, it took me a further five years to start developing one sustainable power generation project and a further two years to complete it. When we began, there were only two of us at "Resus Energy", the company setup as the group's power and energy investment arm. Prior to developing a sustainable energy project, Resus had already invested in a large oil-fired power station. We were a passive investor with operations and management outsourced to external parties.

Based on our strong belief in renewable energy for sustainability, building Resus Energy was not just about building power stations. It was about building a company with strong values and culture based on the principles of sincerity, trust, and sustainability. We strongly believe that these values are important for the survival of both human beings and nature.

Sincerity is precursor to sustainability

Our sincerity is tested constantly particularly when we make "difficult choices". The infrastructure development, such as building power stations, invariably causes serious damage to the environment and displaces human habitats. However, we develop these projects with the objective of improving our lives. As a champion of sustainability, it is painful to see vast areas of land dug up, trees felled, and communities uprooted. These are the times when our sincerity is tested. I always tell our team that an axe in the hands of a Vedda★ (indigenous tribes) is safer than in the hands of a lumber trader. Veddas have used it for centuries and coexisted with the forests, which they fervently protect. They are true sustainability leaders.

As we developed our second project, part of the works fell inside a nature reserve. Our first step was to educate the surrounding villagers about the importance of their bio reserve and its unique biodiversity. Our strategy was at odds with the usual approach adopted by developers of downplaying the environmental damage in order to keep the noise of stakeholders low. The villagers were happy with our approach as some of them said that they did not know their reserve was so important and as beautiful as they saw in our presentation clips. They placed their trust in us. That helped us tremendously in this project and in all new projects that we built in the years that followed.

In the same project, we had to remove a rare "giant-creeper" to clear the way for the water diversion channel. We had permission for that. But we were in pain. We built the channel through the creeper without disturbing it. We feel happy that we found a viable solution and kept our promise to protect nature. Whenever a visitor comes to visit the power station, we showcase this ingenious solution as a symbol of our sincerity to protect nature and the environment. It cost us more, but there are countless benefits in terms of winning the trust of people and gaining their support for our power projects.

Retail businesses encourage consumption, and it is intuitive to say that it is a difficult space for sustainability leadership. Paul Polman, former Unilever CEO (2009–2018) quotes that "We cannot choose between [economic] growth and sustainability – we must have both".[5] His statement reflects pain, and their sincerity in their quest to be a sustainability leader and withstand the test of time.

Patagonia, another retail giant, is taking sustainability in retail to a new level. Some years ago, on Black Friday, Patagonia ran a full-page advertisement in the New York Times with the headline, "Don't Buy This Jacket. Today, we stand on the precipice of a climate crisis to which the fashion industry and Black Friday itself have contributed" (Patagonia, 2020).[6] The drive in Patagonia in espousing less consumption is laudable. CEO, Rose Marcario, was quoted saying, "You can serve the interests of your employees and do what's right for the planet and still make great margins".[7]

There are no shortcuts to sustainability. It cannot be a fad, nor can it be a sham. If the change is not triggered the damage is inevitable.

★The Vedda people are the last indigenous tribe living in the island of Sri Lanka. Dating back to the 6th century BC, the Veddas inhabited the forests and are known as "forest people".

Sustainability is a passion

Against all odds, I was promoting renewables inside a highly diversified family-owned business group in the 2000s. The renewable power projects tend to be capital intensive. Our pursuit to expand "Resus" in renewable energy was threatening to dry up the group's coffers. We were asked to stop. It was a devastating blow to our aspirations and enthusiasm.

In a sudden rush of blood, I offered to resign. I strongly believe that leaders should take difficult decisions if it warrants defending a cause they sincerely believe in. The legacy of leadership goes beyond corporate walls. It follows the leader.

In the wake of my resignation, the group proposed to re-consider our expansion with the condition that we would raise funding from outside sources including own stakes in Resus. During negotiations, what we take-home mattered more than emerging the victor in a battle of egos. The take home for us was the consensus to expand with conditions. I think my offer to resign and deep commitment to sustainability worked.

The initial public offering (IPO) to raise funding for new investments was easier said than done. "Resus" was a cash-cow in the family-owned business group, and whilst the IPO could provide capital for expansion, the expansion would mean the dilution of group's profits. The IPO eventually occurred, and we began inching forward with steady growth and a good deal-flow in terms of investments and power purchase agreements. The group then became jittery again. They offered to exit. Though I profoundly showed the benefit of holding "Resus", the group stood to its guns and in 2014, "Resus Energy" was put up for sale.

That was a devastating blow. I felt the weight of my obligations to the team that built the company; villagers who supported our projects; and those we gave employment to and built a new life around us, on my shoulders. It was also a double-blow for me. It coincided at a time that I was journeying to succeed as the group's CEO, an eye-catching position in a top Sri Lankan conglomerate. But my passion for renewables had grown so strong, I only feared the potential disengagement with "Resus" than the abrupt end to my crusade to reach the top, although no one told me that I was off the ride.

However, it was the acid test for my passion and sincerity, and the values I preached and stood for. The team was eagerly awaiting my next move. I wanted to takeover "Resus". But I had no capital. We were given a month and a half to come up with an offer and conclude the deal. We had to compete. We formed a consortium to bid at lightening-speed. The struggle was far from being over. I and the team had to invest ourselves. I sold all my stock options (ESOPs), liquidated the personal savings and the stock portfolio, and took the retirement benefits. I mortgaged my house and borrowed money. All of that became the bulk of our equity money for acquiring Resus. But it was still insufficient to have a sizeable stake. We frantically reached out to a bank and they agreed to lend twice our equity.

The credibility a leader earns over years pays back at most surprising times. Our consortium partners proposed to lock us in the business for five years. The bank lent twice our investment with only our stake as a surety. Those in effect were statements of terms. They were investing on us and we were investing in our passion, as we staged one of the largest management-buyouts in the country's history. That is the **Power of sustainability.**

Sustainability is the new normal

Resus is not a unique story in the global context. Social distrust of the global economic model is increasing. The walkout by students in Greg Mankiw's Economics class, at Harvard in 2011, leaving an open letter that said, "we found a course that espouses a specific – and limited – view of economics that we believe perpetuates problematic and inefficient systems of economic inequality in our society today"[8] provides a glimpse of the struggle that seeks new narratives for economic success.

Raworth (2017) says

> Humanity's 21st century challenge is to meet the needs of all within the means of the planet . . . ensure that no one falls short on life's essentials . . ., while ensuring . . . we do not overshoot our pressure on Earth's life-supporting systems, on which we fundamentally depend.[9]

In February 2020, members of the activist's group, Extinction Rebellion, dug up the lawns of Trinity College, Cambridge, in protest of "the destruction of nature"[10] against the college's investments in the fossil fuel industry.[11]

In Deloitte's Global Millennial Survey for 2020, a large number of Millennial and Gen Z respondents said that they are focused on key environmental concerns within their own lives. "50 per cent and 41 per cent of Millennials and Gen Z'ers said that they've stopped or are reducing the purchase of fast fashion".[12] Bloomberg says that TikTok stars and YouTube gamers are part of a new wave of young influencers promoting climate change awareness. "Millions of kids and adults from younger generations tune in to live gamer streams and watch TikTok videos . . . and in-between games . . ., creators with hundreds of thousands of followers speak positively about climate-friendly actions".

The mass climate marches in 2014 and 2015 succeeded to pre-empt the UN Climate Change Conference, to pressure politicians into embracing the goal of 100% clean energy. Christiana Figueres, Executive Secretary, UNFCCC, said, "When we saw those massive marches, that's when we knew the people were with us".[13] The Conference, which led to the execution of the Paris Agreement, led to the development of the Sustainable Development Goals (SDGs) – a collection of 17 interlinked goals designed to limit global warming to 1.5 °C by 2030.

People are increasingly vigilant and influential in a quest to redefine the legitimate limits of life. It is driving change. Unless we change, the change will be forced upon us. Social pressure is influencing global policies too.

I believe that all of world's energy demand will be met from Renewables in the future. Whilst it was unimaginable sometimes ago, the technology and creative market options are enabling a 100% renewable energy scenario.

"Resus" had this conviction ten years ago. We transformed ourselves into a renewable energy company, disposing our highly profitable oil-fired power station, and embraced a newfound purpose. Though it put us a notch below the line of returns, we got out of firing oil, it gave us the "head-held-high" posture to navigate to the future – the future that we have bet our life and soul on. Though we do not know the value of spinoffs in renewables yet, we know that in a world that success is redefined in new set of narratives, we would very much be in the center.

Adapt or perish: sustainability is imperative

Climate change is real. In 2019, over 11,000 scientists declared a climate emergency[14] and urged immediate action to avert catastrophic impacts. Grave warnings were sounded of a sixth mass extinction, affecting one-eighth of all species, unless drastic action is taken.[15] However, responding to that is easier said than done.

The consumption-led economic model, often blamed for straining earth's limits, however, has helped global poverty reduction. It brought down the world's population living below $1.90 per day from 42.5% in 1981 to 9.2% in 2017.[16] In Buddhist parlance, "you never preach to those in empty stomach". The problem, however, is that, as Antonio Guterres, UN Secretary-General, says, "Income disparities and a lack of opportunities are creating a vicious cycle of inequality, frustration and discontent across generations".[17] It seems that the earth has taken its big toll to make rich the richer, rather than helping the poor.

Resus is small in size but big in thinking

"Resus" is small in the global context. But no one prevented us thinking big. Our vision says that we "strive to build a commercially sustainable world-class organisation that "cares for people and planet" in meeting the energy needs of the people. We are making a statement. People and the planet are at our core. It is our purpose in effect. There is no scale for sustainability. Small meaningful steps suffice. Collectively, the impact can be big. Let me share two examples.

As we care for people, we started a home-garden project soon after the first pandemic breakout. We have transformed our free spaces at power stations to vegetable gardens. Produce is distributed free to staff. We want staff to be self-sufficient and have access to food. We had apprehensions on food security during lockdown. We are determined to negate that as much as practicable. Good work brings people together. Caring means that.

Similarly, as we care for planet, we began reforestation of a nature reserve. It is also the drainage basins for three of our power stations. It was started small. Integration of intermittent renewables such as wind and solar requires batteries backing up to stabilise the grid. Ninety-seven per cent of the global battery storage is hydropower – not Lithium Ion. But those are reservoirs. The storage in run-of-the-river systems is the drainage basin itself. If basins enable stable runoffs, it can produce stable energy and help fauna and flora to flourish. That is the case when catchments are densely vegetated.

Sustainability offers a world of opportunity

Apart from climate demand, the technological innovations are also disrupting business dynamics. Conventional business models are being rapidly displaced. Sustainability takes a center-stage in this. It offers a whole new range of opportunities to succeed.

Whilst most motor vehicle manufacturers assure us that making fossil-fuel burning vehicles is being phased off, Tesla was selling environmental credits. Its "fastest-growing business isn't putting owners in its Model S and Model-3. It is selling environmental credits that enable its SUV- and truck-making rivals to avoid big emissions fines".[18]

In electricity generation, integration of renewables required backup power stations to be lined up to manage intermittency. However, the use of forecasting, ICT, and artificial-intelligence tools is accommodating more intermittent renewables without having to build expensive backup stations now. However, the technological breakthroughs are also making renewables as well as energy storing cheaper. Solar panel prices have plummeted 250-fold over the last three-and-half decades, and battery storage costs have come down 5.5-fold between 2010 and 2019.[19,20] Renewable energy is full of emerging opportunities.

We paid the highest price in an open tender to secure "Resus". Takeover left me heavily in debt. That's the toll of fulfilling a passion. Then barely a month since, the government changed. The taxes and market interest rates shot up astronomically. Our cash flow forecasts became redundant. Suddenly, we hit a dead wall, as we kept leveraging assets to stay afloat. Our plan for "Resus" at the takeover was growth. We opted not to backtrack, despite the tough economic conditions. But our cash flows were strained.

We kept reaching out to banks and they helped, and we began expanding steadily against all odds. But with a dearth of cash, "Resus" couldn't pushout dividends which I and the team were dependent on to service our personal loans that partly formed our investment. We had to borrow more to settle loans. But then sustainability is also about weathering the storm.

As the old saying goes on to say, I knew that "only time will tell" the success of fulfilling my passion. As I conclude the writing of this chapter, in July 2021, the government has changed again. The taxes and the interest rates have come down. Amidst difficulty, the capacity of our portfolio is poised to reach seven times of that at the takeover. As we are forging, a new journey ahead again amidst a set of new challenges in a world of new opportunities, I feel extremely fulfilled.

Summary

Let me conclude this with a summarised narrative of what ensued in this chapter. Climate change is threatening our existence. The change required is inevitable. We either lead, adapt, or succumb to it, no matter where or who we are. Sustainability provides us the platform for transition. It offers options to succeed. The choice is ours.

Practical exercise: being a sustainability leader

1. Have you ever felt inspired to undertake a sustainability project?
2. What characteristics should you nurture to master the power of sustainability?
3. Reflect on how you would influence those around you to drive sustainability?
4. What are practical limitations in the pursuit of sustainability leadership?

Notes

1   UCLA (n.d.), *What Is Sustainability?* Available at: https://www.sustain.ucla.edu/what-is-sustainability/
2   Goodreads.com (n.d.), *Tim Jackson>Quotes.* Available at: https://www.goodreads.com/author/quotes/177609.Tim_Jackson
3   Great Thoughts Treasury, *A Database of Quotes.* Available at: http://www.greatthoughtstreasury.com/author/tim-jackson
4   WWF (2018), *Living Planet Report - 2018: Aiming Higher.* World Wildlife Fund.
5   Pickering, A. (2018), *Purpose After Polman: How the Poster Child for Purpose Paved the Way for Future Leadership.* Available at: https://sustainablebrands.com/read/leadership/purpose-after-polman-how-the-poster-child-for-purpose-paved-the-way-for-future-leadership
6   Patagonia (2020), *Buy Less, Demand More This Black Friday.* Available at: https://patagonia.medium.com/buy-less-demand-more-this-black-friday-4fd2b6c54d85
7   Financial Times (2018), *The Profitable Company That Cares about the Planet.* Available at: https://www.ft.com/content/1564e99a-5766-11e8-806a-808d194ffb75
8   The Crimson.com (2011), *Students Walk Out of Ec 10 in Solidarity with "Occupy".* Available at: https://www.thecrimson.com/article/2011/11/2/mankiw-walkout-economics-10/
9   Raworth, K. (2017), *Doughnut Economics: Seven Ways to Think Like a 21st-Century Economist.* Random House.
10 Bell, V. (2020), XR Activists Dig Up Lawn Outside Trinity College and Dump the Dirt in Barclays Bank. *Yahoo News.* Available at: https://uk.news.yahoo.com/xr-activists-dig-up-lawn-outside-trinity-college-in-protest-over-development-155227985.html?guccounter=1
11 Hunter, W. (2020), *Varsity. Extinction Rebellion Return to Trinity Lawns as Divestment Protests Continue.* Available at: https://www.varsity.co.uk/news/19729
12 Statista (2020), Young Generation Focused on Climate. *Statista.* Available at: https://www.statista.com/chart/23650/millenial-gen-z-climate-goals/
13 Avaaz (n.d.), *Our Victories.* Available at: https://secure.avaaz.org/page/en/highlights/. Accessed on: June 28, 2020
14 Ripple, W., C. Wolf, T. Newsome, P. Barnard and W. Moomaw (2020), World Scientists' Warning of a Climate Emergency. *BioScience,* 70(1), 8–12. Available at: https://doi-org.ezp.lib.cam.ac.uk
15 IPBES (2019), *Global Assessment Report on Biodiversity and Ecosystem Services.* IPBES. Available at: https://ipbes.net/

16 The World Bank (2020). Available at: https://www.worldbank.org/en/topic/poverty/overview

17 United Nations Department of Economic and Social Affairs (2020), *World Social Report 2020.* Available at: https://www.un.org/

18 Tully, S. (2020), Tesla's Biggest Profit Center is Dangerously Close to Running Out of Power. *Fortune.* Available at: https://fortune.com/2020/09/30/tesla-profit-revenue-environmental-credits-elon-musk/

19 Our World in Data (2020), *Solar PV Module Prices.* Available at: https://ourworldindata.org/grapher/solar-pv-prices

20 Martin, C. (2019), Better Batteries. *Bloomberg.* Available at: https://www.bloomberg.com/quicktake/batteries

Further reading

• Brundtland, G. (1987), *Our Common Future.* Available at: https://sustainabledevelopment.un.org/content/documents/5987our-common-future.pdf

• Davis, G. and C. White (2015), *Changing Your Company From the Inside Out: A Guide for Social Intrapreneurs.* Boston: Harvard Business Review Press.

• Exter, N. (2013), *Employee Engagement with Sustainable Business: How to Change the World Whilst Keeping Your Day Job.* UK: Routledge Explorations in Environmental Studies.

• Levine, D. (2020), Ex-Facebook Executive Starts Group to Help Employees Push Companies on Climate Change. *Reuters,* February 24. Available at: https://www.reuters.com/article/us-climatechange-companies-idUSKCN20I0CA

• Sachs, J., G. Schmidt-Traub, M. Mazzucato, D. Messner, N. Nakicenovic and J. Rockström (2019), Six Transformations to Achieve the Sustainable Development Goals. *Nature Sustainability,* 2(9), 805–814.

INDEX

Abandoned Engineering 297
Abdelrahman, N. 219
Abraham, Thomas xvi-xvii, 22–34
abuse of power 371, 374–375, 376, 378
abuse of women and children 50
accelerators (for company growth) 32–33
Accident Compensation Corporation (ACC) (New Zealand) 275, 276
accountability 371, 374, 378; *see also* transparency
Ackerman, E. 178
action arrow 95–96
action steps to improve leadership skills: analytical thinking 176–177; authenticity 114–115; challenging the status quo 277–278; collaboration 343; community-building 351–352; creative thinking 183, 186–189, 190; diversity and inclusion 302–303; dream fulfillment 267; enhance your presence 138–141; entrepreneurship 42–43; impact investments 393; inclusive thinking 290–291, 292–293; mental fitness 247–248; moral values 103; negotiation skills 331–333; people development 235; power of leadership 19–20; purpose 72; self-confidence 258; sensemaking 199–200; social equity 407–408; social justice 377–378; storytelling 149–151; strategising 162–163; trust 127–129; volunteering 54–56
actors and physical presence 135

Acumen (social impact investments) 102
adaptability, cognitive 41
Adewale, Oyinkan iii
Advisory Board, personal 292
Aerofarms 32
AeroVironment 172–173
Aesop 74, 86
Affordable Housing projects 383
Agency H5 79–80
Agency That Helps Organisations Build Communities, An 352
Agile Lean Life 178
Ahlibank (Oman) 16
Airbnb 28
Airbus 76
Akuro, Wilbroda Awuor 212
Alchemist, The (Coelho) 268
Alcott, Louisa May 265, 268
Alibaba (Clark) 34
Aligned to Achieve (Eiler & Austin) 164
Al Kharusi, Hanaa 16
Allan, B. G. 178
alliances *see* collaboration; partnerships
Alred, G. 217
amateurism 53
American Express 22–23
Amnesty International 381
Ampel, Celia 259
An, R. 57
analytical thinking, power of 166–177
Ancient Indian education 229–230
Ancona, D. 201
Anderson, Chris 141

Angelou, Maya 205, 207, 209
Angola, Africa 51
Annan, Kofi 386, 394
Answer, The (Pease & Pease) 190
Anthro-Vision (Tett) 21
anti-corruption campaigns 371
Aotearoa, New Zealand 62
Appalachian America 89–90
Apple Inc. 335, 339
Applied NeuroCreativity (ANC) 188
Ardern, Jacinda 84, 93–94
Argonon 295–300; Argonon Diversity
   Steering Group 300
Artificial Intelligence (AI) 32, 169,
   181–182
Art of Creative Thinking, The (Judkins) 190
Art of Thinking Clearly, The (Dobelli) 190
Art of War, The (Sun Tzu) 165
Asian Institute of Technology (Thailand)
   9–10
AstraZeneca 6, 354
As You Like It (Shakespeare) 141
Atkinson Vos (all-terrain vehicle company) 81
Attawia, Joey 296
Auckland, New Zealand 271, 276
Aurelius, Marcus Antonius 155, 164
Austin, A. 164
Austin, Bobby 85, 87
Australia: "Bob" Hawke, Prime Minister
   245–246; entrepreneurship 38–39
authenticity 107–117
aviation 94–95; principles of 65–66
Awakening Compassion at Work (Dutton &
   Worline) 82–83, 87, 304
Axiom Precision Manufacturing 39
Azim Premji University 379

B2B2C (business-to-business to consumer)
   models 29
B2C (business to consumer) models 29–30
Bacon, Sir Francis 98, 103
Balaram, J. 178
Balboa, N. 125, 131
BAME employees (black, Asian, minority
   ethnic) 298–299
Banerjee, Abhijit 379
Banfield, John 127
Bangladesh 384
Banker to the Poor (Yunus) 384, 394
Ban Ki-moon 305, 390, 394
Barclays 91
bargaining *see* negotiations
Barnard, P. 419
Barretto, Alan L. iii

BATNA (best alternative to no agreement)
   324, 327
Bazerman, Max H. 333
Bean, Mackenzie 236
Beck, Martha 73
Be Extraordinary (Wild) 103
Begum, Zarina 370, 371
Bell, V. 419
Bellagio, Italy 381
Bennett, Anne 144–145
Bennett, N. 270, 279
Bennis, Warren 21
Between The Monster and The Saint
   (Holloway) 249, 250
Bhardwaj, Anjali xxvii, 369–378, 379
bias 35, 115, 174–175, 247, 290
BiasSync 35
Bidwell, L. 218
Big Data and AI (Pencheva et al.)
   217
Big Questions, Worthy Dreams (Parks) 73
Biondo, A. 249
Biro, M. M. 219
Blackwell, Geoff 84, 87
Blakely, Sara 35–36
Blatt, Ruth 337–338, 343
blended finance 388–389
Blitzscaling (Reid & Yeah) 34
Blue Ocean Strategy (Chan Kim &
   Mauborgne) 165
"Body Language and Presence" (Cuddy)
   141
Bolt, Usain 136–137, 141
Bonay, Philippa 11, 16, 17
Borgonovi, F. 57
Borrin Foundation 275
Borrup, Tom 352
Bossons, P. 219
Botica, Desiree xxv, 335–343
Bourke, C. J. 293
Bourke, Juliet 293, 301, 304
Bowling Alone (Putnam) 53, 57
BPAY Group Australia 127
Brafman, O. 293
Brandenburg, M. 394
Brandenburger, A. 190
Branson, Richard 206
Breedlove, Lynn 409
British Museum 112–113
Brown, Brené 112, 117, 141, 250,
   266–267, 268
Bruckschlögl, Josef xx–xxi, 155–165,
   319–333
Brundtland, G. 420

Building Inclusive Workplaces (Green &
    Young) 293
Bulc, Violeta 358
Bunnings (Australian hardware stores) 128
Burns, Robert 382, 394
Burrows, Karl 62–63, 66, 73
Burstall, James xxiv–xxv, 294–304
Business Queensland 326, 333
Butler, M. 131
Buy Less, Demand More This Black Friday
    (Patagonia) 419
Byron, Lord 136

Cable, D. 293
Cacioppo, J. T. 57
Cacioppo, S. 57
CAF Group 108
Cain, Susan 141
Campbell, Glen 85
Campbell, Joseph 260, 265–266, 268
Canada, diversity in workforce 276
Canham, T. 178
Caputi, P. 249
carer, leadership role 14
Carnegie, Dale 144, 151
Carter, Emma 81, 87
Cartesian Duality 243
Casablanca 339
Cash in the Attic 297
Castelaz, Jim 170
Centre for Social Impact (Chen & Erakovic)
    279
Centre for Women's Business Research 37
Centres for Creative Economy and
    Innovation (Korea) 189
challenges: identification of 172;
    overcoming 242–243, 255, 296; social
    and environmental 386; to the status quo
    269–279
Chan, Albert P. C. 365
Chanel, Gabrielle Bonheur "Coco" 339
change: connection and authenticity 111;
    and diversity and inclusion 297–300; and
    entrepreneurship 27; and leadership 7,
    9–10, 42; and mentoring relationships
    212, 224; and trust 123; *see also*
    innovation; status quo, challenges to
Changing Your Company From the Inside Out
    (Davis & White) 420
Chan Kim, W. 165
character 18, 88, 94–95, 97, 101
Charette, Janice 111–112
charisma 132–133, 141; *see also* presence,
    power of

Charlton, J. 406, 409
Chen, C. M. 293
Chen, Mai xxiv, 269–279
Chen, Z. 219
Cheston, Jessie 75
Chevron 91
China 3–4
Chipman, Claire 257
Choi, Jungkiu 288–289
Chopra, V. 218
Christchurch, New Zealand 93–94
Christensen, C. 45, 164
Christopher, Rate R. 268
Chuang, S. 236
Chui, M. 343
Cicero 234, 236
Citizen Network 408
civic action 51
civil-rights activist 5
Clark, Air Vice Marshall Andrew ii
Clark, C. 394
Classical thought 230–231
Clausen, Mads Roke xvii–xviii, 46–57
Clegg, S. R. 201
Clement of Alexandria 234, 236
climate change 69, 323, 415–417; climate
    activism 137–138
Coaching and Mentoring at Work (Connor &
    Pokora) 219
Coaching and Mentoring in Social Work
    218
Coelho, Paulo 265, 268
cognitive adaptability 41
cognitive biases 174–175, 247
Cohen, R. 394
Colby, S. L. 277, 279
Coleridge, Samuel Taylor 191,
    201
collaboration 335–343; *see also* community,
    power of; partnerships
Collaboration Tips (Adobe Workfront)
    343
*Collaborative Capitalism and the Rise of Impact
    Investing* 394
Collaborative Intelligence (Markova &
    McArthur) 343
collective leadership 6; *see also* team
    collaboration
collective (global) purpose 63, 69
Collins, J. 87
communication *see* negotiations; storytelling
communication, non-verbal 134–136
community, power of 344–352 *see also*
    collaboration; partnerships

community development entities (CDE) 328–329
compassion 16, 48, 78, 80, 81, 82–83, 84–85, 391
competitive edge 295, 301–303
Conceptualising and Measuring Mental Fitness (Robinson et al.) 249
confidence 42, 331; *see also* self-confidence
Confidence Code, The (Kay & Shipman) 257, 258
Confidence Gap, The (Harris) 259
Confucian philosophy 229–230
Congo, Democratic Republic of 348–349
Connor, M. 219
conscious living 69, 70–71
consumer experience 33
context and setting 7
Conway, C. 218
COP26 Conference 323
Corich, Katherine xviii, 61–73
corruption, political 370, 371, 374, 376
Cosmos (Sagan) 178
Costa Rica 306, 315; San José 309
Cote, C. 178
courage 81, 111, 260–267, 276
COVID-19 and Gender Equality (Madgavkar) 315
COVID-19: Collaboration Is the Engine of Global Science 343
COVID-19 pandemic 74–75; and deep thinking skills 17–18; and global collaboration 338; and government transparency 373–374; health and wellbeing 14; impact of 194; and mentoring relationships 224; and risks to business 41; vaccine development 3–4, 185–186, 354
Covishield vaccine 4, 7, 354
Cranwell-Ward, J. 219
Creative Community Builder's Handbook, The (Borrup) 352
Creative Ireland Programme 189
Creative Power of Collaboration, The (Sawyer) 343
creative thinking: and change 269–270; inclusive thinking 290; in organisations 186–187, 188; power of 179–190
Criado Perez, C. 316
Crick, Francis 180
critical thinking skills 17–18
Cruise, Sean iv
Cuddy, Amy 141
culture wars 296–297
Cupertino, California 339

curator, leadership role 13–14
curiosity 18, 98, 188, 234, 292
cybersecurity 174–175

Dalio, R. 164
D'Alpuget, B. 250
Daring Greatly (Brown) 117, 268
data, age of 31–32; *see also* digital technology
Data Analytics 169
Davis, G. 420
de Bono, Edward 269–270, 279
de Carvalho, Sarah 67–68
deep thinking skills 17–18
defining moment 6
de Gaulle, Charles 132, 141
Delivering Through Diversity (Hunt) 315
Demetriades, Marios ii
Democratic Republic of Congo 348–349
Dempsey, M. 293
Denmark: Mothers' Aid 47–48; Voluntary Council 48–49
Denning, Stephen 151
Denning, Steve 143
Denyer, Simon 379
Descartes, René 243
Deshmukh, Sunil xxi, 191–201
Design and Fabrication of the Mars Helicopter Rotor, Airframe, and Landing Gear Systems 178
DesignSingapore Council 189
Detmold, Zoe 39
Detmold Ventures 39
Devi, Sunita 370, 371
D & I (diversity and inclusion) 294–304; *see also* gender equality
Diana, Princess 51
Diary of Anne Frank, The (Frank) 249, 250
digital technology: accelerators and incubators 32–33; age of data 31–32; Artificial Intelligence (AI) 32; digital entrepreneurship 25–34; ecommerce 155–156; and rapid innovation 30–31; shift to 23–25
disability 397; and risk 403–406; and social equity 398–403; United Nations Convention on the Rights for People with Disabilities 400
disruptive change 215, 286, 291
distraction, age of 18–19
Diverse Thinking Capability Audit of New Zealand Boardrooms 274, 279
Diverse Thinking in New Zealand Boardrooms (Chen & Erakovic) 279

diversity and inclusion 294–304; *see also* gender equality
Diversity Wins: How Inclusion Matters (Hunt et al..) 304, 308, 315
Dixon-Fyle, S. 301, 304
DNA research 180
Dobelli, R. 190
Dolan, Gabrielle xx, 142–152
Double X Economy, The (Scott) 316
Doughnut Economics (Raworth) 419
dream fulfillment 6, 260–267
Dreyfus, H. 236
Dreyfus, S. 236
Dreyfus Skill Acquisition model 225–226
Drubner, S. 45
Drucker, P. 45, 394
Duncan, C. 178
Duncan, Clark 34
Durham University, St. Aidan's College 80
Dutton, Jane, 82, 87, 304

Earhart, Amelia 306, 315
eCommerce; *see* digital technology
Economics of Belonging (Sandbu) 57
Edelman (PR firm) 109
Edge of the Sound, The (de Gaulle) 141
Edison, Thomas 270, 279
education for leaders 10–11
educator, leadership role 14–15
Effective Executive (Drucker) 394
Eiler, T. 164
Einstein, Albert 179, 185
electric vehicles 170
Eliasoph, Nina 51, 57
Ellis, Amanda iv
Ellis, M. 293
Emerson, J. 394
Emerson, Ralph Waldo 239, 240, 249
emotional intelligence 247
empathy 84, 109–110
Employability Trust 80
Employee Engagement with Sustainable Business (Exter) 420
empowerment: and entrepreneurship 40; and self-direction in disability community 398–399; for women 312–314
enabler, leadership role 12–13
Enacting Purpose Initiative 73
energy, renewable 412, 414, 416, 418
engagement 127, 287
entrepreneurship 35–44; accidental entrepreneurs 65–66; digital entrepreneurship 25–34

Environmental Protection Agency (EPA) 375
equality 64, 67, 94, 113; contrasted with equity 398; Global Impact Initiative (GII) 381, 383, 389–390; *see also* gender equality
Equileap 315
equity *see* social equity
Erakovic, L. 279
Erasmus 234, 236
Esteve, M. 217
European Commission (EC) 356
European Economic and Social Committee 358
European Foundation for Management Development (EFMD) 76, 83
European Mentoring & Coaching Council (EMCC) 217, 218
European Network of Ambassadors for Diversity in Transport 359
European Union 358
evangelist, leadership role 15–16
Evotec 169
Exploring Career Mentoring and Coaching (Open University) 219
Exscientia 169
Exter, N. 420
Extinction Rebellion 415
extroverts contrasted with introverts 136

Facebook 212
failure and success 263–265
Fairchild, C. 301
fairness 76
Famous Mentors and Mentees That became Very Successful (Uhland) 218
FCB Harlow Butler 221
Fearless (Phillips-Harris) 259
Ferguson, Dr. Niall 223
Ferry, Korn 313, 315
Fessell, D. P. 218
Fifield, A. 103
Fifth Discipline, The (Senge) 164
Figueres, Christiana 416
FinChatBot 32
Finding a Mentor (Robbins) 218
Finding Your own North Star (Beck) 73
Finland 308
Fisher, Roger 117, 326, 333
5 Disciplines of Inclusive Leaders, The (Polonskaia) 316
Five Competitive Forces, The (Porter) 164
Five-Stage Model of Mental Activities, A (Dreyfus & Dreyfus) 236

food access 89–90
Ford Motor Company 166–167
Forrest, Andrew 38
4 Ways to Increase Your Analytical Skills
    (Cote) 178
Four Things I Learned About Mentorship
    From Former CEO of AstraZeneca
    David Brennan (Thakral) 218
Fox, Erica A. 325, 333
Frank, Anne 246–247, 249, 250
Frankl, Viktor 64, 73
Franklin, Benjamin 208
fraud 324–325
Freddie Mercury: The Biography (Jackson) 141
freedom of information 369–378; Report
    Cards on elected representatives 372–373
Freedom of Information Act (U.S.) 375
freelance work 30
Freeman, Morgan 93
Frei, F. 120, 131
Frei, F. X. 117
Frey, W. H. 304
Friedman, Tom 386
Friis-Olivarius, M. 188, 190
From Promise to Practice (UNESCO) 379
From Zero to One (Thiel) 165
Frost, S. 304
Fujimori, Masaya v
Functional Mentoring (Thorndyke et al.) 218
Future of Jobs Report (WEF, 2020) 180
*Future of Work Is Changing: Will Your
    Workforce Be Ready?* 219

Gamble, R. 236
Game of Thrones 142, 151
Gandhi, Mahatma 5, 6, 101, 103, 194
Garcia, Hector 73
Garvey, B. 217
Gates, Bill 386
Gates, Melinda 307, 315
Gelles, David 103
gender equality 305–314; and blended
    finance 388–389
Gender Equality Global Report & Ranking
    (Equileap) 315
*Generation of Mars Helicopter Rotor Model for
    Comprehensive Analyses* 178
George, Bill 109, 113, 117
Gerlach, G. 201
Germany: Angela Merkel 84; Nazi party
    286
Getting to YES (Fisher & Ury) 114, 117,
    326, 333
Get Together (Richardson) 352

Ghandi, V. 131
Giese, R. 279
Gift of Imperfection, The (Brown) 268
gig workers 30
Gilbert, Sarah 3–4, 6, 21
Gill, Alison 78
Gill, M. 218
Gillihan, Seth J. 259
Gino, Francesca 186, 190
Giri, Gautam 373–374
Girls Who Code 289
Gladwell, Malcolm 275, 279
Glaser, R. 125, 131
Glasgow, Scotland 323
Glasgow Climate Pact 323
GlaxoSmithKline 360
Global Civil Society (Kaldor) 57
Global Gender Gap Report 315
Global Impact Initiative (GII) 381, 383,
    389–390
Global Impact Investing Network (GIIN)
    394
Global Millennial Survey (2020) 416
global purpose 63, 69
global warming 69
Glossop, Karen xx, 132–141
goals: career 199, 206, 211; in collaborative
    process 340–341; goalsheets 332; life
    211, 217, 256–258; and negotiating
    332, 357; organisational 12, 156, 356;
    Sustainable Development Goals (SDGs)
    307, 370, 388, 389, 390–391, 416
God Is Not a Christian (Tutu) 57
Golden Rule 75, 86
Goldman, B. M. 117
Goleman, Daniel 118, 119–120, 127, 130,
    131
Golombek, M. 178
Gompers, P. 299, 304
Good Time to Be a Girl, A (Morrissey) 219
Gordon, Dr. Mary 110, 117
Gore, Al 386
Goss, Pete 8
Gover, S. 219
Grameen Bank 384–385
Grant, A. 190
Great Tradition, The (Gamble) 236
Grech-Cumbo, B. 315
Green, Catherine 21
Green, M. 293
Gretzky, Wayne 274
Grip, H. F. 178
Grose, Jim 39
Grove, A. S. 164

Grubhub 29
Gunesekera, Giles xxvii–xxviii, 380–394
Gurukula: An Exposition of the Ancient Indian Education System (Kachappilly) 236
Gurukula system 229–230
Gusic, M. E. 218
Guterres, Antonio 417

Hagan, A. 131
Haigh, Clifford 86
Haka (company) 62–63
Haka Works: Whakapapa (Burrows) 73
Halakha (living in the right way) 100
Hall and Partners 80
Hamilton, David 87
Hamilton, Wanda xix, 107–117
Hancock, B. 293
Happy Child International (HCI) 67
Hardenberg, C. 394
Hard Thing About Hard Things, The (Horowitz) 34
Harris, Chloe Phillips 251–258
Harris, Russ 259
Hart, W. E. 217
Harvard Business School 108
Harvard Law School 333, 334
Harvard University 415
Haskins, Gabrielle (Gay) xviii, 9–10, 45, 57, 74–87, 86, 87, 333
Hasson, Uri 152
Hawke, Robert James Lee "Bob" 245–246
Hawke: The Prime Minister (D'Alpuget) 250
health and wellbeing 14
Health for all. All for health 4, 6
Helen and Teacher (Lash) 353
Heller, Cheryl 170–171, 178
help, asking for 262–263
Hemrajani, Sunder 9, 21
Henson, Kathleen Kenehan 79
Heraclitus 234
Hero's Journey, The (Campbell) 268
hero's quest 265–266
Hero With a Thousand Faces, The (Campbell) 268
Heslop, Neil 108, 117
Hewlett, S. 315
Hewlett, S. A. 304
Hibbs, B. 178
Higgins, M. C. 218
Himalayan trekking club 8–9
Hisrich, R. D. 45
Hoffman, Reid 34
Holder, Emily 379
Holger, D. 304

Hollinger, P. 190
Holloway, R. 249, 250
honesty 81, 92
Honken, N. 236
Horowitz, Ben 34
hospitals and MRSA infections 288
House Hunters International 297
How Diversity Can Drive Innovation (Hewlett) 315
How Maya Angelou Made Me Feel (Tunstall) 217
How to Be a Brilliant Mentor (Szgzyglak) 219
How to Build a Community Poster 352
How to Get Better Results With Inclusive Thinking (Ellis) 293
How to Improve Your Analytical Skills to Make Smarter Life Decisions 178
How to Make a Mind Map 178
How to Win Friends and Influence People (Carnegie) 151
How Will You Measure Your Life? (Christensen) 45
HR (human resources professionals) 200–201, 284–285, 286–287
H-type executives 197–199
Hu, Y. 293
Hughes, Peter 275
Hugo, Victor 380, 394
Human Genome Project 339
Human Resources (HR) Manager mentoring programmes 200
Human Rights Act 270
Human Rights Commission (New Zealand) 275
human trafficking 69; *see also* It's a Penalty
hunger, and feeding the planet 69, 307, 377
hunger for excellence 40
Hunt, Gaillard 379
Hunt, V. 315, 316
Hunter, W. 419

Ibarra, Herminia 113–114, 117
Iceland 308
I & D (inclusion and diversity) *see* diversity and inclusion
Ihde, Adolf 76
Ikigai: The Japanese Secret to a Long and Happy Life (Garcia & Miralles) 73
(I know this to be true) on kindness, empathy, and strength 84, 87
Illustrating Equality vs. Equity 408
impact: high impact collaboration 339–342; high-impact purpose 70; Impact Festivals 182; of kindness 82; measurement of 71; and risk 41–42, 403–404; social impact

170–171; and strategising 161; and trust
129; and volunteerism 54
Impact (Cohen) 394
Impact Investing: An Introduction (Rockefeller
Philanthropy Advisors) 394
impact investments: examples 384–389; at
Global Impact Initiative 383–384; and
leadership skills 391–392; measurement
of 389–390; overview 380–381
Importance of Inclusion in the Workplace, The
(Ferry) 315
Impro: Improvisation and the Theatre
(Johnstone) 141
inclusion and diversity 294–304, 406
Inclusive Talent Management (Frost &
Kalman) 304
inclusive thinking 283–293
incubators 32–33
India 5; beer industry 192; corporate
negotiations 320–321; Delhi, Yale
University project 376–377; economic
growth 1990s 194–195; independence 5;
markets and global brands 192, 194–196;
Mumbai 22–23; Public Distribution
System 370; Right to Information (RTI)
law 370, 371
Infineum 284, 285, 286
influence: a desire to 231; as form of
teaching 232; of kindness 75–76; of
leaders 121–122; and strategy 161
Information for Mentors 218
inner purpose 62, 69
innovation: and creative thinking 180–181,
186–187; and inclusive thinking 288,
290, 301; and power of leadership 7;
rapid 30–31; *see also* change
Innovation and Entrepreneurship (Drucker) 45
Innovator's Dilemma, The (Christensen) 164
In Pursuit of Purpose (Munroe) 73
*Inside Story of the Oxford AstraZeneca Vaccine
and the Race against the Virus, The* 21
inspirer, leadership role 12
Intel® Digital Readiness Programs 190
Intellectual Life, The (Sertillanges) 236
intention 210; intentional self-denial 98;
and social impact measurements 389; *see
also* purpose
Interaction Institute for Social Change 408
Intergalactic Design Guide, The (Heller)
170–171, 178
International Aviation Women's Association
(IAWA) 312–313, 365
*International Best Practices of Public-Private
Partnership* 365

International Initiative for Disability
Leadership 408
International Labour Organization 53, 57
International Space Station (ISS) 355
interviews 145
*Introduction to the Symposium on Mentoring,
An* 217
introverts contrasted with extroverts 136
intuition 196, 198, 328
Inventure – The Purpose Company 69
Invest for Good (Mobius et al.) 394
Invisible Women (Criado Perez) 316
IPBES (Intergovernmental Science-Policy
Platform on Biodiversity and Ecosystem
Services) 419
Irby, B. J. 219
Ireland, *Creative Ireland Programme* 189
Isocrates 234, 236
It's a Penalty 67–68

Jackson, Laura 141
Jackson, Tim 411, 419
Jakes, Bishop 68
Jameel Poverty Action Lab (J-PAL)
372–373
Japan: corporate negotiations 320–321;
Nadeshiko (charity project) 133
Jenner Institute (Oxford University) 4
Jerome 234, 236
Jet Propulsion Lab (JPL) 172–173
Jobs, Steve 149, 151, 212, 335, 339, 343
Johannesburg, South Africa 221
John Lewis Partnership 79
Johns Hopkins University 52
Johnson, W. 178
Johnstone, Keith 141
Johri, Amrita xxvi–xxvii, 369–378, 379
Johri, Dr. Lalit xvi, 3–21, 45, 57, 76, 80,
82, 86, 87, 187, 197, 201, 320–322,
333, 360–363
Joly, Hubert 73
Jordan, J. 178
Joseph Campbell Companion, A 268
Journal of Positive Psychology 261
J.R. Global Associates 18, 320
judgement 17, 163, 209, 247, 253
Judgment in Managerial Decision Making
(Bazerman & Moore) 333
Judkins, R. 190

Kachappilly, Kurian 235
Kahlo, Frieda 136
Kahneman, D. 165, 293
Kaldor, Mary 57

Kalman, D. 304
Kandola, A. 249
Kay, Katty 257, 258
Keates, Kelly xvii, 35–44
Keennon, M. 178
Keller, Helen 344, 353
Kendrick, Michael 397, 408
Kernis, M. H. 117
Khan, Mushira Mohsin 103
Khan, Salman 135
kindness: definitions 77–78; global need for 85–86; impact of in organisations 82–83; influence of 74–76; in organisations 78–83; role models for 83–84; role of in leadership 76–77; small daily acts 69
Kindness in Leadership (Haskins et al.) 45, 57, 86, 87, 333
King, Martin Luther, Jr. 5, 21, 23, 34, 269, 279
Kituyi, M. 45, 343
Klein, J. R. xix, 18, 88–103, 319–333
Klotz, I. 178
Koch, J. 219
Kodak 194
Konieczny, G. 394
Koning, W. J. F. 178
Korea, Centres for Creative Economy and Innovation 189
Kotter, John P. 40, 45
Kovalli, S. 299, 304
Kram, K. E. 218
Kubrick, Stanley 265
Kuhn, Thomas 270, 279
Kumar, Selvan 379
KWAK Telecom Ltd. 157, 162, 324–325

La Guardia Airport 95
Laker, Sir Freddie 206
Lane, Richard 21
Langberg, S. 178
Lara-Alecio, R. 219
Larsen, Jensine xxvi, 344–352
Lash, P. J. 353
LastingImpact.AI 175
Lateral Thinking for Management (de Bono) 279
law firms, boutique 209, 271
Lawrence, Jennifer 135
Lázaro Cárdenas Health Center (Chiapas, Mexico) 375
Leaders Guide to Storytelling, The (Denning) 143, 151
leadership 3–11, 18–21, 40, 76–77, 96, 108–114, 119–124, 121–123; and change 9–10; collective act 6; EVA 21; getting immersed in reality 5; making positive difference 5; and risk 8–9; seizing opportunity 6; striving to achieve dream 6
leadership simulators 8–9
leadership teams 6
leading change 10
LeapFrog Investments 385–386
Leider, Richard 69, 73
Lemoine, J. G. 270, 279
Leopard USA 300
Les Misérables (Hugo) 380, 394
Letters to a Young Poet (Rilke) 251–252, 254, 258
Levine, D. 420
Levitt, Kevin 178
Levitt, S. 45
Lewis, C. S. 94, 103
Lewis, John Spendan 87
Lewis, Mervyn K. 365
Li, F. C. R. 290, 293
Li, M. 218, 219
Lichterman, Paul 51, 57
Life of the Mind, The (Schall) 236
Likierman, A. 201
Lilani, Pinky 112, 117
Lin, C. J. 293
Lintener, Marita xxvi, 354–365
Lion and the Mouse, The (Aesop) 74, 86
listening 80–81, 99, 125, 128, 217, 325, 391
Little Caesar 338
Littleton, C. 217
Little Women (Alcott) 268
Liu, B. 293
Living on Purpose (Steiner) 73
Lloyd, Kris 39
local associations and businesses 47, 90, 170, 182, 320, 359, 372, 375, 385
London, University of 133
London Business School 76
Long Walk to Freedom, A (Mandela) 250
Lorenzo, R. 304
Lozier, Kara 349–350, 353
Lucas, George 265
Lufthansa 355

Made in New York 300
Madgavkar, A. 315
Madison, President James 369–370, 379
Magnetic Stories (Dolan) 152
Make 2017 the Year to Get Serious About Mentoring (Biro) 219

Maki, J. 178
Maltese Falcon, The 339
Mana (Māori concept) 141
Managing Business Relationships, Negotiating Successfully 333
Manawanui Support Limited 408
Mandela, Nelson 67, 73, 113, 220–221, 235, 244–245, 250
Manifesto for a Moral Revolution (Novogratz) 102, 103
Mankiw, Greg 415
Man's Search for Meaning (Frankl) 73
Manual on the Measurement of Volunteer Work (ILO) 53, 57
Māori culture 62, 66, 133, 402
Maple, Sherry ii
Marcario, Rose 413
Markova, D. 343
Mark Twain in Eruption 103
Markway, Barbara 259
Marley, Bill 80
Marriott International 301
Mars, NASA mini helicopter 171–174
Marshall, Marsha xxviii, 396–408
Mars Helicopter Technology Demonstrator 178
Martin, C. 420
Masked Singer, The 297
Massachusetts Institute of Technology 372
Masters, Blake 34
Mateschitz, Dietrich 157
Mathis, Shawn D. xxii, 220–235
Matthews, Paul, xix, 118–131
Mauborgne, R. 165
Mazzucato, M. 420
McArthur, A. 343
McCrindle, M. 131
McDonald, Avril xxiii–xxiv, 260–267
McDonald's 196
McKinsey & Company 284, 301, 308
McLeod, Carolyn 130
Meals on Wheels 50, 382
meaning *see* purpose
mediator, leadership role 13
Meditationes Sacrae (Bacon) 98
Meditations (Marcus Aurelius) 164
Meister, J. C. 219
men raising children 68
mental fitness 239–249; foundational concepts 247; measurement of 241, 242. *see also* mind, life of
mentor, leadership role 15
mentoring: finding a mentor 209–210; future of 215–216; impact of 213–214; inspirational relationships 212; online

contrasted with face-to-face 223–225; overview 205–209; roles of mentors 211
Mentoring--A Henley Review of Best Practice 219
Mentoring During a Crisis (Kram et al.) 218
Mentoring Managers in Organisations (Conway) 218
Mentoring Millennials (Meister & Willyerd) 219
Mercury, Freddy 132
Mere Christianity (Lewis) 103
Merkel, Angela 84
Messner, D. 420
Mexico, Chiapas 375
Michelle Obama's 10 Most Memorable Lines (Weinger) 219
microfinance 384–385
Microsoft Excel 342
Microsoft Teams 342
Mikhaylov, S. J. 217
Millennial Generation, The (Frey) 304
Miller, Nigel 109
Milner, R. J. 218
mind, life of 233–234; *see also* mental fitness
Mind and Heart of the Negotiator, The (Thompson) 333, 334
mindfulness 247
Minimal Viable Product (MVP) 27
Ministry for Women (New Zealand) 275
Ministry of Business, Innovation, and Employment (New Zealand) 275
Miralles, Francesc 73
Misbehaving (Thaler) 165
mission 3; *see also* purpose
Mobius, M. 394
Moeller, Clair J. i
Moment of Lift, The (Gates) 307, 315
Moomaw, W. 419
Moore, Don A. 333
moral values: building moral values 94–100; discovering moral values 92; overview 88–90; power of 100–102; recognizing moral values 93–94; universal 91
Morris, A. 117, 120, 131
Morrissey, H. 219
mothers2mothers 212
Mothers' Aid 47–49
Mother Theresa 212
motivation 18, 40, 82, 124, 214, 243, 319, 322
Motiv Power Systems 170
Moyo, Dr. Dambisa 91
Mr. Peabody and Sherman 284
MRSA infections, hospitals 288

Multiple Sclerosis (MS) 399
Mumbai, India 22–23
Munroe, Myles 61, 73
Murray, Clare 78
Muscular Dystrophy 397, 405–406
Musk, Elon 186
My Beloved World (Sotomayor) 316

Nadeshiko (charity project) 133
Nakicenovic, N. 420
Namadamu, Neema 348–349, 353
Nanayakkara, Kishan xxviii, 410–419
Narayana Health 4, 7, 21
NASA (National Aeronautics and Space
    Administration) 171–174, 185; Mars
    Exploration Program 178; mini
    helicopter for Mars 171–174; and
    public-private partnerships 360
Nash, S. 45
Nassar, Alina xxv, 305–314
Nassar Abogados (law firm) 309
Nationwide Building Society (UK) 79
negotiations: BATNA 324, 327; distributive
    323; failure of 328–331; foundational
    concepts 319–322; integrative 323;
    negotiation skills 325–328; process of
    323–325
Neider, L. L. 117
Neoh, Beng ii
Netflix 28–29
New Delhi, India 370, 372
*New Earth, A: Awakening to Your Life's
    Purpose* (Tolle) 73
New Future of Work, The (Microsoft) 218
New Mindset on Mentoring, A (Kram &
    Higgins) 218
New Risks, New Welfare (Taylor-Gooby) 57
Newsome, T. 419
Newton, Sir Isaac 193
New Zealand: Corich's experience 62–65;
    Disability Rights Commission 399;
    diversity in 271; gender gap 308; Jacinda
    Ardern 84, 93–94
New Zealand Asian Lawyers 273
New Zealand Asian Leaders (NZAL) 273
New Zealand Law Foundation 275
New Zealand Ministry of Education
    (MOE) 275
New Zealand Nurse's Organisation 409
Nightmare Tenants 297
Nobel Prize recipients 272, 349, 370, 376,
    384, 386
Nobel Wisdom (Pratt) 279
Nokia 194

nonviolence, philosophy of 5
Norway 308
Nothing About Us Without Us (Charlton) 409
Novogratz, Jacqueline 102, 103
nursing, professional development 225–228

Oades, L. G. 249
OAMLP (Oxford Advanced Management
    and Leadership Programme) xxix, 11,
    76, 108, 158, 320, 382
Obama, Michelle 216
O'Brien, Mark xxii-xxiii, 239–249
Office of Ethnic Communities (New
    Zealand) 275
Officer, Gary A. iii
Ohno, Taiichi 186
Oldfield, Rebecca xxiv, 283–293
Olympic Games (Tokyo 1964) 144–145
Oman, Ahlibank 16
Onarheim, B. 188, 190
On Becoming a Leader (Bennis) 21
online mentoring 223–225
Only the Paranoid Survive (Grove) 164
OnRole™ 226–227
OnSomble™ 224, 225–227
On War (Von Clausewitz) 165
Onzain, M. 217
Open University 219
Open Your Mind, Open Your Life (Gandhi)
    103
opportunity: defining 166, 172; seizing
    6; for storytelling 145–146; and
    sustainability 417–419
Oprah's Super Soul Conversations 73
orchestration 6, 11–12
orchestrator, leadership role 11–12
Originals (Grant) 190
Ortman, J. M. 277, 279
Osborn, D. 249
Osei-Kyei, Robert 365
Our Common Future (Brundtland) 420
outer purpose 61–62, 64
Outliers (Gladwell) 279
Oxford Advanced Management and
    Leadership Programme (OAMLP) xxix,
    11, 76, 108, 158, 320, 382
Oxford Handbook of Innovation, The 45
Oxford University: Saïd Business
    School xxix, 10–11, 73, 76, 80, 108;
    vaccinology 3–4, 6, 7

Paillusseau, Antoine 32
Pakistan 4
Paladan, N. 45

Palmer, Chen 271
Pande, Rohini 379
Panditrao, Mangesh 31
paradigm shifts 270–271
Paris Agreement 416
Parks, S. D. 73
particularism 52
Partnership Platform (United Nations) 362
partnerships 354–365; network partnerships
    358–359; private-public partnerships
    (PPP) 356–357, 360–364; and social
    purpose 359–360; *see also* collaboration;
    community, power of
Patagonia 413, 419
paternalism 53
Patton, B. 117, 333
peace 75–76, 97, 113, 349
Pease, A. 190
Pease, B. 190
Peisakhin, Leonid 379
Pempejian, J. 178
Pencheva, I. 217
People & Company 352
people development: in Eastern and
    Western philosophies 229–231;
    foundational concepts 231–233; and the
    mind 233–234; online contrasted with
    face-to-face 223–225; OnSomble™
    and Providence St. Joseph case studies
    225–229; overview 220–222
performance: financial 82–83, 301;
    high-performance leaders 112–113;
    KPIs (key performance indicators) 358;
    measurement of 158; and mental fitness
    243–244; performance evaluations
    286–287; report cards for elected
    representatives 372
Perseverance Rover 171–174
personal business development *see*
    entrepreneurship
personal development 41, 230, 362
"personal pentagon" 98–100
Peters, M. P. 45
Phan, J. T. 210, 218
philanthropic insufficiency 52
Philips (and compact disc development) 187
Phillips-Harris, Chloe xxiii, 259
philosophical basis of moral values 89, 109
Pickering, A. 419
Pickles, Kate 353
Pinto, Paul 379
Pipenberg, B. T. 178
planning: and analytical thinking 168–169;
    business plans 42, 358; in collaborative

process 341; personal goals 72, 190; and
    self-confidence 255–256; and strategy 158
Pokora, J. 219
Policy of Excluding Women from Combat
    270
political corruption 370, 371, 374, 376
Polman, Paul 413
Polonskaia, A. 316
Poncet, Jean François 83
Porras, J. 87
Porter, Michael (M. E.) 158, 164
positive differences 3, 5, 188
poverty 89–90
power, abuse of 371, 374–375, 376, 378
power generation 412–415
Power of Impact Investing, The (Rodin &
    Brandenburg) 394
Power of Kindness, The 80–81
Pratt, David 272, 279
Premier League (Football) Charitable Fund
    80–81
presence, power of 132–141
presentations 146
Principles (Dalio) 164
private equity 387–388
private-public partnerships (PPP) 356–357,
    360–364
problem-solving: and analytical thinking
    175, 176; and inclusive thinking
    288–289; and negotiation skills 326,
    331
*Profitable Company That Cares about the
    Planet, The* 419
profit with purpose 385–386; *see also* impact
    investments
*Projections of the Size and Composition of the
    U.S. Population: 2014 to 2060* 279
Providence St. Joseph Health 227–229
public law specialists 271
public speaking 146
purpose: benefits of 70; examples of 67–68;
    finding personal purpose 68–69; global
    or collective purpose 63, 69; high-
    impact purpose 70; impact of 70–71;
    inner purpose 62, 69; outer purpose
    61–62, 64; power of 61–67
Purpose After Polman (Pickering) 419
Putin, Vladimir 136
Putnam, Robert 53, 57

Qi, L. 290, 293
Quaker Faith and Practice (Haigh) 86
Quakers 75–76
Qualcomm 173

Queen (rock band) 132
Quiet Leadership (Rock) 103
Quiet: The Power of Introverts in a World That Can't Stop Talking (Cain) 141
Quintilian 234, 236
Quon, A. 178

Radical Inclusion (Brafman & Dempsey) 293
Rajeswaran, S. 304
Ramakrishnan, Prasad xxi, 166–178
Rapisarda, A. 249
Raworth, K. 415, 419
Ray, Amit 342, 343
recycling 69, 387
Red Bull 157
Red Cross 51
Reeves, M. 304
reflection exercises: analytical thinking 177; authenticity 117; challenging the status quo 278; digital solutions 33–34; entrepreneurship 42–43; gender equality 314; impact investments 394; kindness 86; leadership manifesto 20–21; mental fitness 248; mentoring 210, 217; partnerships 364; sensemaking 201; strategising 164; sustainability 419; trust 130; volunteerism 56
relationship triangle 97–98
relaxation and presence 138–139
Religious Society of Friends 75–76
renewable energy 412, 414, 416, 418
Renton, Washington (Providence St. Joseph Health) 227–229
Resilience 247, 276, 391
Responsible Investment Association Australasia 394
Ressa, Maria 370, 379
Resus Energy 412, 414–415, 417
Rethinking Public Private Partnerships (Lewis) 365
Retrain Your Brain (Gillihan) 259
Return to Love, A (Williamson) 268
Reverse Mentoring 217
Richardson, Bailey 352
Right Mentor Can Change You Career, The (Sastry & Tagle) 218
Right to Information (RTI) Act 370, 371, 372, 374, 375
right to know see freedom of information
Right to Speak, The (Rodenburg) 141
Rilke, Rainer Maria 251–252, 254, 258
Rinehart, Gina 38, 45

Ripple, W. 419
Rising Strong (Brown) 250
risk: and entrepreneurship 41–42; and leadership 8–9; risk-taking 8–9, 163; social risks 49, 52
Robbins, Anthony 210, 218, 262, 268
Robinson, Paula 242, 249
Rock, David 103
Rockefeller Foundation 381
Rockefeller Philanthropy Advisors 394
Rockström, J. 420
Rodenburg, Patsy 141
Rodin, J. 394
Roettger, Dietmar 176
Rogue Elephant (Denyer) 379
Role of Kindness in Small Manufacturing and Engineering Companies in the North West, The 87
Roosevelt, R. 249
Roosevelt, Theodore 248
Rose, Melany 112–113
Rotorcrafts for Mars Exploration (Balaram & Tokumaru) 178
Roulet, T. 218
Royal Bank of Canada 169
Ruiz, Michele 35

Sachs, J. 420
Sagan, Carl 169, 178
Saïd Business School (Oxford University) xxix, 10–11, 73, 76, 80, 108
Saint, S. 218
Sakurai, Chiaki iii
Salamon, Lester 52, 57
sales, shift to digital 23–25
Salt From My Attic (Shedd) 268
Salvador, Brazil 166–167
Sambucci, Luca 174–175
Samoa 65
Samsung Design Innovation Centre 187
Sandbu, M. 57
Sapaugh, Curt 85, 87
Sarkar, S. 201
Sastry, A. 218
Satark Nagrik Sangathan (SNS) 371, 372, 373
Saujani, Reshma 289
Savage, N. 178
Sawyer, Keith 343
Scarface 338
Scarpy, Kathleen 79, 87
Schäfer, Christian i
Schall, J. 236
Schaninger, Bill 284, 293

Schmidt-Traub, G. 420
Schneider, Michael 128
School of X (Singapore) 189
Schriesheim, C. A. 117
Science of Achievement, The (Robbins) 268
Scigliano, D. 219
Scott, L. 316
Secrets of Valley of the Kings 297
self-awareness 3, 19, 109, 111, 139
self-confidence 251–258
Self Confidence Workbook, The (Markway & Ampel) 259
self-control 93, 97
self-direction 399, 400, 402, 403–404, 405, 406
self-investment 41
Sen, Amartya 376, 379
Senge, P. M. 164
sensemaking, power of 191–201
Sensemaking in Organisations (Weick) 201
Sertillanges, A. G. 236
SESAR Deployment Alliance (SDA) 356, 365
7 Steps to Improve Your Analytical Thinking Skills 178
sexual exploitation 67–68
Shafik, Minouche (D. M.) 291, 293
Shakespeare, William 141
Shaw, Ruth 80–81
Shedd, John A. 265, 268
Shepherd, D. 45
Shetty, Dr. Devi Prasad 4, 6
Shipman, Claire 258
Shoptimize 31
Silverman, Lori 143, 152
Simmons, Annette 143, 152
Sims, Peter 117
Sinek, Simon 343
Singapore, DesignSingapore Council, School of X 189
Singh, Deepak 27–28
Singh, Shekar 379
"Single European Sky" 357, 365
SNGLR Group 174
"Soaring through the Glass Ceiling Study" 313–314, 316
social capital 53
Social Design 170–171
Social Economy, The (McKinsey study) 341
social equity: basic concepts 406–407; and disability 398–403; importance of 399–400; promotion of 400–403; and risk 403–406

social impact 49, 54, 97, 161, 170–174, 383, 388–390; *see also* impact investments
social justice 369–378; *see also* Gandhi, Mahatma; Yousafzai, Malala
social risks 49, 52
Sodexo 300
"software as a service" (SaaS) start-ups 25–26
Sokolowski, Wojtek 53SolAero 173
Solving the Global Nurse Shortage (Mathis) 235
Sonak, Anshul xxi, 179–190
Sondergaard, Peter 31
Sony (and compact disc development) 187
Sorell, M. 178
Sotomayor, Sonia 312, 316
South Africa: apartheid 286; *see also* Mandela, Nelson
Southall Black Sisters (SBS) 50–51
Space Odyssey, A 265
SpaceX 186
Spanx 36
Speakers for Schools 300
species biodiversity, decline of 69, 413
Spielberg, Steven 211
Spielvogel, Carl 279
Spotmentor 27–28
Spring Health 171
Squirrel Inc. (Denning) 143
Sri Lanka 375; folk poem 410
Sriskandarajah, Dhananjayan iii
St. Aidan's College, Durham University 80
Standard Chartered bank 288–289
Star Wars 265
State of Working India 2021 (Azim Premji University) 379
status quo, challenges to 269–279, 306
Steele, Ken 103
Steffens, P. 45
Steiner, Brandon 73
Stern, R. 178
Steve Jobs: His Own Words and Wisdom (Jobs) 343
Stiglitz, Joseph 376, 379
Stories for Work (Dolan) 152
Story Factor, The (Simmons) 143, 152
storytelling, power of 142–151
strategising, power of 155–164
Streetcar Named Desire, A 339
Streetlights 300
Stresse, S. 45
Stressed at Work? (Roulet & Gill) 218

Structure of Scientific Revolutions, The (Kuhn) 279
St. Vincent de Paul charity 382
S-type executives 197–198
Su, Felix 379
success and failure 263–265
Sullenberger, Captain Chesley Burnett III 94–95
Sunak, R. 304
Sun Tzu 165
Superdiverity Institute for Law, Policy and Business 271
SuperDIVERSE Women 273
Superdiversity Institute 273
Superdiversity Stocktake (Chen) 273, 275, 279
support *see* community, power of; mentoring
sustainability 410–419; *see also* impact investing
Sustainable Development Goals (SDGs) (UN) 307, 370–371, 388, 390–391, 416
sustainable growth 162
Sweden 308
Swiss Federal Institute of Technology (ETH) 176
SWITCH: From Telling to Trusting With Powerful Leader Conversations (Matthews) 131
Sysdoc 65–66, 336–337, 340–342
Szgzglak, G. 219

Tagle, A. 218
TalentBridge 178
Tapping into the Drug Discovery Potential of AI (Savage) 178
Taylor, Richard 109
Taylor-Gooby, P. 57
team collaboration 11–16
teams *see* collaboration; community, power of; partnerships
technology *see* digital technology
TED talks 151, 152, 266
TED Talks--The Official TED Guide to Public Speaking (Anderson) 141
Telekom Austria 160–162
Telementoring: Taking Learning Global (Scigliano) 219
10 Top Negotiation Examples 334
Ten Pieces of Wisdom From Desmond Tutu 408
tension stories 147
Teow, J. 315, 316
Teseriero, Paula 408
Tesla 418
Teterboro Airport 95

Tett, Gillian 21
Thakral, A. 218
Thaler, R. H. 165
Thiel, Peter 28, 34, 165
thinking: analytical 166–177; deep thinking skills 17–18; *see also* mental fitness; mind, life of
Thinking Fast and Slow (Kahneman) 165, 293
Think Like a Freak (Drubner & Levitt) 45
Thomas, M. 45, 57, 333
Thomas, Mike iv, 77
Thomas Cook (tourism company) 355
Thompson, Leigh 333, 334
Thorndyke, L. E. 218
Thornley, B. 394
3M 91
Thunberg, Greta 137–138, 141
Ti, Eng Hui v
Tien, Y. H. 293
Titus, A. 293
To a Mouse (Burns) 394
togetherness 46, 49, 56
Tokumaru, P. T. 178
Tolle, Eckhart 62, 73
Tomlinson, Neil ii
Tong, F. 219
Topping, James 76
Topping, Phyllis 76
Toyota Production System 186
tragedy stories 146–147
Train Up a Child (Steele) 103
transformational leadership 40
transition stories 147
transparency: and corruption 371; during COVID-19 pandemic 373–374; and social justice 376–377
Transportation Law 309
Trepanier, Dr. Sylvain 227–229, 236
Trinity College, Cambridge 415
triumph stories 146
True North: Discover Your Authentic Leadership (George & Sims) 117
Trump, Donald 136
trust 21; leadership examples 121–122; obstacles to 122–126; in organisational culture 144; power of 118–121, 127–129; roadmap to 129–130
Trust Factor (Zak) 365
truth 92, 116, 148, 248; *see also* authenticity
Tseriero, Paula 399
Tsoukatos, Angela 128
Tu, M. 218, 219

Tully, S. 420
Tunstall, E. D. 217
Turning to One Another (Wheatley) 353
Tutu, Desmond 46–47, 49, 57, 396, 408
Twain, Mark, 92 103
Tyler, J. 178

Uber 28
UCLA (University of California--Los Angeles) 411, 419
Uhland, S. 218
Umoh, R. 218
unconscious bias *see* bias
Unilever 413
Unimogs (all-terrain vehicles) 81
United Nations 5, 307, 355; Climate Change Conference 416; Convention on the Rights for People with Disabilities 400, 409; Department of Economic and Social Affairs 420; Universal Declaration of Human Rights 399
University College London Hospitals (UCLH) 78
University of Auckland 271
University of Bonn 355
University of Chester 77
University of Delhi trekking club 8–9
University of Houston 266
University of Nebraska 218
University of Oxford 4
Upwork 30
Ury, William 114, 117, 326, 333

van der Bas, Maarten 68
van der Merwe, Reinette iv
van der Peet, Father Michael 212
Vedda people 413, 414
Vesalius in Zante (Wharton) 353
Virgin Group 206
Virtual Mentoring and Coaching (Abdelrahman et al.) 219
vision, shared 39–40
volunteers: definitions of volunteer work 53–54; failures of volunteerism 52–53; power of 46–56
von Clausewitz, C. 165
vulnerability 110, 116, 266

Wake Me Up When the Data Is Over (Silverman) 143
Wall, Louisa i
Wall, Thomas 207
Wall, Victoria xxii, 205–217

Want Higher Profits? Hire a Female CEO (Grech-Cumbo) 315
Wardlaw, Lieutenant General Richard i
Warner, Albert 338–339
Warner, Harry 338–339
Warner, Jack 338–339
Warner, Samuel 338–339
Warner Brothers 338–339
waste, reducing 69, 393
Watson, James 180
Wei, X. 293
Weick, Karl (K. E.) 192, 201
Weinger, M. 219
wellbeing and health 14
Wertheimer, Pierre 339
Western Samoa 65
"whakapapa" (Māori concept) 62–63, 66
Wharton, Edith 349, 353
What Are the Types of Negotiation? (Harvard Law School) 334
What Entrepreneurs can Learn from These 4 Mentorship Stories 217
What Great Mentorship Looks Like in a Hybrid Crisis (Tu & Li) 218, 219
What Is a Problem Solving Approach? (Harvard Law School) 333
What Is Sustainability? (UCLA) 419
What's the Right Way to Find a Mentor? (Phan) 218
What the Hell Do We Do Now? (Butler et al.) 131
Wheatley, Margaret (M. J.) 344, 353
Where Do We Go From Here (King) 269, 279
Which Two Heads Are Better Than One? (Bourke) 293, 304
White, Andrew 11
White, C. 420
Why Diversity Matters (Hunt) 316
Why Kindness is Good for You (Hamilton) 87
Why Mentors Matter (Bidwell) 218
Why You Should Find a Great Mentor If You Want to Be Successful (Umoh) 218
Wild, Jennifer 103
Williams, M. 201
Williamson, Marianne 267, 268
Willyerd, K. 219
Wilmot-Sitwell, Alex 298
Winfrey, Oprah 207, 268, 274, 279
Winkler, Matthew 268
wisdom 99–100
"wokeness" 296–297
Wolf, C. 419
Wolters Kluwer publishing house 23–25

women: empowerment 312–314; and
    leadership 16, 35–44, 305–314; women
    in business 35–44, 305–314; *see also*
    gender equality
"Women in Transport" 358, 365
Women in Work Index (Teow et al.) 315, 316
women leaders 16
Women of the Future 80, 112
Woodside Cheese Wrights 39
workforce, evolving nature of 124
WorkSafe (New Zealand) 275, 276
World Bank 4, 420
World Economic Forum 180, 190
World Health Organization 4, 408
World Pulse 346–350, 352
World Report on Disabilities 408
World Social Report 2020 (United Nations)
    420
Worline, Monica 82, 87, 304
Wozniak, Steve 339
Wright, Orville 338
Wright, Wilbur 338

Writings of James Madison, The 379
Wuhan, China 3–4

Yale University 376
Yeah, Chris 34
Year of Living Purposefully, A (Leider) 73
Young, J. 293
Young, Kirsty 293
Yousafzai, Malala 4, 21
Youth Hostel Association of India 8
Yunus, Muhammad 384–385, 386, 394

Zak, Paul J. 144, 151, 365
ZARA 187
Zero to One (Thiel & Masters) 34
Zhu, D. 178
Zhu, H. 57
Zonge, Dr. Ken 36–37
Zonge Engineering and Research
    Organization 36–37
Zuckerberg, Mark 212
Zürcher, Jérôme 175–176

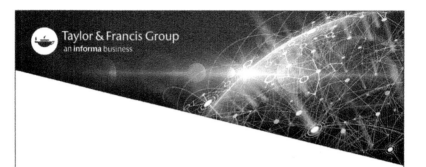

Taylor & Francis Group
an **informa** business

Taylor & Francis eBooks

www.taylorfrancis.com

A single destination for eBooks from Taylor & Francis
with increased functionality and an improved user
experience to meet the needs of our customers.

90,000+ eBooks of award-winning academic content in
Humanities, Social Science, Science, Technology, Engineering,
and Medical written by a global network of editors and authors.

TAYLOR & FRANCIS EBOOKS OFFERS:

A streamlined
experience for
our library
customers

A single point
of discovery
for all of our
eBook content

Improved
search and
discovery of
content at both
book and
chapter level

REQUEST A FREE TRIAL
support@taylorfrancis.com

 Routledge
Taylor & Francis Group

 CRC Press
Taylor & Francis Group